Law, Justice and Human Rights in India

Law, Justice and Human Rights in India

Short Reflections

Kalpana Kannabiran

With a Foreword by

Anand Teltumbde

Orient BlackSwan

LAW, JUSTICE AND HUMAN RIGHTS IN INDIA:
SHORT REFLECTIONS

ORIENT BLACKSWAN PRIVATE LIMITED

Registered Office
3-6-752 Himayatnagar, Hyderabad 500 029, Telangana, India
e-mail: centraloffice@orientblackswan.com

Other Offices
Bengaluru, Chennai, Guwahati, Hyderabad, Kolkata,
Mumbai, New Delhi, Noida, Patna

First published by Orient Blackswan Private Limited 2021

ISBN 978-93-5442-110-5

041566

Typeset in
Adobe Jenson Pro 11/13
by Shine Graphics, Delhi 110 094

Printed at
Avantika Printers Private Limited, New Delhi 110 020

Published by
Orient Blackswan Private Limited
3-6-752, Himayatnagar, Hyderabad 500 029, Telangana, India
e-mail: info@orientblackswan.com

Dedicated in humility and solidarity to
dissenters and conscientious resisters
victims and survivors of structural violence
prisoners of conscience
persons incarcerated without fair trial
victims of custodial torture, 'encounters'
and illegal custody
human rights defenders and advocates
in India

Contents

List of Abbreviations

ABVP	Akhil Bharatiya Vidyarthi Parishad
AFSPA	Armed Forces (Special Powers) Act, 1958
ASA	Ambedkar Students' Association, University of Hyderabad
ASWI	Association of Scientific Workers of India
BC	Backward Class
BJP	Bharatiya Janata Party
CAA	Citizenship (Amendment) Act, 2019
CBI	Central Bureau of Investigation
CJI	Chief Justice of India
CrPC	Criminal Procedure Code
DPO	district panchayat officer
EFLU	English and Foreign Languages University, Hyderabad
FIR	first information report
FRA	Scheduled Tribes and Other Traditional Forest Dwellers (Recognition of Forest Rights) Act, 2006
IAS	Indian Administrative Service
IMA	Indian Medical Association
INSAF	Indian Social Action Forum
IPC	Indian Penal Code
JNU	Jawaharlal Nehru University
LGBTQ	lesbian, gay, bisexual, transgender, queer
LSE	London School of Economics and Political Science
NALSA	National Legal Services Authority
NCRB	National Crime Research Bureau
NCW	National Commission for Women
NFDW	National Federation of Dalit Women
NGO	non-governmental organisation
OBC	Other Backward Class
OCI	overseas citizen of India

OTFD	other traditional forest dwellers
PIL	public interest litigation
PR (College)	Pithapur Rajah's Government College, Kakinada
RSS	Rashtriya Swayamsevak Sangh
SC	Scheduled Caste
SEBC	Socially and Educationally Backward Class
SIMI	Students Islamic Movement of India
SKBR (College)	Sree Konaseema Bhanoji Ramars College
ST	Scheduled Tribe
T-MASS	Telangana Mass and Social Organisations
UAPA	Unlawful Activities (Prevention) Act, 1967
UN	United Nations
UNCRPD	United Nations Convention on the Rights of Persons with Disabilities
UNICEF	United Nations Children's Fund
UPA	United Progressive Alliance
VC	vice-chancellor
VHP	Vishva Hindu Parishad
WCLA	Women in Criminal Law Association
WRD	*World Report on Disability*

Foreword

> *The state practices "violence", the individual must not do so. The state's behaviour is violence, and it calls its violence "law"; that of the individual, "crime".*
>
> —Max Stirner (1995: 176)

The law is an assurance to the powerless that she will be protected from the raw, exploitative instincts of the powerful. And it is with this logic that the bourgeoisie democracies have evolved a maxim of separation and independence of the law-making wing (legislature), the law-enforcing wing (executive) and the adjudicating wing (judiciary) of the governments. It means that although the legislature can make laws and the executive can enforce them, the judiciary can adjudicate on whether the laws are not *ultra vires* of the constitution and whether the application of the laws by the executive is correct or not. Unfortunately, in India, the separation and independence of the two former wings, that is, the legislature and the executive, are structurally jeopardised. The politicians that people elect to legislate laws become supremos of the executive wing at various levels. The manifestation of this structural flaw is seen in the police and the bureaucratic machinery becoming subservient everywhere to political bigwigs. Theoretically, the excesses of this combine could only be checked by the judiciary, which appeared to perform its role by and large independently, subject to its intrinsic caste and class bias. But in recent times, cases of political interference in the judicial process are widely suspected, which culminated in the unprecedented action of four senior Supreme Court judges holding a press conference to expose the rot in the country's highest court (PTI 2018).

This book, a collection of 67 short essays by noted sociologist and women's rights activist, Kalpana Kannabiran, is kaleidoscopic, dealing with most contemporary issues like prisoners' rights, campus violence, women's rights, state impunity, judicial accountability, citizen engagement in law-making, questions of discrimination against Dalits,

Adivasis, persons with disabilities, sexual and religious minorities and questions of culture. All these issues collectively map the contemporary Indian reality and it is important that Kalpana has used her knowledge of sociology and law to dissect their constitution. The fact that contemporary reality is shaped as much by Indian sociology as by the law, India's Constitution and entire statutes often escapes the discourse on these issues. One cannot understand contemporary India, even its problems of caste and communalism, which are often superficially discussed as legacy issues, without looking at the making of the post-colonial state post 1947.

This state was constructed under the halo of the freedom struggle, which had built up vague hopes in people through promises made by Congress leaders, particularly Mahatma Gandhi, who had been its mascot. They expected that once the British were gone, India would be sans exploitation and oppression; it would be truly their own rule (*swaraj*), which would give tillers their lands, workers just wages and would strive to provide all people a decent living and ensure justice. It blinded people from suspecting the contrary development. The rhetoric of socialism, republican homilies and transformative governance were duly sworn by but in reality they were given the easy go-by in favour of the capitalist development of India, keeping the feudal fabric of the society undisturbed. The entire colonial state apparatus—its structure, roles, processes and paraphernalia, along with the statutes and laws including the draconian ones which were derided during the freedom struggle—which was designed with the colonial logic of exploitation, was adopted without any change for the governance of the new state. This glaring dichotomy went largely unnoticed even in intellectual discourse in India. The constitution that was framed with much fanfare was also nothing but a rehash of the previous colonial constitution—the Government of India Act, 1935—with rhetorical flourish and with a strategic masterstroke, projecting Babasaheb Ambedkar, who had emerged as the messiah of the downtrodden, as its chief architect. The epithet would stick as the years passed by despite Ambedkar disowning the Constitution in the harshest possible words within just a couple of years of its adoption. The intelligentsia kept singing paeans to the Constitution even though the reality rapidly ran opposite to what it supposedly professed.

Ambedkar, in his much-applauded maiden speech in the Constituent Assembly, had questioned Jawaharlal Nehru's objective resolution saying that justice—social, economic and political—could be possible without the structure of society being socialist. It was informed by the plan of state socialism he had drafted, vide *States and Minorities* (1947), on behalf of his party, the Scheduled Caste Federation. It proved prophetic. Despite the socialistic claims of the Constitution, inequality galloped, and with it, justice eluded its victims. Today, India is the most unequal society in the world. During the initial decades, inequality tended to decline and even when it rose, the rise was modest. However, after it adopted neoliberal reforms, inequality rose with an accelerated pace. The entire ethos of justice itself was reversed under the force of the neoliberal mania for economic growth. While the resultant economic progress and the competitive rhetoric made the rich and upper middle classes happy, it engendered crises and unrest among the rest. The state that effectively withdrew from its obligation towards the latter increasingly had to resort to force to maintain order, providing fertile ground for fascists to rise. The rise of right reactionary forces all over the world during the past three decades of neoliberalism testifies to this process. In India, these forces manifesting in the form of Hindutva forces are out to undo whatever little democratic achievement it has made and turn the country into a Hindu *rashtra*, a Brahminist fascist state.

Besides the process of fascisation of the state which is ongoing, the justice delivery system, of which the law is the key instrument, plays a major role in making the character of the state. Laws are primarily made by the ruling classes to protect their interests but they do it under the cover of altruism and independence. It lends the system its legitimacy. While people believe in the justness of the system, it is not necessarily just to them. An entire body of laws, which includes sedition, which was decried by most leaders of the Congress, including Gandhi, was adopted without any change from the colonial regime. Soon after the transfer of power, the state went on adding to these 'black laws'. One of the first to be promulgated was the Madras Suppression of Disturbances Act, 1948, to suppress the Telangana peasant uprising, which had begun in 1946, against forced labour, illegal exactions, evictions by feudal landlords and oppression by village Patels. Among others, it developed into an agrarian liberation struggle to get rid of feudal landlordism and the nizam's dynastic rule in the state. The struggle continued even after Hyderabad merged with India. With this law, as many as 4,000 communists and peasant activists were killed and more than 10,000 communists and sympathisers were put behind bars. Later, a spate of such 'black laws', such as the Maintenance of Internal Security Act (MISA), 1971, the Terrorism and Disruptive Activities (Prevention) Act (TADA), 1987, the Prevention of Terrorism Act, 2002, the National Security Act (NSA), 1980 (amended 1984, 1987), the Unlawful Activities (Prevention) Act (UAPA), 1967, the Unlawful Activities (Prevention) Amendment Act, 2004 (as amended), were passed, which effectively neutralised whatever constitutional safeguards that were provided to people. These are just a few familiar ones; if one includes all, Central as well as states' (every state having competitively legislated its own draconian laws), the list may overwhelm the length of this Foreword.

Purported to be for extraordinary situations and extraordinary crimes, they are used against ordinary people in ordinary circumstances with impunity, invariably to suppress their democratic demands. These unconstitutional laws are designed with a protectionist rhetoric against threats (which could be real or imagined) to the integrity of the nation, which itself remains a questionable construct in India. But what they actually protect is the ruling dispensation's ability to bypass human rights. During the last five years of the Bharatiya Janata Party's (BJP) rule, the impunity of the state in resorting to these laws is legion. The most recent example of this is the use of the National Security Act to arbitrarily arrest 160 Muslim men in Uttar Pradesh in the one year that Yogi Adityanath has been its chief minister (Dixit 2108b). As per official data, within 10 months of Adityanath's rule, there have been more than 1,100 police encounters in the state, which caused the deaths of 34 persons, left 265 injured and led to the arrest of 2,744 (Dixit 2018a). The recent Bhima Koregaon case conjured up by Pune police, clearly under orders from the Centre, in which 11 noted human rights activists and intellectuals, including me, have been charged under the dreaded UAPA, is the most blatant case of misuse of this unlawful law. Fabricating a plot out of nothing and implicating the most unlikely people in it bares the objective of the rulers to send a fascist message across the country—that they can do anything to any person and hence should be feared. It would be an understatement to say that the UAPA, that virtually gives an ordinary police official authority to arrest any person, incarcerate her for years and ruin her entire family, is misused rampantly. For instance, the arrest of Delhi University professor G. N. Saibaba (Vatsa 2014; *Scroll.in* 2018), a person with 90 per cent disability, and his comrades, on the allegation of being Naxals, their conviction to life imprisonment, and the judiciary's insensitivity to the entire process, exposes the character of the rule of law in India. Such a verdict would not have been possible without the extreme provisions in the UAPA and judiciary taking a constricted view of it.

In all this, caste, class and community play a major role. The poor Dalits, tribals, Christians and Muslims bear the brunt. The first two communities had the seeming legal protection of the Scheduled Castes and the Scheduled Tribes (Prevention of Atrocities) Act, 1989, hailed as an act with teeth outside of the draconian laws. While the latter are widely applauded by the 'nationalist' crowds, the Prevention of Atrocities Act is grudged by all the non-scheduled communities and is reduced to toothlessness. After its promulgation, there has been a consistent rise in atrocity cases. This illustrates the dynamics of the justice delivery system in India: the law meant to protect the lower strata, when brought in, actually acts against their interests. The condition of Muslims is worse than that of Dalits and Adivasis, they being termed international terrorists. The genesis of any terror act can invariably be traced to politics, but it is never suspected. What is suspected are Muslims. In this process, scores of them are behind bars for years as undertrials and are even sent to the gallows. The increasing incidence of right-wing Hindu terror is blatantly ignored. Recently, in March 2019 (Shantha 2019), 11 Muslim men were acquitted of charges filed under the now-repealed Terrorist and Disruptive Activities (Prevention) Act after 25 years in jail! Their reaction to the verdict, 'Our only mistake was being born Muslim,' reveals the pathetic state of the law administration machinery in India.

The National Crime Research Bureau (NCRB), in its twenty-first report, *Prison Statistics India 2015*, recorded that over 55 per cent of the undertrial prisoners in India are either Dalits (Scheduled Castes [SC]), Adivasis (Scheduled Tribes [ST]) or Muslims. An analysis of this data showed that this number was grossly disproportionate to the combined population of Dalits, Adivasis and Muslims, which amounts to just 39 per cent of the total population according to the 2011 Census. An analysis of the caste-based classification of undertrials from the NCRB report in 2014 revealed that 21.6 per cent are SCs and 12.4 per cent are STs. Dalits and Adivasis—two of the most vulnerable sections of Indian society—make up a considerable number of India's prison population. Although the proportion of these two communities in India adds up to about 24.2 per cent, their share amongst prisoners is considerably higher, at 34 per cent. Dalits make up 22 per cent of prisoners, almost one in four, as against their proportion in the population, of 16.6 per cent. While Adivasis make up 12.4 per cent of prisoners, their share in the general population is 9 per cent. In some states, particularly the BJP-ruled states, this is more pronounced. In Gujarat, which was flaunted by Narendra Modi as the model state to impress people into voting him prime minister, around 32.9 per cent of all convicts and 23.4 per cent of undertrials in Gujarat's prisons are Dalits, a community that forms just about 6.7 per cent of the state's overall population (NCRB's *Prison Statistics India 2013* report). It means that the proportion of Dalits among Gujarat's convicts is nearly 4.9 times higher than their share in the state's population, with its undertrial numbers up to 3.5 times higher. According to this report, of the total 3,808 convicts in Gujarat, 1,251 were Dalits, 624 Adivasis, 1,360 Other Backward Classes (OBC) and 573 'others'. Out of a total of 7,604 undertrials, 1,778 were Dalits, 1,405 Adivasis, 2,718 OBCs and 1,703 'others'.

Within these vulnerable communities, women constitute the major part of the victims. A simple glance at the NCRB reports may stun one with horror. In 2011, there were 228,650 reported incidents of crimes against women, which crossed the 300,000 mark in 2015, an increase of a whopping 44 per cent. Like Dalits, women also may be wary of reporting crimes against them because of the fear of social stigmatisation. And as such, these statistics clearly understate crimes. Many kinds of crimes are committed against women but the most heinous of them may be rape. In India, a woman is raped every 15 minutes (Varadhan 2020). Behind all these rising crimes, the criminality of the justice delivery system can be seen as a common cause.

The author has provided her perceptive commentary on the specific episodes of these crimes in this volume. Its value lies in the insightful exposition of various issues with the help of her seamless application of sociology and law. It opens out the framework of the Constitution to popular appreciation so as to trigger a public debate on the scope of justice and its multiple sites. A must read for those who want to understand and engage with the contemporary reality of India.

Anand Teltumbde
18 March 2019

References

'United Nations Rights Experts Urge India to Release Jailed Delhi University Professor G. N. Saibaba'. 2018. *Scroll.in*, 28 June. Available at https://scroll.in/latest/884552/united-nations-rights-experts-urge-india-torelease-jailed-delhi-university-professor-gn-saibaba (accessed 13 June 2021).

Ambedkar, B. R. 1947. *States and Minorities: What are Their Rights and How to Secure Them in the Constitution of Free India*. Available at http://www.ambedkar.org/ambcd/10A.%20Statesand%20Minorities%20Preface.htm (accessed 29 May 2021).

Dixit, Neha. 2018a. 'A Chronicle of the Crime Fiction That is Adityanath's Encounter Raj'. *The Wire*, 24 February. Available at https://thewire.in/rights/chronicle-crime-fiction-adityanaths-encounter-raj (accessed 16 September 2021).

———. 2018b. 'In Run up to 2019, NSA Is the Latest Weapon Against Muslims in UP'. *The Wire*, 10 September. Available at https://thewire.in/rights/in-adityanaths-up-the-national-security-act-is-latest-weapon-against-muslims (accessed 16 September 2021).

NCRB (National Crime Records Bureau). 2013. *Prison Statistics India 2013*. New Delhi: Ministry of Home Affairs.

———. 2014. *Prison Statistics India 2014*. New Delhi: Ministry of Home Affairs.

———. 2015. *Prison Statistics India 2015*. New Delhi: Ministry of Home Affairs.

PTI. 2018. 'Supreme Court Crisis: All Not Okay, Democracy at Stake, Say Four Senior-Most Judges'. *Business Line*, 18 January.

Shantha, Sukanya. 2019. '"Our Only Mistake Was Being Born Muslim": A 25-Year Fight Against Terror Charges'. *The Wire*, 11 March. Available at https://thewire.in/rights/tada-muslims-terrorism-11-acquitted (accessed 17 September 2021).

Stirner, Max. 1995. *The Ego and Its Own*, ed. David Leopold. Cambridge: Cambridge University Press.

Varadhan, Sudarshan. 2020. 'One Woman Reports a Rape Every 15 Minutes in India'. *Reuters*, 9 January. Available at https://www.reuters.com/article/us-india-crime-women-idUSKBN1Z821W (accessed 16 September 2021).

Vatsa, Aditi. 2014. 'Delhi University Professor G. N. Saibaba is Arrested for "Naxal Links"'. *The Indian Express*, 10 May.

Publishers' Acknowledgements

For granting permission to reproduce copyrighted material in this volume, the publishers and the author wish to make the following acknowledgements.

The Hindu, for the articles reproduced as Chapters 1–6, 8–16, 21–25, 30–32, 34–35, 39, 41–42, 44–45, 49, 52, 54, 59–60, and 65, originally published, respectively, under the titles:

1. 'Adivasis and the Genocide', *The Hindu*, 24 April 2002.
2. 'The Burden of Criminal Neglect', *The Hindu*, 3 January 2015.
3. 'Constitutional Conversations on Adivasi Rights', *The Hindu*, 24 July 2015.
4. 'Without Land or Recourse', *The Hindu*, 23 February 2019.
5. 'Caste, the Academy and Dalit Women', *The Hindu*, 20 June 2001.
6. 'Reservation and the Creamy Layer', *The Hindu*, 24 October 2006.
7. 'Roadmap for Reservation in Higher Education', *The Hindu*, 18 April 2008.
8. 'Atrocities That No Longer Shock', *The Hindu*, 15 October 2013.
9. 'The Scope of Constitutional Morality', *The Hindu*, 4 October 2018.
10. 'The Annihilation by Caste', *The Hindu*, 3 February 2016.
11. 'Post-truths about Rohith Vemula', *The Hindu*, 17 January 2017.
12. 'Creating Enabling Environments', *The Hindu*, 24 June 2011.
13. 'The Rights of Prisoners with Disabilities', *The Hindu*, 20 May 2014.
14. 'Disability is Not Divinity, *The Hindu*, 12 January 2016.

15. 'Right to Privacy as Right to Life', *The Hindu*, 9 November 2017.
16. 'From "Perversion" to Right to Life with Dignity', *The Hindu*, 6 July 2009.
17. 'It's Time to Scrap the Eunuchs Act', *The Hindu*, 28 September 2017.
18. 'Rethinking the Law on Sexual Assault', *The Hindu*, 3 June 2010.
19. 'Girl Punk, Interrupted', *The Hindu*, 24 August 2012.
20. 'A Moment of Triumph for Women', *The Hindu*, 25 January 2013.
21. 'On Human Rights and Radical Evil', *The Hindu*, 30 December 2002.
22. 'UPA Strays off Sonia's Course', *The Hindu*, 10 February 2013.
23. 'Something is Rotten in the States of . . .', *The Hindu*, 13 April 2015.
24. 'An Assault on the Right to Privacy', *The Hindu*, 6 September 2018.
25. 'Constitutional Justice is Non-negotiable', *The Hindu*, 9 December 2019 (co-authored with Justice B. Sudarshan Reddy, included in this volume with his permission).
26. 'Taking Aim at the Messenger: On the Attack on Kancha Ilaiah', *The Hindu*, 5 October 2017.
27. 'Kancha Ilaiah: For Lives Lived in Labour', *The Hindu*, 28 October 2017.
28. 'They Cannot Stop Me from Teaching Marx and Ambedkar: Prof. K. Satyanarayana', *The Hindu*, 9 September 2018.
29. 'Of Lawyers and the Law', *The Hindu*, 9 July 2000.
30. 'Lawyer, Judge and Aam Aadmi', *The Hindu*, 18 January 2014.
31. 'The Court is Not Above the Constitution', *The Hindu*, 23 April 2019.
32. 'Education, Campuses and Violence', *The Hindu*, 29 October 2002.
33. 'What is a University?', *The Hindu*, 16 February 2016.

34. 'Development, Justice and the Constitution', *The Hindu*, 27 July 2011.
35. 'Regulating Cultures through Food Policing', *The Hindu*, 1 May 2012.
36. 'Retrieving the Idea of Citizenship', *The Hindu*, 28 January 2020.

The Wire, for the articles reproduced as Chapters 18, 27, 33, 46, 48, 55–57, 61, and 63, originally published, respectively, under the titles:

1. 'Kashmir and Una Define a New Practice of Politics', *The Wire*, 2 August 2016.
2. 'Denying Women Entry to the Sabarimala Temple Amounts to Untouchability', *The Wire*, 19 July 2018.
3. 'Activists' Arrests a Dire Warning for Anyone Who Dares to Question or Resist', *The Wire*, 30 August 2018.
4. 'When Professional Associations Start Promoting Narrow, Sectarian Agendas', *The Wire*, 2 March 2016.
5. 'Privacy, Sequestered Courts, and the Place of Dissent', *The Wire*, 16 January 2018.
6. 'Urgent Notes from a University in Crisis', *The Wire*, 24 March 2016.
7. 'Let the University of Hyderabad Not Become a Feudal Village', *The Wire*, 16 June 2016.
8. 'One Year after Rohith Vemula's Suicide, a Deepening Crisis in Hyderabad University', *The Wire*, 16 January 2017.
9. 'By Inciting Violence, Paresh Rawal, MP, Must Surely Forfeit His Seat', *The Wire*, 26 May 2017.
10. 'SC/ST Act: A Hostile Environment and an "Atrocious" Interpretation', *The Wire*, 26 March 2018.

Scroll.in, for the articles reproduced as Chapters 19, 40, 43, 64 and 66, originally published, respectively, under the titles:

1. 'Babri Masjid Revisited', *Scroll.in*, 15 November 2019.
2. 'Supreme Court's Refusal to Quash FIR against Anand Teltumbde Damages the Right to Dissent', *Scroll.in*, 25 January 2019.

3. 'To Accuse Activist Harsh Mander of Hate Speech is to Fall Prey to the Barbarity of False Equivalence', *Scroll.in*, 17 May 2020.
4. 'Through the Clouds of Protest, Sightings of Hope', *Scroll.in*, 22 January 2020.
5. 'The Fight to Free Pregnant Student Activist Safoora Zargar is a Battle for India's Very Soul', *Scroll.in*, 9 June 2020.

Economic and Political Weekly, for the articles reproduced as Chapters 7, 26, and 53, originally published, respectively, under the titles:

1. 'Chunduru: On the Road to Justice', *Economic and Political Weekly* 42, no. 39 (29 September 2007): 3915–16.
2. 'Annihilation by Caste: Lessons from Budaun and Beyond', *Economic and Political Weekly* 49, no. 25 (21 June 2014).
3. 'Making the Forked Tongue Speak ... An Ethnography of the Self', *Economic and Political Weekly* 43, no. 16 (19 April 2008): 63–70.

The New Indian Express, for the articles reproduced as Chapters 17 and 36, originally published, respectively, under the titles:

1. 'An Apology to Mohammed Akhlaq', *The New Indian Express*, 16 October 2015.
2. 'Free Speech is the Cornerstone of Constitution', *The New Indian Express*, 22 July 2015.

The Leaflet, for the articles reproduced as Chapters 50 and 51, originally published, respectively, under the titles:

1. 'Redeeming the Constitution', *The Leaflet*, 10 May 2019.
2. 'Juridical Viralities, Courts and the Question of Justice', *The Leaflet*, 14 August 2020.

Citizens against Hate, for the article reproduced as Chapter 20, originally published under the title 'We Shall Not Be Silenced, nor Shall We Ever Forget', in *'Everyone Has Been Silenced': Police Excess against Anti-CAA Protesters in Uttar Pradesh, and Post-violence Reprisal*, March 2020.

Outlook, for the article reproduced as Chapter 29, originally published under the title, 'Judicial Opacity on Women's Entry in Sabarimala is Troubling', *Outlook*, 20 November 2019.

Discover Society, for the article reproduced as Chapter 37, originally published under the title, '"Hard Words Break No Bones": Sedition, Free Speech, Academic Freedoms and Sovereignty in India', *Discover Society*, no. 46 (20 February 2016).

Indian Cultural Forum, for the article reproduced as Chapter 38, originally published under the title, 'Mourning the Loss of Gauri Lankesh', *Indian Cultural Forum*, 14 September 2017.

LSE South Asia Centre, for the article reproduced as Chapter 58, originally published under the title, 'I Don't See What is Happening within Universities as Separate from What is Happening in the Political Arena', *South Asia @ LSE* Blog, 17 May 2017.

Seminar, for the article reproduced as Chapter 62, originally published under the title, 'Of Law, Resurrection and a Future', *Seminar*, January 2017.

LiveLaw, for the article reproduced as Chapter 67, originally published under the title, '#I Can't Breathe: Governance by Annihilation and by Hate', *LiveLaw*, 3 October 2020.

Acknowledgements

The short essays presented in this volume were published as op-eds, commentaries and interviews, for the most part in *The Hindu*. Other essays appeared in *Economic and Political Weekly*, *The New Indian Express*, *Outlook*, *The Wire*, *Indian Cultural Forum*, *Discover Society*, *Scroll.in*, *LiveLaw*, *Seminar*, Citizens against Hate, the *South Asia @ LSE* Blog and *The Leaflet*. I am grateful to the editors of all these publications for the space they provided me to write and for permitting me to republish the essays in this collection. Some of the essays have been edited, some have been abridged—and therefore may not appear here exactly as they did in the original published versions. I have however, not attempted to 'update' them, as the chronology is a sign of the times in which they were written—between 2000 and 2020.

I am grateful to Roopa Sharma, Insiya Poonawala and the Orient BlackSwan team for their patience and warm support in the publication of this volume. I am especially grateful to Meghna C. N. for her meticulous and painstaking editorial support. I thank the anonymous reviewer for suggestions on reorganising the manuscript.

Anand Teltumbde, my good friend, conscience-keeper and radical Ambedkarite philosopher, generously agreed to write the Foreword to this collection, at a time when he was battling a vindictive state, and resisting incarceration. I have no words to express my gratitude to him. As this book goes to print, Anand is in jail, a prisoner of conscience at a critical juncture in our collective life as a constitutional community. His sage voice, his wisdom and his courage guide us, even as we feel acutely the void caused by his detention.

My mother Vasanth and my siblings Chitra and Arvind have been patient with me and have been enormously supportive over a lifetime—intellectually and emotionally. To Raj Mohan, Ramya and Keertana, I owe my greatest debt. They are my inspiration and my strength. This book is for them, with love.

Kalpana Kannabiran
August 2021
Secunderabad

Introduction

Social movements around constitutional rights and the rule of law have foregrounded the close and complex interconnections between law and society in everyday life-worlds. They have also pushed us as scholars in the social sciences to hone our understanding of discrimination, vulnerability, inequality and precarity in relation to the (in)operation of the law and its procedures. While the teaching or learning of law is not a constitutive part of pedagogic practice in the social sciences, there are moments in contemporary history where the kinship with law has been inescapable, not affording any more an opportunity to assume its opacity or its irrelevance to an understanding of society. Although there is early writing that has foregrounded the constitutive position of law in sociology for instance, this did not necessarily inform sociological sensibilities—especially pertaining to empirical realities the sociologist confronted—on Indian society.

As someone formally trained in law, sociology and gender studies, and as a feminist socio-legal counsellor with a women's collective who has straddled multiple domains of social movements as an activist, I often saw the intersections between these domains and found myself thinking through issues from the crevices—building bridges across locations, rather than inhabiting fragmented silos that disciplinary training primes you for. The focus, however, as it developed almost instinctively, was on law through a feminist lens for a lay reader. This engagement, rooted in movement politics, and the frequent confrontation with derogations and injustice, was based on a recognition that empathy and a self-reflexive approach to social location and questions of privilege were indispensable to writing in a deeply graded and unequal society. Emotion, therefore, came to occupy a central place in my exploration of law and its relation to borders of different orders—whether in the context of political dissent, collective violence, crimes against humanity, family violence—and in relation to people and communities who lived and faced the routine oppressions of the state, especially on its securitised borders, in Kashmir, for instance.

In participating in protests, campaigns, advocacy and classroom teaching in sociology for law students, I was simultaneously straddling several domains and was forced to disseminate my learnings from one space to another, rather than see these as self-contained silos. Constitutive of this endeavour and built into the questions that were thrown up from time to time was the critique of power and dominance. Short opinion pieces that built bridges, opened out debates and conversations around the making of law, critiqued judicial deliberations of law and rights, opened up a space for a public discourse on dissent and provided this alternative space for an expansion of deliberative dialogue. Importantly, as several readers pointed out to me over the years, it forced the lay reader, who in the normal course distances herself from 'law', to engage with its language, protocols and practices.

This collection presents 64 opinion articles and three interviews, published between 2000 and 2020. It is organised into two parts. Part A presents chapters on specific issues: Adivasi rights, Dalit rights, rights of persons with disabilities, minority rights, queer rights and women's rights. Part B presents chapters on the overarching debates around human rights, civil liberties and reflections on the Constitution for our futures. Each part is further organised into thematic sections. Within the thematic sections, individual chapters are arranged chronologically. In moving between sections, therefore, one also moves back and forth chronologically.

Contemporary India is the focus of the entire collection. Chapter 1, in the opening section titled 'Adivasis and Gujarat 2002', was written in 2002 after a fact-finding mission to Gujarat after the democidal pogrom that targeted Muslims in the state. Although the focus of this chapter is the Adivasi citizen, the context is collective violence against Muslims. Chapter 30, in the section titled 'Civil Liberties', also speaks to Gujarat in 2002 and was written in its aftermath, reflecting on Upendra Baxi's (2002) book, *The Future of Human Rights*. At the time of writing this Introduction, the embers of Delhi 2020 are still smouldering. The travel of 'democidal politics' (to borrow from Baxi) from state to national government, the mobilisation of the *aam aadmi* (common man) into armed groups (pun intended), '*Jai Siya Ram*' (in Gujarat, 2002) and '*Jai Shri Ram*' (in Delhi, 2020) as the war cries of marauding mobs, and the exploitation of vulnerability by majoritarian governments in both instances, make for compelling reflection.

The debate on the death penalty has been most difficult to sustain, especially in an environment that is resonating with cries for instant retribution in place of a fair trial, where terrorist offences and crimes against women evoke similar responses of public anger and the unabashed celebration of impunity for the police. It breaks to the surface at the most unexpected moments in the most unexpected ways, as, for instance, in the case of the execution of Afzal Guru accused in the Parliament attack case. The ferment in university campuses after 2014 was precipitated by discussions around the injustice of the trial of Afzal Guru, with the Akhil Bharatiya Vidyarthi Parishad (ABVP), the students' wing of the Sangh Parivar, disrupting meetings on campuses across the country that were now labelled 'anti-national' because they condoned the actions of 'terrorists' like Afzal Guru. Yet in 2019, we came full circle with the arrest of decorated Jammu and Kashmir police officer, Davinder Singh, who was named by Afzal Guru as the person who not only tortured him in custody but also forced him to ferry men to Delhi, who later turned out to be the militants who attacked the Parliament (*The Times of India* 2020). The question of the (in)justice of the trial of Afzal Guru and his execution is far from settled.

At the time of writing, the campaign against the death penalty opposed the execution of the men convicted for the rape and murder of Jyoti Singh ('Nirbhaya'), provoking intense grief and rage from Jyoti's mother, who saw justice in the death penalty, no less, even commending the custodial killings in Hyderabad. What is the measure of justice? A new, more stringent law in her name, a trial, a conviction was what Nirbhaya accomplished in death. And yet, the custodial murder of unarmed suspects is seen by her grieving parents as 'more just', and arguments against the death penalty as gross injustice. How might we shift the discourse away from retribution? Arguing against the death penalty is not an argument to forgive perpetrators of crime. It is an argument against the taking of life by the state, and the reinstatement of restitutive justice and humane punitive systems that do not derogate the dignity of those held in custody even for the most heinous crimes.

The earliest essay in this collection, Chapter 44, published in 2000, in the section titled 'Professions and Civil Rights', discusses the suicide of a lawyer in Hyderabad unable to bear sexual harassment by a male colleague. In 2019, we grappled with the derailment of due process by the then chief justice of India, Ranjan Gogoi, in a complaint of sexual harassment against him by a member of his official staff. This case is discussed in Chapters 49 and 50 in the section titled 'Judges are Equal Citizens'. Ironically, while the Vishaka guidelines set out by the Supreme Court of India in 1997 heralded the recognition of sexual harassment at the workplace and prescribed the procedure to deal with this pervasive problem that confronted women at work, courtroom culture has been the most impervious to change. The question of judicial exceptionalism has been a difficult one to push for change on. Especially when the chief justice of India ensures a 'settlement' of a complaint of sexual harassment against himself, blocking due process, we know that courts can also be sites of the fallibility of power, not necessarily sites for the dispensation of justice alone. Our work on speaking to ideas of justice and constitutionalism then involves, importantly, engaging in a public debate that calls judges into account.

Structural violence lies at the heart of our collective engagements with the law—this is the theme around which several of the chapters revolve. The ground covered reflects my own preoccupations with human rights and the rule of law: prisoners' rights, women's rights, state impunity, judicial accountability, citizen engagement in law-making, questions of discrimination against Dalits, Adivasis, persons with disabilities, sexual and religious minorities, questions of culture and university campuses as sites of politics. With respect to campuses, given my location in Hyderabad, and the significance of the struggles waged by Rohith Vemula during his lifetime and in his name after his passing, I have focused on the University of Hyderabad. But these reflections are not limited to that campus alone, as will be evident.

Viewed chronologically, the chapters give a sense of the times, flagging issues for discussion as they have arisen in the public domain. There is a thematic scheme to them as well, within an overarching frame of an idea of justice. Yet, both chronologically and thematically, the chapters run into each other. Caste, free speech, universities, gender, courtroom cultures criss-cross frequently across the sections in which individual chapters may be placed, as they must. The Constitution of India frames my writing, which seeks to promote a deliberative public engagement with its basic tenets. Sociologists might argue that this is self-limiting—fixating on the normative, it has been observed, detracts from a robust understanding of empirical particularities. That is a valid criticism, but my focus in the limited space that an opinion column (which most of these chapters originally appeared as) affords has been to point to ways in which we may use constitution-scapes to build an informed and sustained critique of dominant, majoritarian, misogynist, Hindu-supremacist politics and older practices of state impunity.

There is a sense in which we are going around in circles. The marginalisation of Adivasi communities that is the subject of Section I has been one of the most difficult to seek effective legal redress and constitutional remedies for despite a sustained focus, insurgent law-making and critical ethnography—protection of land rights and the Forest Rights Act, 2006, for instance—and some stunning decisions from the courts, notably *Samatha* (1997)[1] and *Nandini Sundar* (2011)[2] that foregrounded the rights of Adivasis to constitutional protection as never before. But also, Article 19(5), the Fifth and Sixth Schedules of the Constitution, that mandated autonomy for areas with a predominantly Adivasi population. Chapter 4 points to a decision of the Supreme Court that constructed Adivasis as 'encroachers' and directed their eviction from forests—taking us right back to where we began at the time the Constitution was framed. And yet, so much has changed, the shifts perhaps evident from the questions that surfaced for anthropologists and lawyers with the disciplinary locations of the two converging, as we see in the case of *Nandini Sundar*, and in the *Report of the High-Level Committee on the Socio-Economic, Health and Educational Status of Tribal Communities of India* (2014) chaired by sociologist Virginius Xaxa.

Section II, 'Blocked by Caste', demonstrates the swinging of the debate on caste discrimination between reservation and atrocity. Although caste has been at the centre of the sociology curriculum in India for decades, the work of Babasaheb Ambedkar, Savitribai and Jotiba Phule, Periyar and other anti-caste philosophers did not enter classrooms until Dalit students active in Ambedkarite groups on campuses and outside began to demand it. Chapter 5 examines the contestations around the formulation of caste as a form of racial discrimination in the context of the World Conference against Racism in Durban, South Africa, in 2001.

The debate on merit, reservation and the 'creamy layer' has centred on reservations especially in professional education. The tremors around the Mandal Commission Report continue right into the present, interspersed with gruesome atrocity—Chunduru, Laxmanpur Bathe, Khairlanji, the impunity with respect to manual scavenging, to recall a few. Finally, reservations and atrocity converge in the struggles of Vemula and the cascading movement of Dalit students around social justice and Ambedkarite philosophies on university campuses from 2016 onwards. This is a discussion that travels between the sections on caste, human rights, university campuses and citizenship—in an important sense, straddling the pervasiveness of caste and the snowballing of resistance to caste orders in contemporary India. Lynching of cattle traders, the lynching of Mohammed Akhlaq and the turbulence around beef festivals on campuses by Dalit students bridge our discussion of Dalit rights with minority rights where among other issues, the politics of food has translated into a matter of life and death, as I discuss in Chapter 60, 'Regulating Cultures through Food Policing'. Gender and the figure of the Dalit woman are at the centre of the debate on caste, in different ways—the murder of the two young girls in Badaun, the women and children of the Bhotmange family in Khairlanji, and the resilience of Radhika Vemula, for instance.

Disability rights, the subject of Section III, continues to be a neglected space of academic engagement with institutional arrangements, curricular content and teaching methods exhibiting gross hostility to persons with disabilities especially in education, employment and public spaces. Within the human rights movement as well, the perception of disability as not being a human rights issue came to a head in the case of G. N. Saibaba—a person with severe disabilities and multiple related medical conditions that require high support—presently in solitary confinement, convicted of offences under the draconian Unlawful Activities (Prevention) Act (UAPA), 1967. The case of Saibaba forced us to ask what the meaning of the right to personal liberty under the Constitution of India was for a person with disabilities. And also, how does one think of disability in higher education—in the social sciences, humanities and law especially, but also in the medical sciences and reproductive health. It is these multiple preoccupations that jostle for space in the section on disability.

The rights of religious minorities in India, especially Muslims, has never been under greater threat than at the present moment. The chapters in Section IV, 'Minority Rights', look at different moments in the politics of hate and the deeply discriminatory politics of jurisprudence on minority rights. With the violence against Muslims in Delhi in February 2020, in Uttar Pradesh in 2019 and the steady rise in religious intolerance under the Hindutva majoritarian government in India, there is utmost urgency in engaging with the question of minority rights in contemporary India. The chapters in this section begin with a reflection on the lynching of Mohammed Akhlaq and end with a reflection on the firing on anti-Citizenship (Amendment) Act (CAA) protesters in Uttar Pradesh, as also on Delhi, 2020. The slope we as a people have hurtled down and our entrapment in governance by hate is open to view. The criminalisation of dissent, especially evident in the incarceration of Sharjeel Imam, and the equivocation around his arrest raise serious questions about the need to revisit our understanding of solidarity and its basis.

The loss of life, the brutality and the mayhem Muslims in India are being subjected to by Hindus on a rampage is planned and premeditated. And yet, the violence of Hindutva politics claims the lives of both Hindus and Muslims, as Asim Ali (2020) and Jawed Naqvi (2020) argue in separate ways, but Muslims are targeted in distinctly different ways on a different scale altogether, a statement supported by considerable evidence gathered especially by peoples' tribunals and citizen hearings on different episodes of collective violence over the past two decades, culminating in the violence around the Citizenship (Amendment) Act, 2019, in Delhi in February 2020. In the darkest moments that confront us all especially in the context of the CAA, Muslims have placed themselves at enormous risk—facing dispossession, social humiliation and annihilation—in challenging an unjust law that undermines the fundamental basis of the Constitution of India.

The year 2019 was catastrophic in terms of rights derogations. The Babri Masjid judgement,[3] the Bhima Koregaon case transfers,[4] the judicial callousness on Kashmir,[5] the judicial eulogies of power (Yamunan 2020) and prevarications in matters of justice (Sebastian 2020) leave us just so terribly angry, distraught, helpless and furious at the capture of institutions—the state, the police, the judiciary, the administration, the legislatures—that keeps those not being targeted in a chokehold while Muslims are being subjected to deadly attack on several fronts at once. Nissim Mannathukkaren's (2020) argument on the 'barbarity of false equivalence' bears infinite reiteration:

> Moral equivalence completely obscures the root causes of a problem.... Thus, six years of relentless hate-mongering against Muslims is seen to be of no consequence in creating an absolutely inflammable social sphere.
>
> In no period of Indian political history after Partition has so much hate pervaded the public sphere. WhatsApp groups and Twitter timelines have become a cesspool of the most morbid fantasies of hate against Muslims, all purveyed by otherwise "civil", "decent" "educated" and "family-oriented" Hindus.

Gender rights in India—the focus of Sections V and VI—can be clearly seen in terms of movement politics around (a) women's rights from the mid-1970s to the present (the reform of rape laws in 2013), and (b) queer rights from the mid-2000s, but gaining traction with the judgement of the Delhi High Court in *Naz Foundation* in 2009[6] and the *Navtej Singh Johar* case in the Supreme Court in 2018.[7] Within the larger space of queer rights, the transgender question has been particularly a cause for concern in Telangana, which till the present has an extremely repressive legislation, the Andhra Pradesh (Telangana Area) Eunuchs Act, an act of the nizam's dominion, that continued in operation. It is on this law that the section on queer rights focuses, while also discussing in some detail the implications of the decision in *Naz Foundation*, opening out the judgement for the lay reader. The section on women's rights has a wider scope ranging from rape law reform and feminist resistance to the fraught issue of women's entry into the Sabarimala temple. This section also, importantly in my view, presents for the reader an account of the making and unmaking of laws through resistance struggles and movements that deliberate on the structure and content of specific legislations—the Justice Verma Committee (2013) and the new law on sexual assault are case in point.

The chapters in Part A on understanding discrimination set the context for the issues of civil liberties, professional ethics, judicial responsibility, and free speech discussed in Part B of the collection.

The seven sections that comprise Part B focus on civil liberties, human rights and law. The chapters in this part attempt to open out specific cases of state violence and impunity—the genocidal state, debates on the death penalty, extra-judicial murder, for instance, the centrality of free speech and associational freedoms to deliberative democracy, especially in the context of the rise of right-wing nationalism and the use of sedition laws to silence dissent. Also important in this part is the rise of hate speech that fuels violence against dissenters and minorities on the ground.

The chapters in Part B also look at questions of judicial accountability, although they are immediately relevant to the arguments presented in Part A as well. The understanding on which these articles were written was that there must be an informed critique and engagement with judicial decisions. Judges are neither above nor outside the law. If courts of law are then the first available recourse to justice, how have lawyers and judges fared—indeed how have institutions of justice fared—in the defence of fundamental freedoms?

The debate on dissent and free speech came to a head in early 2016, immediately after the death of Rohith Vemula. Universities and institutions of higher education across the country were central to the new and radical practice of politics that spoke the Constitution and spoke truth to power in unprecedented ways, with Dalit, Adivasi and minority students at the forefront of the struggle for *azaadi* (freedom). How might we situate the university in a democracy in turmoil, and what might be the lessons we learn from that experience? And finally, through all of this, what are the futures of the Constitution in India?

From custodial killings misnamed as 'encounters' to the death penalty, from the banning of free speech to the slapping of charges of sedition, from the anticipation of violence and assault on the part of human rights defenders like Kancha Ilaiah to their murder on the streets, like Gauri Lankesh, the period since 2014 has been one of deep crisis for any minimalist adherence to the rule of law and due process.

Resistance is at the heart of democracy. Yet, even as we celebrate the resistance by students of Jawaharlal Nehru University, Aligarh Muslim University and Jamia Millia Islamia in the face of brutal state terror strikes, even as we celebrate the resistance of the women of Shaheen Bagh and the cascading of Shaheen Baghs across the country, we remain hemmed in by the unspeakable violence in Assam over the National Register of Citizens, the lockdown of Kashmir post the abrogation of Articles 370 and 35A, the police firing on unarmed protestors in Uttar Pradesh, the mass violence against Muslims in Delhi in 2020, the continuing incarceration of dissenters during the pandemic, bringing this state action within the meaning of aggravated punishment. And we witness the derailment of constitutional commitment to dignity in the case of Hathras, reinstating caste-Hindu supremacy as the method of rule in India under Hindutva. The country mirrors the gated, surveilled, securitised campus. The sections on universities and free speech were written in response to specific instances of the criminalisation of speech of protestors and the validation of hate speech. The colonial law on sedition acquires an increasing legitimacy and traction under a political dispensation that not merely eschews debate, but actively obstructs deliberative dialogue.

The chapters in Part B thus look closely at the right to life and personal liberty in the times of hate politics. How do these curbs on personal liberties and the derogation of the right to life by state and non-state actors alter our sense of who we are as citizens of this free country, and what might we do to retrieve a constitutional sensibility that is publicly owned and adopted? In the final analysis, how do we move towards occupying the Constitution-as-commons? The concluding chapters in this part speak of the ways in which insurgent interpretations of the Constitution challenge courts and governments alike, positing a people's understanding of the Constitution as the fundamental basis for citizenship.

In bringing these essays together, I attempt to share a sense of my journey within and outside academia, viewing social realities from the perspectives of the borderlands, and attempting to understand the Constitution (indeed the law) as a tool that speaks to these realities and gives these perspectives voice and visibility. These ideas have grown out of collective conversations in rights movements—I hope this collection contributes in some small way to the groundswell of resistance that speaks truth to power in so many different ways in India today.

Kalpana Kannabiran
August 2021

Notes

1. Samatha v. State of Andhra Pradesh & Ors, AIR 1997 SC 3297.
2. Nandini Sundar & Ors v. State of Chhattisgarh, (2011) 7 SCC 547.
3. M. Siddiq v. Mahant Suresh Das & Ors, 2019 SCC OnLine 1440.
4. Romila Thapar & Ors v. Union of India & Ors, WP (Cr.) No. 260 of 2018.
5. Anuradha Bhasin v. Union of India & Ors, (2020) 3 SCC 637.
6. Naz Foundation v. Government of NCT of Delhi & Ors, (2009) 160 DLT 277.
7. Navtej Singh Johar v. Union of India, AIR 2018 SC 4321.

References

'Davinder Singh: Senior Jammu & Kashmir Police Officer who was Arrested with Two Terrorists'. 2020. *The Times of India*, 13 January. Available at https://timesofindia.indiatimes.com/india/davinder-singh-senior-jk-police-officer-who-was-arrested-with-two-terrorists/articleshow/73223012.cms (accessed 17 September 2021).

Ali, Asim. 2020. 'Left and Liberals Should Stop Looking for the Perfect Victim in Delhi Riots'. *The Print*, 2 March. Available at https://theprint.in/opinion/left-and-liberals-should-stop-looking-for-the-perfect-victim-in-delhi-riots/373837/ (accessed 19 July 2021).

Baxi, Upendra. 2002. *The Future of Human Rights*. New Delhi: Oxford University Press.

Justice Verma Committee. 2013. *Report of the Committee on Amendments to Criminal Law*.

Mannathukkaren, Nissim. 2020. 'The Barbarity of False Equivalence'. *The Wire*, 8 March. Available at https://thewire.in/communalism/delhi-riots-communalism-false-equivalence (accessed 9 March 2020).

Ministry of Tribal Affairs, Government of India. 2014. *Report of the High-Level Committee on Socio-Economic, Health and Educational Status of Tribal Communities of India*.

Naqvi, Jawed. 2020. 'Bigotry: A Handy State Asset'. *Dawn*, 3 March.

Sebastian, Manu. 2020. 'Delhi Riots Case Hearing: How Things Changed in a Day with Change of Bench?'. *LiveLaw*, 27 February. Available at https://www.livelaw.in/top-stories/delhi-riots-case-hearing-how-things-changed-in-a-day-with-change-of-bench-153214 (accessed 5 March 2020).

Yamunan, Sruthisagar. 2020. 'Judge's Praise for Modi: If Justices Veer from Professed Values, Can Criticism of This be Punished?'. *Scroll.in*, 23 February. Available at https://scroll.in/article/954059/judges-praise-for-modi-if-justices-veer-from-professed-values-can-criticism-of-this-be-punished (accessed 5 March 2020).

Part A

Understanding Discrimination

I

The Adivasi Experience

1

Adivasis and Gujarat 2002*

The violence in the rural areas of Gujarat took on a very different form from that in the cities, especially Ahmedabad. In eastern Gujarat, the violence—looting and arson—was largely carried out by Adivasis against Muslims.

Chhotaudepur town is surrounded by 48 villages that have been directly affected by the violence, of which we visited two and met people from several other villages. There are 2,300 people in the relief camp, all of whom moved here over a month ago from villages where Adivasis constituted a numerical majority.

Panwad village has a population of about 11,000, of which Muslims number about 1,000. There are Muslims, Adivasis, Baniyas, Lohars and Prajapatis in the village, Adivasis being in the majority. Muslims were engaged in vehicle businesses—renting trucks, tempos, jeeps, etc.—and the brick business, and a few families were engaged in agriculture. Around Panwad there were several villages with two or three Muslim families. As the trouble began on 28 February, these families started coming to Panwad for shelter. At 2:30 p.m. on 10 March, Adivasis from neighbouring villages began gathering in Panwad. Then the attacks began. Local leaders—all non-Adivasis—were issuing orders. The police offered no protection to the Muslim families. Two trucks and six jeeps were parked in the police station compound for safe custody while five vehicles were stationed in front of the police station even before the trouble began. All these vehicles were burnt even as

---

* Originally published as 'Adivasis and the Genocide', in *The Hindu*, 24 April 2002.

Written after an extensive fact-finding mission as part of the Indian Social Action Forum (INSAF) team that visited Gujarat after the mass genocidal violence against Muslims in 2002, this essay foregrounds the urgency of forging a broad-based alliance that brings together all marginalised groups.

the police watched. Panwad's Muslims were forced to leave the village that day.

When we visited the village on 3 April, the devastation was shocking. The houses had been burnt and reduced to rubble after being looted. In the soot, on what remained of the walls, were slogans declaring 'Hindustan' to be the land of the Hindus in abusive language. We were told that there were instructions from Kiritbhai Shah, a local leader, that nobody should take photographs without his consent and that one should have a written permit to do so. All the Hindu houses in Panwad had a small, framed picture of Radha and Krishna, possibly to identify them as Hindu houses.

In Kadwal, 55 houses were destroyed. The village mosque was razed to the ground and the books in it were burnt. 'Jai Siya Ram' was inscribed on the ground among the debris. We met the *mukhia* (headman) of Kadwal and some women from the village at the relief camp in Chhotaudepur. One woman said, 'After the Sabarmati Express was burnt, we didn't sleep one night. Adivasis had been given money to do this eight days earlier. What do they know of the difference between a *mandir* [temple] and a *masjid* [mosque]?'

Kawant village has a population of approximately 10,000, of which 1,200 are Muslims. Although there was no trouble there initially, every day the pressure on the Adivasis of the village mounted, with one or two families being attacked. On 11 March, the police told the Muslim families that they must move to a safe place if they wanted protection and sent 900 of them to Bodeli town, 40 kilometres away, under escort. The 300 Muslims who remained in the village were shifted to Baroda, 115 kilometres away, on 12 March. The looting went on for four days. The village mukhia told us that the police in Bodeli put pressure on them to leave because they felt they were creating problems. So 900 of them took off in different directions.

An Adivasi schoolteacher in Joj said,

> Adivasis are innocent. They were given liquor and money and forced to participate in the arson. We later spoke to the Adivasis who took part. They said they had been used. There were young boys and men. No women. The women stood and wept silently, watching the destruction. One woman from the blacksmith community asked the rioters to stop the violence. Her house was also burnt down.

Some of the Muslim families asked to leave had lived in the village for 38 years. The village *sarpanch* (headman) is an Adivasi member of the Bharatiya Janata Party (BJP). While we did find that Adivasis had in fact been involved in the looting and arson in large numbers, the people affected by the riots did not hold the Adivasis responsible for the violence. They also recognised that the Adivasis did not really have the choice of refusing and were threatened and coerced into participating in the arson by Vishva Hindu Parishad (VHP) activists supported actively by the police. Where in the country is it possible for Adivasis to muster up gallons of petrol, set fire to vehicles in the presence of the police and get away?

In the village hierarchy in this entire region, the Adivasis were the most disadvantaged and were to a great extent economically dependent on the Muslims, largely moneylenders and traders. The goodwill between the two groups was mainly like that of patron and client and had an economic base that went back several decades. This, together with the traditional positioning of the Adivasi communities, leads us to clear patterns in the violence in tribal areas. With one exception—no Muslim was killed in the violence in the region. The involvement of Adivasis was limited to economic crimes—looting and arson. No rapes or assaults on women were reported from these areas. Muslims in the relief camps were emphatic in their assertion that the Adivasis did not touch them. In the case of a woman named Bilkis, an Adivasi family offered her shelter and gave her clothes to wear, while Hindus of her village allegedly raped and killed all the women in her family. In Panwad, while the Adivasis were responsible for arson, the affected people in the relief camp in Chhotaudepur named three non-Adivasi Hindus who gave orders during the looting. This was further borne out during our visit to the village when we were told quite menacingly that Kiritbhai (one of the three) had said that no photographs should be taken of the village. The person who accompanied us to the village and showed us the aftermath of the violence was an Adivasi activist from the village.

Against this history, the reasons for the turnabout by the Adivasis could have two facets. One, the relationship of economic dependence is a class relation that has the clear potential of being exploitative. And here, the community identity of the person with economic power is largely irrelevant—the Baniya and the Muslim moneylender fulfil identical needs in the village economy in an identical manner. This potential conflict can then be channelled in any direction. Second, a very important trend in the mobilisation strategies of the Sangh Parivar that is critical to understanding the violence in Gujarat is the mobilisation of Dalits and Adivasis against Muslims and their recruitment into one of the organisations of the Sangh Parivar at the lowest level, paid and mobilised to attack Muslims in village after village.

That we have even allowed this poison to penetrate this deep is a matter of serious reflection for all democratic forces in the country. The situation in Gujarat foregrounds the urgency of forging a broad-based alliance that brings together all marginalised groups and the progressive political formations that mobilise these groups in Gujarat, because we need now, more than ever before, to find strength in numbers.

2

The Burden of Criminal Neglect*

The *Report of the High-Level Committee on Socio-Economic, Health and Educational Status of Tribal Communities of India* (Ministry of Tribal Affairs 2014), under the chairmanship of sociologist Virginius Xaxa, was circulated in December 2014. The 431-page report details the situation of tribal communities: Scheduled Tribes, de-notified tribes and particularly vulnerable tribal communities. Taking on board the findings and demands of social movements, non-governmental organisations (NGOs), researchers and bureaucrats, the report consolidates what we already know about the situation of tribal communities in this country. Without detracting from its significance as an archive, it is important to revisit some basic questions at this moment that have been brought to the fore yet again.

Of the forest area in this country, 60 per cent is in tribal area. Of the 58 districts with forest cover greater than 67 per cent, 51 are tribal districts. Three states—Odisha, Chhattisgarh and Jharkhand—account for 70 per cent of India's coal reserves, 80 per cent of its high-grade iron ore, 60 per cent of its bauxite and almost 100 per cent of its chromite reserves. Of those displaced by dams, 40 per cent are tribal peoples (ibid.: 49–50). A look at violent conflict, whether in Fifth Schedule states or in Sixth Schedule states, shows that 'the state is involved in all of these conflicts in some way or another' (ibid.: 50). Not surprisingly, the areas where these wars are being waged (with the state as party) are tribal areas with rich mineral reserves. The Armed Forces (Special Powers) Act (AFSPA), 1958, guarantees impunity to state perpetrators of extrajudicial murder and assault, and there are a large number of peaceful mass movements against the appropriation of tribal homelands by the state and by corporations.

* Originally published in *The Hindu*, 3 January 2015.

While there is a generally discernible occupational shift in tribal communities, the committee observes, the focus of national state agencies on mainstream categorisations of agricultural labourers, cultivators and the omnibus category of non-farm workers masks the finer details of tribal work-worlds and therefore obstructs an understanding of shifts therein. The need for tribal communities to have continued and uninterrupted access to forests for livelihoods and the responsibility of the state in securing these livelihoods, ensuring their viability, and providing an account of their diversity; creating enabling conditions for the dignity of work and sustainability; and plans for protecting and removing both conflict and livelihood degradation caused by the repressive presence of the forest bureaucracy in tribal areas are issues that merit greater attention.

The absence of state accountability and responsibility are at the core of the problem.

Governance of Tribal Areas

The question of autonomy in Scheduled Areas has been set out in the Fifth and Sixth Schedules of the Constitution. In Fifth Schedule areas, the Tribes Advisory Council—a body with elected and community representatives from Scheduled Tribes—is to advise the governor on matters of administration and governance in Scheduled Areas. Extensive review has shown that although governors are vested with enormous powers with respect to Fifth Schedule areas, they have been found uniformly tardy in the matter of submission of reports and in respecting the constitutional guarantee of autonomy to tribal areas—leading the high-level committee to recommend the setting up of a cell 'in order for the Governor *to properly carry out the duties of the post* vis-à-vis protection of the tribes' (Ministry of Tribal Affairs 2014: 74; emphasis mine) with a whisper that this cell should not just turn into another bureaucratic institution with little interest in tribal affairs. The deliberations of the Tribes Advisory Councils have been found to be tokenistic, and the councils themselves filled with bureaucrats and ministers instead of representatives of tribal communities with effective voice. Even with the Autonomous Councils in the Sixth Schedule states, which have a more robust formal autonomy, the committee finds that 'there is a huge discrepancy between the formal rules guaranteeing autonomy and the informal workings of autonomy on the ground' (ibid.: 87).

As a remedy, the committee recommends that Governors' Cells be set up in all Fifth Schedule states to assist the governor (ibid.: 73), although details about the functioning of such cells set up in Chhattisgarh, Jharkhand, Maharashtra and Rajasthan are not yet known.

What might be the modalities for an ad hoc 'cell' to show a constitutional authority the right path to 'good governance'?

Data reproduced in the report from the years 1981–82 showed a dropout rate of 91.65 per cent before the completion of tenth standard, with a participation in higher education of 1.62 per cent among the Scheduled Tribes (ibid.: 157–59, 175). While flagship programmes and policies have been introduced with laudable objectives, the committee observes that inadequate infrastructure, poor teaching and learning materials, lack of focus on teacher education, the impact of armed conflict on teacher absenteeism and school functioning, and practices of discrimination and stigmatisation in schools have affected tribal children most adversely. Added to this is the rampant and routinised corruption in the government schooling system, an issue that has not been addressed, but one that has an immediate and disastrous effect on children's and teachers' wellbeing. All of these together hold tribal children in a chokehold, pushing them back into ghettoised suboptimal learning possibilities and grinding poverty.

Adivasi Life-Worlds

Where does the solution lie? Might common schools be an answer? Should schooling continue in the 'separate and unequal' mode? And most importantly, the state and adult citizens hold the responsibility for protecting the rights of all children in trust. It is no longer a question of quibbling over numbers—of schools, teachers, dropouts, enrolment, etc. If the outcome is that tribal children do not get a decent education, the state is responsible both for the absence of due diligence and for direct derogation of the fundamental rights of children. On another level, the question is not merely one of the exposure of tribal children to the world outside; more critical is the need to promote an understanding of diverse tribal life-worlds in all children through a restructuring of education.

Tribal land alienation and dispossession are at the crux of the crisis tribal communities face across the country—acquisition of land by the state using the principle of 'eminent domain', manipulation of records and incorrect interpretation of law, encroachment of tribal land by non-tribal people and immigrants, creation of national parks, and armed conflict resulting in forced migration and eviction from homelands. There are questions related to the routinisation of arbitrary arrest, illegal detention and torture in custody of tribal people living in conflict areas. There are no figures publicly available on the demographic profile of prisoner/detainee populations in Fifth Schedule areas. The important guarantee under Article 21 of the Constitution—the right to life and personal liberty—is in a state of perpetual suspension in tribal areas. If one were to go by the data and observations put forth by the high-level committee, once more we learn that the state is waging war at every level against tribal communities across states. Added to this is criminal neglect and violent corruption that has systematically obstructed the delivery of public goods and services. There is a proliferation of reports, of bureaucratic writing generally, as an end in itself.

What are we to do with this information? The government set up a committee that found the state complicit both directly as perpetrator and through the absence of due diligence in the genocidal neglect of tribal peoples.

Where do we go from here?

Reference

Ministry of Tribal Affairs, Government of India. 2014. *Report of the High-Level Committee on Socio-Economic, Health and Educational Status of Tribal Communities of India.*

3

Constitutional Conversations on Adivasi Rights*

Even 67 years after Independence, the problems of Adivasi communities are about access to basic needs. These include, but are not restricted to, elementary education, community healthcare, sustainable livelihood support, the public distribution system, food security, drinking water and sanitation, debt and infrastructure (see Ministry of Tribal Affairs 2014). For them, equality of opportunity remains largely unfulfilled. In this context, it is important to stress that the values of tribal culture are transmitted in a manner that protects the right of the bearers of knowledge to determine the terms of the transmission without exploitation or commodification. Nor can the Adivasis' unhindered access to land and forests, including full access to the commons, especially in Scheduled Areas, be understated. Tribal communities have, over the decades, witnessed the fragmentation of their habitats and homelands and the disruption of their cultures through predatory tourism. All this has left them shattered and impoverished. Entire communities across states have been dispossessed systematically through state action, and have been reduced from owners of resources and well-knit, largely self-sufficient communities to wage earners in agriculture and urban agglomerates with uncertain futures. Yet, we can scarcely forget that the rights of tribal communities in India are protected by the Constitution and special legislations.

Rights Enumerated

While most of these protections are available to groups named in the Constitution (Scheduled Tribes) Order, 1950, there are some tribal

* Originally published in *The Hindu*, 24 July 2015.

communities that fall within the categories of Scheduled Castes and Other Backward Classes and some that don't fall into any of these categories. Within the category of Scheduled Tribes, there are over 500 groups listed, of whom roughly 70 are part of the sub-classification, Particularly Vulnerable Tribal Groups, a small cluster of groups that include the Jarawas of the Andaman Islands, the Chenchus of Andhra Pradesh and Telangana, and the Baigas of Chhattisgarh. These groups face an acute crisis of survival, evident in their rapidly dwindling numbers (Ministry of Tribal Affairs 2014: 59–63, 316–18). Therefore, they are in need of special protection even within the larger Scheduled Tribe (ST) category, protections in relation to non-tribal communities as well as in relation to other tribal communities. Notwithstanding these complex intersections and overlaps (and exclusions in some instances), tribal communities, especially the STs, are the subject of special constitutional attention.

The right of tribal peoples to development through pathways that affirm their autonomy and dignity, as set out in Article 21 and under the Fifth and Sixth Schedules of the Indian Constitution, is often seen as the core of Adivasi rights. And indeed, they are. The oft-quoted *Samatha* judgement of 1997, rich in its defence of the rights of Adivasi communities to their homelands, posits an inter-reading of Articles 14 (equality), 15 (non-discrimination), 16 (equality of opportunity), 17 (abolition of untouchability), 21 (life and liberty), and 23 (right against exploitation) from the Fundamental Rights chapter of the Constitution, and Articles 38 (securing a just social order), 39 (guiding principles of policy) and 46 (promotion of educational and economic interests of Scheduled Castes (SCs), Scheduled Tribes (STs) and other weaker sections) from the Directive Principles of State Policy.[1]

The constitutional arguments advanced in the High Court of Andhra Pradesh resisting the Polavaram dam centred on whether the state could alter (diminish) the boundaries of a Scheduled Area without presidential assent. Submergence, in fact, alters boundaries, causes disappearance of villages and village institutions, and renders people from these communities vulnerable through dispossession by displacement—all of which are the subject of special protections for the STs. The largest volume of litigation in Scheduled Areas has to do with non-tribal occupation of tribal land and the blatant derogation of land transfer regulation laws. Financial inclusion poses the third major problem: despite policy commitments to financial inclusion of vulnerable communities as a measure to lift them out of debt bondage and predatory moneylending and usury, moneylenders continue to thrive in tribal areas.

Hidden Provision

It is in this overall context that I flag an unused constitutional provision as perhaps holding a key to the justiciable, mandatory protection of the interests of the STs as distinct from other marginalised groups.

Article 19 of the Constitution is commonly understood, through text and case law, as a provision that protects freedom of speech, expression, assembly, association, movement, residence and calling. The first clause of Article 19 reads as follows:

> 19(1) All citizens shall have the right
> (a) to freedom of speech and expression;
> (b) to assemble peaceably and without arms;
> (c) to form associations or unions;
> (d) to move freely throughout the territory of India;
> (e) to reside and settle in any part of the territory of India; and
> (f) omitted
> (g) to practise any profession, or to carry on any occupation, trade or business.[2]

Clauses 19(2) to (4) set out the reasonable restrictions to speech, assembly and association in the interests of public morality, decency and integrity and sovereignty of the state—these aspects and their restrictions are what figure most often in animated fashion in debates around Article 19.

Clause 5 of Article 19 reads as follows:

> 19(5) Nothing in sub clauses (d) and (e) of the said clause shall affect the operation of any existing law in so far as it imposes, or prevent the State from making any law imposing, *reasonable restrictions on the exercise of any of the rights conferred by the said sub clauses* either in the interests of the general public or for the protection of the interests of any Scheduled Tribe. (Emphasis mine.)[3]

In other words, an important part of Article 19 protections have to do specifically with protection of interests of STs (Clause 5) as distinct from other marginalised groups through limitations on right to freedom of movement [sub-clause 1(d)] and right to freedom of residence [sub-clause 1(e)]. This, I would argue, when read with existing protections (for instance as set out in *Samatha* or similar cases) offers a core and express fundamental right protection to Adivasis (as distinct from legal/statutory protection) from a range of state and non-state intrusions in Scheduled Areas as well as from the perennial threat of eviction of Adivasis from their homelands.

It is the interests of STs that are paramount in this fundamental right provision, which is presented importantly as a restriction on an enumerated right that is clear and specific—not a restriction of a general nature, namely, the 'sovereignty and integrity of India' or 'public order', 'decency' or 'morality', as is the case with the other constituent freedoms in Article 19.

Understanding the situation of tribal communities is key to understanding the Constitution, its framework and its possibilities in the fullest sense. Perhaps it is time to reinvigorate our reading of the Constitution in the troubled times we live in. We may find answers to other questions as well around an idea of justice that we grapple with every day.

Notes

1. *Samatha*, AIR 1997 SC 3297.
2. India Const. art. 19, cl. 1.
3. Ibid., art 19, cl. 5.

Reference

Ministry of Tribal Affairs, Government of India. 2014. *Report of the High-Level Committee on Socio-Economic, Health and Educational Status of Tribal Communities of India.*

4

Without Land or Recourse*

The order of the Supreme Court issued on 13 February with respect to the claims of forest-dwelling peoples in India—the Scheduled Tribes and Other Traditional Forest Dwellers (OTFD)—is a case of the Supreme Court speaking against itself. In effect, the court has ordered the eviction of lakhs of people whose claims as forest dwellers have been rejected under the Scheduled Tribes and Other Traditional Forest Dwellers (Recognition of Forest Rights) Act, 2006, or FRA. That this order negates the claims of citizens under special protection of the Constitution, namely, the Scheduled Tribes and other vulnerable communities, already pushed by gross governmental neglect precariously to the edge, is another matter altogether. The question before us today centres on the responsibility of the Supreme Court in upholding constitutional claims and equal citizenship.

The Background

The order in question was issued in the case of *Wildlife First & Ors*. The question before the court, as stated in the order of 2016 when the matter was last heard, pertained to 'the constitutional validity of the [FRA] and also the questions pertaining to the preservation of forests in the context of the above-mentioned Act'.[1] The details regarding claims made under the FRA that were placed before the court by the petitioner in 2016 showed that of the 44 lakh claims filed before appropriate authorities in the different states, 20.5 lakh claims (46.5 per cent) were rejected. The order of 2016 went on to observe, 'Obviously, a claim in the context of the above-mentioned Act is based on an assertion that a claimant has been in possession

* Originally published in *The Hindu*, 23 February 2019.

of a certain parcel of land located in the forest areas.'[2] True. A claim is made either for individual or community rights by the people/communities covered by the FRA. This is a plain reading of the act, which is unambiguous on this score.

From here, however, that order did a jurisprudential somersault to observe,

> If the claim is found to be not tenable by the competent authority, the result would be that the claimant is not entitled for the grant of any *Patta* [land title] or any other right under the Act *but such a claimant is also either required to be evicted from that parcel of land or some other action is to be taken in accordance with law.* (Emphasis mine.)[3]

This is the material part of the order. In other words, the claimant cannot contest the decision of the authority, says the court. With respect to action to be taken against those 'unauthorisedly in possession of forest land', the states were then asked by the Supreme Court to report on concrete measures taken to evict the Scheduled Tribes and Other Traditional Forest Dwellers from the forest. In the very next paragraph, which pertains to the state of Tamil Nadu, the order referred to action against those people whose claims had been rejected as 'eviction of encroachers'.

What Now?

In the present order of February 2019, the Supreme Court specifically directs governments in 21 states by name to carry out evictions of rejected claimants without further delay and report on or before 12 July 2019. There are several questions that must be foregrounded for immediate attention.

The most obvious one has to do with the meanings attached to the rejection of claims. According to the 2014 *Report of the High-Level Committee on Socio-Economic, Health and Educational Status of Tribal Communities of India* (Ministry of Tribal Affairs 2014), constituted by the government of India (Xaxa Committee), 60 per cent of the forest area in the country is in tribal areas—protected by Article 19(5) and the Fifth and Sixth Schedules of the Constitution. With specific reference to claims under the FRA, reiterating the findings of several other studies that have documented the deep procedural flaws in processing claims, the Xaxa Committee observed,

> [c]laims are being rejected without assigning reasons, or based on wrong interpretation of the "OTFD" definition and the "dependence" clause, or simply for lack of evidence or "absence of GPS survey" (lacunae which only require the claim to be referred back to the lower-level body), or because the land is wrongly considered as "not forest land", or because only forest offence receipts are considered as adequate evidence. The rejections are not being communicated to the claimants, and their right to appeal is not being explained to them nor its exercise facilitated. (Ibid.: 310)

The mere rejection of claims by the state therefore does not add up to a finding of the crime of 'encroachment'—the sheer volume of rejections should instead set alarm bells ringing in the court of procedural improprieties.

Interestingly, in this case it appears as if a private party, Wildlife First, is pitted against the state. A closer examination reveals that it is, in fact, Wildlife First and the state together which have joined forces against the most vulnerable communities in the country living in areas constitutionally protected from encroachment even by the state—can we forget the stellar *Samatha* judgement of the Supreme Court in 1997?[4]

Why must we worry about this order of the Supreme Court in 2019? As has been widely reported (Sethi 2019), the immediate result will be the forced eviction of over one million people belonging to the Scheduled Tribes and other forest communities. Importantly, the area marked for eviction falls under areas designated under the Fifth and Sixth Schedules of the Constitution—there is no reference to the implications for governance in the Scheduled Areas and whether the Supreme Court, in fact, has the authority to order evictions of Scheduled Tribes from Scheduled Areas. In a democratic country with citizens (not subjects) and a written constitution which is affirmed by the people who are sovereign, how can we countenance the dismantling of an entire constitutional apparatus that prescribes the non-derogable boundaries to Adivasi homelands and institutional mechanisms that promote autonomy and restrain interference in governance?

Against the Safeguards

At an even more fundamental level, we are speaking of special protections under the Constitution—even more today than ever before. The presence of Article 19(5) in the Fundamental Rights chapter of the Constitution, which specifically enjoins the state to make laws 'for the protection of the interests of any Scheduled Tribe' is vital. How has the Supreme Court ordered the eviction in complete disregard of this core and express fundamental right protection to Adivasis (as distinct from legal/statutory protection), which protects them from a range of state and non-state intrusions in Scheduled Areas as well as from the perennial threat of eviction from their homelands? Is it not the supreme obligation of the Supreme Court to protect the Scheduled Tribes and other vulnerable communities from the grave harms of violent dispossession?

Finally, in the recent judgements of the apex court on the right to privacy and Section 377, the court has sung paeans to autonomy, liberty, dignity, fraternity and constitutional morality—the pillars of transformative constitutionalism. It is the same court in the same era that has now ordered the dispossession of entire communities protected under the Constitution. We, as citizens, have every reason to worry.

Notes

1. Wildlife First & Ors v. Ministry of Forest and Environment & Ors, WP (C) No. 109 of 2008, decided on 13 February 2019 (SC).
2. Ibid.
3. Ibid.
4. *Samatha*, AIR 1997 SC 3297.

References

Ministry of Tribal Affairs, Government of India. 2014. *Report of the High-Level Committee on Socio-Economic, Health and Educational Status of Tribal Communities of India.*

Sethi, Nitin. 2019. 'SC Orders Forced Eviction of More Than 1 Million Tribals, Forest-dwellers'. *The Wire*, 20 February. Available at https://thewire.in/rights/sc-orders-forced-eviction-of-more-than-1-million-tribals-forest-dwellers (accessed 17 September 2021).

II

Blocked by Caste

5

Caste, the Academy and Dalit Women*

The ongoing debate on caste and race is taking place in the context of a larger advocacy on discrimination and Dalit human rights. It has centred on the articulation of caste as discrimination, and the various forms of that discrimination—exclusion, untouchability, denial of constitutional rights and guarantees, violent subjugation and histories of slavery—as resonant of internationally recognised forms of racism. This chapter will focus on two aspects of the issue: questions for the sociology of caste and the articulation of caste as race by Dalit women.

Caste has formed the centrepiece of sociology for close to a century now. While the practice of caste has been opposed and consistently resisted by movements in the country, caste as a knowledge system in sociology has tended to follow the well-worn paths of a 'depoliticised' social anthropology, creating sharp disjunctures between social practice and knowledge systems within the academy. Further, the disaggregation of social practice in the curriculum of sociology, into various 'topics' and 'papers', by situating caste, for instance, in Indian society or in social institutions, and the politics of caste within social movements, erases the potential for a radical pedagogy, and renders invisible the radical politics of anti-caste movements within the academy even while 'teaching' them. While this has undoubtedly begun to change, the power of traditional authority on caste is difficult to dismantle. We also know from our experience over the last half century at least that sociologists have periodically been called into the service of the

---

* Originally published in *The Hindu*, 20 June 2001.

This essay was part of the international debate around whether caste discrimination is a form of race discrimination, in the context of the World Conference against Racism, held at Durban in August–September 2001.

state, particularly to supply 'knowledge of society' that could then inform policy. And this knowledge must, by definition, lend itself to disaggregation and be apolitical, in short, the knowledge that the sociologists generate is expected to maintain the status quo.

In reiterating its stand that caste and race are not only dissimilar, but also practices that cannot be compared, let alone brought within the purview of the same international instruments, the Indian government is relying on this knowledge that has been produced by the discipline of sociology (see *The Hindu* 2001). The assertion by Dalit activists mobilising for the Durban conference that their concern is not with 'sociological categories' but with lived experience feeds directly into a 'separate spheres' argument and allows sociology to continue with its project of producing knowledge in the service of power, legitimising the exercise in the process (for different views and contestations on the Durban conference, see Thorat and Umakant 2004). It is time now to call the academy into question, and to engage with systems and processes that produce knowledge, by providing alternative paradigms of knowledge, theory and understanding, and asserting their legitimacy within the academy.

It is time to remind ourselves that the theorising of caste has its intellectual history not in the 'scientific' work of anthropologists of European origin and their 'native' heirs, but in the political work of Indian ideologues who were committed to the establishment of an egalitarian social order, and who, in that endeavour, saw caste as the single most powerful obstacle to the realisation of that commitment—Jotiba Phule, Savitribai Phule, Pandita Ramabai, Periyar and Ambedkar, to name the most influential ones. The Phules' accounts of caste in the nineteenth century are grim. Ambedkar's concerns in the twentieth century centred on finding ways in which independence could bring freedom to the oppressed—affirmative action and positive discrimination being a first step.

Arguments on homogeneity, the measures of likeness and commonalities, and the parameters of comparison are settled within the academy, hence interventions must engage with these arguments, if for no other reason than to have a long-term impact on the content of education. One of the arguments, naturally from scholars of caste, put forth against the move to bring caste within the purview of the

Convention on the Elimination of All Forms of Racial Discrimination has been that the Scheduled Castes are not a homogenous category (for example, Béteille 2001). Outside the realm of this scholarship, but within the realm of reality, no social group is completely homogenous across region and time. The Scheduled Castes are no exception. Yet, it is perfectly legitimate to assert the commonality of experience across cultural, linguistic, regional, national and ethnic diversity. Ambedkar's coining of the word 'Dalit' was part of this exercise in unifying the oppressed and forging a common cause. The current move to bring caste within the ambit of the Racism Convention is not a move by the United Nations alone. It is, far more importantly, an assertion by Dalit groups across the country, part of an effort to realise the visions of anti-caste movements.

The second concern of this chapter is to underscore the efforts of the National Federation of Dalit Women (NFDW) in bringing this issue into focus. In the draft 'Declaration on Gender and Racism', from February 2001, the federation resolved to fight the specific oppression of women from marginalised groups, whose situation as Dalit/indigenous/minority is only compounded by their being women. Apart from the fact of social exclusion at various levels, the NFDW (2001) asserted that '[d]escent based discrimination based on caste results in the violent appropriation of and sexual control over Dalit women by men of the dominant castes, evident in the systematic rape of Dalit women and the perpetuation of forced prostitution in the name of religion through the devadasi system.'

In a context of increasing religious nationalism, fundamentalism and dominant caste chauvinism, of globalisation and its disastrous consequences for the poor (almost exclusively Dalit), of the abdication of democratic governance by the state, the declaration asserts that the situation of Dalit women is particularly troubling. The draft declaration calls upon governments to review and reform national laws related to violence against women, to gather statistical information on the status of Dalit women, to offer them protection, to redistribute land to women of marginalised groups, and to work alongside the international community on issues of discrimination. An extremely significant point in the declaration, and one that ties in with the first part of this article, is the concern of the NFDW over the engineering of partisan, hegemonic representations of history in textbooks and curricula at all levels.

The effort of the federation to forge a broad-based common platform with other groups that suffer systematic exclusion in an increasingly virulent right-wing environment is both courageous and radical, while at the same time engaging with and calling into question the disaggregation of knowledge within the academy. The campaign for the inclusion of caste within the definition of racism is, in fact, a rewriting of caste as a knowledge system that derives directly from lived experience and the politics of that experience.

References

'Caste and the Durban Conference'. 2001. *The Hindu*, 31 August.

Béteille, André. 2001. 'Race and Caste'. *The Hindu*, 10 March.

NFDW (National Federation of Dalit Women). 2001. 'Declaration on Gender and Racism'. Unpublished draft, February.

Thorat, Sukhadeo, and Umakant, eds. 2004. *Caste, Race and Discrimination: Discourses in International Context*. New Delhi: Indian Institute of Dalit Studies and Rawat Publications.

6

Reservation and the Creamy Layer*

The 19 October 2006 Supreme Court judgement, *M. Nagaraj*,[1] on reservations for Scheduled Castes and Scheduled Tribes forces us to review the notion of 'creamy layer' that appears over the past decade or so to have become the cornerstone of jurisprudence on affirmative action and reservations in India. By that token, this concept has become accepted in dominant mainstream discourse as well—from job interviews to casual conversations.

There are fundamental flaws in the concept itself. First, a concept can only become operative if there is an attempt at definition, and when there is some deliberation/argumentation about the definition. The concept of creamy layer was first declared as part of majoritarian common-sense, validated by the fact of its conception, and extended, interpreted and applied in different contexts in an apparently self-explanatory manner. While there was an attempt to identify defining criteria for the creamy layer *after* the concept was declared, both the declaration and the identification of defining criteria was in relation to the Other Backward Classes (OBCs), itself a contentious exercise. It has now been used in relation to the Scheduled Castes and Tribes, again without definition.

What is the concept of the creamy layer in this context? What are the signposts of this concept, beyond the fact that a small section of Dalit and Adivasi people over the past two generations *at best* have managed to secure tertiary education and enter the professional world and public employment? The crux of affirmative action rests on the fact of caste-based discrimination, that is, on grave social disabilities arising from caste status. The very formulation of the concept of creamy layer, an exercise in dominance, disaggregates discrimination

* Originally published in *The Hindu*, 24 October 2006.

and narrows its articulation down to economic status alone, thus distorting the realities of disadvantaged castes—in this case, Dalit and Adivasi realities.

Second, and linked to the problem of the lack of definition, instead of enabling understanding of a situation (as concepts should), it obstructs understanding by equating knowledge to stereotype, a powerful dominant stereotype being that Dalits do not share benefits at the community level and therefore must be 'ruled' in this matter by the non-inclusive public domain of which institutions of justice are a part. What this discursive perpetuation of the stereotype does is that it also masks the unwillingness of dominant castes to share resources equally with Dalits/Adivasis. In fact, this stereotype serves to divert attention away from the exclusionary practices of dominant castes.

In the interests of equality, the concept of creamy layer must be tested for its general applicability. From the Dalit/Adivasi standpoint, let us deploy the concept of the creamy layer without fear or favour. What do we find? The entire public domain—in education, industry, employment—has been captured by the creamy layers of Indian society (the cream of the cream, men of these classes) that seek to consolidate their intergenerational concentration of privilege by whittling down claims to affirmative action to a bare minimum and absolving themselves of any responsibility for the continuing oppressions that Dalit communities face in contemporary India. In fact, there is a denial that such oppressions even exist. What we have then is the monopolising of resources by the dominant creamy layers and the exclusion of families with one generation of tertiary education and secure employment from access to reservations. This then perpetuates inequality in the so-called 'open' category as well, which from the Dalit standpoint, is a 50 per cent or more reservation for the dominant castes, which few are willing to acknowledge.

Third, it furthers an anti-historical view of discrimination, by rejecting the relevance of past experience of violent exclusion as the basis of affirmative action, thus turning the historical logic of constitutionalism on its head. This heightened visibility of the concept of the creamy layer with reference to affirmative action goes hand in hand with the failure by governments and courts to provide justice to victims of gruesome violence by the creamy layers of our society—Karamchedu, Chunduru, Melavalavu, Jhajjar, the list is long. How does one explain the unequal application of the concept? Or is the equality of the concept located in the fact of the denial of claims to justice?

The systematic denial of justice with respect to atrocities is inextricably linked to the whittling down of entitlements through the arbitrary application of undefined concepts. It is necessary not to lose sight of the totality of the Dalit/Adivasi experience—across generations and an experience which continues well into the present, whether one looks at the performance of the most degrading forms of labour, the use of violence with impunity, or their daily struggles against discrimination once they enter public employment and tertiary education.

The concept of the creamy layer obfuscates the fact of caste discrimination within institutions of education, employment and justice. It is assumed that once a person enters public employment, promotions/elevation will be a matter of merit. Yet, we have been witness to the systematic obstruction of promotional opportunities and normal career advancement routes to Dalits, even at the highest levels (for details, see NCSC 2013). The problem of lack of representation in the judiciary remains unresolved (see, for instance, Chandru 2016; Buaria 2020). Reports about the ways in which Dalits/Adivasis in these public domains are obstructed from performing their routine responsibilities abound.

Fourth, it is a concept that is applied on the other, not on the self. Essentially, what the jurisprudence of the creamy layer reveals is that the architects of the concept and its proponents—both in the judiciary and in civil society—are principally from non-SC/ST backgrounds, and are therefore outside the sphere of application of the concept. They apply the concept to describe the life-worlds of those unlike them, life-worlds that reflect the consequences and costs of their own privilege. We are back then to the caste system of the pre-Constitution era where the interpretation of the law is not a matter of deliberation, or argumentation (to echo Sen 2006), but is a matter of diktat—meanings are assigned and declared to be true.

There are of course a few exceptions, even in the current debate, where votaries are not from dominant sections but from the very marginalised groups that are being 'ruled', and herein lies the irony—the very presence of a miniscule number of Dalits/Adivasis in the propagation of the concept of the creamy layer results in their own exclusion, a consequence that dominant votaries do not bear. This last group then applies the concept on the self and by that token excludes the self as an unworthy claimant of affirmative action. They, by their very presence in the propagating spaces, are the creamy layer that must be excluded. There must not be an opportunity for a critical mass to develop among Dalit communities. The most effective way of ensuring this is by articulating a concept as vacuous yet insidious as the creamy layer.

Within Dalit and Adivasi communities, groups in the spirit of our argumentative traditions have engaged in animated deliberation on the distribution of benefits. Notwithstanding the inconclusiveness of the debates, the fact is that there is a debate and contestation—the struggles of the Madiga Reservation Porata Samiti (Madiga Employees Federation n.d.) are an excellent example. And yet, when the resolution of these claims is placed before the government, there is no attempt to resolve the issue, the major consideration being the political stakes of dominant parties involved. What sets these processes of deliberation apart from the blanket declaration of the concept of the creamy layer is that Dalit groups in each state/region engage in political dialogue on this issue with a painstaking documentation of why, how and to whom benefits must be distributed in each sector in their contexts. More importantly, it is a debate between groups positioned similarly on the social scale, and subject to similar practices of exclusion by the dominant society. There is, within Dalit and Adivasi communities, a diversity of responses to affirmative action and the need to distribute privileges both at the individual and collective levels, which must enter the account. It is important to recognise the difference between this contestation within Dalit communities and the resolutions thereof and the proclamation of inequality from without. It is a question of legitimate voice and responsibility.

This brings us to the final point, which is that we cannot afford to forget the consistency of Dalit/Adivasi engagement in resistance and deliberative politics and their critique, across several generations of the systems that oppressed them, at enormous cost personally and collectively. It is also extremely important not to lose sight of the spirit of Ambedkar's legacy especially with respect to the Constitution. Thinking about affirmative action is about memory and forgetting. Amnesia in this instance is a privilege that emanates from dominance.

Note

1. M. Nagaraj v. Union of India, (2006) 8 SCC 212.

References

Buaria, Rhythm. 2020. 'Need for Reservations in the Higher Judiciary of India'. *The Wire*, 29 October. Available at https://livewire.thewire.in/politics/need-for-reservations-in-the-higher-judiciary-of-india/ (accessed 19 July 2021).

Chandru, K. 2016. 'Judges, Castes and Social Justice'. *The Hindu*, 16 March.

Madiga Employees Federation. n.d. 'Madigas Movement'. Available at http://www.madiga.net/p/movement.html (accessed 19 July 2021).

NCSC (National Commission for Scheduled Castes). 2013. *Reservation in Promotion for Members of Scheduled Castes*. Available at http://ncsc.nic.in/files/Reservation%20in%20Promotion.pdf (accessed 19 July 2021).

Sen, Amartya. 2006. *The Argumentative Indian: Writings on Indian History, Culture and Identity*. New Delhi: Penguin.

7

Chunduru

*On the Road to Justice**

The most significant development that marks the sixtieth anniversary of Indian independence, for Andhra Pradesh, and indeed for India, is the decision of the special court, under the Scheduled Castes and the Scheduled Tribes (Prevention of Atrocities) Act, 1989, convicting over 50 persons accused of attacking Dalits in Chunduru, 21 of whom were found guilty of murder and sentenced to imprisonment for life.[1] The decision came 16 years after the attack, in what is the first major case in Andhra Pradesh to be brought under the SC/ST (Prevention of Atrocities) Act, 1989. This is, in fact, what set the case apart from the earlier cases of collective violence and grave assault against Dalits in Karamchedu, Neerukonda and Padirikuppam.

Around noon on 6 August 1991, a mob of 400 persons belonging to the upper castes were believed to have attacked Dalits in the village of Chunduru in the most brutal manner, killing eight persons and throwing their bodies into the Tungabhadra Drain Canal. A key eyewitness was shot dead by the police within days of the massacre. Some of those assaulted survived. The reality of the violence was so gruesome that the doctor who performed the post-mortem committed suicide soon after. It was widely believed to be because he was unable to cope with what he had seen. The trigger for this attack, like the trigger for the attack on Dalits in Karamchedu six years earlier, was

---

* Originally published in *Economic and Political Weekly* 42, no. 39 (29 September 2007): 3915–16.

This essay was written immediately after a visit to Chunduru, following the decision of the special court at Chunduru, constituted under the Scheduled Castes and the Scheduled Tribes (Prevention of Atrocities) Act, 1989.

trivial—an altercation between youths of both communities in a cinema hall in the village, to which the people from the dominant caste took exception (APCLC 1991). But clearly, the trigger is not indicative at all of the genesis of the violence or its snowballing into barbaric proportions that shock the human conscience. There was national outrage at the attack (see, for example, Jonathan 2013; Janyala 2016). The Dalit movement offered unstinting support in the immediate aftermath of the attack, as did other peoples' movements.

The first thing one sees on entering the main village is an elevated ground with nine mud graves marked 'Raktakshetram' in the central crossroads, the place where the victims were buried, which serves as a grim daily reminder of the barbarity of the attack for all those living in the village—those who lived through the violence and the generation that was born since—and all visitors. The government's decision to allow the burial of victims here on 10 August 1991 was met with stiff opposition from the highest quarters outside the village. It is not the lush green fields, the idyllic natural beauty that surrounds Chunduru that stays in the mind. In fact, the violence of that beauty is chilling. The quiet, still faces of those who have lived with the reality of the violence—their quiet acknowledgement of moral support from visitors and the apparently unobtrusive, yet grave, defining presence of Raktakshetram rips through the placid, seductive landscape and interrupts coherent thought.

For the Dalit people of Chunduru, however, it has been a long, arduous and painful struggle to wrest justice from a hostile system in a hostile society. Besides coping with the brutality of the attack and continuing to live with the consequences and the memories in the same village, they have had to devise strategies at every stage to clear the road to justice of obstacles.

The first major struggle was to bring the special court, under the Prevention of Atrocities Act, to Chunduru. Where people have already suffered enormous loss and are then required by the court to recount the loss in accordance with norms that are completely alien to them, norms that do not make space for the trauma of the experience or the retelling of that experience, the physical location of the court becomes vital in reassuring survivors or in disempowering them. Dalits in Chunduru wanted the special court to be set up in the village itself and fought a legal battle in the high court to win that demand because, predictably, the accused resisted that move. There is no doubt that the moral courage and conviction of witnesses, survivors and indeed the entire Dalit community in the village was strengthened by the reassuring presence of the court in their midst. The physical location of justice was no longer the distant town; participation in or even merely witnessing the proceedings no longer involved travel time and costs, and most importantly, deliberations over justice happened at the site of loss.

The second major battle had to do with the appointment of prosecutors. While generally human rights lawyers have been reluctant to represent the government in a state known for its scant regard for the rule of law, especially in matters of state violence, the appointment of a person with a demonstrated commitment to human rights as prosecutor was an important step towards victory—and one that was unsuccessfully challenged and opposed by the accused. This result underscores the importance of the presence of human rights advocates in prosecutorial offices in cases of collective, structural crime.

The final hurdle was placed when the accused petitioned the high court opposing the appointment of a judge to the special court on the grounds that since he belonged to the Dalit community, he would be biased against the accused. This was an inversion of all official assumptions about the objectivity and neutrality of the judge in the justice delivery system. Even while the matter was being heard in the high court, by a remarkable coincidence, the judge was administratively transferred out of the special court.

The problems and consequences of delay in the commencement and completion of trial in criminal cases have been discussed and deliberated upon at great length in legal academia. Chunduru demonstrates the painful and difficult consequences of delay in cases of mass crime and atrocity against people who are poor and socially and politically vulnerable—especially Dalits. Sixteen years is a long time. An entire generation did not live to experience the verdict. But for those that did, the struggle between the memory of loss and the imperatives of survival from day to day cannot be forgotten. Living as they did in the same village, with the people and the monuments that mark the loss—the families of those accused of the assault, the cinema hall which was the immediate trigger and which has since been converted into a school, the graves, the stupa in memory of Anil Kumar who was shot dead, the streets, the fields, the canal, indeed the village itself—the Dalits of Chunduru have had to strike a balance between memory and survival, and have had to walk that tightrope at enormous personal cost for a decade and a half. As the special public prosecutor in this case, B. Chandrasekhar, observed in a personal conversation, the Dalits of Chunduru have had to bear the burden of national interest even while struggling from day to day and keep their faith against all odds.

The struggles by mass movements for justice have been critical to enlarging the possibilities for justice itself—nowhere is this more evident than in the case of Chunduru. People like Jaladi Moses (who lost two brothers in the massacre) in Chunduru, human rights stalwart K. G. Kannabiran (who appeared in the high court every time the accused appealed on one ground or another) and prosecutors like Chandrasekhar who kept the case alive, are people who are committed to the annihilation of caste. In the face of atrocity, apart from mass protest, it is necessary to build alliances to keep prosecutions alive and effective—an effort which calls for an outlay of enormous time, intellectual and physical energy and material costs over a long period, undergirded by the moral commitment to annihilate caste.

And justice itself is so many things—the 'victory' in the court of trial is both the culmination of a struggle and the beginning of the delivery of justice.

Note

1. State (Sub-divisional Police Officer, Tenali) v. Modugula Sambi Reddi & 218 Ors, Sessions Case No. 36/1993, decided on 31 July 2007 (Court of Special Sessions Judge-cum-IV Additional Sessions Judge, Guntur).

References

APCLC (Andhra Pradesh Civil Liberties Committee). 1991. *The Chundur Carnage*.

Janyala, Sreenivas. 2016. '24 Years On, This AP Village Still Can't Put Massacre Behind It'. *The Indian Express*, 24 February.

Jonathan, Samuel P. 2013. 'Tsunduru Dalit Massacre: A Blood-Soaked Chapter in Modern History'. *The Hindu*, 7 August.

8

Roadmap for Reservation in Higher Education*

The Constitution (93rd Amendment) Act, 2005, by which Article 15(5) was inserted in the Constitution, was challenged in the Supreme Court, as also was the Central Educational Institutions (Reservation in Admission) Act, 2006 (Act 5 of 2007), which provides for reservation in admissions to the Scheduled Castes, the Scheduled Tribes and the Other Backward Classes to certain central institutions established, maintained or aided by the Centre.[1] Section 5 of Act 5 of 2007 provides for an increase in seats in the open category to 'compensate' those 'lost' to reservation.

The Reasoning

The arguments challenging reservation can be summarised as follows: admissions to educational institutions should be based purely on merit; the impugned act attempting affirmative action is to be treated as 'suspect legislation'—unreasonable, arbitrary, capricious and contrary to Articles 14 and 21—and must undergo the tests of 'strict scrutiny' and 'compelling state necessity'; the 'creamy layer' principle should be applied to the OBCs as well as the SCs and the STs; non-exclusion of the creamy layer is illegal; quotas should not be a punishment for the unreserved categories; minority institutions should not be exempt from the 'common burden of reservation' for the SCs, the STs and the Socially and Educationally Backward Classes (SEBCs); the OBCs have not suffered the indignities borne by the SCs and the STs and therefore cannot be treated on an equal footing; since the problem of backwardness is located in the arena of primary education, reservation

* Originally published in *The Hindu*, 18 April 2008.

is necessary only up to the Class 12 level, after which individuals join the ranks of the forward by virtue of education; and the provision of additional seats amounts to 100 per cent reservation, since the increase of seats to assure undiminished access to the unreserved category will match exactly the seats reserved.

The arguments defending the quota focused on a liberal interpretation of the Constitution and urged the court to consider the fact that the provision of reservation to disadvantaged groups was being made 56 years after the Constitution came into force. In terms of proportion, the OBCs, and the SCs and STs comprised more than 27 per cent and 22 per cent of the population, respectively—the reservation proposed, therefore, was not disproportionate to the comparative population figures. The concept of creamy layer could not be applied to the SCs and the STs, while for the OBCs, its application was restricted to the ambit of Article 16(4), with specific reference to employment. Applying the creamy layer principle to educational institutions would mean that the advanced castes would eliminate any challenge to their leadership in the professions and services; it is utopian to expect that by ignoring caste it would perish because the caste system plays an important role in every conceivable activity of private life. Importantly, it was also argued that the primary objective of reservation was to bring about equality of status and opportunity in order to create a level playing field among groups positioned differently on the social scale—not poverty alleviation or universal education, which is part of a very different set of issues.

There was an acknowledgement on both sides, however, of the intractability of caste and the difficulty of mapping its exact contours. Should one look for vulnerability to atrocity? Is there a nexus between caste and occupation? Is education the solution to social exclusion? Does wealth bridge barriers between castes? What is the character of the class–caste nexus? Can it be reasonably assumed that there will be a correlation between the SEBCs and the disadvantaged castes?

The issues discussed by the judges, in four separate judgements, centred on questions of the constitutionality of the 93rd Amendment, especially in terms of its implications for minority and unaided institutions and its conflict with the provisions of Article 15(4), the definition and identification of the backward classes, especially the relevance of the method adopted in *Indra Sawhney* (Mandal case), the place of caste in the determination of backwardness, and, most importantly, the relevance of the troublesome concept of creamy layer to reservations for both the SCs/STs and the SEBCs.[2]

While all the judges upheld the constitutionality of Article 15(5), the chief justice observed that the question of whether any exemption granted by the provision was violative of equality guaranteed by Article 14 would arise only when an educational institution believed that its fundamental right to equality had been violated by the exemption accorded to the minority institutions that petitioned the court.[3] No institution had raised this argument on its own behalf. Justice Dalveer Bhandari, taking the opposite course which led to a similar conclusion, severed the reference to unaided institutions, although no such institution approached the court, 'in the larger public interest', arguing that the inclusion of unaided institutions contravened the protections under Article 19 and therefore violated the basic structure.[4]

On the central question of the definition of 'backward class' and its identification, especially the validity of using caste to identify class, the Supreme Court reiterated that it arrived at a point in *Indra Sawhney*, after a string of cases starting with *Champakam Dorairajan* (1951), that caste could be the starting point for determining the socially and educationally backward classes. Any reference to the backward classes immediately thrusts to the centre of the debate the concept of creamy layer. Chief Justice K. G. Balakrishnan held that while the creamy layer principle was not part of the general principle of equality, it had the limited and specific purpose of identifying the backward classes entitled to reservation. It would have to be applied as the court was bound by the decision of the larger bench in *Indra Sawhney*. However, he observed, the SCs and the STs were a separate class that could not be brought within the ambit of the creamy layer identification.[5]

Justice Bhandari, however, held differently in the matter of creamy layer with respect to the backward classes, that the principle of creamy layer emanated from the broad doctrine of equality itself. He expressed no opinion in the matter of SCs and STs, although he discussed it at some length.[6]

In a postscript to his brief judgement, Justice R. V. Raveendran, concurring with the judgement of the chief justice, raised and left open the question of whether members of the reserved categories who get selected in open competition on merit should be counted against the 27 per cent quota under an enactment enabled by Article 15(5).[7] He, along with Justice Bhandari, ruled that unfilled seats should revert to the general category.

Continuing Concerns

Counting persons who gain admission in the open category against the quota would defeat the purpose of reservation and, in effect, decrease the quota below the stipulated level. Also, this measure would make the very principle of creamy layer redundant, directly contradicting the present stand of the court. The exemption of institutions listed in the Schedule to Act 5 of 2007, the minority institutions, and now, unaided private institutions, goes against the spirit of equality and considerably shrinks the space for entitlements of persons from vulnerable groups. It is not so much a question of the measure of equality between institutions *inter se* that is critical in access to education, as of the measure of equality between citizens differently placed because it is citizens who bear the brunt of discrimination and exclusion. After all, reservation is an inseparable part of the principle of equality and where equality is concerned, no institution can be outside its ambit.

Notwithstanding these concerns, this judgement has an important bearing on the entire system of higher education, especially institutions of excellence, because it challenges the idea that merit exists in a vacuum—outside of social location and equality of opportunity. Opening these institutions to Dalit and Adivasi students especially will bring in dimensions of diversity and counter-hegemonic thinking that will enrich the quality of education imparted there and strengthen democracy.

Notes

1. Ashoka Kumar Thakur v. Union of India & Ors, (2008) 6 SCC 1; Indra Sawhney v. Union of India 1992 SUPP (3) SCC 217; State of Madras v. Champakam Dorairajan AIR 1951 SC 226.
2. *Ashoka Kumar Thakur.*
3. Ibid., para. 102 (per Balakrishnan, J.).
4. Ibid., paras. 132–33 (per Bhandari, J.).
5. Ibid., paras. 160–61 (per Balakrishnan, J.).
6. Ibid., para. 6 (per Bhandari, J.).
7. Ibid., para. 1 (per Raveendran, J.).

9

Atrocities That No Longer Shock*

The response by the state to the 2012 Delhi gang rape case was immediate and effective—a commission to review legislative protections and recommend amendments, and a new enactment (Amnesty International 2013). The judiciary responded similarly—death penalties for the accused, and although there was indignation about the 'leniency' towards the juvenile involved in the crime, there was overall a sense of satisfaction that the ends of justice had indeed been met. But all through this saga, the persistent voice of Dalit intellectuals and activists kept asking why Khairlanji did not provoke this kind of national outrage and why India is unmoved by the most gruesome massacres of Dalits (for example, Telang 2013; Teltumbde 2013).

The 9 October 2013 verdict of the Patna High Court in the Laxmanpur Bathe massacre (Gaikwad 2013) brings this question up yet again; a painful reminder of the continuing legitimacy of the caste system and aggravated assault, making a mockery of the rule of law.

On a plain reading of this judgement,[1] it is not disputed that 58 persons—men, women and children, all Dalits—were killed in a concerted attack on the night of 1–2 December 1997, after being shot by a mob of over a hundred men armed with guns believed to be a part of the Ranvir Sena, the private army of the dominant caste landlords (Chaudhuri 2012). It is also not disputed that survivors in this village were eyewitnesses who had lost entire families in the massacre and had narrowly escaped murder themselves. There was a delay by the police in recording statements; persons identified by the eyewitnesses were not named in the statements in the first instance; there was a delay of three days in reaching the first information

* Originally published in *The Hindu*, 15 October 2013.

reports (FIRs) to the chief judicial magistrate; there was blood in the homes of the victims and survivors, 'copious blood' on the banks of the river Sone, and blood smeared on a boat on the riverbank; the murderous mob shouted slogans in praise of Ranvir Baba, believed to be the protector of the Bhumihar Brahmins, and dispersed at the sound of a whistle; footprints of 100–150 persons on both banks of the river suggested to the investigating officer that the mob had crossed the river towards Sahar, but he did not cross the river in his investigation. The investigating officers recorded statements by the survivors which said that several of the men named as perpetrators were members of the Ranvir Sena, and had criminal antecedents.

Delay

The case was committed to the court of sessions in 1999, but typically, as with many atrocity cases, the trial did not begin for 11 years, till the high court issued fresh instructions in November and December 2008. By this time, of the 91 witnesses, 38 had turned hostile. Of the 50 accused sent up for trial in 1999, 44 finally faced trial, some having died in the interim. The sessions court sentenced 26 persons to death in 2010 after convicting them of murder, criminal conspiracy and atrocity—13 years after the massacre.

The witnesses cited a dispute over wages and standing crop as the reason for the attack—the demand was for an increase in wages from 1.5 kilograms of food grain to 3 kilograms.[2] The perpetrators were not an unknown mob from a strange and distant land. They were landlords in the same and neighbouring villages, who the victims and their families knew well and worked for. They were all from the dominant, landowning castes.

They attacked in the dead of night, flashing torches to search for the victims. Although the witness-survivors hid themselves to escape attack, they recognised the men and named them. But they also witnessed unimaginable violence and lost several members of their families in the attack. Their testimonies during the investigation speak of their hurtling from one house to another discovering more bodies than survivors, and the sound of wailing that rent through the night.

Loopholes

The Patna High Court speaks of loopholes in the evidence on record: the delay in reaching the FIRs to the chief judicial magistrate; the fact that names were not recorded in the first visit, on the day after the massacre, from witnesses who had lost all their family members in the attack; the impossibility of recognising perpetrators from places of hiding; the impossibility of risking one's life to climb up to a terrace to identify people in the mob; the impossibility of fixing the identities of individuals in a mob from a distance; inaccuracies in recording the exact location of hiding during the massacre; and absence of evidence of any dispute between the dominant landowners and the Dalit wage-workers.[3] Where do these refutations leave us?

Fifty-eight people in a small Dalit hamlet were massacred. There is no denying that. The attackers, says the high court, were unknown men from Sahar, across the river Sone in Bhojpur district, who have not been apprehended. Instead, the wrong people, who bear no responsibility for the crime, have been convicted, says the court. How can we be sure?

This is the trouble with caste atrocity. The fact that perpetrators are in an immediate relation of dominance with victims and survivors and are easily recognised counts for nothing. Can we even begin to understand the courage and determination of poor and traumatised Dalits? The outcome of this case demonstrates yet again how difficult it is to keep a case alive, to keep memories raw and open in the face of an almost certain betrayal by the state, and how tough it is to keep fighting against the conspiracy—between upper caste perpetrators, their collaborators in the establishment and their apologists in a caste-ridden society.

Why not Khairlanji? Why not Karamchedu? Why not Laxmanpur Bathe? Why does this country not come to a grinding halt in the face of atrocity of the worst kind? Justice can only be said to be done when those that are most vulnerable are able to access it without difficulty. It is our collective failure and a national shame that we allow the space for this travesty again and yet again.

Notes

1. State of Bihar v. Girja Singh & Ors, Death Reference No. 5 of 2010, decided on 9 October 2013 (Pat. HC), arising out of Sessions Case No. 2 of 1999, decided on 7 April 2010 (by 1st Additional Sessions Judge, Patna).
2. Ibid., para. 11.
3. Ibid.

References

'India: New Sexual Violence Law Has Both Positive and Regressive Provisions'. 2013. *Amnesty International*, 22 March. Available at https://www.amnesty.org/en/press-releases/2013/03/india-new-sexual-violence-law-has-both-positive-and-regressive-provisions-2/ (accessed 19 July 2021).

Chaudhuri, Zinnia Ray. 2012. 'Explained: What is the Ranvir Sena and Why it is Feared'. *DNA*, 4 June. Available at https://www.dnaindia.com/india/slideshow-explained-what-is-the-ranvir-sena-and-why-it-is-feared-1697737 (accessed 14 June 2021).

Gaikwad, Rahi. 2013. 'Patna High Court Acquits All 26 in Dalit Massacre Case'. *The Hindu*, 9 October.

Telang, Priyadarshi. 2013. '"Nirbhaya", New Delhi and Priyanka, Khairlanji'. *Round Table India*, 16 September. Available at https://roundtableindia.co.in/index.php?option=com_content&view=article&id=6899:nirbhaya-new-delhi-and-priyanka-khairlanji&catid=119&Itemid=132 (accessed 19 July 2021).

Teltumbde, Anand. 2013. 'Delhi Gang Rape Case: Some Uncomfortable Questions'. *Economic and Political Weekly* 48, no. 6 (9 February): 10–11.

10

The Scope of Constitutional Morality*

Writing in 1988, Upendra Baxi's lines remain disconcertingly relevant today:

> The issue of the rights of sweepers and scavengers has never entered the mainstream legal consciousness in the country.... Nor have the Bar and the Bench, and the mushrooming legal aid and advice programmes shown any awareness of the exploitative conditions of work imposed upon the scavengers and sweepers under the employment of municipal corporations or related local bodies.... [T]he exploitative conditions of work constitute governmental defiance of the law and the constitution, which can be best summed up as a crucial component of overall governmental lawlessness in the country since Independence. (Baxi 1988: 173–74)

We struggle against the caricaturing of this extremely stigmatising, violently exploitative and degrading form of forced labour by a government and civil society that showcases empty rhetoric and ceremony around 'cleanliness', while decimating an entire class of citizens through callous neglect, with impunity.

There has been a steady rise in deaths of conservancy workers, and a steadier normalisation of the risks to life they bear on a daily basis. Why do sewer deaths not bring the country to a grinding halt, as they should? Will a general strike of all conservancy workers across the country bring the country to a halt? Because then, it will not any more be a question of prime-time jingles on a clean India, the focus will shift to each of us to take the moral and physical responsibility of cleaning our own sewers and keeping ourselves free of the risk of toxic death—self-preservation.

To return to Baxi's concerns on the place of law, Article 17 of the Constitution of India states: 'Untouchability is abolished and its

---

* Originally published in *The Hindu*, 4 October 2018.

practice in any form is forbidden. The enforcement of any disability arising out of Untouchability shall be an offence punishable in accordance with law.'[1] This is a fundamental right and therefore justiciable and enforceable by courts, which shall call governments into account.

In 2009, the Delhi High Court, in *Naz Foundation*, invoked Ambedkar's delineation of constitutional morality in asserting the urgency of decriminalising consensual sexual relations proscribed by Section 377 of the Indian Penal Code (IPC). The Delhi High Court cited a second provision as well: Article 15(2), which prohibited any form of horizontal discrimination, drawing again from the experience of untouchability that obstructed the universal use of public places, restaurants, water sources, etc.[2] In September 2018, we witnessed a triumphal return of the idea of constitutional morality as a guiding principle for constitutional interpretation. The five-judge bench of the Supreme Court of India in the case of *Navtej Singh Johar* deployed this framework to reaffirm the rights of lesbian, gay, bisexual, transgender, queer (LGBTQ) and all gender non-conforming people to their dignity, life, liberty and identity.[3]

The genealogy of Ambedkar's signposting of constitutional morality may be traced to the strength of anti-caste resistance and the abolition of untouchability and caste discrimination. It is from this context that constitutional wisdom was applied to analogous situations of oppressions based on sexuality and sexual personhood. It is time now for us to call the government to account through a recursive method that takes us to the original constitutional proscription of untouchability, armed with the wisdom of the *Navtej Singh Johar* case.

The first aspect that must be marked is the importance of judicial empathy. In a violently exclusionary society, where radical readings of the Constitution breathe life into lives that are otherwise bereft of hope, the application of the Constitution to lives as lived is an extremely emotional moment. We saw each of the judges on the bench speaking eloquently to the power of emotion and empathy. We have people from India's most oppressed castes dying painful deaths without dignity in the sewers of the same city where the court sits every day. There is neither accountability nor due diligence on the part of the state. The time for the expression of judicial empathy is now. Justice Indu Malhotra's lines are apposite: 'History owes an apology to the members of this community and their families, for the delay in providing redressal for the ignominy and ostracism that they have suffered through the centuries.'[4]

Given the urgency, with people dying daily despite constitutional and statutory protections, how do we right these historical wrongs, or at least 'set the course for the future'? We are all agreed that the *de minimis* approach is bad law—rule by law rather than rule of law, as it should be, to echo Justice D. Y. Chandrachud.[5] The fact that it is still possible for people to be sent into sewers without protection, and to be forced to perform degrading labour is enough for us to sit up and take note. Chief Justice Dipak Misra set out four cardinal corners of the Constitution: individual autonomy and liberty, equality sans discrimination, recognition of identity with dignity, and right to privacy. In addition, he also underscored the centrality of fraternity to the constitutional value system.[6] These five signposts require us to contemplate and act on the meanings and expressions of 'intrinsic dignity' for conservancy workers and *safai karamcharis*. If 'self-determination and the realisation of one's own abilities' lie at the core of personhood, how would forced, unsafe and degrading labour, and persistent untouchability figure in this new constitutional imaginary? In the case of the safai karamcharis, we are today witness to the 'violation of their fundamental rights ... which strikes at the very root or substratum of their existence' (Chief Justice Misra),[7] and there are no visible pathways to freedom in this virulent caste society. Lest we forget, untouchability is a crime under the Constitution.

Important for citizen consideration today is the fact that the Supreme Court, in deciding on the unconstitutionality of Section 377, recognised that the four corners of the Constitution rest on a social reality steeped in prejudice, stereotypes, parochialism, bigotry, social exclusion and segregation. If decriminalising 'unnatural' sex is a necessary precondition for democracy, abolition of untouchability in all its forms remains an unrealised constitutional right even while it lends indispensable tools to combat other grounds of discrimination.

The lesson on the importance of intersections in constitutional reasoning today is brought home to us in this case in yet another way. There is recognition by the court that majoritarian governments/sections work hard to keep oppressive structures in place, and the firm acknowledgement that it is the duty of the court to place questions of liberty, equality and dignity out of the reach of majoritarian impulses. The sanction for manual scavenging lies at the heart of majoritarian mindsets and structures. It is part of an ideological framework that permeates the institutional apparatus of government. If, as Chief Justice Misra observes, 'the sustenance of fundamental rights does not require majoritarian sanction',[8] can we call for some constitutional-procedural deliberation on the 'progressive realization of rights'[9] in this instance? The principle of non-retrogression in the matter of fundamental rights has now been unequivocally stated. But on our streets, we only observe it in the breach, especially in the case of safai karamcharis.

To end with Ambedkar (2016 [1949]): 'We must remove this contradiction at the earliest possible moment or else those who suffer from inequality will blow up the structure of political democracy.'

Notes

1. India Const. art 17.
2. *Naz Foundation* (2009) 160 DLT 277.
3. *Navtej Singh Johar*, AIR 2018 SC 4321.
4. Ibid., para. 20 (per Malhotra, J.).
5. Justice K. S. Puttaswamy (Retd) v. Union of India, (2017) 10 SCC 1, paras. 127–28 (per Chandrachud, J.).
6. *Navtej Singh Johar*, AIR 2018 SC 4321, para. 4 (per Misra, J.).
7. Ibid., para. 19 (per Misra, J.).
8. Ibid., para. 190 (per Misra, J.).
9. Ibid., para. 253(ix) (per Misra, J.).

References

Ambedkar, B. R. 2016 [1949]. 'Why B. R. Ambedkar's Three Warnings in His Last Speech to the Constituent Assembly Resonate Even Today'.

Scroll.in, 26 January. Available at https://scroll.in/article/802495/why-br-ambedkars-three-warnings-in-his-last-speech-to-the-constituent-assembly-resonate-even-today (accessed 10 July 2021).

Baxi, Upendra. 1988. 'Untouchability: Constitution, Law and Plan'. In *Law and Poverty: Critical Essays*, ed. Upendra Baxi, 165–74. Bombay: N. M. Tripathi.

11

The Annihilation by Caste*

Even as we come to terms with the death of Rohith Vemula (Chukka 2016), we are witness to the unprecedented churning that he set in motion even as he left—educating, agitating, organising in death as in life.

From all his writing and his associations, there is no doubt whatsoever that Rohith identified himself as the Dalit son of a Dalit mother, as a Dalit Ambedkarite scholar and organiser, and as a co-traveller encountering the oppressions, discrimination and exclusion experienced by his Dalit compatriots in the university campus and outside. For those uneasy with his erudition, his performance and his total identification with the Dalit identity, there had to be some way to discredit his politics in death.

Searching for this crucial flaw was even more important because what Rohith's treatment amounts to, resulting in his death, comes within the definition of caste atrocity, under the Scheduled Castes and the Scheduled Tribes (Prevention of Atrocities) Act, and has grave implications for those named in the FIR registered after his death. Whether or not Rohith named people in his suicide note is not material at this point. What is important to consider is whether the chain of events leading to his death gives reason to presume the possibility of discrimination based on caste coming within the definition of atrocity and leading to his death by suicide.

Caste as the Core

There is no dispute about the facts. Contrary to what ministers Smriti Irani or Sushma Swaraj might assert, this entire issue has to do with

---

* Originally published in *The Hindu*, 3 February 2016.

discrimination based on caste—the struggles of the Ambedkar Students' Association (ASA), Rohith's political and personal struggles, the institutionalised discrimination that Dalit students have been subjected to at the University of Hyderabad, curricular and co-curricular neglect of the social basis of discrimination in institutions of higher education, constant and disproportionate punitive action against Dalit students, their academic neglect and isolation, the simultaneous stigmatisation of 'reserved' candidates and the vilification of Dalit students like Rohith who qualify in the open category but persist in identifying themselves as Dalit, the unusual and excessive interest of the Union government in the criminalisation of Dalit student activists who organise as Dalits on campuses, and most importantly, the institutionalised humiliation of Dalits in academia (MHRD 2016; *Report of the People's Tribunal* 2016). Ministerial ignorance cannot be excused.

Dalit or Not?

Officers and reporters have ferreted out Rohith's father and paternal family in an overzealous attempt to roll back the demand that this is a Dalit issue (Mondal 2016). The old patriarchal argument that since his father was Vaddera, he was Vaddera, negates Dalit women's struggles in a caste order. In this case, it obliterates the experience of struggle against bondage, violence and humiliation of two generations—of Radhika Vemula and her children—their fortitude and determination to defeat the oppressions of caste at all costs. And when they are on the threshold of an unimaginable victory, we witness, yet again, annihilation by caste. An injustice compounded and bolstered by the institutional and political denial of discrimination or atrocity.

There is no need to labour the point about whether the actions that led to Rohith's suicide *prima facie* attract the provisions of the SC/ST (Prevention of Atrocities) Act. All that is needed at this point is to understand whether the act of suicide by a Dalit points to abetment by a non-Dalit. A complaint may be registered invoking the act if this fact is established. If the police refuse, the court can intervene. Rohith has a non-Dalit father and a Dalit mother. While there has been a long line of cases in the various high courts and the Supreme Court on this question, the most recent one, decided by a two-judge bench of the Supreme Court, consisting of Justices Aftab Alam and Ranjana Prakash Desai, is the law. In *Rameshbhai Dabhai Naika* (2012), the question before the Supreme Court was 'what would be the status of a person, one of whose parents belongs to the scheduled castes/ scheduled tribes and the other comes from the upper castes[?]'.[1]

The concluding paragraph of the judgement is self-explanatory:

> [I]n an inter-caste marriage or a marriage between a tribal and a non-tribal the determination of the caste of the offspring is essentially a question of fact to be decided on the basis of the facts adduced in each case.... [I]t is open to the child of such marriage to lead evidence to show that he/she was brought up by the mother who belonged to the scheduled caste/scheduled tribe.[2]

Did his father's non-Dalit status give him an 'advantageous start in life'[3] or did he suffer 'the deprivations, indignities, humilities and handicaps like any other member of the community to which his/ her mother belonged?'[4] Additionally, was he treated like a member of the community to which his mother belonged—not only by that community, but by people outside the community as well?

Rohith suffered exclusions, humiliation and discrimination along with other Dalit students on the campus and in the wider community. Yet, he refused to allow caste to break or confine him—and that was his most poignant struggle. The most important aspect of this struggle—its defining feature—was that it carried forward the tenacious struggles for a life with dignity for the children of Radhika Vemula, who pointed her children to the stars, daring them to dream. In a moment of utter collective regret, irreparable loss and grief, this family points the way to the annihilation of caste.

Notes

1. Rameshbhai Dabhai Naika v. State of Gujarat & Ors, (2012) 3 SCC 400, para. 1.
2. Ibid., para. 43.
3. Ibid., para. 6.
4. Ibid., para. 43.

References

Chukka, Vikram. 2016. 'The Chain of Events Leading to Rohith Vemula's Suicide'. *The Wire*, 19 January. Available at https://thewire.in/education/the-chain-of-events-leading-to-rohith-vemulas-suicide (accessed 15 June 2021).

MHRD (Ministry of Human Resource Development). 2016. *Laying of the Report of the Justice Ashok Kumar Roopanwal (Retd) Commission of Inquiry and Memorandum of Action Taken Thereon on the Table of Both the Houses of Parliament*. Available at https://www.education.gov.in/sites/upload_files/mhrd/files/document-reports/JusticeAshokKumarRoopanwalReport.pdf (accessed 9 July 2021).

Mondal, Sudipto. 2016. 'Rohith Vemula: An Unfinished Portrait'. *Hindustan Times*, January.

Report of the People's Tribunal on Caste Discrimination & Police Action in University of Hyderabad. 2016. Available at http://sanhati.com/articles/17555/ (accessed 15 June 2021).

12

Post-truths about Rohith Vemula*

Rohith Vemula left us on 17 January 2016. The Ambedkar Students' Association activist at the University of Hyderabad was a young Dalit leader of strong political convictions—opposed to the Hindu Right and committed to Ambedkarite anti-caste philosophy and democratic politics and, importantly, associational freedoms. There is no doubt that Rohith has in death, as in life, brought anti-caste resistance to the centre of deliberative democratic politics on campuses across the country, and brought new meanings to bear on the power of associational freedoms at a time when we are rapidly losing sight of it.

We are told a year after his passing that the government of Andhra Pradesh has decided that Rohith was Vaddera—an OBC, not a Dalit (Mitta 2016; Apparasu 2017). This is the discovery of a (post-)truth when the person is no longer alive to make an assertion to the contrary. When there is a certificate, witnesses, and a Supreme Court decision on the inheritance of caste status for Dalits and Adivasis from the mother, the government 'discovers' evidence to the contrary. Why this overdrive?

What is an Atrocity?

There is a case of atrocities registered against the vice-chancellor (VC) of the University of Hyderabad under the Scheduled Castes and the Scheduled Tribes (Prevention of Atrocities) Act, 1989. We now have an amended act with a covering letter that states that it is being strengthened to make it more effective.[1] Section 3 of the Scheduled Castes and the Scheduled Tribes (Prevention of Atrocities) Amendment Act, 2015, defines 'economic boycott' as '(i) a refusal

* Originally published in *The Hindu*, 17 January 2017.

to deal with ... other person; or (ii) to deny opportunities including access to services ...; or (iii) to refuse to do anything on the terms on which things would be commonly done in the ordinary course.'[2] 'Social boycott' is defined as including acts against a person 'to isolate him from others'.[3] A 'victim' is any individual belonging to a Scheduled Caste or Scheduled Tribe 'who has suffered or experienced physical, mental, psychological, emotional or monetary harm ... and includes his relatives, legal guardian and legal heirs'.[4]

Section 4 of the Amendment Act expands the definition of atrocity. When a person not belonging to a Scheduled Caste or Tribe 'by words either written or spoken or by signs or by visible representation or otherwise promotes or attempts to promote feelings of enmity, hatred or ill-will against members of the Scheduled Castes or the Scheduled Tribes'; 'prevents him from using or having access to a place of public resort to which other members of the public or any section thereof have a right to use or access to'; 'obstructs or prevents' an SC/ST member in any manner with regard to 'entering any educational institution, ... shop or place of public entertainment or any other public place'; or 'imposes or threatens a social or economic boycott of any person or a family or a group belonging to a Scheduled Caste or a Scheduled Tribe', he shall be punishable.[5]

Punishments and Rewards

In the aftermath of the differences between ASA and ABVP activists on campus, Bandaru Dattatreya, minister of state for labour and employment, wrote to Smriti Irani, the minister for human resource development:

> The Hyderabad University ... has become a den of casteist, extremist and anti-national politics.... [W]hen Yakub Memon was hanged, a dominant students union, that is, Ambedkar Students' Association has held protests against the execution. When Shri Shushil Kumar, President, ABVP in the campus protested against this, he was manhandled.... What is more tragic is that the University Administration has become a mute spectator to such events. (Quoted in *The Quint* 2016)

The incident occurred on the night of 3 August 2015; the proctorial board censured both groups of students on 12 August. Yet, on the basis of the ministerial communication in which the ASA is described as 'casteist, extremist and anti-national', and the ABVP, by implication, its opposite, the new VC constituted a subcommittee in contravention of procedure and issued a suspension order against the ASA on 16 December 2015, naming five students, that said, 'the above students ... are not permitted to participate in the students' union elections, enter the hostels, administration building and other common places in groups' (Chukka 2016). There was no order against the ABVP students. Less than a week after the suspension order, Rohith sent a chilling handwritten letter to the VC titled, 'Solution for Dalit Problem', in which he recommends termination of life as the only option available to Dalit students—himself included (*India.com* 2016). It evoked no rapid administrative reversals.

Dattatreya is a politician who will promote his political interests. The minister for human resource development shares Dattatreya's political anxieties and therefore issues communications to the universities (Jain 2016). They are at a distance from the university and not members of the university community.

It is the university administration led by the VC that is at a proximate distance and directly connected in terms of responsibility and culpability in actions of this nature. It is no argument to say after the fact that there is no discrimination on campus. The events strongly suggest the opposite. It is also not the ASA that is casteist, from a close examination of the materials on record. For this rhetoric to be absorbed by a liberal arts institution is tragic.

What is also worrisome is the nexus of punishments and rewards. Following the government's bidding (for that is what it appears to be from all accounts), we have seen the terrifying spiral of punishments (see *Report of the People's Tribunal* 2016). We have seen rewards for the VC: an award for excellence in academic work (PTI 2017) despite findings of plagiarism (Vasudevan 2016), and for excellence in institution-building. We have also seen the gift of de-certification of a victim (Apparasu 2017) that drastically diminishes criminal culpability in a case involving a grave institutional wrong, since the only way to extricate him from criminal proceedings is to alter the certification. All these point to the Central and state governments acting in unison. Institutional dignity and autonomy lie in ruins.

Notes

1. Ministry of Tribal Affairs, F. No. 16/5/2016-CP&R (issued on 18 February 2016).
2. The Scheduled Castes and the Scheduled Tribes (Prevention of Atrocities) Amendment Act, 2015, sec. 3(i)(bc).
3. Ibid., sec. 3(ii)(eb).
4. Ibid., sec. 3(ii)(ec).
5. Ibid., sec. 4(i).

References

'Prepare for Dalit Euthanasia, Said Rohith Vemula in Searing Letter to University of Hyderabad VC, Just Weeks before His Death'. 2016. *India.com*, 19 January. Available at https://www.india.com/news/india/dalit-euthanasia-rohith-vemula-letter-to-university-of-hyderabad-vc-873626/ (accessed 15 June 2021).

'Rohith Vemula's Suicide Reveals Letters from Bandaru, HRD Office'. 2016. *The Quint*, 19 January. Available at https://www.thequint.com/news/hot-news/rohith-vemulas-suicide-reveals-letters-from-bandaru-hrd-office#read-more#read-more (accessed 15 June 2021).

Apparasu, Srinivasa Rao. 2017. 'Rohith Vemula Not a Dalit, Says Collector; Andhra Govt to Cancel SC Certificate'. *Hindustan Times*, 14 February.

Chukka, Vikram. 2016. 'The Chain of Events Leading to Rohith Vemula's Suicide'. *The Wire*, 19 January. Available at https://thewire.in/education/the-chain-of-events-leading-to-rohith-vemulas-suicide (accessed 15 June 2021).

Jain, Mayank. 2016. 'Read the Letters HRD Ministry Sent Hyderabad University about "Anti-national" Activities on Campus'. *Scroll.in*, 19 January. Available at https://scroll.in/article/802107/read-the-letters-hrd-ministry-sent-hyderabad-university-about-anti-national-activities-on-campus (accessed 15 June 2021).

Mitta, Manoj. 2016. 'How This Self-Proclaimed Pro-Dalit Government Has All but Buried the Rohith Vemula Case'. *Scroll.in*, 31 December. Available at https://scroll.in/article/825545/how-this-self-proclaimed-pro-dalit-government-has-all-but-buried-the-rohith-vemula-case (accessed 25 July 2021).

PTI (Press Trust of India). 2017. 'Hyderabad University VC Receives Award from PM Modi at Indian Science Congress'. *The Indian Express*, 3 January.

Report of the People's Tribunal on Caste Discrimination & Police Action in University of Hyderabad. 2016. Available at http://sanhati.com/articles/17555/ (accessed 15 June 2021).

Vasudevan, Mukunth. 2016. 'Hyderabad University VC Admits to Plagiarism'. *The Wire*, 5 April. Available at https://thewire.in/education/hyderabad-university-vc-admits-to-plagiarism (accessed 15 June 2021).

III

Disability Rights

13

Creating Enabling Environments*

> *Disability need not be an obstacle to success.... It is my hope that ... this century will mark a turning point for inclusion of people with disabilities in the lives of their societies.*
>
> —Stephen Hawking (2011: Foreword, *World Report on Disability*)

The inauguration of the United Nations Convention on the Rights of Persons with Disabilities (UNCRPD) in 2008 signalled the recognition of disability as a human rights issue. Research in different countries has demonstrated the ways in which disability is a development issue as well by mapping its bidirectional link to poverty (see WHO and World Bank 2011). The World Health Organisation's *World Report on Disability* (WRD), prepared in response to a request by the World Health Assembly, affirms the work of disability rights advocates and attempts to fill the knowledge and information gap on disability.

The lack of a standard measure of disability across countries makes definition, comparisons and statistical estimates of incidence a challenging task. Combining the 2010 population estimates and the 2004 disability prevalence estimates of the World Health Survey and Global Burden of Disease study, the WRD estimates that there are over a billion people, that is, 15 per cent of the world's population (including children), living with disability (ibid.: 29). The National Disability Policy of India estimated in 2006 that the disabled constitute 2.13 per cent of the country's population (Ministry of Social Justice and Empowerment 2006).

It is now widely understood that environment determines a person's experience of disability—either as a facilitator or barrier.

---

* Originally published in *The Hindu*, 24 June 2011.

But what do we mean by 'environment'? The International Classification of Functioning, Disability and Health, which the WRD draws on, maps environmental factors ranging from technological and built environments to emotional and psycho-social environments that influence active participation. Importantly, this classification makes a distinction between capacity and actual performance, the gap between which could be indicative of the environmental barriers that need to be eliminated.

Accessibility is a concern that cuts across different domains of environment and must reach persons across disabilities. While it is widely acknowledged that accessibility standards are indispensable to inclusion and non-discrimination on grounds of disability, these have largely been left to the goodwill of institutions—state and private. The WRD observes, 'Laws with mandatory access standards are the most effective way to achieve accessibility' (WHO and World Bank 2011: 175).

Disability audits of public and healthcare services, of existing and proposed policies and of institutions and organisations, have pointed to the practices of exclusion and indirect discrimination resulting from a lack of sensitivity to the needs of people with disabilities. A global survey in 2005 showed that of 114 countries, 37 had no training in place for rehabilitation professionals and 56 had not updated the medical knowledge of healthcare providers on disability (ibid.: 110). Aggravating these barriers in the structural and systemic environment are mental barriers—negative stereotypes and stigmatisation—that question the right to choice, family life, adoption and such for persons with disabilities (ibid.: 6).

While there is a general tendency to homogenise disability and flatten out the diversity of conditions and capabilities, disability is, in fact, stunningly diverse and encompasses the child with learning disabilities, the injured soldier and the elderly man with severely impaired mobility, not to speak of survivors of violence and the mentally ill.

The distinction between disability and ill health is an important one. The WRD cites an Australian National Health Survey in which 40 per cent of people with severe or profound disability rated their health as good, very good or excellent (ibid.: 8). Yet, unarguably, ensuring the prevention of health conditions that lead to disability is a development concern. The World Health Survey, cited in the WRD, draws attention to attitudinal, physical and systemic barriers that impede the access of the disabled to healthcare, drawing on the findings of research in Uttar Pradesh and Tamil Nadu that pointed to cost, lack of local services and transportation as being the top three obstacles to using health facilities (ibid.: 62–63). The financing of healthcare, making it affordable and making medical equipment accessible to the disabled remain urgent concerns. The failure of service providers to communicate in appropriate formats or with sensitivity to the needs of disabled care-seekers might result, as it did in Zimbabwe, in the exclusion of the disabled from routine screening and counselling services (ibid.: 72). Care coordination, in this context, is extremely important, and short-term increases in service delivery costs are compensated by efficiency and effective delivery in the long term.

The exposure of children to multiple risks, compounded by children screening positive for a high risk of disability being denied access to adequate childcare and nutrition, foregrounds the criticality of the family in providing care to children who are disabled and those facing increased risk. A 2005 study by the United Nations Children's Fund (UNICEF) estimated 150 million children with disabilities. Data from specific countries also suggest a higher risk in children belonging to ethnic minorities (ibid.: 36). There is a sizeable enrolment gap between children with and without disabilities, with figures across Asia, Europe, Africa and South America showing higher enrolment rates for non-disabled children across age groups (ibid.: 207–08). School problems, the report found, revolved around curriculum, pedagogy, inadequate training of teachers, physical barriers, labelling, violence, bullying and abuse (ibid.: 209).

The denial of equality, dignity and autonomy to persons with disabilities lies at the core of disability rights as human rights. An important finding of the WRD, and one that confirms our experience in India, is that persons with disabilities are at a greater risk of being targeted by violence. In the United States, the risk is four to ten times more. Among the various forms of violence, sexual violence, especially against intellectually challenged persons who are in institutional care, is a major concern. The *Chandigarh Administration* case is an example.[1]

Even more serious is the 'legitimate' incarceration of the mentally ill and the denial of fundamental rights under the Constitution. This treatment is echoed in the Disability Rights International report on the mentally ill in Paraguay, which documented life-threatening abuses and incarceration in dehumanising conditions (ibid.: 146). In this regard, the Italian experience of deinstitutionalising the mentally ill and equipping general hospitals to care for mentally ill patients, thus integrating mental healthcare with general healthcare, merits special mention. Although the coverage is far from adequate, the enactment of legislation and the drawing up of concrete plans of action supported by budgetary allocations and inter-sectoral professional services show the way forward (ibid.: 106). This trend towards deinstitutionalising has also been followed in some countries in eastern Europe, notably, Romania.

Article 12 of the UNCRPD places an obligation on governments to put in place adequate mechanisms for effective, supported decision-making by persons with disabilities, ensuring thereby that they do not lose legal capacity on grounds of disability.[2] The WRD finds large gaps in meeting support needs across the world—China, for instance, reported a shortage of personnel; and 30 countries (including Iraq, Madagascar, Mexico, Sudan, Thailand and Tanzania) reported having fewer than 20 sign language interpreters (ibid.: 140). The Disabled Children's Action Group, set up by parents of children with disabilities to address the needs of children from black and coloured communities in South Africa in 1993, is an example of how a mutual support group can actually change the contexts in which children grow up (ibid.: 143).

This report is particularly relevant for us in India at a time when we are witnessing a concerted effort to put an effective and comprehensive national law in place.

Notes

1. Suchita Srivastava & Anr v. Chandigarh Administration, (2009) 14 SCR 989.
2. Convention on the Rights of Persons with Disabilities art. 12, 3 May 2008, 2515 UNTS 3.

References

Ministry of Social Justice and Empowerment. 2006. 'National Policy for Persons with Disabilities'. No. 3-1/1993-DD.III.

WHO (World Health Organisation) and World Bank. 2011. *World Report on Disability*. Foreword by Stephen Hawking. Geneva: WHO.

14

The Rights of Prisoners with Disabilities*

We have a slew of cases around prisoners' rights that emphasise their right to dignity and their right against cruel and degrading punishment, which have been understood to violate the right to life, guaranteed by Article 21 of the Indian Constitution. In complying with the standards set out in constitutional jurisprudence on this matter, the offence for which the person has been apprehended or convicted is immaterial. The standard is clear. No person shall be subjected to degrading, inhuman or cruel punishment that is violative of human dignity; the duty of care to be exercised in this matter during pre-trial custody is of a much higher order. These are standards applicable to all custodial situations and to all persons, irrespective of caste, sex, race, religion or place of birth.

Treatment in Custody

The *Veena Sethi* case in the early 1980s brought to light the treatment of prisoners with mental illnesses and their prolonged incarceration for periods ranging from 16 to 30 years in custody.[1] This is far in excess of sentences given to them in most of these cases, without bringing them any substantive relief beyond release from illegal custody and transport and food expenses till they reached home. That was long before there was a consciousness or political articulation of the rights of persons with disabilities, which, importantly today, includes civil and political rights for prisoners with disabilities.

---

* Originally published in *The Hindu*, 20 May 2014.

This chapter is the first in a series addressing the incarceration of G. N. Saibaba.

We have seen some reports on the arrest of G. N. Saibaba and the conditions under which he is being held in custody (Vatsa 2014; *Scroll.in* 2018). The fact that needs close and urgent examination here is not whether he has Maoist 'links' or whether he is a 'sympathiser' or even whether a university professor can be harassed in this manner (although we must separate his troubles in the university from his treatment by the officers of the criminal justice system). What needs our immediate attention is even more fundamental: as a person with disabilities who requires constant assistance and support, what are the standard minimum rules that must temper the decision to take him into custody, in order that the treatment meted out to him is not construed as cruel, degrading and inhuman?

It would be useful for the authorities who have taken Saibaba into custody to be informed of India's commitment to the UN Convention on the Rights of Persons with Disabilities. Article 4(1)(d) enjoins States Parties 'to refrain from engaging in any act or practice that is inconsistent with the present Convention and to ensure that public authorities and institutions act in conformity with the present Convention'.[2] What are the specific protections for persons with disabilities in relation to state custody? Article 15(1) of the UNCRPD is immediately relevant: 'No one shall be subjected to torture or to cruel, inhuman or degrading treatment or punishment.'[3] Article 15(2) of the convention places an obligation on the state to protect persons with disabilities from cruel degrading or inhuman treatment and punishment. It says, 'States Parties shall take all effective legislative, administrative, judicial or other measures to prevent persons with disabilities, on an equal basis with others, from being subjected to torture or cruel, inhuman or degrading treatment or punishment.'[4]

The norm of substantive equality, well established through constitutional jurisprudence in India, speaks of the principle of equality that necessarily includes special treatment for persons who are vulnerable. The denial of special provisions, appropriate assistance and specialised healthcare access to a person with disabilities in custody, who uses a wheelchair and has special healthcare needs arising from chronic illness, comes firmly within the meaning of degrading, inhuman and cruel treatment in derogation of the state's obligation under the UNCRPD.

Particularly where a prisoner with disability requires support and assistance for daily living, placing such a prisoner in solitary confinement and denying the right to accessible facilities for personal care and hygiene is violative of the right to dignity and bodily integrity—both guaranteed under Article 21 of the Constitution, but also under Article 17 of the UNCRPD. The latter simply and pertinently states that '[e]very person with disabilities has a right to respect for his or her physical and mental integrity on an equal basis with others'.[5]

The rights of persons with disabilities legislation that ought to set out these standards in clear and unequivocal terms has been ever in the making in India.[6] The absence of specific legislation, however, need not deter us from the path of justice. Article 14 of the Constitution that sets out the substantive right to equality before law, and Article 21 that sets out the framework for the right to life (with dignity)—as it specifically applies to prisoners—should at this time be read with the UNCRPD, which India has ratified. This is till the time that we put in place policies and national legislation that mandatorily provide for special services and basic needs that prisoners with disabilities might require, and prioritise the conditional and compassionate release of prisoners with high support needs.

Vulnerability of Women

Recognising the vulnerability of women in custodial situations, the Criminal Procedure Code (CrPC) provides very different standards for their involvement in criminal investigations. There are also special standards for the treatment of women prisoners and pregnant women in custody. The demand for treatment that is sensitive to the rights of persons with disabilities to dignity and physical integrity and to their specific needs is therefore not unprecedented. Where prison and custodial facilities are not equipped at all to deal with the specific needs of persons with disabilities, arrest and detention in custody should be a measure of last resort, clearly not the case where Saibaba is concerned. The investigating authorities must release him from custody forthwith and carry out any investigations they may require without infringing on his right to human dignity and fundamental freedoms, and in full compliance with the CrPC, the Constitution and the UNCRPD.

Notes

1. Veena Sethi v. State of Bihar, (1982) 2 SCC 583.
2. Convention on the Rights of Persons with Disabilities art. 4, cl. 1(d), 3 May 2008, 2515 UNTS 3.
3. Ibid., art. 15, cl. 1.
4. Ibid., art. 15, cl. 2.
5. Ibid., art. 17.
6. This was later passed as the Rights of Persons with Disabilities Act, 2016.

References

'United Nations Rights Experts Urge India to Release Jailed Delhi University Professor G. N. Saibaba'. 2018. *Scroll.in*, 28 June. Available at https://scroll.in/latest/884552/united-nations-rights-experts-urge-india-to-release-jailed-delhi-university-professor-gn-saibaba (accessed 13 June 2021).

Vatsa, Aditi. 2014. 'Delhi University Professor G. N. Saibaba is Arrested for "Naxal Links"'. *The Indian Express*, 10 May.

15

Between the Divine and the Diabolical

*Disability Rights over the Edge**

In the 65 years since its adoption, the Constitution of India has provided the opportunity and space for an enlarged and expansive enunciation of basic rights, moving to an interpretive tradition that upholds the spirit of the fundamental rights to life, liberty and equality with dignity, among others. Although there have been contestations, peaks and troughs in the ways the Constitution has been interwoven with lives and worlds, there is little doubt that it has provided the framework for an assertion of fundamental rights, importantly against the state, but also against private actors, providing the standard of constitutional morality that must in all cases defeat public, including religious, morality. This is especially critical where the latter is found to perpetrate stigmatised identities and labelling that diminishes the dignity of persons and oppresses them in untold ways.

Constitutional Morality in Crisis

We have been witness in the past months to the virtual negation of the constitutional spirit in every sphere of our public life—by constitutional authorities of every kind—with impunity. State authorities, supported by constitutional heads of nation and states, justices and priests in unison invoke and propitiate mother goddesses instead of constitutional rule. And constitutional courts see criticism of government and police as contemptuous conduct. Behold the disablement of a constitutional democracy.

---

* Originally published as 'Disability is Not Divinity', in *The Hindu*, 12 January 2016.

This chapter is the second in a series addressing the incarceration of G. N. Saibaba.

In this melee, there is something else that merits our close attention. The year 2015 comes to a close on a note of crisis, as we witness a rollback of hard-won recognition of disability rights in India by the very constitutional authorities entrusted with safeguarding and advancing them.

Divine, Not by Human Design

On 27 December, as part of the fifteenth edition of his radio address, *Mann Ki Baat,* Prime Minister Narendra Modi spoke for one-and-a-half minutes about disability:

> Those in whom *paramatma* [the Almighty] has created a deficiency in the body, those for whom some part of the body does not work properly, we call them "*viklaang*" [disabled person], and we know them as "viklaang". But sometimes, when we get to know them, we realise that although there is the deficiency that we see with our eyes, *ishwar* [god] has given them some extra power, there is a different kind of *shakti* [power] that paramatma has created within them which we cannot perceive with our eyes. But when we see them at work, or we see their capability, we are taken aback, "*Arre wah*! [Oh wow!] How does he manage to do this?" Then I had a thought: From our eyes we feel that he is viklaang, but from experience we find that he has some extra power, *atirikt shakti*. Then I had another thought: why don't we, in our country, replace the word "viklaang" with the word "*divyaang*" [divine body]? These are those people who possess divinity—*divyata*—in one or more parts of their body; whose bodies are possessed by divine power [*divyashakti*], which those of us with normal bodies [*saamaanya shareer*] do not have. I really like this word. Compatriots, can we adopt divyaang instead of viklaang in common usage? I hope you will take this forward. (Modi 2015; translation mine)

In other words, that which is divinely ordained shall not be questioned. It is immutable and inheres in the body of the disabled person, not in their treatment—the 'deficiency' and the 'divyashakti'—conjoined twins that constitute the disability stereotype.

Diabolical, 'to the *Anda* Cell!'[1]

In an order passed on 23 December 2015, the Nagpur Bench of the Bombay High Court passed an order rejecting the bail application of

G. N. Saibaba on medical grounds stressing his involvement in 'serious crime' and the activities of a 'banned organisation' as overriding any concerns for his physical health and wellbeing while in state custody, going to the extent of saying that all efforts to secure bail for him on medical grounds are 'nothing but a subterfuge'.[2] It is useful to bear in mind at this stage, however, that we are speaking of a person who has been placed under arrest but has not yet undergone trial, and certainly not been convicted for a terrorist offence or offence under the Unlawful Activities (Prevention) Act.

Be that as it may, the court accepts the fact that 'the applicant suffered 90% disability from his childhood. He had also undergone cardiac surgery about 8 to 10 years before'.[3] The medical certificate relied on by the court states that Saibaba suffered from a 'known case of post polio residual paralysis with chief complaints of reduction in left shoulder movements and pain in back for which he has managed conservatively with supportive medication'.[4] He was advised to go through regular treatment for three months and also advised by the doctor in the super-speciality hospital at Nagpur to undergo a coronary angiography. On the basis of these medical records the court concludes that the 'present health condition of the applicant ... is *perfectly normal* and is in the same position as it was when he was in jail' (emphasis mine).[5]

The fact that his disability and attendant medical conditions place Saibaba at an unfair disadvantage in conditions of custody and solitary confinement—that the standard of care required for a person with severe disabilities is of a different order from the standard of care for a non-disabled person; that the standard is not met by simply ensuring the maintenance of status quo (although even this is contested by the applicant); that conditions of incarceration aggravate the risk to life disproportionately in the case of a person with disabilities—are considerations that do not enter the balance sheet drawn up by the constitutional court. The tenor seems to be that the diabolical acts the complainant is alleged to have sympathised with (his direct involvement is not on record) offset any need for state (and judicial) benevolence. The Constitution hangs in suspended disbelief.

Conclusion

Trapped in the cusp between the divine and the diabolical, it is time, yet again, for us to understand afresh that the disproportionate disadvantage, exclusion and stigmatisation suffered by persons with disabilities is a result of discrimination against them, and are caused by cultural, social and physical barriers that obstruct their effective participation in social and political life. Disability is not a divine gift—this assertion is a grave misreading of the place of rights in realising human dignity and the role of the state in ensuring protection against discrimination. In the same vein, it is important to recognise that accessibility, and support services for persons with severe and profound disabilities especially, are indispensable to the protection of their right to life, bodily integrity and dignity under the Constitution of India. Incarceration of persons with severe disabilities aggravates their physical and psychosocial suffering disproportionately in comparison to other prisoners, defeating the fundamental right to equality, and for this reason must only be used as a measure of last resort, if at all. We need an honest acknowledgement, at least by constitutional courts, that our prisons are simply not equipped to provide custodial treatment that does not erode the fundamental right to life, equality and dignity of prisoners with disabilities. There is an urgency with which we must wrest constitutional ground for disability rights in these hard and strained modern times. Importantly, we need a re-education on the Constitution at the highest echelons of our juridical-political order.

Notes

1. As described by Suresh (2019), '[A]nda cell is a colloquial term for a high-security compound inside a prison that is egg-shaped. The cells inside are often tiny and dimly lit, with sparse ventilation and little space for movement. They are … a form of solitary confinement. Its purpose is often to segregate criminals accused of serious offences, such as terror suspects, from the rest of the inmates.'
2. Dr Gokarakonda Naga Saibaba v. State of Maharashtra, through PSO, PS Aheri, District Gadchiroli & Anr, Criminal Application

(BA) No. 785/2015, decided on 23 December 2015 (Bom. (NB) HC), para. 11.
3. Ibid., para. 11.
4. Ibid., para. 11.
5. Ibid., para. 12.

References

Modi, Narendra. 2015. *Mann Ki Baat.* Radio broadcast. All India Radio, 27 December.

Suresh, Nidhi. 2019. 'Prisoner Mirza Himayat Baig Recounts Solitary Confinement inside an Anda Cell'. *The Caravan*, 31 October.

16

Right to Privacy as Right to Life*

In the right to privacy judgement, Justice Chandrachud held:

> Life and personal liberty are inalienable to human existence.... The human element in the life of the individual is integrally founded on the sanctity of life.... A constitutional democracy can survive when citizens have an undiluted assurance that the rule of law will protect their rights and liberties against any invasion by the state and that judicial remedies would be available to ask searching questions and expect answers when a citizen has been deprived of these, most precious rights.[1]

Violation of Right to Life

In 2014, Delhi University professor G. N. Saibaba was arrested under the Unlawful Activities (Prevention) Act and held in Nagpur Central Jail till the Supreme Court granted him bail in 2016. In March 2017, he was convicted by the Gadchiroli sessions court and sentenced to life imprisonment for alleged offences under the same act, and returned to custody in the anda cell of Nagpur Central Jail (Dahat 2017).[2] His appeal against the conviction is pending before the Nagpur Bench of the Bombay High Court (Jain 2017). While the grounds of his conviction are debatable, the immediate concern is regarding the question of miscarriage of justice on other grounds. Saibaba has severe disabilities and multiple related health conditions and has high support needs. Placing him in solitary confinement with no support violates his right to life, bodily integrity and autonomy under Article 21, although his conviction only imposes

---

* Originally published in *The Hindu*, 9 November 2017.

This chapter is the third in a series addressing the incarceration of G. N. Saibaba.

restraints on personal liberty. This inhuman treatment is punishment far in excess of the sentence awarded by the court.

It is now time to ask searching questions about the sentence, and appeal to the court for the application of constitutional due process so as to not endanger his right to life.

The deplorable conditions in Indian prisons are well known. It is settled law now that prisoners may be deprived of personal liberty according to procedure established by law, but that does not include a derogation of their right to dignity. The privacy bench reiterates the words of Justice Krishna Iyer in the *Prem Shankar Shukla* case:

> The guarantee of human dignity, which forms part of our constitutional culture, and the positive provisions of Articles 14, 19 and 21 spring into action when we realise that to manacle man is more than to mortify him; it is to dehumanize him and, therefore, to violate his very personhood, too often using the mask of "dangerousness" and security.[3]

The right to life cannot be restricted to mere 'animal existence'. How do we begin to understand the sanctity of life, dignity and bodily integrity for a person with disabilities? If handcuffing is an extraordinary and excessive restraint on an ordinary prisoner, what constitutes excessive restraint beyond the writ of law for a person with disabilities?

The Supreme Court holds unequivocally that in adopting the Constitution, the people of India do not surrender the most precious aspects of the human persona—namely life, liberty and freedom—to the state on whose mercy these rights would depend. Each of these aspects—life, liberty and freedom—must be considered together and/or severally as the case may be. Where there is a sentence on personal liberty, the citizen does not surrender his life to the mercy of the state.

If, as the right to privacy judgement asserts, privacy 'as an integral part of the right to human dignity is comprehended within the protection of life as well',[4] it is necessary for every court to develop a sensibility towards and understanding of what constitutes human dignity and protection of life for persons located differently in the social order. For, an important aspect of this judgement, which is now law in India, is respect for human diversity and pluralism. Albeit with reference to a different case, the court observed that neither the fact that very few persons bear certain attributes nor the test of 'popular acceptance ... furnish a valid basis to disregard rights which are conferred with the sanctity of constitutional protection'.[5] Saibaba may well be the only person in his situation. That in itself is reason for the courts to intervene actively in his favour and remove him immediately from the situation of precarity and irreversible harm.

In light of the decision of the Supreme Court on the right to privacy, particularly its comments on the *Suresh Kumar Koushal* judgement on Section 377 of the Indian Penal Code[6] and the *habeas corpus* case,[7] one cannot help but hope that the Nagpur Bench of the Bombay High Court, in considering Saibaba's appeal against his conviction, similarly examines the judegment and deliberates on the relationship between fact, law, popular rhetoric and proportionality therein.

Entitled to Bail

Most importantly, however, it is hoped that the court examines disability as grounds for the grant of bail, as distinct from (but related to) 'medical grounds'. This entails, according to the Rights of Persons with Disabilities Act, 2016, 'respect for inherent dignity, individual autonomy ... and independence of persons' and 'accessibility'.[8] Section 2(s) of the act defines a person with disability as 'a person with long term physical, mental, intellectual or sensory impairment which, in interaction with barriers, hinders his full and effective participation in society equally with others'.[9] In conditions of custody, such persons must be protected from any hindrance to the exercise of bodily integrity and autonomy with dignity—this lies at the core of the right to privacy. Unavailability of such a guarantee within custodial facilities entitles the prisoner with disabilities to bail.

Saibaba's predicament is best described in his own words:

> I am frightened to think of the coming winter.... As temperature goes down excruciating pain continuously in my legs and left hand increases. It is impossible for me to survive here during the winter that starts from November ... I am living here like an animal taking its last breaths. Somehow eight months I managed to survive. But I am not going to survive in the coming winter. I am sure. It is of no use to write about

> my health any longer.... No one understands 90% disabled person is behind bars struggling with one hand in condition and suffering with multiple ailments. And no one cares for my life. This is simply criminal negligence, a callous attitude. (Saibaba to his wife, 17 October 2017)

At the time of his conviction and the proceedings so far, we did not have the constitutional wisdom of the privacy bench before us. In weighing the question of restraint on personal liberty against the risk to life, bodily integrity and dignity, the court scene in *The Merchant of Venice* (Act 4, Scene 1) spins into view: 'Therefore prepare thee to cut off the flesh/Shed thou no blood, nor cut thou less nor more/But just a pound of flesh.' A Daniel come to judgement.

Notes

1. *K. S. Puttaswamy*, (2017) 10 SCC 1.
2. State of Maharashtra, through PSO, PS Aheri, District Gadchiroli v. Mahesh Kariman Tirki & Ors, Sessions Case No. 13 of 2014 & Sessions Case No. 130 of 2015, decided on 7 March 2017 (Court of Sessions Judge, Gadchiroli).
3. Prem Shankar Shukla v. Delhi Administration, AIR 1980 SC 1535, para. 1, cited in *K. S. Puttaswamy* (2017) 10 SCC 1, para. 97.
4. *K. S. Puttaswamy*, (2017) 10 SCC 1, para. 26.
5. Ibid., para. 126.
6. Suresh Kumar Koushal & Anr v. Naz Foundation, (2014) 1 SCC 1, cited in *K. S. Puttaswamy*, (2017) 10 SCC 1, paras. 124–28.
7. ADM Jabalpur v. Shivkant Shukla, (1976) 2 SCC 521, cited in *K. S. Puttaswamy*, (2017) 10 SCC 1, para. 92.
8. Convention on the Rights of Persons with Disabilities art. 3, 3 May 2008, 2515 UNTS 3, quoted in the Rights of Persons with Disabilities Act, 2016.
9. The Rights of Persons with Disabilities Act, 2016, sec. 6(s).

References

Dahat, Pavan. 2017. 'Ex-DU Professor Saibaba Sentenced to Life for Maoist Links'. *The Hindu*, 7 March.

Jain, Meetu. 2017. 'Bombay High Court to Hear G. N. Saibaba's Appeal against Life Sentence Verdict'. *India Today*, 6 December. Available at https://www.indiatoday.in/india/story/bombay-hc-to-hear-gn-saibaba-appeal-against-life-sentence-verdict-1101615-2017-12-06 (accessed 19 July 2021).

Shakespeare, William. 1993. *The Merchant of Venice* (The Complete Works of William Shakespeare). Created by Jeremy Hylton. Available at http://shakespeare.mit.edu/merchant/full.html (accessed 13 June 2021).

IV

Minority Rights

17

An Apology to Mohammed Akhlaq*

I feel personally responsible for Mohammed Akhlaq's death. In his death are the embers of my deeply cherished values, my faith in the power of secular reason and the power of resistance, and I see the defeat of my ability to question and demand answers for profound wrongs. Some months ago, when I wrote about free speech in the context of the right of an intellectual to question religion (Kannabiran 2015), I was accused by a fairly erudite liberal (or so I thought) scholar of being a 'secular fundamentalist'. I was troubled, not so much by the accusation as by what it signalled about the scholar making the accusation. I panicked about how dangerously close the liberal intelligentsia was sliding to a position that is not only irretrievable, but also a position that draws legitimacy from the blood of its victims. These victims are not intellectuals alone. While writing is expression, it is culture that is expression par excellence—food is at the heart of culture, as is worship. Critique by a rationalist, the suspicion of beef in a Muslim home, temple entry by a Dalit, invite death, no less (*The Hindu* 2015). The thirst for the blood of the victim, a moving target, is insatiable.

Independent India saw the imprisonment of poets and writers in the 1970s. But there was resistance. However, majoritarian, dominant-caste hate speech, the hallmark of the three decades since the 1990s, is ascendant now as never before and there is a snuffing out of dissent as never before. Technologies of cyber communication are harnessed in unprecedented ways, sealed through a cosy and growing homosociality between political and corporate musclemen (see Gopalakrishnan 2015). The camera is witness.

* Originally published in *The New Indian Express*, 16 October 2015.

There is murder on the streets—of free-thinking intellectuals and ordinary citizens who just go about their business from day to day—eating what they have always eaten and what they like to eat, wearing what they like to wear, sometimes daring to marry out of choice, at other times, daring to espouse a political viewpoint (for example, *Hindustan Times* 2015; Puniyani 2015). There is fear in the hearts of many who write—a very real, palpable fear of the murderous mob on the rampage—a mob with people from our city, our town, our village, our caste, our family, our state, our country, governments we have elected, sometimes in uniform and at other times not, and they are out for the kill. Those that are not crippled by fear have chosen silence as resistance—What is left to say? Who is listening? Does it matter any more that the basic right to life of citizens of this democratic country has been trafficked to faceless mobs by those who are under oath, entrusted with the security of the people of the country?

In the era of the Constitution, we are asked to be thankful when our daughters are not assaulted; murder is not any more a question of crime, targeted murder is not aggravated atrocity—the protest over a gruesome, unpardonable murder is just a blemish on India's platinum shine, a mere embarrassment to our messiahs out to win the world. Hate is the way of life in shining India. And impunity is a method of government.

My mind wanders back (what can the mind do but wander in this frightening time?) to the discussions around the Rowlatt Satyagraha in 1919, and recalls one exchange especially:

> Raizada Bhagat Ram: To my mind [the meetings during the satyagraha were peaceful] due to the soul-force of Mr Gandhi.
>
> Michael O'Dwyer: [*raising his fist*] Raizada *Sahib*, remember, there is another force greater than Gandhi's soul-force. (*Punjab Disturbances* 1920, vol. 1, quoted in Bhalla 1997: 52.)

Independent India has seen an acceptance and exploration of Gandhi's 'soul-force' as well as trenchant critiques of it, notably in the Ambedkarite tradition. There are other critiques as well. Yet, central to the entire range of writings by conscientious resisters of different hues was the firm belief in justice and peace.

But our times have changed. O'Dwyer's fist pales into insignificance, an empty gesture. Our tongues ripped out, we watch the painful incineration of our most dearly held beliefs and freedoms. At a time when the air is thick with the cinematic smog of a golden age, a hoary Indian past, history fades into mythology; the arrow grows heads, morphing into a trident; science drowns in the treacherous waters of miracle; divine birth tales, far from being an immaculate matter of blind faith, are proof that science has no history, that it is immutable, and the figure of Karna signals an ascendent genetic science in a mythic era, just as the figure of Ganesha removes constitutive obstacles in the way of modern medicine. This funereal smog chokes off the last remnant of the argumentative Indian; it chokes off the voices of those that asserted over centuries that their right to faith included the right to question; it decimates those that dare to speak truth to power.

So today, starvation takes on new meaning and a new life. It is not only those that cannot afford food that will starve. It is also the rest who will not eat lest they pay with their lives. I remember my good father saying long ago that there was no bigger travesty of justice than imprisoning a writer, thus denying her the opportunity to practice her craft. Thankfully, he is not alive to witness a time when the freedom to practice a craft or trade is way beyond the horizon—this is the time when people are killed for eating.

And while citizens die at the hands of murderous mobs that direct governments, and scholarship acquires a saffron monotone, the cameras click away, eager to capture the millionth image of carefully manicured, coiffured power—the bloodstained image of Brand India.

Make not in India. Not till we have yanked ourselves back onto the road to freedom.

References

'Rationalist Narendra Dabholkar's Murder Unsolved 2 Years On'. 2015. *Hindustan Times*, 20 August.

'The Dadri Lynching: How Events Unfolded'. 2015. *The Hindu*, 3 October. Available at https://www.thehindu.com/specials/in-depth/the-dadri-lynching-how-events-unfolded/article7719414.ece (accessed 25 July 2021).

Bhalla, Alok. 1997. 'A Dance of Grotesque Masks: A Critical Reading of Manto's "1919 Ke Ek Baat"'. In *Life and Works of Saadat Hasan Manto*, ed. Alok Bhalla, 28–54. Shimla: Indian Institute of Advanced Study.

Gopalakrishnan, Amulya. 2015. 'Dadri Reopens Debate on Online Hate Speech'. *The Times of India*, 9 October.

Kannabiran, Kalpana. 2015. 'Free Speech is the Cornerstone of the Constitution'. *The New Indian Express*, 22 July.

Puniyani, Ram. 2015. 'Who Killed Govind Pansare?'. *The Indian Express*, 11 March.

18

Kashmir and Una Define a New Practice of Politics*

July 2016 has been a month of turmoil for all of India. As we move into August, the month of *azaadi* (freedom), some thoughts on where we are today. The hunting down of Burhan Wani and the unforgiveable massacre and assault of unarmed protesters in Kashmir that followed (Irfan 2016) has been the tipping point in Kashmir's tolerance and utter patience with a persistently violent Indian state. As I read report after painful report of the profound trauma unleashed on Kashmiri people, I was reminded of the moving testimonies and stories of lives told by Iffat Fatima in her film *Khoon Diy Baarav* (2012)—too much bloodshed, too much pain, and injustice beyond repair, or even comprehension. What else does one say but that the government has committed a grave criminal wrong against an entire people—and we wait and watch, and say in words and through silence what simply has so little meaning any more. The utter pointlessness of writing a byline on Kashmir—and yet, we must write and respond in the best or the only way that we can and put our strengths behind the people and their indomitable courage. I am reminded of an inane question a viewer asked Iffat when her film was screened in Hyderabad in December 2015: 'It is very good that you have travelled so far out to talk to so many people. But what is missing in your film is the voice of army personnel. Did you attempt to talk to any of them? You show the outposts from a distance.' She simply answered 'no'. But I was angry that it was even possible to ask that question after seeing the film.

It is this assumption of 'neutrality' that has been the undoing of public discourse in the rest of the country on Kashmir. In a film about

* Originally published in *The Wire*, 2 August 2016.

disappearances, and arbitrary arrests, and checkpoints, and the routine, habitual, everyday assault of the ordinary Kashmiri man, woman, child, the person on the street, by security personnel, the 'voice' of the army *is* these actions and signposts—the visual, the physical; *impunity is the voice and the speech of the army and indeed the Indian government in Kashmir.* It is only when we shut this voice out that we begin to hear the voice of the people—those who spoke to Iffat, entire villages in mourning that cascaded to Burhan's funeral and those who brave lethal weapons of 'crowd control' and suffer grievous hurt and yet pour onto the streets in protest asserting the right to mourn collectively and publicly—as also the very few outside who attempt to speak the language of solidarity (a language for the most part bereft of words by now).

In a startling irony, I came across a farcical post on Facebook a week ago that talked of the BJP and its cow protection armies triggering a parliamentary debate on the banning of pellets because cows that strayed within firing range were blinded—and that the demand was also that callous Kashmiri owners of cows be prosecuted for wilfully sending their cows out to face the fire. And I broke down thinking it could well be a factual report—what is this country we live in, where even such an absurdity is well within the realms of the possible in our own imagination and in what we see around us? And where humour is no humour at all but cause for deep, deep sadness?

Speaking of cows and tipping points, the gruesome violence in Una (Vaya 2016) has given birth finally to a resistance beyond measure. We have had the illustrious Bezwada Wilson in the news in the past week for receiving the Magsaysay Award for his lifetime's work to abolish manual scavenging and degrading labour performed by Dalits (*The Hindu* 2016). While Kashmiris brave bullets on the streets, Dalits in Gujarat have called the largest, and most notable labour strike in recent memory—no Dalit will lift dead carcasses any more. 'The *gau rakshaks* [cow protectors] beat us because they think the cow is their mother. Well, then, they should take care of her and pick up her carcass when she dies,' they say (Daniyal 2016). In other words, take the merit and the dirt, both. This is no small strike. It is, to borrow from Joan Mencher (1974), 'the caste system [turned] upside down'.

So the gau rakshaks and their *sarkari rakshaks* [state police] can take full responsibility and ensure safe passage for their deceased mother-cows, lending their shoulders and bidding them a ceremonial-ritual farewell in their journeys to the afterworld.

And Dalits will finally hold their heads up in pride and march towards lives with dignity. But Dalits shall also now take pride in the fact that contrary to the pre-ordained order of learning in a caste society, it is they who have educated the dominant castes (yet again, but this time in an unforgettable way) on the road to fulfil their moral-filial obligations and earn merit in this life and the hereafter. This should soon extend from carcasses of animals to the human dead (it has already spread to human waste)—cremation grounds, burial grounds, all places that depend on Dalits to handle impurity so that the upper castes can enjoy undiluted merit bolstered with unsullied purity. The scales have tilted and the upper castes shall bear the polluting burdens of their purity. If this is accomplished we are a huge step closer to the annihilation of caste.

An interview with BJP MP Vinay Sahasrabuddhe in the *Times of India* (2016) is telling: '*Gau raksha* has been a popular theme and is a guiding principle of our Constitution.' In an article in the *Indian Express*, minister T. C. Gehlot is quoted as saying that gau rakshak squads are social organisations, but the trouble in Una was that they rushed off on the basis of a rumour instead of stopping to 'find out its veracity and then go' (Nair 2016). So is it okay for squads to go after ascertaining the truth? And they take recourse to Article 48 of the Constitution of India that enjoins the state to organise agriculture and 'prohibit the slaughter of cows and calves and other milch and draught animals'. But that is not all that Sahasrabuddhe says. He also hastens to assert, 'Una is an isolated incident. There is no reason to draw sweeping conclusions and portray a frightening scenario.' We must note that this comes after the declaration of a strike by Dalits. So what is frightening? Not the gruesome murder and flogging of Dalits and Muslims. That is routine and everyday—it evokes neither comment nor fleeting attention. What is frightening, especially to the ruling party and its fringe armies on the prowl, I suggest, is the consequences of the strike. The Dalit mobilisation post Una is not an isolated incident. Nor will it just disappear. It is here to stay and indeed bears unimaginable consequences for the arrogance and impunity of caste domination. Article 17 of the Constitution of India—the abolition of untouchability—is a fundamental right, our guiding principle, and overrides completely the 'guidelines' of Article 48: 'Untouchability is abolished and its practice in any form is forbidden.'[1]

Between Kashmir and Una, we have before us a new turn in the practice of politics—the deep regret is, of course, that it has cost us too much. We have lost way too much on the road to azaadi already.

Note

1. India Const. art. 17.

References

'Gau Raksha a Guiding Principle of Constitution ... but No One Can Defend Violent Incidents like Una ... Dalits Integral to BJP'. 2016. Interview by Akhilesh Kumar Singh. *The Times of India*, 2 August.

'Magsaysay Award for Wilson, T. M. Krishna'. 2016. *The Hindu*, 27 July.

Daniyal, Shoaib. 2016. '"Your Mother, You Take Care of It": Meet the Dalits behind Gujarat's Stirring Cow Carcass Protests'. *Scroll.in*, 23 July. Available at https://scroll.in/article/812329/your-mother-you-take-care-of-it-meet-the-dalits-behind-gujarats-stirring-cow-carcass-protests (accessed 14 June 2021).

Fatima, Iffat, dir. 2012. *Khoon Diy Baarav*. Film screening, December Film Festival, Hyderabad, 4 December 2015. C. D. Deshmukh Auditorium, Council for Social Development (CSD).

Irfan, Shams. 2016. 'Scenes from Burhan Wani's Funeral'. *The Wire*, 24 July. Available at https://thewire.in/politics/the-funeral-burhan-wani (accessed 14 June 2021).

Mencher, Joan. 1974. 'The Caste System Upside Down or the Not-So-Mysterious East'. *Current Anthropology* 15, no. 4 (December): 469–93.

Nair, Shalini. 2016. 'Gau Rakshaks like Any Other Social Organisation: Social Justice Minister'. *The Indian Express*, 28 July.

Vaya, Surabhi. 2016. 'As Dalit Protests in Gujarat Continue, a Look at What's Behind Them'. *The Wire*, 27 July. Available at https://thewire.in/politics/dalit-agitation-gujarat-una (accessed 14 June 2021).

19

Babri Masjid Revisited*

We live in unimaginably difficult times. We must therefore confront difficult questions, and give voice to our misgivings, especially where it concerns questions of constitutionalism and justice. For in an important sense, an idea of justice and the hope that constitutional sensibilities will trump the politics of hate is all we have in our democracy toolkit today. Elusive, faltering, but possible, eminently so. It is in this frame of mind that I share some of my thoughts on the Babri Masjid case that was decided by the Supreme Court of India on 9 November (*The Hindu* 2019).

Context is always critical. Whether or not the court can take note in its deliberations on specific cases, as citizens, we must understand judicial decisions—whether unanimous or dissenting—as embedded within a larger context, and therefore as reinforcing the context or causing a constitutional disruption. And judicial dissent is an immeasurable treasure in these times.

We live in a time when the Union home minister issues an open call to arms to the foot soldiers of the ruling party against an elected state government that dares to implement the 2018 decision of the Supreme Court—the reference is, of course, to Sabarimala (Philip 2018). The Supreme Court is not supreme, they say through this, and with impunity. Even at the time of writing, the Sabarimala issue, again precipitated by the Sangh Parivar with the Central government as its flagbearer, is referred by the Supreme Court to a larger bench (Rajagopal 2020), the only saving being that it was not a unanimous decision. Dissent is the safety valve in a democracy, as a judge observed last year (Ananthakrishnan 2018).

---

* Originally published in *Scroll.in*, 15 November 2019.

The state of Jammu and Kashmir is dismantled, the abrogation of Article 370 proclaimed, and people of an entire state are placed under occupation; and the Supreme Court has not yet, after over three months of lockdown, intervened to restore people's constitutional rights in the region. While the matter of the abrogation is itself a serious one, post abrogation, why have fundamental rights been in a state of suspension, and why is there a deafening judicial silence on this? Again, the Supreme Court is not supreme, the government seems to say, with impunity. Judicial silence disables justice through what I have elsewhere called 'jurisprudential dissociation'—an interpretive strategy in India to circumvent providing critical protections to vulnerable communities against discrimination and loss of liberty, even while acknowledging in unequivocal terms, in the same case, that it was the duty of the court to protect the fundamental rights of every citizen (Kannabiran 2012).

We can scarcely forget that the ruling party at the Centre and in the state of Uttar Pradesh was at the forefront of the demolition of Babri Masjid in 1992 and had unequivocally declared that a Ram temple shall be built in its place even while the Supreme Court was hearing the case (*Business Standard* n.d.). From the Sabarimala experience, we know by now what that means. Quick on the heels of the Supreme Court verdict on Ayodhya, the Hindu Mahasabha is already pressing for the withdrawal of criminal cases against *kar sevaks* (persons who offer labour as service) involved in the demolition and the ensuing violence; and has demanded that they be given government pensions, and that lists of kar sevaks be installed in the temple that will be built at the site where Babri Masjid once stood in Ayodhya. For, they assert, 'The Supreme Court gave its judgement in favour Shri Ramlalla' (PTI 2019). And despite judicial assurances to the contrary, the VHP's claim in respect of 3,000 other mosques (Venkataraman 2019) is cause for deep concern and anxiety.

This then is a small part of the context in which a 1,045-page 'unanimous' decision is delivered by the Supreme Court on Babri Masjid, where the constitutional bench did not name the author of the judgement, and even more curiously, included an anonymous 116-page 'Addenda' at the end of the judgement, which is literally (through its placement in the judgement) the last word. It functions as a jurisprudential exception, reinforcing and reiterating the 'faith, belief and trust of the Hindus' that the 'disputed structure is the holy birthplace of Lord Ram',[1] after the judgement has weighed evidence and arrived at its decision on the basis of purportedly 'rational' principles. It therefore returns focus to the supremacy of Hindu theological considerations, and will determine the reading of the judgement as long as it remains unexpunged. It is tragic that this was a unanimous decision with no dissenting voices within the apex judiciary.

It has been argued that the Places of Worship (Special Provisions) Act, 1991, and the explicit provision in Section 3 therein that '[n]o person shall convert any place of worship of any religious denomination or any section thereof into a place of worship of a different section of the same religious denomination or of a different religious denomination or any section thereof',[2] will be a restraint to conduct under the present regimes. It is true, as the court observes, that the act imposes a 'non-derogable obligation towards enforcing our commitment to secularism under the Indian Constitution';[3] it is also true that the act itself guarantees the principle of non-retrogression. But adherence to the letter and spirit of these principles, statutes and indeed the Constitution presumes a political dispensation that subserves constitutional values. We also have no guarantee that courts will place the public good, due process, and the call of the Constitution above all else with a sense of urgency in the event of derogation, if recent courtly moves in the matter of personal liberty and right to life are any indication. As Faizan Mustafa and Aymen Mohammed (2019) have observed in their measured critique of the judgement, 'Though the apex court accepted that a wrong had been done … in the final order, it had to give the entire disputed site to the Hindu plaintiffs though the law of equity says that one who seeks equity must come with clean hands.'

Several senior commentators have dwelt at length on the minutiae of the judgement. While some have been circumspect (for example, Mustafa and Mohammed 2019) on the extent to which it has been crafted on a keen understanding of the rule of law and due process, others have been laudatory (for example, Baxi 2019b) over this unparalleled achievement of declaring the title in favour of the deity Ram Lalla and offering Muslims a compensatory allotment—which

Baxi (2019a) terms 'an exercise of power and duty to do complete justice'. Yet others have been vocal in their critique and accused of being 'incendiary' for being sharply critical. The polarisation of communal interests was evident in the case—in fact, the title suit itself is a result of this polarisation and a political consequence of the programschrift of the Sangh Parivar—the litigants on the Hindu deity's side all active functionaries of the various arms of the Parivar. To disregard this critical aspect of the claim is to refuse to see the elephant in the room.

The court repeatedly identifies the parties by the religion of the petitioners, not by the name(s) of individual petitioners, so despite assertions by senior scholars to the contrary, constitutional othering has been entrenched through this judgement, unfortunately so. The question of judicial empathy is at the centre of this case. What are the expressions of empathy and its effects? Is it weighted equally in relation to all parties to the dispute? And how is empathy (or the lack of it) in this instance interlocked with questions of equity (or the lack of it)?

Rather than looking at this question in the aftermath of the judgement in the frames of 'constitutional othering' (that is, examining whether and to what extent the Muslim is named and divested and the Hindu named and endowed), it is extremely important for our collective dignity to shift the terms of the discourse. This cannot be done by just deciding that this business is done and dusted and moving on.

The judicial loquacity of this decision stands in stark contrast to the judicial deflection in matters related to, say, Kashmir. Why? Babri Masjid is a title suit for a 1,500-square yard plot of land which masks two episodes of mass violence—in 1949, at the peak of Partition violence, and in 1992, when Hindutva politics rose to a violent, genocidal crescendo in the country (*Outlook* 2018). Kashmir is an entire state and its people. Both cases involve profound and targeted communal violence—genocidal in the first case, democidal in the second. Both cases concern a similar usurpation of possession, a similar 'occupation'—and the judicial loquacity and deflection have an identical effect. This is the reality that stares us in the face.

Contexts have personal consequences and spin-offs, and have the power to alter individual consciousness. It is therefore critical for us to reassemble our plural intellectual and moral reserves. Irrespective of my personal faith or conscience, which I have a guarantee under the Constitution to profess, Babri Masjid is an intrinsic part of my heritage, the desecration of which has caused deep injury to me; the desecration of the Golden Temple (see Singh 2021) was deeply injurious in a similar way; the desecration of religious symbols and structures in Goa (*The Times of India* 2015) causes harm and suffering not only to believers but to the Indian conscience.

All these demolitions/desecrations happened in independent India, under the watch of the Constitution, often at the behest of mainstream political parties and/or elected governments. That they are deeply injurious to our collective psyche and wellbeing is a consequence that bears infinite recall. To fall into the trap of disaggregating harms and gains by religious identity, and placing ourselves in that template is the worst possible harm we can do to ourselves. The responsibility to safeguard religious freedoms in all their plurality, and to ensure the principle of non-discrimination within our faiths is our collective responsibility under the Constitution, a citizen's responsibility—we can scarcely abdicate this right to interpretation by courts, or to conservative political formations that do not represent syncretic cultures and plural communities of believers, or even allow courts and governments to draw us into an adversarial classification.

Notes

1. *M. Siddiq*, CA Nos. 10866–10867 of 2010, decided on 9 November 2019 (SC), 930, 'Addenda'.
2. The Places of Worship (Special Provisions) Act, 1991, sec. 3.
3. *M. Siddiq*, CA Nos. 10866–10867 of 2010 (SC), para. 82.

References

'Christian Group Meets Parrikar over Church Attacks'. 2015. *The Times of India*, 9 February.

'Full Text of Ayodhya Verdict'. 2019. *The Hindu*, 9 November. Available at https://www.thehindu.com/news/resources/full-text-of-ayodhya-verdict/article29929786.ece (accessed 14 June 2021).

'Tracing the History of Babri Masjid: From 1528 to Today'. 2018. *Outlook*, 6 December.

'What is Ayodhya Case?'. n.d. *Business Standard*. Available at https://www.business-standard.com/about/what-is-ayodhya-case (accessed 14 June 2021).

Ananthakrishnan, G. 2018. 'Elgaar Parishad Probe: Dissent Safety Valve of Democracy, Pressure Cooker Will Burst If Not Allowed, Says SC'. *The Indian Express*, 31 August.

Baxi, Upendra. 2019a. 'Award of Five Acres for Masjid in Ayodhya is an Effort to Do Complete Justice'. *The Indian Express*, 12 November.

———. 2019b. 'Ayodhya Verdict Must be Seen Dispassionately from the Prism of Law, Constitutionalism'. *Outlook*, 25 November.

Kannabiran, Kalpana. 2012. *Tools of Justice: Non-discrimination and the Indian Constitution*. New Delhi: Routledge.

Mustafa, Faizan and Aymen Mohammed. 2019. 'Ayodhya Verdict: Several Positives for the Muslim Plaintiffs'. *The Hindu*, 12 November.

Philip, Shaju. 2018. 'Amit Shah Asks on Sabarimala: Why Issue Orders That Can't be Enforced?'. *The Indian Express*, 28 October.

PTI. 2019. 'Hindu Mahasabha Seeks Withdrawal of Cases against "Kar Sevaks" Involved in Babri Masjid Demolition'. *The Hindu*, 13 November.

Rajagopal, Krishnadas. 2020. 'Sabarimala Case: Supreme Court Upholds Referring Religious Questions to Larger Bench, Frames 7 Questions of Law'. *The Hindu*, 10 February. Available at https://www.thehindu.com/news/national/sabarimala-case-supreme-court-upholds-referring-religious-questions-to-larger-bench-frames-7-questions-of-law/article30780943.ece (accessed 17 September 2021).

Singh, Pritam. 2021. 'Wounds That Never Heal: Remembering Operation Bluestar'. *The Wire*, 6 June. Available at https://thewire.in/history/wounds-that-never-heal-remembering-operation-bluestar (accessed 19 July 2021).

Venkataraman, K. 2019. 'What Does the Places of Worship Act Protect?'. *The Hindu*, 17 November.

20

We Shall Not Be Silenced, nor Shall We Ever Forget*

We, in India, find ourselves trapped today in the slushy quicksand of a catastrophic moment, held down, immobilised and facing annihilation by the venomous tentacles of a Hindutva state veering on the edge of fascism—that knows no limits. Muslims are the target of assault—by the police and armed forces, the Parliament, the people in government (see, for instance, Shah 2018; Jayal 2019; Mamdani 2019). The largest section of the judiciary is unwilling to set out the non-negotiability of the Constitution before a state that is unbending in its derogation of the rule of law. The soft targets proliferate—students, dissenters, Hindus who offer refuge to Muslims while mobs are on a rampage—to encompass all the others who walk with and stand with Muslims, and all who stand against the forces of the predator state.

Because of its rootedness in the ideology of Hindu supremacy, it is Muslims who are the most under threat, the most under assault, and the most in danger of being targeted by a politics that seeks to annihilate them as a class. There is an important distinction we need to draw between individual targets and the collective target—the scale of violence, its consequences and its brutality are incomparable. For indeed, what we see now is the crest of Hindutva supremacist politics. Its method of rule is impunity. And it runs and powers the national government. But more importantly, the spread of crimes of hate—ranging from speech to lynching to collective violence to state violence in the name of religion—and the alarming rise of Hindu supremacist banded groups and their silent supporters make any resistance life-threatening, for minorities more than for anyone else.

---

* Originally published in *'Everyone Has Been Silenced': Police Excess against Anti-CAA Protesters in Uttar Pradesh, and Post-violence Reprisal*, 97–103, Citizens against Hate, March 2020.

And yet we know that although this is a battle soaked in the blood of Muslims and dissenters, although the human suffering that has been unleashed is unimaginable, although it will take long years to build the long road to freedom yet again, we will do what it takes to get there.

The reign of terror unleashed by the government of Uttar Pradesh on Muslims in the state in December 2019 is chilling—police excesses and post-violence reprisals on anti-CAA protesters took the form of incidents of arson, fatalities, injuries, medical treatment denied, the desecration of the dead through forced burials, and terror unleashed in the name of the Hindu state. This act of state terror, stoked by the chief minister of the state, puts it outside the domain of mere police excess (*Citizens for Justice and Peace* 2020). Let us stop for a moment and look at the list of those who died: Of the 23 persons who died, all Muslims, one was an eight-year-old child who died in the stampede, and 21 persons were between 20 and 45 years of age. Of the men who were killed, 17 of the 22 men were 30 years of age and below; 11 of them below 25 years. Barring the child, Sagheer, all the rest had bullet injuries in the head, face, chest, abdomen and shoulder. Clearly, the police were shooting to kill, as evident from bullet wounds in the upper body, and there was, to use the words of Human Rights Watch (2019), 'deadly use of force on protesters'. No FIRs were registered against police personnel for causing death by shooting. On the other hand, kin reported facing intimidation, with false cases being foisted on them to deter them from naming the police as responsible for the deaths (Citizens against Hate 2020).

This is a familiar sequence acted out in the case of fake encounters, and there are cases in courts in different states that have ruled with varying degrees of adherence to the rule of law, at least since the infamous Emergency of 1975. What one witnesses today in the cases before us, of Uttar Pradesh and even more recently the murders on the streets of Delhi, however, is the direct incitement to violence by top state functionaries and elected representatives (*The Hindu* 2020). The incitement has progressed from dog whistles to public calls to violence, and has evoked no response of sympathy or righteous anger over the killing of ordinary citizens, nor an invocation of the rule of law to ensure justice and redress. The police force has been aided by the foot soldiers of the Sangh Parivar, on the payroll of the state: 'police *mitra*' (friends of the police), they call them in Uttar Pradesh, the special police officers that the Supreme Court of India in *Nandini Sundar v. State of Chhattisgarh* (2011) called out in unequivocal terms. In a state torn apart by the police and army in the name of combatting the Maoist insurgency, the Supreme Court observed that there was a 'yawning gap between the promise of the principled exercise of power in a constitutional democracy and the reality of the situation in Chhattisgarh'.[1] In the case of Uttar Pradesh before us, we have special police officers, armed by the state, attack peaceful protesters and ordinary, mostly poor, citizens who were going about their daily routines, in a most diabolical fashion. It is not a coincidence that barring few exceptions, the assault has been on Muslims, and all the dead are Muslim. The note of caution sounded by the Supreme Court in *Nandini Sundar* on disciplining power, the rigour of constitutionalism, the accountability of power, and the non-negotiability of promoting constitutional values and vision are torn asunder by the right-wing Hindu majoritarian state.

What does this violence on unarmed protesters signal?

The Indian Parliament in December 2019 passed the Citizenship (Amendment) Act, 2019, that redefines the terms of Indian citizenship in far-reaching ways. Section 2 of the Citizenship Act, 1955, defines an 'illegal migrant' as a person who enters the country without valid legal documents, or enters with valid legal documents but overstays the stipulated period of valid stay[2]—these are the only two situations contemplated by the act at its inception. Subsequent amendments after the Assam Accord, setting deadlines for migrants in Assam to qualify for citizenship and again introducing the overseas citizen of India (OCI) category, stayed within the original non-denominational template.

However, in December 2019, this section was amended by the Hindu majoritarian Parliament under the BJP to read as follows:

> Provided that any person belonging to Hindu, Sikh, Buddhist, Jain, Parsi or Christian community from Afghanistan, Bangladesh or Pakistan,

> who entered into India on or before the 31st day of December, 2014 and who has been exempted by the Central Government by or under clause (c) of sub-section (2) of section 3 of the Passport (Entry into India) Act, 1920 or from the application of the provisions of the Foreigners Act, 1946 or any rule or order made thereunder, shall not be treated as illegal migrant for the purposes of this Act.[3]

The amendment to the Third Schedule of the Citizenship Act, 1955, that stipulates a minimum time period for application for citizenship, consists of the insertion of a proviso that states:

> Provided that for the person belonging to Hindu, Sikh, Buddhist, Jain, Parsi or Christian community in Afghanistan, Bangladesh or Pakistan, the aggregate period of residence or service of Government in India as required under this clause shall be read as "*not less than five years*" in place of "*not less than eleven years*".[4] (Emphasis mine.)

Through this diabolical move, the binary of citizen and non-citizen officially morphed into a binary of refugee (*sharanarthi*) and illegal infiltrator (*avaidh ghuspethiya*, variously translated as illegal migrant, intruder, infiltrator), solely predicated on religion, as home minister Amit Shah himself clarifies:

> I wish to make this clear. There should be no confusion among the people and no confusion in the media ... *There is a distinction between ghuspethiye and sharanarthi*. Any person who leaves one country and goes to another in order to protect his dignity (*maanyata*), his identity (*astitva*), his self-respect (*svamaan*), his religion (*dharm*), is a sharanarthi. A person who enters a country illegally for livelihood or other reasons is a ghuspethiya. There is no confusion at all in the mind of the Bharatiya Janata Party on this matter. (Shah 2018; translation and emphasis mine.)

It must be remembered that the Citizenship Act, 1955, makes no such distinction. While several definitions were contemplated, Alladi Krishnaswami Ayyar drew the attention of the house to the two principles on which the law of citizenship may be based: *lex sanguinis* (blood and race, regardless of place of birth) and *lex soli* (grounds of birth) (Rao 1968: 151). The suggestion of the advisory committee was to adopt the *lex soli* principle, which was commended by Sardar Vallabhbhai Patel, who

> referred to the struggle against racial discrimination in South Africa ... and to the demand of Indians settled there on the ground of their birth. He cautioned the members not to take a narrow view of the subject and introduce racial phraseology in the Constitution.... "It is important," he said, "to remember that the provision about citizenship will be scrutinized all over the world." (Ibid.: 152)

Given the backdrop of Partition, it was generally felt that the definition of citizenship must be broad enough to accommodate persons with 'some kind of territorial connection with the Union, whether by birth, or descent, or domicile' and who 'had not made his permanent abode in any foreign country' (ibid.: 158, 162). Even at this difficult time, the ethnic/racial basis and distinctions between religious faith of the seeker of citizenship did not enter the account at all.

From that foundational position, we have now been forced into hearing the term 'ghuspethiya' (which is a call to violence) used for all those who are deemed to be outside the borders of the Hindu nation. This is no longer India that is being spoken about. The spectre of the potential or actual ousting from citizenship into statelessness along with its concomitant denial of livelihoods, dignity and fundamental freedoms and vulnerability to violence, especially, but not only, state violence is particularly chilling. The presumption on which state action under Hindutva proceeds is on the sealing of borders on the basis of religious homogeneity and the ousting/annihilation of the Other.

In the case of Uttar Pradesh, we must remember that we are not speaking of the immigrant at all. We are speaking about the gruesome violence visited by the state on 'birthright citizens', to borrow Martha Jones's (2018) brilliant term, who are Muslims by faith—citizens who have an intergenerational claim to this country, without any need whatsoever of having to prove it. Mahmood Mamdani's (2019) insistence on the fact that 'the CAA is a demonic rather than a benign legislation' bears infinite repetition, especially after the mass violence against Muslims that unfolded in Uttar Pradesh, Jamia and Delhi between December 2019 and February 2020, where 'the official discourse thus seeks to present Muslims as a politically and morally legitimate target for persecution by a government-mobilised majority'. Since expulsion and detention is not possible in the case of

Muslim birthright citizens, this incarceration of the Constitution of India by the Hindutva state drives their annihilation through the politics of maiming (Puar 2017), with very tenuous possibilities, if at all, for justice.

Importantly therefore, even as we document the specific derogations of procedures established by law and due process in the Uttar Pradesh cases, as also we must with Delhi 2020 that followed close on its heels, and even as we push for concrete legal action and prosecution of officers of the state, we cannot stop with that. It is not the police, the armed militias, and banded mobs that are acting on their own. There is a chain of command. There is concrete evidence of a chain of command.

Our responsibility as the conscience-keepers of this country is two-fold: First, and most immediately, we must push for the pinning of command responsibility on the elected leaders of the BJP, who, through brazen acts of omission, commission and incitement, have sanctioned the use of deadly force with intent to maim, and cause death and dispossession of large sections of ordinary, peaceful citizens. This is not a riot. It is not police excess or police action alone. It is a *crime against humanity*. Second, we must do everything in our power to rebuild a different idea of India, an idea rooted in the spirit of the Constitution. We find ourselves in the dark pit of a fractured society, where we simply count religious inscriptions on bodies, and express solidarity, doubts, equivocations, allegations and accusations on that basis. As we remember the dead and their extreme suffering, as also those who suffer with them and are condemned to futures of suffering under this regime, we need to stop for a moment and ask ourselves, who are the 'we'? For the 'we' and the 'them' cannot under the Constitution be defined in terms of religious belonging. This must be a country that ousts precarity, not one that ousts/annihilates people condemned to live on the edge of precarity. It must be defined in terms of a shared humanity, and deep mutual respect and dignity. There is really no other way forward.

Notes

1. *Nandini Sundar*, AIR 2011 SC 2839, para. 1.
2. The Citizenship Act, 1955, sec. 2(b).

3. The Citizenship (Amendment) Act, 2019, sec. 2.
4. Ibid., sec. 6.

References

'India: Deadly Force Used Against Protesters'. 2019. *Human Rights Watch*, 23 December. Available at https://www.hrw.org/news/2019/12/23/india-deadly-force-used-against-protesters (accessed 3 March 2020).

'Is UP at War with It's Own People?'. 2020. *Citizens for Justice and Peace*, 25 February. Available at https://cjp.org.in/is-up-at-war-with-its-own-people/ (accessed 14 June 2021).

'Kapil Mishra's Controversial Speech Played in Delhi High Court'. 2020. *The Hindu*, 26 February.

Citizens against Hate. 2020. *"Everyone Has Been Silenced": Police Excess against Anti-CAA Protesters in Uttar Pradesh, and Post-Violence Reprisal.* Available at https://citizensagainsthate.org/wp-content/uploads/2020/03/Citizens-Against-Hate-Everyone-Has-Been-Silenced.pdf (accessed 14 June 2021).

Jayal, Niraja Gopal. 2019. 'Faith-Based Citizenship: The Dangerous Path India is Choosing'. *The India Forum*, 13 November. Available at https://www.theindiaforum.in/article/faith-criterion-citizenship (accessed 14 June 2021).

Jones, Martha S. 2018. *Birthright Citizens: A History of Race and Rights in Antebellum America*. Cambridge: Cambridge University Press.

Mamdani, Mahmood. 2019. 'Uncovering the CAA's Larger Stratagem'. *The Hindu*, 31 December.

Puar, Jasbir K. 2017. *The Right to Maim: Debility, Capacity, Disability*. Durham and London: Duke University Press.

Rao, B. Shiva. 1968. *The Framing of India's Constitution: A Study*. New Delhi: Indian Institute of Public Administration.

Shah, Amit. 2018. 'Press Conference on National Register of Citizens', 31 July. Available at https://youtu.be/z5p85_d_IWE (accessed 30 November 2019).

V

Queer Rights

21

From 'Perversion' to Right to Life with Dignity*

Constitutional morality is not a natural sentiment. It has to be cultivated. We must realise that our people have yet to learn it.

—B. R. Ambedkar (1948; quoted in *Naz Foundation*, para. 79)[1]

The recent judgement of the Delhi High Court, on 2 July 2009, in *Naz Foundation*, is a milestone in the jurisprudence on diversity and pluralism in India. Importantly, it also inaugurates intersectional jurisprudence that examines questions of constitutionalism in relational terms that underscore inclusiveness. By this token then, it is not merely a judgement that bears significance for the rights of lesbian, gay, bisexual and transgender peoples. It makes the articulation of LGBT rights a torchbearer for a more general understanding of discrimination, oppression, social exclusion and the denial of liberty, on the one hand, and the meaning of freedom and dignity, on the other.

The Yogyakarta Principles on the Application of Human Rights Law in Relation to Sexual Orientation and Gender Identity, launched on 26 March 2007, were drafted by experts from 25 countries, representative of all regions of the world. These principles delineate in painstaking detail the obligation of states to respect, protect and fulfil the human rights of all persons regardless of their sexual orientation or gender identity. On 18 December 2008, the United Nations General Assembly was presented with a statement endorsed by 66 states from around the world reaffirming in substance the Yogyakarta Principles. It is these international efforts, along with the movement for LGBT

* Originally published in *The Hindu*, 6 July 2009.

rights within India, that provided the context and arguments for the decriminalisation of homosexuality.

Drawing on Ambedkar, the court rejected the argument that homosexuality was contrary to public and popular morality in India, upholding constitutional morality instead, the diffusion of which was contingent on Ambedkar's ideas of notional change, as evident in the lines quoted above. To quote from the judgement: 'The Constitution of India recognises, protects and celebrates diversity. To stigmatise or to criminalise homosexuals only on account of their sexual orientation would be against the constitutional morality.'[2] Linked to this is the observation of the court on the question of the horizontal application of rights, with specific reference to Article 15(2), a barely remembered but critical part of Article 15: No citizen shall obstruct another from access to public places on grounds of caste, sex and other specified grounds.[3] This purposive and intersectional reading of Article 15(2), hitherto restricted largely to practices of untouchability vis-à-vis Dalits, opens out an important strategy in constitutional interpretation.

Applying the UN human rights framework to an understanding of sexual orientation and gender identity, the judgement sets out three categories: (a) non-discrimination; (b) protection of private rights; and (c) the ensuring of special general human rights protection to all, regardless of sexual orientation or gender identity.[4]

Perhaps the most important issue the judgement addresses is the meaning of 'sex' in Article 15(1) of the Constitution of India: 'The state shall not discriminate against any citizen on grounds only of religion, race, caste, sex, place of birth or any of them.'[5] Does the term 'sex' in this context refer to attribute or performance? Is sex to be applied in a restricted fashion to gender or can the multiple resonances of its common usage be taken into account, so that sex is both gender (attribute) and sexual orientation (performance)? This is particularly significant because, as the judgement demonstrates through an extensive review of case law and principles from different parts of the world, gender and sexual orientation are an intrinsic and inalienable part of every human being; they are constituents of a person's identity. In the words of Justice Albert Sachs of South Africa, the Constitution 'acknowledges that people live in their bodies, their communities, their cultures, their places and their times' (in *National Coalition for Gay and Lesbian Equality v. Minister of Justice*).[6] It is this composite identity of every person that is affirmed through a nuanced reading of 'sex' in Article 15(1): 'We hold that sexual orientation is a ground analogous to sex and that discrimination on the basis of sexual orientation is not permitted by Article 15.'[7]

Justice P. N. Bhagwati's delineation of the right to dignity in *Francis Coralie Mullin*, that 'the right to life includes the right to live with human dignity and all that goes along with it, namely, the bare necessaries of life ... expressing oneself in diverse forms, freely moving about and mixing and commingling with fellow human beings',[8] provides the starting point for the discussion on the importance of self-respect, self-worth and privacy to human social life, recognised nationally and internationally. And privacy is particularly important in the area of sexual relationships, where the thumb rule is simply that '[i]f, in expressing our sexuality, we act consensually and without harming one another, invasion of that precinct will be a breach of our privacy' (*Paris Adult Theatre I v. Slaton*, USA).[9]

The criminalisation of homosexuality, the judgement says, by condemning in perpetuity an entire class of people, forcing them to 'live their lives in the shadow of harassment, exploitation, humiliation, cruel and degrading treatment at the hands of the law enforcement machinery' denies them 'moral full citizenship'.[10] Because Section 377 is aimed at criminalising private conduct of consenting adults, the court held that it comes within the meaning of discrimination, which 'severely affects the rights and interests of homosexuals and deeply impairs their dignity'.[11] It is 'unfair and unreasonable and, therefore, in breach of Article 14 of the Constitution of India'.[12]

The right to public health is another aspect of human rights that is seriously undermined through the criminalisation of same-sex behaviour. There are two parts to this right, both of which lead back to the fundamental right to life under Article 21. The first is the right to be healthy. In this context, the concerns of the National AIDS Control Organisation are pertinent. Fear of law enforcement agencies obstructs disclosure, which in turn impedes HIV/AIDS prevention programmes and increases the risk of infection in high-risk groups.

The second part of the right to health is more expansive and includes the right to control one's health and body, the right to sexual and reproductive freedom, the right against forced medical treatment and the right to a system of health that offers equality of opportunity in attaining the highest standard of health. While several documented testimonies of LGBT persons speak of the treatment of their sexual orientation as a psychiatric/mental disorder (see, for instance, Pradhan, Ayyar and Bagadia [1982] that reports psychiatric treatment to 'cure' homosexuality), the judgement importantly affirms the findings worldwide that sexual orientation is an expression of human sexuality—whether homosexual, heterosexual or bisexual. 'Compelling state interest', instead of focusing on public morality, the judgement says, 'demands that public health measures are strengthened by de-criminalisation of such activity, so that they can be identified and better focused upon'.[13]

Asserting that there is no presumption of constitutionality where a colonial legislation is concerned, the judgement holds that Section 377 fails the test of 'strict scrutiny' which would require proportionality between the means used and the aim pursued. And when it is a question of 'matters of "high constitutional importance"' like the rights of LGBT persons, the courts are obliged to discharge their sovereign jurisdiction, in this case, reading Section 377 down to apply only to child sexual abuse.

It is pertinent to point out here that the Andhra Pradesh (Telangana Area) Eunuchs Act specifically targets eunuchs and hijras in far more direct ways than Section 377 does. We hope that the momentum of the movement for LGBT rights will turn its full force on obsolete legislations like this as well, so that transgender communities in areas where such laws are in force begin to enjoy the fullest freedoms and life with dignity.

Notes

1. Constitutional Assembly Debates, vol. 7, 1948, quoted in *Naz Foundation,* (2009) 160 DLT 277, para. 79.
2. Granville Austin, *The Indian Constitution: Cornerstone of a Nation,* quoted in *Naz Foundation,* (2009) 160 DLT 277, para. 80.

3. *Naz Foundation*, (2009) 160 DLT 277, para. 104.
4. Ibid., para. 42.
5. India Const. art 15, cl. 1.
6. National Coalition for Gay and Lesbian Equality & Anr v. Minister of Justice & Ors, 1999 (1) SA 6 (CC), para. 117 (S. Afr.), quoted in *Naz Foundation*, (2009) 160 DLT 277, para. 47.
7. *Naz Foundation*, (2009) 160 DLT 277, para. 104
8. Francis Coralie Mullin v. The Administrator, Union Territory of Delhi, (1981) 2 SCR 516, quoted in *Naz Foundation*, (2009) 160 DLT 277, para. 27.
9. Paris Adult Theatre I v. Slaton, 413 US 49, 63 (1973) (USA), quoted in *Naz Foundation*, (2009) 160 DLT 277, para. 41.
10. *Naz Foundation*, (2009) 160 DLT 277, para. 52.
11. Ibid., para. 93.
12. Ibid., para. 98.
13. Ibid., para. 86.

References

Pradhan, P. V., K. S. Ayyar, and V. N. Bagadia. 1982. 'Homosexuality: Treatment by Behaviour Modification'. *Indian Journal of Psychiatry* 24 (1): 80–83.

Yogyakarta Principles: Principles on the Application of International Human Rights Law in Relation to Sexual Orientation and Gender Identity. 2007.

It's Time to Scrap the Eunuchs Act*

The Andhra Pradesh (Telangana Area) Eunuchs Act, 1329 F (Act No. XVI of 1329 F), an enactment 'for the registration and control of eunuchs'[1] must be struck down immediately as it violates every principle of natural justice. This move acquires particular urgency in light of the recent judgement of the nine-judge bench of the Supreme Court of India on 24 August 2017 in *Puttaswamy*, upholding the fundamental right to privacy.

Description and History

The Eunuchs Act, enacted in the nizam's dominions has been in force since 1919 explicitly to control 'eunuchs', that is, people who were both males 'in female dress' *and* those who had undergone 'emasculation'.[2]

Section 1A of this act states, 'The word "eunuch" shall, for the purpose of this Act include *all persons of the male sex who admit to be impotent or who clearly appear impotent* on medical inspection' (emphasis mine).[3] Section 2 of the act provides for the maintenance of a register by the government that will contain 'the names and place of residence of *all eunuchs residing in the City of Hyderabad or at any other place* ... and who are reasonably suspected of kidnapping or emasculating boys, or of committing unnatural offences or abetting the commission of the said offences' (emphasis mine).[4] It is reasonable to presume that the definition of unnatural offences that applied was that of Section 377 IPC. Section 4 of the act titled 'Registered Eunuch Found in Female Clothes', reads as follows:

> Every registered eunuch *found in female dress* or *ornamented* in a *street or a public place* or in *any other place* with the intention of being seen from

* Originally published in *The Hindu*, 28 September 2017.

> a street or public place or *who dances* or *plays music* or takes part in *any public entertainment* in a street or a public place may be arrested without warrant and shall be punished with imprisonment for a term which may extend to two years or with fine or both. (Emphasis mine.)[5]

Section 5 provides for the punishment of a eunuch with imprisonment if it is found that he 'has with him or in his house or under his control' a boy who is less than 16 years old.[6] There is no exception made for the possibility that this boy may be a biological or adoptive child of said person. Section 6 provides that:

> [t]he District Magistrate may direct that any such boy be delivered to his parents or guardian, if they can be discovered, *and they are not eunuchs; if they cannot be discovered or they are eunuchs, the Magistrate may make such arrangement as he thinks necessary* for the maintenance, education and training of such boy. (Emphasis mine.)[7]

Sections 5 and 6 explicitly bar eunuchs from the right to relationship, family, child custody and parental autonomy. Finally, Section 7 penalises consensual and non-consensual emasculation and abetment to emasculation with imprisonment for a term, which may extend to seven years.[8]

Constitutional Framework

The Constitution of India, in Article 15, lists 'sex' as a ground of non-discrimination. However, the constitutional category of 'sex' has not been defined as restricted to male and female alone. It may therefore be constructively interpreted to offer full constitutional protection to all persons and citizens of all genders as the case may be. It may be recalled that the 2009 *Naz Foundation* judgement of the Delhi High Court, deliberating on the constitutionality of Section 377 IPC, applied the United Nations (UN) human rights framework to an understanding of sexual orientation and gender identity, setting out three categories of protection: (a) non-discrimination; (b) protection of private rights; and (c) ensuring special general human rights protection to all regardless of sexual orientation or gender identity.[9] The constitutional reasoning of this decision is immediately relevant to the Eunuchs Act.

Although the *Naz Foundation* judgement was struck down by the Supreme Court in *Koushal*, the privacy bench opens the *Koushal* judgement for detailed re-examination. With reference to the reasoning in *Koushal* that 'a miniscule fraction of the country's population constitutes lesbians, gays, bisexuals or transgenders and in last more than 150 years less than 200 persons have been prosecuted',[10] the privacy bench, speaking through Justice Chandrachud, observed that this cannot be regarded as a valid constitutional basis for disregarding a claim based on privacy under Article 21 of the Constitution and 'is not a sustainable basis to deny the right to privacy'. Importantly, he observes, 'The purpose of elevating certain rights to the stature of guaranteed fundamental rights is to insulate their exercise from the disdain of majorities, whether legislative or popular.'[11]

With regard to the second part of the reasoning in *Koushal* that Section 377 is a largely unenforced provision, the privacy bench observes:

> [S]exual orientation is an essential component of identity. Equal protection demands protection of the identity of every individual without discrimination.... The de minimis hypothesis is misplaced because the invasion of a fundamental right is not rendered tolerable when a few, as opposed to a large number of persons, are subjected to hostile treatment.... The chilling effect on the exercise of the right poses a grave danger to the unhindered fulfilment of one's sexual orientation, as an element of privacy and dignity.[12]

With specific reference to the transgender community, the judges refer specifically to *National Legal Services Authority (NALSA)*,[13] observing, 'NALSA indicates the rationale for grounding of a right to privacy in the protection of gender identity within Article 15. The intersection of Article 15 with Article 21 locates a constitutional right to privacy as an expression of individual autonomy, dignity and identity.'[14]

Justice J. Chelameswar, in his judgement, affirms that the 'right to privacy consists of three facets i.e. repose, sanctuary and intimate decision'[15] and includes 'the freedom of certain groups ... to determine their appearance and apparel'.[16] Justice R. F. Nariman observes that of the three aspects that are at the core of the fundamental right to privacy, 'The privacy of choice, which protects an individual's autonomy over fundamental personal choices',[17] is one.

The Eunuchs Act Must Be Struck Down

There is widespread evidence that the existence of the Eunuchs Act has resulted in a pervasive and continuing practice of criminalisation, illegal detention, torture in custody and extreme coercion, which includes a perennial threat of arrest. It is also a fact that transgender persons are routinely subjected to sexual assault and sexual violence but fear registering FIRs because of the stigmatisation and vulnerability consequent on this draconian legislation, which shapes the attitudes and conduct of law enforcement officers. The Eunuchs Act has a chilling effect on the assertion of their right to privacy, dignity and freedom by transgender persons.

The Supreme Court of India has opened up a definitive space in constitutional interpretation that makes the declaration of unconstitutionality of this law by the High Court of Andhra Pradesh and Telangana urgent. We need to take necessary steps to safeguard the fundamental rights of transgender persons in the state of Telangana. In Justice S. K. Kaul's words: 'The old order changeth yielding place to new.'[18]

Notes

1. The Andhra Pradesh (Telangana Area) Eunuchs Act, 1329 F (Act XVI of 1329 F).
2. Ibid., sec. 4, 7.
3. Ibid., sec. 1A.
4. Ibid., sec. 2.
5. Ibid., sec. 4.
6. Ibid., sec. 5.
7. Ibid., sec. 6.
8. Ibid., sec. 5, 6, 7.
9. *Naz Foundation*, (2009) 160 DLT 277, para. 42.
10. *Suresh Kumar Koushal*, (2014) 1 SCC 1, para. 43.
11. *K. S. Puttaswamy*, (2017) 10 SCC 1, para. 126 (per Chandrachud, J.).

12. Ibid., paras. 127–28 (per Chandrachud, J.).
13. National Legal Services Authority (NALSA) v. Union of India & Ors, (2014) 5 SCC 438.
14. *K. S. Puttaswamy*, (2017) 10 SCC 1, para. 84 (per Chandrachud, J.).
15. Ibid., para. 36 (per Chelameswar, J.).
16. Ibid., para. 38 (per Chelameswar, J.).
17. Ibid., para. 81 (per Nariman, J.).
18. Ibid., para. 83 (per Kaul, J.).

VI

Women's Rights

23

Rethinking the Law on Sexual Assault*

The Criminal Law (Amendment) Bill, 2010, being proposed to bring about changes in the criminal laws with respect to protections against sexual assault, has been a subject of discussion and popular misinterpretation in the recent past. While the move by the government to re-examine the law on sexual assault is long overdue and the opening up of this subject a welcome step, it is necessary to underscore the concerns raised by rights advocates across the country.

Human rights groups combating sexual assault, women's groups and groups working on child rights, have come together to reflect on the extent to which this bill addresses concerns on the ground, to identify major gaps, and propose an alternative that might eliminate the gaps and ambiguities to the maximum extent possible. This critical engagement with legislative drafting is especially important in view of the fact that it has taken 30 years to put the issue on the floor of Parliament a second time, and 10 years after the Law Commission of India made fairly concrete recommendations in its 172nd report, 2000.

In the 30 years since the Mathura and Rameeza cases launched the first major campaign for the reform of rape laws in the early 1980s (see Kannabiran 2008), experiences of sexual assault that have been reported have changed dramatically and in troubling ways. If impunity

* Originally published in *The Hindu*, 3 June 2010.

Human rights groups, women's groups and groups working on child rights came together in Mumbai to reflect on the extent to which the proposed Criminal Law (Amendment) Bill, 2010, addressed concerns around sexual assault on the ground. This chapter sets out those concerns for a public discussion, and predates the campaign for a stringent and comprehensive law on sexual assault that followed the fatal assault on Jyoti Singh in Delhi in December 2012.

for armed forces personnel accused of assault sets up a major hurdle to bringing justice to survivors (Manipur [Mehrotra 2010] and Kashmir [Asia Watch and Physicians for Human Rights 1993]), sexual assault during episodes of collective violence (Gujarat [Concerned Citizens Tribunal 2002] and Kandhamal [College of Social Work 2010]) or as part of caste atrocity (Rajasthan [Vij 2007] and Khairlanji [Teltumbde 2008]), custodial sexual assault on women with intellectual disabilities (Chandigarh),[1] on transgenders (Karnataka [PUCL-K 2003]), on children—girls and boys (Nautiyal and Mal 2010), and sexual assault on and/or humiliation of men in custody (Amnesty International India 1992) and situations of collective/targeted violence have posed serious problems for rights advocates in the absence of provisions in the law to prosecute perpetrators.

These concerns that emerged in the course of combating rights violations have given birth to the effort to think through—collectively—parameters for a law on sexual assault that will be comprehensive to the maximum extent possible. The large and diverse group engaged in this exercise is, of course, aware that this is no easy task, and is aware also of the fact that both the process of drafting provisions and canvassing the draft will be educative for those engaged in it and for those who must receive it—in government, Parliament, institutions of justice and communities. There is also a hope that the deliberations around the new legislation will not be trivialised and made a mockery of in Parliament and the media, like the women's reservation bill debates.

The entire effort to reach this point is over a decade old, and begins with the petition to the Supreme Court, on whose directions the Law Commission put out the 2000 report. The key themes in the effort that has been under way in the current drafting phase for three months are: (a) to set out a statement of objects and reasons that will provide an interpretive guide to prosecutors and the legal fraternity; (b) to formulate tentatively the definition of sexual assault and aggravated assault that effects a clear shift from the limitations of the existing formulations in the IPC on outraging modesty and rape; and (c) to think through the gradation of punishments, and procedural and evidentiary standards that reflect the gravity of the experience of sexual assault and provide just redress without putting the complainant on trial.

Broadly, the ongoing effort to formulate a new law aims at situating sexual assault within the constitutional right to life, dignity and bodily integrity along with evolving international jurisprudence that sees rape as a form of torture when committed in custody or in situations of occupation/conflict. It also attempts to set out the social contexts within which such violence occurs, underlining the fact that it is always an exercise of power that is used to target women, children and persons who are socially vulnerable. Coercive circumstances—economic, political and social dominance, positions of authority and situations of custody ranging from state institutions to the family—enhance the power of the perpetrator. An important part of the discussions focuses on the fact that sexual violence occurs along a continuum that ranges from sexual harassment to aggravated assault. For this reason, there has been some discussion (as yet unresolved) on whether the title of the chapter should read 'sexual violence' or 'sexual assault'.

Drawing on the experience of advocates and groups pushing relentlessly for the prosecution of those involved in mass crimes in Gujarat in 2002, the debates recognise the fact that sexual violence is not limited to penetration but includes sexual humiliation, which has aggravated consequences for victims and their families (International Initiative for Justice 2003). The category of sexual humiliation as an assault on bodily integrity and dignity is one that needs to be articulated carefully and in a manner that does not fall into the trap of 'honour discourse' that has defeated women's rights to equality for decades.

Victims have faced an uphill task of proving that they did not consent to sexual intercourse and that they were, in fact, assaulted. The first battle was to remove a consideration of past sexual history as a factor that establishes the credibility of the complainant. The second major battle was to determine what constituted 'resistance' to rape. In providing support and redress to victims, rights advocates have found that coercive circumstances often disable any possibility of offering resistance, even where consent is withheld. What is the substantive meaning of consent? While it simply means 'unequivocal voluntary agreement', can it be weighted when the victim is in coercive circumstances? How is the issue of consent dealt with in the case of a woman with intellectual or psychosocial disabilities that inhibit or obstruct her ability to consent or withhold consent to sexual intercourse? Drafting protections against child sexual assault poses the biggest challenge to this effort.

In dealing with aggravated sexual assault, the pinning of command responsibility on a public servant would lead to more effective exercise of due diligence in preventing the crime. Given the range of cases before us, it is important to study the failures of omission and commission, in order to delineate clearly what command responsibility consists of in cases of aggravated sexual assault.

Broadly, rather than viewing 'sexual assault' as a mechanical substitute for 'rape' under Section 375 of the IPC, the effort of rights groups has been to think through the feasibility of formulating a chapter on sexual violence/atrocity that will define a range of such violence in a manner in which the focus shifts from the penetrative logic of definitions hitherto used to the assaultive nature of sexual violence. Effecting this shift has implications for procedural law and the law of evidence as well—carefully calibrating the shift in burden of proof and eliminating the two-finger test, for instance—both of which are being examined alongside the penal code provisions, with a clear understanding that procedural and evidentiary guarantees upholding universal human rights standards will not be derogated in the course of redefining the law on sexual assault.

Note

1. *Suchita Srivastava* (2009) 14 SCR 989.

References

Amnesty International India. 1992. *Torture, Rape and Deaths in Custody*. Index No. ASA 20/006/1992. Available at https://www.amnesty.org/download/Documents/192000/asa200061992en.pdf (accessed 25 July 2021).

Asia Watch and Physicians for Human Rights. 1993. *The Human Rights Crisis in Kashmir*. New York: Human Rights Watch.

College of Social Work. 2010. *Study of the Conditions of Women Affected by Communal Violence in Kandhamal District, Orissa*. Mumbai: Nirmala Niketan.

Concerned Citizens Tribunal. 2002. *Crime against Humanity: An Inquiry into the Carnage in Gujarat,* 3 vols. Mumbai: Citizens for Justice and Peace.

International Initiative for Justice. 2003. *Threatened Existence: A Feminist Analysis of the Genocide in Gujarat.* Available at https://www.onlinevolunteers.org/gujarat/reports/iijg/2003/ (accessed 17 June 2021).

Kannabiran, Kalpana. 2008. 'Sexual Assault and the Law'. In *Challenging the Rule(s) of Law: Colonialism, Criminology and Human Rights in India,* ed. Kalpana Kannabiran and Ranbir Singh, 78–118. New Delhi: Sage.

Law Commission of India. 2000. *172nd Report on Review of Rape Laws.* DO No. 6(3)(36)/2000_LC(LS).

Mehrotra, Deepti Priya. 2010. *Restoring Order in Manipur: The Drama of Contemporary Women's Protests.* New Delhi: Zubaan.

Nautiyal, Pallavi and Arun Mal. 2010. 'Towards Protection of Children against Sexual Abuse: No Child's Play'. *NUJS Law Review* 3, no. 1 (January–March): 77–92.

PUCL-K (Peoples' Union for Civil Liberties, Karnataka). 2003. *Human Rights Violations against the Transgender Community.* Available at http://www.pucl.org/reports/human-rights-violations-against-transgender-community (accessed 17 June 2021).

Teltumbde, Anand. 2008. *Khairlanji: A Strange and Bitter Crop.* New Delhi: Navayana.

Vij, Shivam. 2007. 'Bhanwari Devi: A Mighty Heart'. *Tehelka,* 13 October.

24

Girl Punk, Interrupted*

It is not for a good work that we stone you but for blasphemy.

—John 10:33; quoted by Maria Alyokhina, of the band Pussy Riot, at the band members' trial, Moscow (2012)

We live in an age of so-called 'trials' and in an age of so-called 'freedom'. We resist in differing degrees, but the eerie timelessness of the questions that remain unresolved, and their monotonous repetition in different languages through different methods in different countries, is disconcerting.

The imprisonment, 'trial' and conviction of the three members of Pussy Riot, a Russian feminist punk band that spoke resistance politics against the power of Vladimir Putin, has been widely covered in the media (*BBC News* 2012; Smith-Spark 2012). The closing statements of these three young women recall the stormy battles that women have fought—feminist battles, even before they had a name—and continue to fight across the world. The statements challenge, above all, the reductionist construction of feminism rife in popular representation across media. This is an attempt to contextualise the echoes of those statements in India.

This chapter attempts to draw connections between the trial of the band, Pussy Riot, in Russia in 2012, and feminist mobilising in India, arguing that the Russian experience is a reminder that women and feminist politics have been an essential part of the struggle against oppressive systems in India too, from Chipko to Posco.

There has historically been a connection between orthodox religion, its patriarchs, particular forms of politics and state formation, as Yekaterina Samutsevich (2012) reminds us. Likewise, there has

---

* Originally published in *The Hindu*, 24 August 2012.

historically been a connection between political orthodoxy and its patriarchs (which mirrors the forms and modes of power of orthodox religion and the structures of authoritarian states, both). While part of the resistance to this—in the form of *bhakti* (literally 'devotion', here, refers to spiritual traditions of reform that challenged Hindu orthodoxy), Sufism or religious sects—has located itself outside orthodox religion and in opposition to it, another significant part has appropriated the cultural symbols of orthodoxy to represent resistance, which has then been used to challenge the repressive state—Bangalore Nagarathnamma's publication of the subversive literary work of the medieval poet-performer Muddupalani is an early example from the Indian subcontinent (see *The Telugu Archive* 2019). But after this, there has been a string of writing and performance and storytelling by women that has attempted to do precisely this: rupture the seamlessness of a dominant narrative that invests both the power of repression and the power of resistance in patriarchal formations—led most times by men, sometimes by women.

Speaking Out against Repression

The late 1970s and early 1980s, for instance, saw a number of women writers and political activists interrogating the orthodox patriarchal foundations of resistance movements—which rest not on gender alone, but importantly on gender in combination with caste, tribe, religion and class. We continue to have women speaking against the repressive state—Irom Sharmila in Manipur (Mehrotra 2010); or about being trapped by it in insidious ways that need no reason or logic since it wields raw, unaccountable power—Pinki Pramanik in West Bengal;[1] or being tortured for torture's sake (that happens too, here)—Soni Sori of Chhattisgarh (Amnesty International India 2012), to name only three. We have, of course, witnessed the frightening confluence of religious orthodoxy, fundamentalist politics and state formation in Gujarat and continue to experience the aftershocks of that mass hate crime. In rising to the defence of those who have lost life, liberty and dignity, we are critiquing the ideologies of governance that seem to say, 'The show can go on … This is democracy.' Managing to say this effectively, to make people sit up and listen, is 'punk' in our time—put differently, punk is the mask of feminism today.

Whether with the 'pink *chaddi*' campaign (Susan 2009) or with the slutwalks in India (PTI 2011), we have witnessed animated debates about what the locations of the 'real' Indian feminism are. In a country where it is still possible for the head of a state's police force to go on record saying that women provoke assault because of the way they dress, clearly the locations of feminism are many, and each is important and contributes in one way or another to the larger picture. The most poignant response to this statement was by 17-year-old Varsha, who ended her open letter to the officer by warning him that he would soon wake up one morning to a slutwalk in front of his house (Gandikota 2011). The officer has perhaps woken up in a panic a few times after reading that—certainly a slutwalk outside your window is something to panic about—at least till your force arrives to lock the sluts away!

Maria Alyokhina (2012) echoes my fears when she says that what worries her most of all is that the opinion of the younger generation is not taken into consideration: 'Modern education institutions teach people from their childhood to live automatically, do not introduce key issues appropriate to the age, foster cruelty and intolerance to dissent. From the childhood a person forsakes his liberties.' This 'impedes the realization of inner freedom'.

Have we forgotten somewhere that teaching children the value of freedom is critical to the feminist project? Every religion, in its own way, foregrounds 'humility' as a positive value. Most of our cultures have distorted and translated this into abject obedience that must be branded onto children leaving them scarred for life (ontological humility and existential humility, to use Alyokhina's words). Needless to say, social vulnerability exacerbates the denial of basic freedom and rights. I am reminded here of early radical feminist philosopher Shulamith Firestone's (1970) observation that patriarchy cannot tolerate liberation for women or for children.

A Lesson

If there is one lesson feminism teaches, it is never to lose sense of ourselves as citizens. It is not about this one struggle. It is about every single struggle against oppressive systems, or those that are unaccountable, and therefore dangerous to human security and wellbeing. In trying to convince people that they must campaign for the protection of the only juniper reserve in the Krasnodar region of Russia, against the whims of Dmitry Medvedev's wife, Pussy Riot reminds us of our numerous difficult battles to retain control over our forests, our rivers and our environment—from Chipko to the campaign against Bt crops, from Narmada to the anti-Posco struggles, to Kudankulam and Jaitapur. That feminist politics is a necessary part of the challenge to the patriarchal, corporate–state complex is one aspect of the struggle we can never lose sight of—that there are women at the forefront of these struggles who determine their course is an important point. In the very act of doing this, through their presence as conscientious resisters, they pose the biggest challenge to the established order. Or as Nadezhda Tolokonnikova says, '[O]ur performances are a kind of civic activity amidst the repression of a corporate political system that directs its power against basic human rights and civil and political liberties' (quoted in Taylor 2012). The scope of feminist performance and its habitations, as we see, is infinite.

The way in which the corporate political system erodes basic rights is nowhere more evident than in Chhattisgarh. In following the trials and tribulations of Soni Sori, and in trying so hard to come to terms with our complete inability to bring some measure of justice to her (Amnesty International India 2012), in understanding the predicament of the several like her who remain unnamed and unseen, do Alyokhina's (2012) words—'prison is Russia in miniature'—echo our despair? But we know that what is on trial is the repressive state, not these women.

And finally to return to the epigraph: the charge of blasphemy is addressed to Christ. In a total inversion, it is now used by the Russian Orthodox Church, and certified and attached to the criminal file of the three women who have been convicted. Whether women speak with a forked tongue or with guarded tongue, the moment they speak resistance, blasphemy is the charge ('hooliganism' and 'religious hatred' added on)—the orthodoxy will stand the scriptures (religious and ideological) on their head to hold the charge. That is the power of feminism, and Pussy Riot has reminded us of it today.

Note

1. Pinki Pramanik v. State of West Bengal & Anr, 2014 SCC OnLine Cal. 18832.

References

'A Tale of Two Devadasis'. 2019. *The Telugu Archive,* 22 May. Available at https://medium.com/@theteluguarchive/a-tale-of-two-devadasis-603ee867a172 (accessed 19 July 2021).

'India: Release Soni Sori on International Women's Day'. 2012. *Amnesty International India,* 7 March. Available at https://www.amnesty.org/en/press-releases/2012/03/india-release-soni-sori-international-women-s-day/ (accessed 25 July 2021).

'Pussy Riot Members Jailed for Two Years for Hooliganism'. 2012. *BBC News,* 17 August. Available at https://www.bbc.com/news/world-europe-19297373 (accessed 19 July 2021).

Alyokhina, Maria. 2012. 'Pussy Riot: Maria Alyokhina's Closing Statement'. *Critical Legal Thinking (CLT),* 20 August. Available at https://criticallegalthinking.com/2012/08/20/pussy-riot-maria-alyokhinas-closing-statement/ (accessed 25 July 2021).

Firestone, Shulamith. 1970. *The Dialectic of Sex: The Case for Feminist Revolution.* New York: William Morrow.

Gandikota, Varsha. 2011. 'Mr DGP, You're Asking for a Slutwalk'. *Deccan Chronicle,* 30 December.

Mehrotra, Deepti Priya. 2010. *Restoring Order in Manipur: The Drama of Contemporary Women's Protests.* New Delhi: Zubaan.

PTI. 2011. 'Delhi Stages "Slutwalk" against Sexual Violence'. *The Hindu,* 31 July.

Samutsevich, Yekaterina. 2012. 'Closing Statement at the Pussy Riot Trial'. *Lemon Hound,* 16 August. Available at https://lemonhound.com/2012/08/16/yekaterina-samutsevich-closing-statement-at-the-pussy-riot-trial/ (accessed 19 July 2021).

Smith-Spark, Laura. 2012. 'Russian Court Imprisons Pussy Riot Band Members on Hooliganism Charges'. *CNN,* 18 August. Available at https://edition.cnn.com/2012/08/17/world/europe/russia-pussy-riot-trial/index.html (accessed 19 July 2021).

Susan, Nisha. 2009. 'Why We Said Pants to India's Bigots'. *The Guardian,* 15 February.

Taylor, Adam. 2012. 'Here's What Russian Punk Band Pussy Riot Said at the Conclusion of Their Controversial Blasphemy Trial'. *Insider*, 10 August. Available at https://www.businessinsider.com/pussy-riot-trial-nadezhda-tolokonnikovas-closing-statement-2012-8?IR=T (accessed 17 June 2021).

25

A Moment of Triumph for Women*

Starting with Tarabai Shinde's spirited defence of the honour of her sister countrywomen in 1882 (O'Hanlon 1994), women's movements in India have been marked by persistent and protracted struggles. But despite this rich and varied history, we have, in recent weeks, found ourselves shocked at the decimation of decades of struggle.

A Transformation

At a time when despair and anger at the futility of hundreds of thousands of women's lifetimes spent in imagining a world that is safe drive us yet again to the streets; at a time when our daughters get assaulted in the most brutal ways and our sons learn that unimaginable brutality is the only way of becoming men; at a time when we wonder if all that intellectual and political work of crafting frameworks to understand women's subjugation and loss of liberty through sexual terrorism has remained imprisoned within the covers of books in 'women's studies' libraries; at a time like this, what does it mean to suddenly find that all is not lost and to discover on a winter afternoon that our words and work have cascaded out of our small radical spaces and transformed constitutional common sense?

The *Report of the Committee on Amendments to Criminal Law*, headed by Justice J. S. Verma (2013), is our moment of triumph—the triumph of women's movements in this country. As with all triumphs, there are always some unrealised possibilities, but these do not detract from the fact of the victory.

* Originally published in *The Hindu*, 25 January 2013.

Rather than confining itself to criminal law relating to rape and sexual assault, the committee has comprehensively set out the constitutional framework within which sexual assault must be located. Perhaps more importantly, it also draws out the political framework within which non-discrimination based on sex must be articulated, and focuses on due diligence by the state in order to achieve this as part of its constitutional obligation, with the Preamble interpreted as inherently speaking to justice for women in every clause.

If capabilities are crucial in order that people realise their full potential, this will be an unattainable goal for women till such time as the state is held accountable for demonstrating a commitment to this goal. Performance audits of all institutions of governance and law and order are seen as an urgent need in this direction.

The focus of the entire exercise is on protecting the right to dignity, autonomy and freedom of victims of sexual assault and rape—with comprehensive reforms suggested in electoral laws, policing, criminal laws and the Armed Forces (Special Powers) Act, 1958, and the provision of safe spaces for women and children.

Arguing that 'cultural prejudices must yield to constitutional principles of equality, empathy and respect' (Justice Verma Committee 2013: 55), the committee, in a reiteration of the *Naz Foundation* judgement, brings sexual orientation firmly within the meaning of 'sex' in Article 15, and underscores the right to liberty, dignity and fundamental rights of all persons irrespective of sex or sexual orientation—and the right of all persons, not just women, against sexual assault.

Reviewing leading cases and echoing the critique of Indian women's groups and feminist legal scholars—whether in the case of Mathura or even the use of the shame–honour paradigm that has trapped victim-survivors in rape trials and in *khap panchayat*s (council of clan elders)—the committee observes: '[W]omen have been looped into a vicious cycle of shame and honour as a consequence of which they have been attended with an inherent disability to report crimes of sexual offences against them.' (ibid.: 84)

In terms of the definition of rape, the committee recommends retaining a redefined offence of 'rape' within a larger section on 'sexual assault' in order to retain the focus on women's right to integrity, agency and bodily integrity. Rape is redefined as including all forms of non-consensual penetration of sexual nature (ibid.: 111). The offence of sexual assault would include all forms of non-consensual, non-penetrative touching of sexual nature. Tracing the history of the marital rape exception in the common law of coverture in England and Wales in the 1700s, the committee unequivocally recommends the removal of the marital rape exception as vital to the recognition of women's right to autonomy and physical integrity irrespective of marriage or other intimate relationship. Marriage, by this argument, cannot be a valid defence—it is not relevant to the matter of consent and it cannot be a mitigating factor in sentencing in cases of rape. On the other hand, the committee recommended that the age of consent in consensual sex be kept at 16, and other legislation be suitably amended in this regard.

Voices from Conflict Zones

Rights advocates in Kashmir, the states of the Northeast, Chhattisgarh, Gujarat and other areas that have witnessed protracted conflict and communal violence have for decades been demanding that sexual violence by the armed forces, police and paramilitary, as well as collective assault by private actors be brought within the meaning of aggravated sexual assault. This has been taken on board, with the committee recommending that such forms of sexual assault deserve to be treated as aggravated sexual assault in law (Justice Verma Committee 2013: 220). Specifically, the committee recommends an amendment in Section 6 of the AFSPA, 1958, removing the requirement of prior sanction where the person has been accused of sexual assault.

Clearly, a sensitive and committed police force is indispensable to the interests of justice. But how should this come about? There have been commissions that have recommended reforms, cases that have been fought and won, but impunity reigns supreme. If all the other recommendations of the committee are carried through, will the government give even a nominal commitment that the chapter on police reforms will be read, leave alone acted on?

The Delhi Case

The gangrape and death of a young student in Delhi in December 2012 has raised discussion on the question of sentencing and punishment yet again. The first set of questions has to do with the nature and quantum of punishment. Treading this issue with care, the committee enhances the minimum sentence from seven years to ten years, with imprisonment for life as the maximum. On the death penalty, the committee has adopted the abolitionist position, in keeping with international standards of human rights, and rejected castration as an option. The second question has to do with the reduction of age in respect of juveniles. Despite the involvement of a juvenile in this incident, women's groups and child rights groups were united in their view that the age must not be lowered, that the solution did not lie in locking them up young. Given the low rates of recidivism, the committee does not recommend the lowering of the age, recommending instead, comprehensive institutional reform in children's institutions.

The report contains comprehensive recommendations on amendments in existing criminal law, which cannot be detailed here except in spirit. The significance of the report lies not so much in its immediate translation into law or its transformation of governance (although these are the most desirable and urgent), but in its pedagogic potential—as providing a new basis for the teaching and learning of the Constitution and criminal law and the centrality of gender to legal pedagogy.

References

Justice Verma Committee. 2013. *Report of the Committee on Amendments to Criminal Law.*

O'Hanlon, Rosalind. 1994. *A Comparison between Women and Men: Tarabai Shinde and the Critique of Gender Relations in Colonial India.* New Delhi: Oxford University Press.

26

Lessons from Badaun and Beyond*

The murder of two children in Badaun, Uttar Pradesh (*The Indian Express* 2014a), forces us to re-examine our understanding of aggravated assault, murder, sexual assault, atrocity, annihilation *by* caste and structural violence that is constitutive of the rogue state—not *an* exceptional state, but *the* rogue state as the norm in a caste ridden society. This is not an isolated story. These children were not victims of exceptional violence and brutality. Rather, routine heightened violence and torture of the worst kind are constitutive of caste society, with the condonation (indeed, the tacit acceptance of the necessity) of such violence written into inaction and equivocation at every level.

We believed, as advocates of women's rights, that laws would show the road to social change, to 'notional change', to use Ambedkar's (2004 [1936]: section 20, paragraph 8) words. So we fought, long and hard, to secure reforms in rape laws in the early 1980s; to wrest more effective protections against domestic violence through criminal law and, in 2005, a civil legislation; to secure protections for children against child sexual abuse; to curb the practice of sex-selective abortions; to secure property rights for women; to fight relentlessly in courts for better recognition of women's dispossession in the family through maintenance claims; to claim a space of dignity at workplaces. These struggles grew in new directions to recognise the entitlements of Adivasi women to forest rights, Dalit women to land rights and the rights of women with disabilities to reproductive choice, freedom and bodily integrity. At a broad level, one witnesses a cascading of women's rights in law and a sharpening of their rights claims.

A closer and more careful look, however, points to the stubborn persistence of aggravated targeted violence against women belonging

---

* Originally published as 'Annihilation by Caste: Lessons from Budaun and Beyond', in *Economic and Political Weekly* 49, no. 25 (21 June 2014).

to vulnerable social groups, forcing us to ask: Have we really achieved anything through all these years—decades, in fact—of struggle?

My raging grief is about the loss, the deaths of these children, both girls (but there are accounts of a boy killed here as well, not so long ago, after being brutalised); it is about the unspeakable torture they were subjected to, of which sexual assault was a part; it is about our collective inability, as people committed to the annihilation of caste, to make any difference in a context where caste atrocity is, at best, a spectacle for consumption and speculation, where images of children who have been brutally assaulted and murdered are traded by the media in unthinkable ways and their experience negated by the rogue state ... Where does one begin to roll this back?

Although the writing on the Badaun violence has opened out several discussions (see Parashar 2014)—from eliminating open defecation to increasing helplines to castigating the government of Uttar Pradesh—I think this is an issue that goes far beyond the sexual politics of the Samajwadi Party, or the tasks before the toilet ambassadors of the Ministry of Rural Development. Can we forget that Mathura was sexually assaulted in the toilet of a police station? While unarguably women need access to secure basic facilities, this issue is quite separate from their vulnerability to sexual assault (see Kannabiran 2008; AFP 2014; MacAskill and Mehrotra 2014). Days have rolled into years and years into decades with us speaking out about the sexual politics of each of our political parties and their treatment of sexual assault. The only difference perhaps is that the Samajwadi Party has perfected the art and woven it densely into statecraft.

Early reports of the Badaun murders suggested the victims were Dalit children. Later reports identified their caste as a backward caste (*The Indian Express* 2014b). The questions seemed to circulate around whether these murders were situated within the *legal* definition of 'atrocity' in the Scheduled Castes and the Scheduled Tribes (Prevention of Atrocities) Act, 1989—and of course they were not, because the children who had been killed did not belong to a Scheduled Caste. So although the Prevention of Atrocities Act is the single legislation that attempts to address targeted assault based on caste, the technicality of classification put these murders and aggravated sexual assaults in the category of a 'lesser' crime. But was it a lesser crime?

Related to this is the question of whether the sexual assault and murder of women and children should be understood in terms that are common and unmindful of class or social category. Is it material to our understanding that these children belonged to a lower caste than the perpetrators? Is it accidental that the perpetrators belonged to the local dominant caste, and shared social location with the police and indeed the party in government? Is it coincidental that a policeman from the dominant caste was one of the perpetrators?

Should we, in the light of the facts of this case, re-examine what 'broken people' means in a context where caste dominance renders entire groups powerless and vulnerable to grievous hurt and murder (which includes sexual assault in several instances) even though they may not belong to a Scheduled Caste?

Discussions around the Criminal Law (Amendment) Act, 2013, both in the context of the Justice Verma Committee and some years before, in 2010, raised the specific question of sexual assault as part of targeted violence against women belonging to Scheduled Castes, Scheduled Tribes and minorities. Khairlanji (Teltumbde 2008), Vakapalli (Human Rights Forum 2013), Gujarat (IIJ 2003), Kandhamal (HRLN 2008) and Chhattisgarh (Amnesty International India 2012) were troubling reminders that in India, all women faced the threat of sexual violence, but a large number of women faced aggravated sexual violence as part of the everyday, with no recourse to redress or even recognition of a wrong, and harm being done because they were Dalit, minority or Adivasi. The caste system guaranteed impunity to those in dominance in the constitutional era. Yet, this problem, although powerfully articulated, remained unaddressed in the law. Dalit groups and anti-caste intellectuals raised the question of the inequality of protest. Why did the country not come to a standstill after the Khairlanji massacre, which, in sheer terms of numbers assaulted and killed, was far graver? The Delhi victim had demonstrated resistance that earned her the sobriquet 'Braveheart'. The Bhotmange family in Khairlanji too had paid dearly for demonstrating their resistance. Both belonged to working class families. On both sides, there was pain and suffering and loss. The Delhi victim's suffering led to the immediate constitution of a committee, legislation in her name, and trial and convictions at the speed of light. Despite the Bhotmange family's suffering, aggravated sexual assault as part of targeted caste violence was not included in the new expanded definition of sexual assault, and justice continues to elude the sole survivor (Telang 2013).

For the Bhotmange family, the struggle that led to their annihilation was a struggle against caste domination in the belly of the beast, so to speak, by challenging its supremacy through education and small attempts at building family assets in their native village. This critical difference must guide our understanding of the socio-political basis of sexual violence, assault and murder. While all murders result in loss of life and human suffering, targeted murder against members belonging to a social group that is vulnerable is more serious because it reflects a systemic pattern that systematically reinforces power and subjugates entire communities through violence.

Finally, in 2014, the Scheduled Castes and the Scheduled Tribes (Prevention of Atrocities) Amendment Ordinance, promulgated as a result of relentless campaigning by Dalit groups, broadened the definition of caste atrocity: questions of dignity, of self-respect and bodily integrity, of freedom from exploitation and sexual subjugation, and freedom from sexual assault were opened out in the framework of a law that symbolised the demand of Dalits and Adivasis to make the right to non-discrimination non-negotiable and non-derogable. In an important sense, the ordinance is a Dalit manifesto. So there have been significant shifts and developments in the law, particularly where it concerns sexual assault. The debates on sexual assault have been loud and clear and widespread. One would assume from this that there is a 'climate of deterrence'—because women do not want to keep quiet about these matters any more.

Paradoxically, our assumptions are without basis. With the rapid-fire action after December 2012, the new laws in place and vibrant resistance movements pulling out all stops to force a new common sense on caste, both caste dominance and the subjugation of women (and caste dominance through the subjugation of women), are getting stronger and more violent, if at all. Impunity remains the order of the day. When young girls go missing in the dead of night, and families rush to complain fearing the worst and hoping to prevent it, policemen sit back voyeuristically, making a spectacle of grief and fear. That is impunity at its worst. And with all our struggles and our 'victories', we have not changed that.

There is a routinisation of administrative action following these episodes of gruesome violence. Suspensions, official proclamations of sympathies, official fact-finding missions by statutory bodies, arrests, all of these roll into action the moment it is clear that families and communities will insist on justice. The sound bites are steady in their frequency and their monotony, and we know that once those children are laid to rest, these actions will roll back sooner rather than later. The family and community will be diminished by their suffering, crippled by pain and the memory of harm and loss, while the agencies of the callous and criminal state will sit back, waiting for its next voyeuristic experience. For those of us who struggle against violence, the fear of where 'they' will strike next persists.

'The life of the law,' said Justice Oliver Wendell Holmes (1923 [1881]: 1), 'has not been logic: it has been experience.' Who will take a count of the experience of Dalit women and girls—in terms of lives lost and a collective future facing annihilation through the violence of normal times?

We know from Ambedkar and from bearing witness to countless incidents of caste violence that '[c]astes form a graded system of sovereignties, high and low' (Ambedkar 2004 [1936]: section 21, paragraph18), and power is asserted through violence along the ladder of graded inequalities. Because 'caste is impregnable' (ibid.: section 22, paragraph 25), the sexual appropriation of women, through endogamous marriage, bondage and female servitude, and habitual assault on women of dependent castes form part of the common sense of the caste system. This also is the way in which resistance is policed, endlessly, in an eerily repetitive, timeless fashion—'[T]he worst evil of this code of ordinances is that the laws it contains must be the same yesterday, today, and forever' (ibid.: section 23, paragraph 5). Age has never been a bar for sexual assault. And impunity is guaranteed to perpetrators of targeted assault—through police complicity/calculated inaction (as the case may be), through prosecutorial negligence, through judicial misdemeanour and through the disabling of justice claims in constitutional courts with easy recourse to legal technicalities. There are startling parallels between Khairlanji and Badaun.

The true import of the words of anti-caste philosophers hits us more and more rudely with each passing day. With the annihilation of caste not happening, what we are witnessing is annihilation *by* caste. In a country ruled by caste in the constitutional era, annihilation *by* caste is a self-perpetuating patriarchal project that reinvents itself constantly, stalking the powerless and those that resist, blocking their flight from caste, generation after generation. The creation of an atmosphere of terror *and* sexual terrorism is the means through which an entire people are kept subjugated—this is not the place to recount the horrific methods of terror deployed by the dominant castes.

Notwithstanding the technical inapplicability of the Prevention of Atrocities Act to the Badaun murders, what is telling is the extreme vulnerability of Dalit-Bahujan communities—in the state of Uttar Pradesh. Far from being an indication of the ineffectiveness of Dalit-Bahujan mobilisation in Uttar Pradesh, it is rather a sign of the encrusted power of the dominant castes and an indication of how Sisyphean the struggle is. It is neither inappropriate nor inaccurate to characterise this as an attack on Dalit children—in the context of caste atrocity, the term Dalit encompasses the Dalit-Bahujan experience of caste discrimination and structural violence.

And that is really at the heart of the contradictions that Badaun throws up—there is a commonality of experience in disentitlement and vulnerability across Dalit-Bahujan groups that quotidian separations in administration and law negate. But those are the limits of the law. There are also shifting gradations of status, class and power within this large category, these contestations absorbing the ideology and methods of caste in inter-caste relations. Is it methodologically possible to offer protection and legal redress to victims across the ladder of graded inequalities and graded exclusions except through blanket criminal law provisions? And yet, viewing assaults such as these in terms of the Indian Penal Code alone reduces the gravity of the offence by removing the targeted nature of the assault from consideration and defining it outside the purview of caste atrocity.

And finally we come to the rogue state. How many times have we seen this? Karamchedu, Chunduru, Khairlanji, Badaun . . . Mathura,

Rameeza, Bhanwari ... Different states at different times, different courts of different jurisdictions, and the story is the same. Despite the constitutional ban on untouchability and protections against discrimination based on caste, the patriarchal caste order constitutes the state. Democracy lies trapped in the clutches of the two-headed state—the hibernating constitutional order, and the live and throbbing rogue state that actively participates in the project of annihilating *by* caste across the lines of party and ideology—where caste is the unifying ideology and the fundamental logic of governance.

The road that we leave behind is soaked in the blood of victims and built through generations of servitude, and the road that lies ahead is blocked by caste. This takes me to the heart of Ambedkar's (2004 [1936]: section 20, paragraph 8) assertion that the only road to freedom, life and indeed humanity is the annihilation of caste, for all, because violence and the habit of impunity dehumanises the dominant—not only the perpetrators and their cohorts but also the nonchalant bystanders and the distant, studiously indifferent viewers—and annihilates entire classes of vulnerable peoples in full public view with impunity.

References

'Badaun Gangrape and Murder: How the Incident Unfolded'. 2014a. *The Indian Express*, 2 June.

'Victims Not Dalits: UP Tells MHA'. 2014b. *The Indian Express*, 3 June.

'India: Release Soni Sori on International Women's Day'. 2012. *Amnesty International India*, 7 March. Available at https://www.amnesty.org/en/press-releases/2012/03/india-release-soni-sori-international-women-s-day/ (accessed 25 July 2021).

AFP (Agence France-Presse). 2014. 'Badaun Girls' Tragic Story Points to Risks Women Face in Rural India'. *Hindustan Times*, 1 June.

Ambedkar, B. R. 2004 [1936]. *The Annihilation of Caste*. Columbia Center for New Media Teaching and Learning. Available at http://ccnmtl.columbia.edu/projects/mmt/ambedkar/web/ (accessed 16 June 2014).

Holmes, Oliver Wendell. 1923 [1881]. *The Common Law*. Boston: Little, Brown.

HRLN (Human Rights Law Network). 2008. *Genocide in Kandhamal: Ethnic Cleansing of Christians by Hindutva Rightwing Forces in Orissa*. Available at https://idsn.org/uploads/media/Orissa_report_-_Human_Rights_Law_Network.pdf (accessed 25 July 2021).

Human Rights Forum. 2013. *The Terrible Cost of an Inhuman Counter-Insurgency*. Hyderabad: Human Rights Forum.

IIJ (International Initiative for Justice). 2003. *Threatened Existence: A Feminist Analysis of the Genocide in Gujarat*. Available at https://www.onlinevolunteers.org/gujarat/reports/iijg/2003/ (accessed 17 June 2021).

Kannabiran, Kalpana. 2008. 'Sexual Assault and the Law'. In *Challenging the Rule(s) of Law: Colonialism, Criminology and Human Rights in India*, ed. Kalpana Kannabiran and Ranbir Singh, 78–118. New Delhi: Sage.

MacAskill, Andrew and Kartikay Mehrotra. 2014. 'Badaun Rape: Police Mocked Father of Girl Raped and Killed'. *Mint*, 2 June.

Parashar, Swati. 2014. 'Not Merely Toilets: Reframing the Badaun Rape Debate'. *The Hindu Centre for Politics and Public Policy*, 13 June. Available at https://www.thehinducentre.com/the-arena/article6110846.ece (accessed 20 June 2021).

Telang, Priyadarshi. 2013. '"Nirbhaya", New Delhi and Priyanka, Khairlanji'. *Round Table India*, 16 September. Available at https://roundtableindia.co.in/index.php?option=com_content&view=article&id=6899:nirbhaya-new-delhi-and-priyanka-khairlanji&catid=119&Itemid=132 (accessed 19 July 2021).

Teltumbde, Anand. 2008. *Khairlanji: A Strange and Bitter Crop*. New Delhi: Navayana.

27

Article 17 is at the Heart of the Matter*

Article 17 of the Constitution of India is an unprecedented constitutional protection without a parallel: '*Abolition of Untouchability*. Untouchability is abolished and its practice in any form is forbidden. The enforcement of any disability arising out of Untouchability shall be an offence punishable in accordance with law.'[1]

What is 'untouchability'? At its base, untouchability is based on social humiliation, pollution ideologies, and the belief that ascriptive, immutable characteristics are defiling. The people most deeply and inter-generationally affected by the routine, aggravated violence and exclusion that constitute the practice of untouchability are people from the Scheduled Castes or Dalits. However, because untouchability provides the logic for and structures relations in the caste system, untouchability practices spread out along the scale of graded inequality between castes, and notably between men and women

---

* Originally published as 'Denying Women Entry to the Sabarimala Temple Amounts to Untouchability', in *The Wire*, 19 July 2018.

The Lord Ayyappa temple in Sabarimala, Kerala, prohibits women who are of menstruating age (that is, 10 to 50 years) entry into the temple—a prohibition enforced under Rule 3(b) of the Kerala Hindu Places of Public Worship (Authorisation of Entry) Rules, 1965: 'Women who are not by custom and usage allowed to enter a place of public worship shall not be entitled to enter or offer worship in any place of public worship.' The Indian Young Lawyers' Association filed a petition in the Supreme Court challenging this rule in 2006. After a hiatus, finally, in October 2017, a three-judge bench of the Supreme Court referred the matter to a Constitution Bench, which commenced hearings on the case on 17 July 2018. This chapter focuses on one key aspect of the proscription that merits serious constitutional consideration.

in the caste order. The legal/constitutional understanding, indeed the definition of untouchability, could only be arrived at through a painstaking process of description, legal ethnography and consequent legislative drafting. The Scheduled Castes and the Scheduled Tribes (Prevention of Atrocities) Act, 1989, and the amendments therein, enacted in 2015, are one of two direct illustrations of this constitutional unravelling of Article 17. The definition of atrocity has 29 clauses, each delineating a specific form of atrocity, of which three refer specifically to forms of gendered humiliation and violence against women—sexual assault, sexual humiliation and forced temple dedication. The second legislative illustration is the earlier one—the Protection of Civil Rights Act, 1955.

It has long been acknowledged that the caste system is powered by specific forms of subjugation of women—within castes, and between castes—which impose insurmountable disabilities and entrench the public humiliation of women. Ambedkar (2002 [1917]) opens out this gendered basis of the caste system in his classic 1917 essay, 'Castes in India'—where he speaks importantly of the systemic, routine and reinforced humiliation of women (of all castes) as the fulcrum on which the perpetuation and reinforcement of the caste system itself rests, citing specifically the examples of *sati* (immolation of a widow on the funeral pyre of her husband), enforced widowhood and pre-pubertal marriage of girls.

This then must inform our understanding of the reach of Article 17. It applies certainly and irrevocably to untouchability practices in relation to Dalits and Adivasis. But importantly, it also speaks to a whole apparatus of humiliation, violence, exclusion and subjugation that draws on caste-based ideologies of purity and pollution, which apply in very specific ways to women across caste.

About a decade ago and again more recently, the Tirumala Tirupati Devasthanam decided to bar women barbers from employment on the grounds that their menstrual cycles are polluting, citing the Hindu scriptures which hold that women are in an unclean state during menstruation and hence must not touch devotees (Gopinath 2005; *The Indian Express* 2006). Since it is impossible to tell when which women are menstruating, the best solution was to bar women from employment as barbers altogether. This is about proscribing touch, and physical and visual contact based on the ideology of the caste-untouchability complex, and the enforcement of economic disabilities.

Women under the Constitution have a right to equality before the law and the right against discrimination based on sex. To use the ideology of purity and pollution is a violation of the constitutional right against untouchability, Article 17. It is important to understand the intersectional deployment of pollution practices in Hindu society in order to grasp the full import of Article 17.

The guardians of Lord Ayyappa in Sabarimala took this a step further and barred women's entry altogether. In the petition against this rule being heard by the Constitution bench of the Supreme Court (Rajagopal 2016), the first question framed by the three-judge bench for consideration of the Constitution bench is '[w]hether the exclusionary practice which is based upon a biological factor exclusive to the female gender amounts to "discrimination" and thereby violates the very core of Articles 14, 15 and 17 ... ?'[2]

While this is well taken as the first question to be addressed, the most relevant constitutional provision among the three cited above is Article 17. Women are not merely banned from temple entry because they are women. It is not merely the 'biological factor exclusive to the female gender'. Women are banned because orthodox Hindu texts expound on the multitudinous ways in which women pollute upper caste environments during their menstrual cycles and after childbirth, and must be placed outside human social, physical and visual contact during these periods. The exclusion is an actual proscription of touch and sight. And since it is impossible to regulate menstrual cycles of women devotees, they are banned from temple entry altogether owing to the actual or potential threat of pollution.

This is not, therefore, merely a question of equality before law or discrimination based on gender or biology. It is the gender-specific enforcement of untouchability on Hindu women across caste with recourse to the scriptural prescriptions on the maintenance of caste order. The laws of Manu notoriously say, 'When he has touched a Candala, a menstruating woman, an outcaste, a woman who has just given birth, a corpse ... he purifies himself by bathing.' And again,

'A Candala, a domestic pig, a cock, a dog, a menstruating woman and a eunuch must not look on Brahmans while they are eating' (quoted in Dumont 1970: 52). This is the cornerstone of the practice of untouchability that is quoted today to justify keeping women out of Sabarimala because of their 'polluting' presence.

But as a people, we inherited the legacy of human dignity above all else when we gained independence. And the absolute, non-negotiable rejection of untouchability is the bedrock of that legacy. We have been fighting the practice of untouchability (which is far from gone) using the Constitution. Today, the scriptures that propagated untouchability are being quoted above the Constitution. If menstruation is a defilement, we are back to speaking about ascriptive categories that militate against notions of human dignity guaranteed in the Preamble and reaffirmed by the privacy bench. It is important to recognise that untouchability practices implicate women across the ladder of graded inequality in very specific ways, which is why this cannot be construed as just a form of gender-based discrimination. Its power lies in its entrenchment in caste.

With this in view, let us take a more careful look at the question of justification of scriptural and religious traditions of caste-based proscriptions. The Protection of Civil Rights Act, 1955, is 'an Act to prescribe punishment for the (*Preaching and Practice of "Untouchability"*) for the enforcement of any disability arising there from and for matters connected therewith' (emphasis mine).[3] Section 2(a) of the act defines 'civil rights' as 'any right accruing to a person by reason of the abolition of "untouchability" by article 17 of the Constitution';[4] Section 3 speaks specifically to the offence of obstructing persons on grounds of untouchability from entering public places of religious worship.[5] The most important provision for our present purposes is Explanation II of Section 7, which states that:

> a person shall be deemed to incite or encourage the practice of "untouchability"—(i) if he, directly or indirectly, preaches "untouchability" or its practice in any form; or (ii) if he justifies, whether on historical, philosophical or religious grounds or on the ground of any tradition of the caste system or on any other ground, the practice of "untouchability" *in any form*. (Emphasis mine.)[6]

Importantly, this legislation provides different grounds from the Prevention of Atrocities Act, in that it does not delimit the reach of the practice of untouchability, nor does it enumerate its specific forms, recognising only that the ideology of untouchability, embedded at the centre of the caste system, will perpetrate and reinforce unanticipated and unenumerable forms of proscription and humiliation. The term 'untouchability' is emphasised throughout the legislation, simply to denote a complex of systemic practices that draw their legitimacy from the caste system. What exactly these systemic practices are or might be are not specified, the presumption being that these will be illustrated by empirical facts brought before the court from time to time. The constitutional mandate that this legislation serves therefore, if viewed alongside Article 17, is the proscription of untouchability—in whatever form.

Ours is a justice system that is based on non-discrimination. This case is not, in my view, one of a conflict between individual rights and group rights. The singular absolute standard is the prohibition of untouchability in all its forms, whether it affects individuals or groups or indeed classes. In terms of judicial reasoning in the Sabarimala case, this is a proscription based on the supremacist ideology of caste orders. It is necessary *to constructively hold Article 17 in place at the centre*, in its intersection with gender (as also with Articles 14, 15 and 21) in order to open out further pathways to constitutional renaissance as (to quote from a recent judgement of Chief Justice Misra), 'a constant awakening as regards the text, context, perspective, purpose, and the rule of law',[7] asserting constitutional morality and the dignity of women, across caste of a particular faith in this case, as an overriding constitutional goal.

Notes

1. India Const. art. 17.
2. Indian Young Lawyers Association & Ors v. The State of Kerala & Ors, WP (C) No. 373 of 2006, decided on 28 September 2018 (SC), para. 7.
3. The Protection of Civil Rights Act, 1955.
4. Ibid., sec. 2(a).
5. Ibid., sec. 3.

6. Ibid., sec. 7, Explanation II.
7. Government of NCT of Delhi v. Union of India & Anr, (2018) 8 SCC 501, para. 273 (per Misra, J.).

References

'Interviews for Women Barbers Today'. 2006. *The Indian Express*, 18 July.

Ambedkar, B. R. 2002 [1917]. 'Castes in India'. In *The Essential Writings of B. R. Ambedkar*, ed. Valerian Rodrigues, 239–62. New Delhi: Oxford University Press.

Dumont, Louis. 1970. *Homo Hierarchicus: The Caste System and Its Implications*. New Delhi: Vikas.

Gopinath, Vrinda. 2005. 'It's a Bad Hair Day for Subbarami Reddy'. *The Indian Express*, 11 August.

Rajagopal, Krishnadas. 2016. 'New Bench to Hear Sabarimala Entry Case'. *The Hindu*, 8 July.

28

Graded Patriarchies and Graded Inequality

*Sabarimala**

The debate on women's rights within religious institutions, and the interpretative curtailment of access to places of worship has surfaced yet again in the case of Sabarimala (*Business Standard* 2018). This decision needs to be placed within its historical context.

This is, on the face of it, a partisan prohibition that is rooted in women's biology. For 40 years from minority to menopause, women are barred from entering the temple of Ayyappa at Sabarimala. There is no comparable proscription on men. This bar on women's entry is justified on grounds of the antiquity of the custom—it predates the Constitution. But can antiquity alone be a rational justification? In keeping with the constitutional guarantee of equality, dignity and non-discrimination, as also freedom of faith and conscience, a custom such as this (like practices of untouchability and sati) is manifestly arbitrary. Can courts in a constitutional democracy—even when the bench by default, if not design, is mostly made up of dominant caste, Hindu males—afford to weigh in on the side of dominance—male and caste? In considering the argument of the opponents to women's entry that the bar on women is part of the essential features of a religion, the question before the court really is, can exclusion be an 'essential feature' in a constitutional era, and can constitutional courts uphold an exclusionary bar that is deemed to be an essential feature?

It is a fact indeed that most female believers comply with the rule of exclusion, with several actively opposing temple entry. Even if this segment constitutes the 'majority' of female believers, is that sufficient justification for upholding an exclusionary practice and for defining a

* Unpublished essay, October 2018.

religious denomination in exclusionary ways? The struggle for temple entry has been a long and difficult one, still unfinished, with Dalits to this day being denied equal access to places of worship in different parts of the country. The proscription against entering a place of worship within a community of believers is an act of structural violence. We cannot have it on the basis of caste, nor can we have it on the basis of gender. Coming to the gender question, we are poised in a historical moment when gender has moved outside the binary of male–female. How does this proscription rooted in binary constructions of gender play out in a 'gender galaxy' (Shah et al. 2015)? Who identifies 'men'? Is it a matter of self-identification? If that is the case, the gender distinctions are already dismantled, when transgender persons attempt to enter the temple. If it is the *thantri* (head priest) who will determine who is 'male', a transgender person ruptures that boundary by their presence. These are complex matters that require deliberation, especially in the post-*Naz Foundation* history of constitutionalism.[1]

Once we have resolved this difficulty (can it be resolved?), we return to a prior point where the argument is made that most women support the bar. When the securitised gatekeeping of religious institutions is in place (with its attendant threats of violence, coercion, deployment of state power, vigilantism and weaponised enforcement), the anticipation of violence obstructs the exercise of choice by women. The 'majority' argument can only be tested when all controls and coercion are lifted and the decision is left totally to individual women believers. Once that is done, if there is even one woman who dissents—either by choosing a different interpretive route for *naishtika brahmacharyam* (a person who takes a vow of celibacy) or a different interpretation of conduct, her view counts. Dissent has been the cornerstone of religious reform, and Kerala has witnessed this history as well.

The *de minimis* argument put forth by a counter-constitutional Supreme Court in *Suresh Kumar Koushal*[2] (which recriminalised homosexuality after *Naz Foundation*) was overturned in *Navtej Singh Johar* in 2018.[3] Further, the right to privacy judgement[4] asserts that the *de minimis* approach is bad law—it is not numbers, but the possibility of unjust exclusion that matters. It is for individual believers to decide (a) whether they are sturdy enough to trek to the hilltop; (b) whether they want to enter the temple; and (c) whether they concur with the

Brahminical male view that a pious woman's mere presence poses a threat to divine celibacy.

What, we might ask, are the implications of investing sexual desire in deities, to be controlled by the deities' male keepers?

There are structural and systemic differences between temple entry where it concerns women as a class, and where it concerns Dalits. However, in a caste-supremacist society where graded patriarchies interlock with graded inequalities, the ideologies of pollution and impurity are visited in different, yet similar ways on women across caste, Dalits and Dalit women—as we see in the fraught case of temple entry. Gender ideologies that structure caste supremacy can scarcely be wished away.

We have had a long and tenacious anti-caste resistance in the country that has focused on the question of dignity for women and the abolition of caste as the only route to dignity for Dalits. Jotiba Phule, Tarabai Shinde, Savitribai Phule, Rakhmabai, Narayana Guru, Ayyankali, Iyothee Thass, Periyar, B. R. Ambedkar and so many, many more. Our understanding of justice within the context of religious prescription draws from the articulation of constitutional morality rooted in these struggles.

Notes

1. *Naz Foundation*, (2009) 160 DLT 277.
2. *Suresh Kumar Koushal*, (2014) 1 SCC 1.
3. *Navtej Singh Johar*, AIR 2018 SC 4321.
4. *K. S. Puttaswamy*, (2017) 10 SCC 1.

References

'SC Lifts Ban on Women's Entry in Sabarimala Temple: Here's the Story So Far'. 2018. *Business Standard*, 17 October.

Shah, Chayanika, Raj Merchant, Shals Mahajan and Smriti Nevatia. 2015. *No Outlaws in the Gender Galaxy* (e-book). New Delhi: Zubaan.

29

Judicial Opacity on Women's Entry in Sabarimala*

It was just days before Chief Justice Gogoi retired that the review petition on the Sabarimala case was decided by a majority of 3:2 (Nivedhitha 2019). The September 2018 judgement—a 4:1 majority decision in favour of women's entry into the temple—now goes before a larger bench for a relook. It is apt, when we consider these contrary outcomes, to recall some basic tenets in constitutional interpretation set out since 2009, marking the turn towards 'transformative constitutionalism'. These include: the consideration of *analogous grounds of discrimination* as impermissible (that is, any form of discrimination akin to what is clearly listed as illegal, say, untouchability),[1] the principle of *non-retrogression* in the delineation of fundamental rights (that is, a right, once granted, cannot be reversed),[2] the unequivocal rejection of the *de minimis* argument (the idea that something is too trivial for the law to consider) in keeping exclusions in place,[3] an expansive reading of the Ambedkarite formulation of constitutional morality,[4] and the unanimous 2017 declaration by a nine-judge Constitution bench of the Supreme Court that the right to privacy (which, the court elaborated, meant dignity, autonomy, choice, and the right to be left alone, free of surveillance) is a fundamental right.[5] Each of these principles is immediately relevant to how the Sabarimala case is moving.

The intervening year between the two judgements has seen attempts by women to enter the temple in the face of violent threats, ferocious trolling, hate speech and fortification of the hill and its environs (Babu 2018). The Constitution and the Supreme Court pale

---

* Originally published in *Outlook*, 20 November 2019.

into a haze in this muscle-flexing and chest-thumping. The nation becomes a mere *dangal* (wrestling arena).

Last week's judgement, on 14 November 2019, reiterating for the most part the reasoning of Justice Malhotra's dissent in 2018, is a setback on many counts. There is a protocol for review petitions—they should be circulated to the same bench that delivered the judgement, the basic purpose being to rectify an error of judgement or a miscarriage of justice. However, Chief Justice Gogoi—not part of the 2018 bench—announces a departure from that right in the opening paragraph, saying several new writ petitions were tagged on to the review: 'The endeavour of the petitioners is to resuscitate the debate about what is essentially religious, essential to religion and integral part of the religion.' While this is itself an overreach, in the next paragraph, he extends the question to Dawoodi Bohra women,[6] Muslim women's entry into mosques/dargahs and Parsi women. Each of these cases is *sub judice* and specific, and without doubt must be ruled in favour of women's claims to equal personhood. But this cannot be done via an omnibus 'judicial policy befitting [the court's] plenary powers to do substantial and complete justice'.[7] The policy must be enunciated on a case-by-case basis with recourse to precedent, settled law and principles therein as and when the matters are brought before the court.

Besides, the judgement raises the question whether the Kerala Hindu Places of Public Worship (Authorisation of Entry) Rules, 1965, governs Sabarimala at all. For those of us who have followed and celebrated the victory of struggles for temple entry a century ago, struggles that are foundational to the Constitution, this is deeply shocking, especially because the specific case of places of public resort is covered by Article 15(2). Exclusion on grounds of menstrual taboos of pollution can be seen as an expression of untouchability proscribed by Article 17, as Justice Chandrachud held in *Indian Young Lawyers Association*,[8] or that it is *analogous* to practices of untouchability (as recently argued in Bindal 2019). Either way, it attracts Article 15(2), especially after 'analogous grounds' have been recognised as discrimination.

Justice Nariman, speaking for himself and Justice Chandrachud, reiterates the majority reasoning of 2018, outlining the 'greatest common measure of agreement'[9] along the following lines: that Ayyappa devotees do not constitute a separate religious denomination under Article 26; that Article 25 guarantees 'equal entitlement of all persons to profess, practise and propagate religion';[10] that exclusionary practice, 'even if it be founded in religious text, is subordinate to the constitutional values of liberty, dignity and equality';[11] that '[n]otions of "purity and pollution", which stigmatise individuals, have no place in a constitutional order';[12] that the Devaswom board's 1955–56 notifications prohibiting women's entry are *ultra vires* Section 3 of the Kerala Hindu Places of Public Worship (Authorisation of Entry) Act 1965, (Kerala Act No. 7 of 1965), and are even otherwise unconstitutional.[13] On whether the prohibition of women between ages 10 and 50 constitutes an 'essential religious practice',[14] Justice Nariman clarifies that it must refer to essential Hindu practices and not specific practices of particular temples, and goes on to note: 'Nothing has been shown to us ... from any textual or other authorities' that such exclusion is an essential part of the Hindu religion.[15] In general, he found the arguments presented for review were 'a mere rehash' of past arguments and 'can by no means be said to be an error apparent on the face of the record'.[16]

Four of the five judges who delivered the 2018 judgement were on this review bench. Three held their earlier position—Justices Malhotra, Nariman and Chandrachud. Inexplicably, Justice A. M. Khanwilkar, who signed with then Chief Justice Misra in favour of women's entry in 2018, reversed his position, with no explanation on the reasons for the drastic shift—whether error or misjudgement. As he has not authored a judgement in the 16 Constitution benches he has been part of, we have no way of deciphering his individual view. His reversal is critical in overturning the majority view. It could well have been 2:3 instead of 3:2. This judicial opacity is troubling, to put it mildly.

The court has not stayed the verdict of 2018, and it is reasonable for women of all ages to presume they can worship in the temple if they so wish. Will they be allowed to? That's a different question altogether, with a telling convergence of views between the state government, the Centre and the Congress leadership. No closet patriarchy, this. The core issue must be restated: it's not whether women want to worship at the temple. Not even about Sabarimala generally. It is specifically about the dehumanising menstrual prohibition in this temple. Left to themselves, women believers may choose either way. They always have. There can be no rationalisation of the coercive proscription. The god does not need keepers of his celibacy, nor do women need menstruation monitors.

Notes

1. *Naz Foundation*, (2009) 160 DLT 277.
2. *Navtej Singh Johar*, AIR 2018 SC 4321.
3. *K. S. Puttaswamy*, (2017) 10 SCC 1.
4. *Naz Foundation*, (2009) 160 DLT 277; *Navtej Singh Johar*, AIR 2018 SC 4321.
5. *K. S. Puttaswamy*, (2017) 10 SCC 1.
6. Kantaru Rajeevaru v. Indian Young Lawyers Association, (2020) 3 SCC 52, para. 2.
7. Ibid., para. 4.
8. *Indian Young Lawyers Association*, WP (C) No. 373 of 2006 (SC), para. 75 (per Chandrachud, J.).
9. *Kantaru Rajeevaru*, (2020) 3 SCC 52, para. 10 (per Nariman, J.).
10. Ibid., paras. 7, 17.
11. Ibid., para. 7.
12. Ibid.
13. Ibid.
14. Ibid., para. 18.
15. Ibid.
16. Ibid., para. 19.

References

Babu, Ramesh. 2018. 'Sabarimala: Police Out in Strength as Temple to Open for Five Hours Today'. *Hindustan Times*, 5 November.

Bindal, Amit. 2019. 'Sabarimala and the Flattening of Religious Community'. *Seminar* 721 (September).

Nivedhitha, K. 2019. 'Sabarimala Review: The Curious Case of Review Petitions' Adjudication'. *The Leaflet*, 21 November. Available at https://www.theleaflet.in/sabarimala-review-the-curious-case-of-review-petitions-adjudication/ (accessed 20 June 2021).

Part B

Civil Liberties, Human Rights and Law

VII

Civil Liberties

30

On Human Rights and Radical Evil*

'State is the name of the coldest of all cold monsters. It even lies coldly, and this lie crawls out of its mouth: "I, the state, am the people."' Friedrich Nietzsche's (2006 [1883]: 34) words ring chillingly true today. 1984, Dangs, Prevention of Terrorism Act, Gujarat, Sikhs, Muslims, Christians, Dalits, Kashmir, Narmada, women ... all this is *dharma* (pious obligation). All else is, to quote Narendra Modi, 'appeasement'.[1] And in this see-saw between 'justice' and 'appeasement', the space for rights, both on the ground and in our thoughts, has been steadily whittled down, to the point of extinction. And this is not to say we don't see the human suffering in all these and the countless other 'episodes' of violence perpetrated or shielded by the state. Thanks to the globalisation of mass media, especially television, we do. In the very process of producing the spectacle of suffering, the mass media erases the possibility of any structural understanding of suffering, says Baxi in *The Future of Human Rights* (2002).

There are lessons to be learnt from each and every struggle. Human rights and civil liberties struggles in India especially have taught us how we can use institutions of justice, the courts especially, creatively, to wrest political rights from an unwilling state in a democracy, and they have also taught us important and valuable lessons in enforcing accountability from the state and its agencies. Women's movements, Dalit struggles, and the struggles of tribal peoples have demonstrated to us the power of the biographies of those who have suffered/survived

---

* Originally published in *The Hindu*, 30 December 2002.

This essay was inspired by Upendra Baxi's (2002) book, *The Future of Human Rights*. The context was the aftermath of Gujarat 2002. While there was no question that the genocide in Gujarat was radical evil, what was far worse was the amnesia that set in during election week later that year.

violence in its most extreme, persistent, pervasive forms, making these testimonies of suffering social texts that become tools for change. Obliterating the distinction between peacetime and war for entire populations that suffer from and live in this environment, Baxi (2002: 146) says,

> The lived reality of sex trafficking, sweat labour, serfdom, workplace discrimination, sexual harassment, dowry murders, rape in peace time as well as a means of doing "politics", torture of women and experimental medicalisation of their bodies (also displacement, child labour, denials of rights to housing, health, education, gainful employment ...) all these and related devices of state and society, present problems of routinisation of terror.

Yet international law makes a doctrinal distinction between the international law of war and peace, reserving languages of pain and suffering for the development of international humanitarian law, while invisibilising them in times of peace.

In an era of globalisation, when visions of alternatives to global capitalism are just devoured, Baxi argues, the question of human rights is relegated to a moral language (social justice, equity, redistribution) that is overworn and fails to evoke any positive response from the globalising middle classes. Lawyers and law students, for instance, the traditional constituency for human rights advocacy, increasingly move rapidly into the vortex of chromium and steel high-tech corporations, defending both the interests of global capital and the proliferation of repressive legislation and administration, and irresponsible government.

Recognising and contending with the fact of distinct regimes within 'human rights', each with its own discursive formations and definitions of what constitutes a violation, has been a critical part of human rights movements as also the transgression of the boundaries of these distinct regimes and these definitions. Domestic violence and starvation induce terror and, by virtue of this blurring, coexist as violations alongside torture, leaving, I would argue, the fundamental question unanswered: Who are the terrorists?

Hannah Arendt (quoted in Baxi 2002: 27), writing in the aftermath of the Holocaust, spoke of radical evil as a 'structural element in the realm of human affairs' in which human beings 'are unable to forgive what they cannot punish and ... unable to punish what has turned out to be unforgivable'. For Baxi (2002: 28), radical evil 'is the imposition of suffering beyond redress, remorse and rights, and even recall', leading to an organised moral amnesia, which undermines the very foundations of human rights. While there is no question that the genocide in Gujarat (Concerned Citizens Tribunal 2002) is radical evil, as all genocides are, what is far, far worse and absolutely unforgivable, is the amnesia that set in during election week and has already settled in. Gujarat is at peace. Our globalised electronic media incessantly beams images of a beaming Chief Minister Modi, runs reports of plans for progress and development in Gujarat, and all else is forgotten. All those thousands of Sikhs who were killed in the streets in 1984 are forgotten (PUDR and PUCL 1984). The families that witnessed the violence are told that they did not see, because what they saw did not happen. Delhi is at peace. That the state (in all its naked and brutal power) is in the hands of a group of people with the worst possible criminal record, and that most of our other states share that record by either actively participating or tacitly supporting the Gujarat gang or the Delhi gang or countless other such gangs are facts that get completely swamped by this euphoric amnesia. This is not peace, it is catastrophic for human rights groups, and for the people of this country. It matters little whether Modi is OBC or L. K. Advani is Sindhi. What matters is the fact that there have been gross violations of human rights that must be redressed.

It is in the context of radical evil then that human rights resistance is located, and in confronting and interrogating violations, human rights paradigms open up further sites of resistance—by asserting the rights of all peoples to self-determination—'a right to *voice*, the right to bear witness to violation, a right to immunity against *disarticulation* by concentrations of economic, social, and political formations' (Baxi 2002: 46; emphasis as in original). This immediately foregrounds an ethic of power, which prevents the imposition of violence whether in the name of sovereignty, imperialism or patriarchy or, in our times, community. Baxi argues,

> [E]ngaged human rights discourse makes possible a deeper understanding of the politics of difference.... It insists that the Other is not dispensable.

> It sensitizes us to the fact that the politics of Otherhood is not ethically sensible outside the urgency of the maxim: "Ask not for whom the bell tolls; it tolls for thee". It insists with Rabbi Israeli Salanter that "the material needs of my neighbour are my spiritual needs". (Ibid.: 156)

This finally brings us to the question of the interdependence of human rights, which very simply, is that the same order of rights inhere in each person. In an age when identities are fluid and multiply at an alarming pace, when cultural spaces and indeed the nation itself is shrinking through increasing exclusion even while it expands through globalisation, when the only precarious road to survival often is community ghettoisation, we need to remind ourselves constantly of the non-negotiability of basic rights and just governance in each of our contexts.

Note

1. There has, since 2002, been no rollback from this view of 'appeasement', as suggested in a 2013 interview with Reuters, quoted in Mishra (2013).

References

Baxi, Upendra. 2002. *The Future of Human Rights*. New Delhi: Oxford University Press.

Concerned Citizens Tribunal. 2002. *Crime against Humanity: An Inquiry into the Carnage in Gujarat*, 3 vols. Mumbai: Citizens for Justice and Peace.

Mishra, Akshaya. 2013. '2002 Gujarat Riots and Modi: The Continuing Absence of Grace'. *Firstpost*, 12 July. Available at https://www.firstpost.com/politics/2002-gujarat-riots-and-modi-the-continuing-absence-of-grace-952357.html (accessed 23 June 2021).

Nietzsche, Friedrich. 2006 [1883]. *Thus Spoke Zarathustra*, ed. Adrian Del Caro and Robert B. Pippin, trans. Adrian Del Caro. Cambridge: Cambridge University Press.

PUDR (Peoples Union for Democratic Rights) and PUCL (Peoples Union for Civil Liberties). 1984. *Who are the Guilty? Report of a Joint Inquiry into the Causes and Impact of the Riots in Delhi from 31 October to 10 November 1984*. New Delhi: PUDR and PUCL.

31

The Abolition of the Death Penalty*

On 20 November 2012, India was one of 39 countries that voted against the UN General Assembly draft resolution which called for the abolition of the death penalty (Singh 2012). On 21 November 2012, Ajmal Kasab was hanged after being pronounced guilty of perpetrating terrorist attacks in Mumbai on 26 November 2008 (Kulkarni and Abbas 2012). Afzal Guru was executed on 9 February 2013 (PTI 2013). Although there is a world of difference between the two cases, there are questions that arise in common in relation to the death penalty. The debate on the death penalty is in focus yet again, and as before, there are votaries for and against. Although the arguments on both sides are well-worn and familiar, we might look at them again in the hope of gleaning new insights.

Increasingly, we find public responses that equate judicial outcomes and 'justice' to immediate and quick retribution. So when men accused of causing grievous hurt and loss of life to women through acid attacks are simply killed in police encounters, we hear popular applause and appreciation for the heroism of the police (for example, *The Times of India* 2008). When political prisoners are sentenced to death, it is an impossible battle, especially if they happen to be labelled as 'extremists', because the combined might of the state and dominant forces closes in on them, muzzling dissent and debate. When a man is hanged for rape and murder, we see a palpably deep satisfaction in a significant

---

* An abridged version of this chapter was originally published as 'UPA Strays off Sonia's Course', in *The Hindu*, 10 February 2013.

This essay on the death penalty, submitted for consideration for publication on 2 December 2012 after the execution of Ajmal Kasab, was published in *The Hindu* in abridged form in February 2013 after the execution of Afzal Guru.

number of people that 'justice' has been done. When someone accused of terrorist attacks is hanged, we dance in the streets and distribute sweets because the 'ends of justice' have been met. And then, there is a baying for more blood, throwing into immediate risk those *languishing* on death row after trials that have been manifestly unfair, and those who have been on death row decades after conviction with their lives hanging by a thread.

Where does this drawing of blood stop? Is retributive justice the way to go in a democratic country that prides itself in its unprecedented historical legacy of interrogating violence in fundamentally non-retributive ways?

It is important, of course, to examine the legal position on the death penalty, and to assess on a case-by-case basis whether the death sentence has been awarded in accordance with procedure established by law. We have had legal scholars deliberate on this in some detail (see Amnesty International India and PUCL-TN&P 2008). Yet, what constitutes the 'rarest of the rare', enough to merit death, is a matter of judicial discretion and political conviction.

There is, however, a larger question the death penalty raises. Is justice coterminous with procedure established by law? Does justice have to do only with the written text of the law, or is it also about the practice of politics and about governance? What is the place of the moral and the ethical in the articulation of justice?

I will attempt here to pose some questions about the death penalty in particular, and punishment in accordance with the law in general, urging a separation between emotion and the task of sentencing, in a manner of speaking.

What better place to begin than post-2002 Gujarat? Maya Kodnani was convicted for perpetrating mass crimes and sentenced to imprisonment for life, but not sentenced to death (Harris and Kumar 2012), and although some of us believed that she must be brought to trial and convicted for her horrible crimes, we were relieved that she was not sentenced to death. Not because the crime was less serious in any way than the crimes committed by Kasab, but because we believed that the ends of justice are not served by taking life. Further, we believed that the sense of loss that results from crimes—whether against the individual body, or against collectivities—can never really be recovered, no matter what the punishment. The pain of loss remains, so does the grief. There can be no equivalence between the lives of Dhananjoy Chatterjee and Hetal Parekh, nor can there be any equivalence between the lives of Ajmal Kasab and Hemant Karkare or Vijay Salaskar (see Chattopadhyay 2004; *CNN* 2008). Nor is the personal history of the accused relevant to the present discussion. Whether he grew up in neglect, or was abused, or was a spoilt, rich brat who never learnt the rules of social intercourse is not material to sentencing, even while it may be relevant to understanding the social contexts and trajectories of crime.

Penalties in the law are not meant to compensate for the loss of life and less still to mitigate loss. They are meant to restore a sense of order and reinstate a sense of the moral by putting persons who cause varying degrees of disruption to trial and convicting them. These are connected, no doubt, in that the person believed to be responsible for causing the loss of life is the person being brought to trial. But this is a connection with limits set by the framework of justice.

This brings me to the fundamental contradiction in the current debate on the death penalty. The eschewing of the death penalty is not a matter of judicial reason alone. It is not the prerogative of courts. In fact, the writ of the courts is limited. It is essentially a matter of politics. With the United Progressive Alliance (UPA) in power, on what basis did the government vote to retain the death penalty? On what basis did the former president turn down a mercy petition? On what basis does the UPA government push for the rejection of mercy petitions by the president?

These questions have a context that we have lost sight of. Sonia Gandhi, the chairperson of UPA, has gone on record in a letter to President K. R. Narayanan (Janwalkar 2011) arguing strongly in favour of clemency for those convicted in the Rajiv Gandhi assassination case, and she also spoke on behalf of both her children, one of whom is now a Member of Parliament representing the Congress party, and an acknowledged leader. The pain and loss was deeply personal. But it was also political. It concerned the assassination of a former prime minister and leader of the Opposition. In taking this principled stand,

Sonia Gandhi was also putting the practice of politics and the public good above the personal loss she and her children suffered. In doing this she drew a radical convergence between the personal and the political that should have become the guiding principle for the entire Indian Parliament's political stand on the death penalty. In what is a deep and unexplainable contradiction, the government led by her party has undermined her own stand on this matter. Was there a discussion? What is the justification for this contradiction?

The loss of memory of deliberative politics has tragic consequences in our time. Memory is not honoured or kept alive by taking life 'lawfully' (or 'justly' even if unlawfully). There is no justice in the death penalty. We need today, more than ever, to remember that there is a principle Sonia Gandhi and her children have established in the matter of the death penalty—a principle that separates personal anger and grief from the idea of justice. It is this principle that should guide parliamentary and governmental deliberations on the death penalty—and indeed also guide presidential deliberations on clemency, thereby setting new measures for the practice of politics—and indeed governance in India.

References

'Colleagues: Slain Terror Chief "Superb," a "Daredevil"'. 2008. *CNN*, 29 November. Available at https://edition.cnn.com/2008/WORLD/asiapcf/11/28/india.terror.chief/index.html (accessed 25 July 2021).

'Three Acid Attackers Shot in AP Encounter'. 2008. *The Times of India*, 14 December.

Amnesty International India and PUCL-TN&P (People's Union for Civil Liberties [Tamil Nadu & Puducherry]). 2008. *Lethal Lottery: The Death Penalty in India*. Amnesty International.

Chattopadhyay, Suhrid Sankar. 2004. 'The Case of Death Sentence'. *Frontline*, 27 August.

Harris, Gardiner and Hari Kumar. 2012. 'Stiff Sentence for Former Gujarat Minister'. *The New York Times*, 31 August.

Janwalkar, Mayura. 2011. 'Death Row Appeal Cites Sonia Letter Asking for Pardon for All Four'. *The Indian Express*, 3 September.

Kulkarni, Kaustubh and Naeem Abbas. 2012. 'Mumbai Attacker Ajmal Kasab Executed Secretly, Sparks Celebrations'. *Reuters*, 21 November.

Available at https://www.reuters.com/article/india-kasab-death-execution-idINDEE8AK01N20121121 (accessed 23 June 2021).

PTI. 2013. 'A Timeline of the Afzal Guru Hanging'. *Mint*, 9 February.

Singh, Yoshita. 2012. 'India Votes against UNGA Move to Abolish Death Penalty'. *Outlook*, 20 November.

32

Something is Rotten in the States of . . .*

The following is an account given by Penderel Moon, an Indian Civil Service officer who served in Punjab, of the violence during Partition.

> *Q*: Some schoolboys were flogged and you gave directions that the biggest six boys were to be selected for that purpose.
> *A*: I said, generally speaking, take the six biggest.
> *Q*: Do you think that is a reasonable thing to do?
> *A*: Yes, I think so, under certain conditions.
> *Q*: It was a mere accident that a boy being big should invite on himself punishment.
> *A*: It was his misfortune.
> *Q*: His misfortune was that he was big?
> *A*: Yes. (Moon 2013: 188)

Moon speaks of how six schoolboys, suspected of having participated in the disturbance, were flogged in Bahawalpur sub-jail at the magistrate's instructions. India carries this colonial legacy of treatment in custody even today. Law and order enforcement is still defined by arbitrariness and impunity in executive action.

The custodial killing of five Muslim undertrials who were on their way to court in Nalgonda, Telangana, on 7 April (Rao and Ramu 2015), and the extrajudicial massacre of 20 woodcutters in Andhra Pradesh (Rangarajan 2015) brings grief to those of us who have engaged long and hard with questions of civil liberties and the non-negotiability of total transparency and accountability where the police and armed forces in the country are concerned. The

---

* Originally published in *The Hindu*, 13 April 2015.

undivided state of Andhra Pradesh stood out in the huge gains made by the movements for civil liberties at an enormous cost and loss of life of human rights defenders. The two fledgling states have, in a trigger-happy manner, wiped that history out without a trace. We are back to where we began in the early 1970s.

Immunity from Prosecution or Impunity?

It may be too much to expect any trace of remorse or a sense of wrongdoing by the two governments. Our own sense of hopelessness is evident in our minimalist demands: all we want is an impartial enquiry. There is dissent from Tamil Nadu, the state that the woodcutters belonged to. But what did Tamil Nadu do with those accused of providing shelter and support to Veerappan?

In the Veerappan case (Sharma, Satyamurty and Palaniappan 2004), as in the Seshachalam forest massacre (Rangarajan 2015), there was evidence that officers at the highest level were involved. This evidence was painstakingly put out by human rights defenders.

While we mourn the custodial killing of the five Muslim undertrials, can we afford to ignore the startling ways in which the incident reminds us of the Hashimpura massacre in 1987? The shock of those acquittals (Kumar 2015), and the pain of hearing the extremely forthright accounts of former police officer, Vibhuti Narain Rai, is still palpable, but its lessons lie elsewhere—mass custodial killings carry the guarantee of impunity and immunity from prosecution, the bloodshed of those killed and those who defended them unto death notwithstanding. Besides, while targets keep shifting, the continuing communalisation of the police force is a matter of very grave concern in an increasingly intolerant social and political environment.

In his characteristically unequivocal manner, noted civil libertarian, K. G. Kannabiran (2004: 1), says in the opening page of his book *Wages of Impunity*,

> [t]here is an overwhelming play of violence as power and power as violence, sometimes in breach of the law and sometimes as a tool for its enforcement. If violence in society is perceived as a breach of the law, the law itself is equally violent and in fact has an even more debilitating

> effect because of its systematic and thorough ruthlessness backed by official sanction.

Today, I miss him more than ever before, even while I heave a sigh of relief that he does not have to witness this blatant and cruel undoing of his arduous labour in states that were both his home as well as his battlefield.

Anonymity of Police Personnel

We have court rulings; the battles have been in courts, in the media, in the streets, over the bodies of victims—and yet there is a sense of déjà vu. These are not the same officers or the same policemen; they are a generation far removed, one that has come into consciousness and gained an education that included, importantly, the meaning of human rights. Yet they do not understand the basic constitutional tenet that the right to life is 'non-derogable' and non-negotiable, and that the authority to wield arms does not come with the authority to kill. We know the identities of the victims. Why do we not know the identities of the police personnel involved in these massacres? While we know from reports that the jail personnel and other officers celebrated the deaths of the 'dreaded' undertrials, or narrowly escaped being scratched by the stones pelted by the woodcutters, we only know who the dead are. There is an inversion of threat, with the generic 'police force' being endangered by chained undertrials and stone pelting woodcutters—and now by angry families and defenders. Their disappearance into anonymity is not a sharing of guilt or responsibility within the force, but a sharing of impunity from the very bottom to the very top.

The forests have stood witness to combing and encounters. In the declared fight against mafias, it is the Adivasis and wage labourers, the unarmed and vulnerable, who die or are dispossessed. Our cities bear witness to the fact that increasingly, it is Muslim youths who are incarcerated or killed, irrespective of which party is in power. 'Terror' is the new communal label. And we have no count because the poor are just an aggregate, lives that do not matter either to a state born out of struggle or to a state which boasts of a forward-looking government.

Our immediate task is to push for prosecutions in both these incidents, but we also have a larger task on hand, a bigger challenge. How should we start all over again to build momentum for a movement that forces discipline and accountability on the state? How do we force governments to take responsibility for safeguarding the constitutional right to life and liberty of all citizens? Most importantly, how do we re-school ourselves and the coming generations to drop our thresholds of tolerance for state impunity and state violence?

References

Kannabiran, K. G. 2004. *Wages of Impunity: Power, Justice and Human Rights*. Hyderabad: Orient Longman.

Kumar, Nirnimesh. 2015. 'Hashimpura Massacre Accused Set Free'. *The Hindu*, 21 March.

Moon, Penderel. 2013. 'Divide and Quit'. In *The Partition Omnibus*, David Page, Anita Inder Singh, Penderel Moon and G. D. Khosla. New Delhi: Oxford University Press.

Rangarajan, A. D. 2015. '20 Woodcutters from TN Gunned by AP Police'. *The Hindu*, 7 April.

Rao, G. Srinivasa and Marri Ramu. 2015. 'Five Undertrial Militants Shot Dead in Nalgonda'. *The Hindu*, 7 April.

Sharma, Ravi, Satyamangalam G. Satyamurty and V. S. Palaniappan. 2004. 'The End of Veerappan'. *Frontline*, 19 November.

33

And We Must Say It Again ... And Yet Again*

The searches and arrests made on 27 August 2018 were shocking (Kothari and Shelke 2018). Not unexpected, but the brazenness of state action hit those of us committed to civil rights and the rule of law rudely. As I sat numbed, wondering what there was left to say that had not already been said, I started a slow and painful process of recall and remembering that took me year by year back to the Emergency years of my childhood, which is when I began to bear witness to state rage and impunity, but more importantly, to the power of resistance against impunity. Waging war against the state—an arbitrary state, a violent and lawless state—is the righteous war to entrench the Constitution. It is a war where conscience and courts are the only weapons to confront the arsenal of the state in all its armed might.

We have, since yesterday, been hearing news reports of conspiracies. What is 'conspiracy'? According to the online Oxford Dictionary (Lexico n.d.), 'A secret plan by a group to do something unlawful or harmful. [For example,] "a conspiracy to destroy the government".' A conspiracy theory is, 'A belief that some covert but influential organisation is responsible for an unexplained event.'

Clearly dictionary and legal meanings of conspiracy are obsolete. Not necessarily—not at all any more—the secret meeting of minds to a common criminal purpose. We live in times of open and declared conspiracy to wage war against dissenting citizens, human rights defenders and against minorities—Dalits and Muslims. The criminal meeting of minds armed with the guarantee of protection from prosecution and the guarantee of impunity to carry out systematic,

* Originally published as 'Activists' Arrests a Dire Warning for Anyone Who Dares to Question or Resist', in *The Wire*, 30 August 2018.

targeted assaults supported by the state or arbitrary action by the government. We have just witnessed an interstate police force that is stunningly rapid in its action of searches, seizures, harassment, criminal intimidation and arrests of students and human rights defenders. This same force is rendered immobile in the face of conspiratorial mob violence and criminal assaults/murder of human rights defenders, as we saw with Swami Agnivesh (Tewary 2018) and Umar Khalid (Trivedi 2018).

The most diabolical aspect of the spate of arrests is its speed and its resilience to justice and fairness. We have witnessed for decades that the confinement to custody is swift and accomplished in a swoop (daytime, not necessarily in the dead of night anymore). But once shackled, liberty is the most difficult to restore, getting totally mired in procedures and criminal procrastinations in the criminal justice system, designed to keep people locked up, disregardful of the law, at any cost—as we have seen in the case of Saibaba (*Scroll.in* 2018) and others in that case, including later his lawyer, Surendra Gadling (Johari 2018), and so many more.

The biggest and most effective conspiratorial bogey that rationalises this kind of brutal state action is the conspiracy to kill a leader. There need be no objective assessment of this allegation. The subjective fear that all does not bode well is sufficient. But, this subjective fear is not a fear of physical death as much as it is of political decimation. We saw this in the run-up to the Emergency in a very different way. The roots of that fear do not lie in the actions of the individuals arrested or their families' repositories of seditious materials. The roots of that fear lie in the political constituencies whose attention must now be deflected from the common and gross ills of the regime.

Who else but the violent, fearsome Naxals may be invoked? But of course, when you are moving the scene of action from Dandakaranya to Delhi, Goa, Pune, Hyderabad, there is a new species of Naxal that the ruler's genie must conjure up—fearsome because of their utter proximity to our everyday lives. The Naxals now do not 'infest' only the forests. We have a proliferation of 'urban Naxals'. If you respect the Constitution, demand the rule of law, petition against unlawful procedure and illegal detention or against arbitrary state action—you are an urban Naxal. You can be a lawyer, a professor in a law school, or a professor of big data analysis in a leading school of management, or a 78-year-old writer and poet who has been a prisoner of conscience in the past, has faced conspiracy trials and been acquitted because of lack of evidence—who has been following up Saibaba's case with messianic zeal—or an editor of the front-running *Economic and Political Weekly*, it doesn't really matter.

For the day and a half since this travesty of justice has been at work, every one of us has shifted our sharp and critical gaze from the powers that be to the specific cases of arrests, caught in extricating those trapped in this round of action. Our attention has been deflected and the attention of people generally has shifted too, from the powers to this new monster in our midst, the urban Naxal.

We need to read this state action for what it is. It is a dire warning that anyone who dares to question, to speak up, to resist—at a time when everyday resistance is the only way to survive with dignity—will put themselves at risk as urban Naxals. We, as a people, are trapped today between lynch mobs, anonymous assassins and arbitrary state action. We are being ordered to be complicit through our silence and inaction. This sounds quite alarmist—but if we take stock of the situation we have landed ourselves in, we can see that this is true. So this is not only about Swami Agnivesh, or Father Stan Swamy, or Umar Khalid, or Sudha Bharadwaj, or Anand Teltumbde, or Arun Ferreira, or Gautam Navlakha. It is about every one of us and the country we live in.

References

'United Nations Rights Experts Urge India to Release Jailed Delhi University Professor G. N. Saibaba'. 2018. *Scroll.in*, 28 June. Available at https://scroll.in/latest/884552/united-nations-rights-experts-urge-india-to-release-jailed-delhi-university-professor-gn-saibaba (accessed 23 June 2021).

Johari, Aarefa. 2018. 'A Poet, a Lawyer, a Professor: These are the Five Activists Held for Sparking Bhima Koregaon Clashes'. *Scroll.in*, 8 June. Available at https://scroll.in/article/881849/a-poet-a-lawyer-a-professor-these-are-the-five-activists-held-for-sparking-bhima-koregaon-clashes (accessed 25 July 2021).

Kothari, Vishwas and Gitesh Shelke. 2018. 'Raids in 7 Cities, 5 Activists Arrested; More Could Be Raided in Coming Days, Say Police'. *The Times of India*, 29 August.

Lexico. s.v. 'conspiracy (*n.*)'. Oxford University Press. Available at https://www.lexico.com/definition/conspiracy (accessed 23 June 2021).

———. s.v. 'conspiracy theory (*n.*)'. Oxford University Press. Available at https://www.lexico.com/definition/conspiracy_theory (accessed 23 June 2021).

Tewary, Amarnath. 2018. 'Swami Agnivesh Attacked in Jharkhand'. *The Hindu*, 17 July.

Trivedi, Saurabh. 2018. 'JNU Student Umar Khalid Attacked in Delhi; Police Recover Pistol'. *The Hindu*, 13 August.

34

Democratic Futures in Peril

*An Assault on the Right to Privacy**

The right to privacy was declared a fundamental right under the Constitution of India by a nine-judge bench of the Supreme Court in the case of *Justice K. S. Puttaswamy v. Union of India* in August 2017.[1] Exactly a year later, on 28 August 2018, we were witness to searches and arrests that have shocked the national conscience and forced the apex judiciary to remind the government that 'dissent is the safety valve of a democracy' (Ananthakrishnan 2018).

I focus here on the specific derogations of the right to privacy in the case of the raid and eight-hour house search-cum-seizure in the case of Professor K. Satyanarayana of the English and Foreign Languages University (EFLU), Hyderabad (Sasikumar 2018). A brief account of the search to set the context: At 8:30 a.m. on 28 August, a posse of around 20 police personnel from Maharashtra and Telangana in three vans knocked on his door with what they claimed was a search warrant in Marathi, a language Satyanarayana neither spoke nor understood. He was not informed of the charges against him. They forced themselves into his home and occupied it for the next eight hours, questioning him and his wife Pavana, on their dress, their personal beliefs, their marriage. They searched their bedroom and opened letters they had written to each other, with the Telangana police reading them aloud and translating them for the Maharashtra personnel. They questioned him on his caste identity and Pavana on her marriage to a Dalit, insisting on examining and commenting on their marriage certificate, commenting on the absence of 'signs' of

* Originally published as 'An Assault on the Right to Privacy', in *The Hindu*, 6 September 2018.

marriage on her (*sindoor* [vermillion worn on the head by married women] and jewellery). They insisted that Satyanarayana keep the washroom door unlocked, and change his clothes in their presence. They barred entry to all and refused to permit them to step out of the house. One day before this, their landline stopped working and their mobile phones had interrupted reception. They confiscated all his research and teaching materials and his computers—even the one his seven-year-old daughter Tara used, and family photographs. Although Satyanarayana requested the police to complete the search before his daughter returned home from school, to protect her from the trauma of the search, they refused to comply. What Satyanarayana lost that day is incalculable. In terms of work alone, it was a daylight heist of his professional assets, hard-earned and put together over two-and-a-half decades—e-books, papers, unpublished manuscripts, course materials and teaching resources. The last straw was, of course, questioning him on his reading habits and his academic practice, on why he had books on Ambedkar, Mao Zedong, Karl Marx; on why he had to read at all.

When he finally got access to a Marathi translator around 5 p.m., by which time the search and seizure was completed, Satyanarayana realised that the warrant had nothing to do with him. It only stated that his father-in-law, Varavara Rao, who another team of police personnel had already placed under arrest at his home at the same time, was residing with him. They forcibly entered Satyanarayana's home, having had him under surveillance prior to the search, therefore, the police knew they did not have legal grounds or authority to enter or monitor his movements.

A closer look at what happened that day of course tells us a story of the total and absolute infringement of the right to privacy, in complete derogation of Satyanarayana's right to dignity and personal integrity. My general arguments presented here are immediately relevant to all the seven persons targeted on 28 August, five of whom were arrested and two subjected to the most humiliating searches and seizures. The two who were not arrested, Teltumbde and Satyanarayana, are both widely respected intellectuals—Dalit pedagogues who have been instrumental in crafting radically new approaches to the understanding of anti-caste philosophies and have resisted the ongoing assault on higher education in enduring ways.

I will attempt here to place this experience in the context of the right to privacy judgement of the Supreme Court, in the hope that the court will initiate a moral and material recuperation of dignity and materials in the difficult times we live in today, upholding the constitutional renaissance it has set in motion, in the national interest.

The core value that the judgement is built around is *dignity as the right to life*. How may dignity be understood? Drawing on the Preamble, which states, 'We the people of India, having solemnly resolved ... to secure to all its citizens.... Fraternity assuring the dignity of the individual and the unity and integrity of the Nation', Justice A. M. Sapre opens out the idea of dignity:

> The expression "Dignity" carried with it moral and spiritual imports. It also implied an obligation on the part of the Union to respect the personality of every citizen and create the conditions in which every citizen would be left free to find himself/herself and attain self-fulfilment....
>
> Dignity of the individual was, therefore, always considered the prime constituent of fraternity, which assures the dignity to every individual. Both expressions are interdependent and intertwined.
>
> In my view, unity and integrity of the Nation cannot survive unless the dignity of every individual citizen is guaranteed. It is inconceivable to think of unity and integration without the assurance to an individual to preserve his dignity. In other words, regard and respect by every individual for the dignity of the other one brings the unity and integrity of the nation.[2]

Justice Sapre then goes on to observe that the right to privacy is a natural, inalienable right which inheres in every human being from birth, without which a meaningful life with dignity is not possible.[3] The duty of care to be exercised by the state in its treatment of citizens has hinged on the right of citizens to be free of state intrusion, surveillance through domiciliary visits, and to be treated with care.

Justice Chelameswar affirmed that the 'right to privacy consists of three facets i.e. repose, sanctuary and intimate decision'[4] and includes 'the freedom of certain groups ... to determine their appearance and apparel'.[5] Justice Nariman observed that of the three aspects that are at the core of the fundamental right to privacy, '[t]he privacy of choice, which protects an individual's autonomy over fundamental personal choices',[6] is one.

Because free speech is the biggest threat in India today, Justice S. A. Bobde's words are apt: 'Privacy must also mean the effective guarantee of a zone of internal freedom in which to think.... The vigour and vitality of the various expressive freedoms guaranteed by the Constitution depends on the existence of a corresponding guarantee of cognitive freedom'.[7]

Earlier cases reaffirmed by the Supreme Court in 2017 have held that the right to privacy includes the right to safeguard personal intimacies of the home, the family, marriage, child rearing and education.

In the case of Satyanarayana then, there has been a gross violation of the sanctity of the home, marriage, relationship, expressive freedoms, cognitive freedoms and bodily integrity through the assaultive gaze of the police even at intensely private moments in daily routines, through surveillance, and through a deliberate, intentional public humiliation on the campus of an intellectual, a Dalit intellectual, where he lives and works, in full public view, and obstruction in his performance of his official duties as a teacher. What can be worse than this, and what reparations can the court order?

Notes

1. *K. S. Puttaswamy*, (2017) 10 SCC 1.
2. Ibid., paras. 8–10 (per Sapre, J.).
3. Ibid., paras. 25–26 (per Sapre, J.); reiterated in para. 107 (per Chandrachud, J.).
4. Ibid., para. 36 (per Chelameswar, J.).
5. Ibid., para. 38 (per Chelameswar, J.).
6. Ibid., para. 81 (per Nariman, J.).
7. Ibid., para. 22 (per Bobde, J.).

References

Ananthakrishnan, G. 2018. 'Elgaar Parishad Probe: Dissent Safety Valve of Democracy, Pressure Cooker Will Burst If Not Allowed, Says SC'. *The Indian Express*, 31 August.

Sasikumar, Neeraja. 2018. '"Persecuting the Dalit Intellectual": A Student Recounts Police Raid at Prof. Satyanarayana's House'. *Outlook*, 1 September.

35

Constitutional Justice is Non-negotiable*

On 6 December 2019, the country was rudely awakened to the news of the deaths, in an encounter early in the morning, of the four accused in the rape and murder of a young veterinarian in Hyderabad (Kurmanath 2019)—an incident, which happened on 27 November 2019, triggering an angry response across the country with demands for speedy justice. Some politicians demanded the public lynching of rapists. Members of the public were justifiably anguished that a gruesome crime such as this was even possible in the heart of a vibrant metropolis. It brought back memories of a similar and gruesome sexual assault on a young woman in Delhi in December 2012 (PTI 2017). Just before the veterinarian's murder, in Asifabad close to Hyderabad, another woman of about the same age was sexually assaulted and murdered by three men (Singh 2019); she belonged to an extremely vulnerable nomadic community that eked out a living from wage labour and petty vending. These cases are just two in a long list where women across India have been killed and maimed in the most brutal fashion while we have had a stringent, amended rape law in place and also fast-track judicial processes.

Sexual assault is pervasive, these incidents tell us, and the response must be systemic, not episodic.

In moments such as this, families react with deep anger and grief. Most times this is exhibited through a demand for instantaneous retribution. For several affected families, death is the only answer to

---

* Originally published in *The Hindu*, 9 December 2019.

This essay, co-authored with Justice B. Sudershan Reddy, retired judge of the Supreme Court of India, raises the very difficult issue of the need to keep sight of the rule of law in the most trying circumstances. This essay has been included in this volume with the permission of Justice Reddy.

rape. It is also a fact that this is not a universal view. Grief at loss and pathways to healing speak through different tongues, and we need to be mindful of this fact.

The Larger Picture in Mind

In thinking through the course of justice, it is extremely important for us to rise above the heat of the moment and provide moral reassurance and comfort to families, while keeping sight of the rule of law and constitutional tenets. The ends of justice are not served by wanton killing and retributive bloodlust. The course of justice cannot be determined by the grief and grieving of victims' families. Justice lies in supporting them in their moment of grief and pain, and insisting on due process that brings suspects and accused to trial through a robust, stringent and competent criminal investigation.

This is the challenge before governments and the criminal justice administration, especially the police.

After the December 2012 incident, in response to the widespread demand for a more stringent law and fast-track courts, the law on rape was amended substantially based on the recommendations and deliberations of the Justice Verma Committee. The Criminal Law (Amendment) Act, 2013, or Nirbhaya Act, as it was christened, is testimony to the possibility of translating public angst into just law. That is a victory for the movement against rape that Nirbhaya's family must celebrate as their own.

A Note for the Indian Police

There is a procedure prescribed by the law for criminal investigation. This is a procedure embedded in constitutional principles and honed over decades of thinking on keeping constitutionalism alive and throbbing through the most testing times. Article 21 of the Constitution of India—'No person shall be deprived of his life or personal liberty except according to procedure established by law'[1]—is fundamental and non-derogable. The police, as officers of government, are bound by the Constitution—there are no exceptions.

The case at hand: four suspects were apprehended and shot in custody within a week, without the criminal investigation having commenced in any substantive way. They were shot purportedly when they tried to escape during an exercise of reconstruction of crime at the scene of offence—so even that very preliminary step in criminal investigation had not been completed. The police personnel—unnamed, except for a commissioner of police—have caused the investigation of the crime of rape and murder to abate by killing the suspects.

Before we examine the problems in this action, let us refresh our memory of a core constitutional precept as set out in the Salwa Judum case in 2011: '[M]odern constitutionalism posits that no wielder of power should be allowed to claim the right to perpetrate state's violence against any one, much less its own citizens, unchecked by law, and notions of innate human dignity of every individual.'[2] This is the touchstone of the constitutionally prescribed rule of law, which police officers are schooled in as part of their foundational training.

The Supreme Court of India, by resurrecting Justice H. R. Khanna's dissent in *Puttaswamy* in 2017, has prescribed the interpretation of Article 21: It is non-negotiable, non-derogable, and is not suspended even during conditions of Emergency. We are not living under declaration of Emergency, so the duty of care is more onerous on the police.[3] Any argument on the actions being carried out in 'purported discharge of official duties' especially involving the death of unarmed persons in custody cannot stand the narrowest test of Article 21.

There is no law in force in India that authorises the police to kill. The plea of self-defence cannot be used to rationalise a targeted, premeditated killing of suspects in custody. This plea is bound to the apprehension of death at the hands of the suspects at the time that the suspects are shot. There is nothing to suggest that the four suspects posed a threat to the lives of the police personnel since they were admittedly in custody and, therefore, presumably unarmed. The police have confessions of the suspects while in custody, the evidentiary value of which must be evaluated by the court; but we have, on the other hand, an open declaration by the police of shooting and causing death. As was argued in the encounters case before the High Court of Andhra Pradesh, the discussion on the law was never whether there should be indictment and trial when homicide is committed in self-defence. The debate was on whether a plea of self-defence where excessive force is used should be tried for manslaughter or murder.[4] This has been deliberated on at length in the High Court of Andhra Pradesh and the full bench decision on encounters can scarcely be forgotten especially because these are unarmed commoners in custody.

A Part of Democracy

Where does that leave us? The case of the rape and murder of the veterinarian abates with the killing of all four suspects. This, without giving a chance for the law to operate. However, we now have a fresh case of the murder of four unarmed suspects in custody that must be investigated with police personnel required to stand trial. The pathways of justice are not linear or without obstacles. But we have, as a people, chosen the route of democracy and the Constitution, so we really have no option but to school ourselves in constitutional morality. For, as Ambedkar (2002 [1948]: 484) cautioned in anticipation, constitutional morality must replace public morality. It is not easy, because it is not a natural sentiment. But it is non-negotiable.

Notes

1. India Const. art. 21.
2. *Nandini Sundar*, AIR 2011 SC 2839, para. 3.
3. *K. S. Puttaswamy*, (2017) 10 SCC 1.
4. AP Civil Liberties Committee v. The Government of AP, 2009 (2) ALD 1.

References

Ambedkar, B. R. 2002 (1948). 'Basic Features of the Indian Constitution'. In *The Essential Writings of B. R. Ambedkar*, ed. Valerian Rodrigues, 473–94. New Delhi: Oxford University Press.

Kurmanath, K. V. 2019. 'Disha Murder Case: All Four Accused Killed in "Encounter"'. *Business Line*, 7 December.

PTI. 2017. 'Delhi Gang Rape Case: Chronology of Events'. *The Hindu*, 5 May.

Singh, S. Harpal. 2019. 'Anger in Agency over Yellapatar Gang Rape, Murder'. *The Hindu*, 8 December.

VIII

Free Speech

36

Free Speech is the Cornerstone of Constitution*

I strongly condemn the notice issued by the police on the advice of an assistant public prosecutor to Kancha Ilaiah and the editor and publisher of a Telugu daily that published his article titled 'Is God Not a Democrat?'(*Deccan Chronicle* 2015). This move was on the basis of a complaint received by two individuals under Sections 153A and 295A of the Indian Penal Code.

Ilaiah is a well-known, highly respected and erudite scholar who has challenged conservatism, orthodoxy and social exclusion in unprecedented ways. It is extremely important in a democracy to be able to disagree, dissent and debate contrary thoughts and ideas without fear of police action, intimidation or state repression. While the move by individuals filing the complaint is undoubtedly ill-advised, it is even more serious that the police have thought it fit to register an FIR against him under these sections.

Free speech and the resistance to censorship have a long history in this country—and it is our right as citizens under the Constitution of India to speak our minds and trigger debate, especially on politics and social injustice. It is no accident that the complainants belong to the VHP—but that is beside the point. Speaking out against caste and speaking of the rights of Dalits and the oppressed classes can never be interpreted as creating enmity between castes in this country. The enmity is perpetuated without respite by the dominant castes through concerted efforts at subjugating Dalits through gruesome violence and discrimination. And matters of religion have historically been at the centre of animated debate and questioning. Can we forget Kabir?

---

* Originally published in *The New Indian Express*, 22 July 2015.

Speaking for the self-respect and dignity of Dalits is a fundamental right under the Constitution and a cornerstone of justice. Can we afford to forget the figure of Ambedkar in the Constituent Assembly? While citizens belonging to the dominant social groups might forget the primacy of the Constitution, can policemen in a constitutional democracy afford to think outside its framework?

On what basis did the police officer in the Sultan Bazar police station satisfy himself that the complaint had substance enough to merit an arrest warrant, converted while being served into a notice of appearance? The biggest mistake the political elite, law enforcers and governments make is when they begin to believe that fear can be induced so easily into the defenders of democracy, that threats, intimidation or even arrest will dissipate protest and disappear radical ideas and dissent in this country.

Reference

'Police Issue Notice to Kancha Ilaiah, Daily'. 2015. *Deccan Chronicle*, 21 July.

37

'Hard Words Break No Bones'

*Sedition, Free Speech, Academic Freedoms and Sovereignty in India**

A 2015 report by PEN International opens with the following lines:

> In India today it is surprisingly easy to silence people with whom you disagree. An overlapping network of vague, overbroad laws and a corrupt and inefficient justice system have given rise to an environment in which speech can be quickly censored.... This is a shameful state of affairs for the world's largest democracy. (PEN International, PEN Canada and IHRP 2015: 2)

Indeed it is, but there is more to this story. I will attempt in this short, rather disjointed essay to undertake a brief journey into the past—to recover the memory of history at a time when history is in peril; and reflect on our present predicament.

The 1960 film from Universal Studios, *Spartacus,* based on a novel by Howard Fast tells the story of a slave rebellion against the Roman republic in the first century BC led by the gladiator Spartacus. The most memorable scene in the film shows the Roman general promising freedom to recaptured slaves if they put Spartacus forward. Kirk Douglas as Spartacus steps forward: 'I am Spartacus'—he is quickly followed by every one of the slaves present. This scene has over the years become iconic especially in times when repressive state regimes work with lists of persons who are singled out, identified, profiled, framed and criminalised for their dissent.

---

* Originally published in *Discover Society,* 20 February 2016.

The quotation in the title of this chapter is from Niharendu Dutt Majumdar v. The Emperor, (1942) 43 Cri LJ 504.

The question of academic freedom, imperilled today by the rise to state power of the Hindu Right in India, throws up several urgent questions for our consideration. There are also several parts to academic freedom that require opening out: the right to question, the right to know, the spirit of inquiry, the right to dissent and the full acknowledgement of academic endeavour as a practice of politics. At its core, it is a defence of rigorous scholarship, of uninhibited creative expression that is transgressive by definition, and of the open classroom that allows for a flow of ideas and disagreements. There is also the vital link to education, higher education in particular, that academic freedom is tied to: the institutional structures of higher education, the freedom of association for all campus communities, and the right to the freedom of expression without fear of punitive action either within the protocols of higher education (assessments, hiring practices, admission policies, etc.), or through the abdication of institutional governance to the repressive apparatus of the state.

Using state power to disembowel the autonomy of universities and institutes, and using political power and governmental machinery to delegitimise the gains of social sciences, humanities and the sciences in favour of obscurantism in a new parade each day of the emperor in his new clothes, is by far the biggest assault we have seen on academic freedoms, and one that will have far-reaching consequences for our collective futures. In recognition of the fact that resistance against authoritarian and oppressive regimes in post-colonial India has inevitably found its most stunning expressions on university campuses, with education, knowledge production, dissent and critical thinking interlocked in social and political thought, there are renewed efforts to harness campuses in the service of the state—through mob assaults, administrative arbitrariness, hiring practices, curtailment of financial subsidies in higher education, sudden and drastic changes in admission policies and criminalising robust debates on campuses. But also, importantly, through a narrow bureaucratisation of higher education that proceeds on a truncated distortion of knowledge and intellectual pursuit in terms of census-driven, immediate, measurable returns, delegitimising the pursuit of history, philosophy, literature and explorations of the seamlessness of knowledge and life, their interconnections and their essentially transgressive, irreducible character.

Dissent, which lies at the core of even a minimalist idea of academic freedom, is, in this new era, constructed as 'incitement to violence' and a 'threat to national security' (with institutions being co-opted into the ring), opens the doors to state and mob violence that has 'been incited'. The undermining of dissent, free speech and academic freedom is triggered through this construction of expression as incitement. Violence, raw violence itself, now decriminalised, subserves the upholding of 'national honour' (now synonymous with security of state) and is outsourced to anyone with a capacity for violence as pastime—these are our self-proclaimed 'patriots'. This is the rule of law in what we believe to be (and what the PEN International report describes as) 'the world's largest democracy'. The only credential check for acting in the name of the state is the limitless capacity for physical and verbal violence, and menacing conduct—this violence can today legitimately be used just about anywhere. There is no institution that guarantees protection to persons in custody despite evidence of torture and assault, as police, the army and a servile media collude with perpetrators of this ugly violence that has neither name nor knows any limit. Justitia stands blindfolded, holding scales that tilt dangerously on the side of gross injustice, sponsored violence and organised misrule. We have known and seen this treatment of political dissidents in the past and have resisted it—it is marked now by its frightening spread and escalation through mobs on the street and the complete co-optation of the mass media with very few brave exceptions.

Academic freedom and free speech, both are now matters of life, death and liberty like never before—victims to the cataclysmic shift in the framing of higher education by those that rule; educate, agitate, organise, in the seventieth year of India's independence, are replaced with indoctrinate, terrorise, criminalise.

There is a proliferation of names on lists and an accumulation of lists that travel seamlessly between proctorial boards, intelligence agencies, fringe groups, organised gangs in professional garb, and goons on the prowl on the streets of our cities. You are damned if you are in custody. You are damned if you are not in custody. Fear stalks the streets and homes and universities—and yet, the voice of reason persists despite blocking news of protests, complicities with this unlawful exercise of power within institutions, brazen profiling, criminal intimidation, fabrication of evidence and direct incitement to violence and communal profiling on TV channels—'The country wants to know, my viewers also want to know', is the opening line of the anchor's intimidation on camera, and the scholar-academic who speaks truth to power, because of the challenge she poses to authoritarian rule, is the target. We can scarcely forget the proliferation of the moral police in the academy—within institutions of higher education—who have crawled out of the woodworks to assert that everything is normal and any trouble is the work of the 'foreign hand'—Marx, Pakistan, the West ... We are back to where we began with our struggles for fundamental freedoms and democratic rights in India in the early to mid-1970s, but we have lost ground in an unprecedented fashion.

Why have universities come to occupy centre stage? It might be useful to look at the triggers. University campuses shall not reproduce publics where Dalit students are 'a part apart' (to echo Ambedkar 2014 [1982]: 261). This is the crux of the cascading resistance within campuses. What has thrown universities (and institutions of higher education) in India into crisis in the past two years, it cannot be forgotten, are questions raised by Dalit students on the hanging of Afzal Guru, discussions on Kashmir, the death penalty and caste-based discrimination that is evident in the creation of *agraharas* (Brahmin quarters) and *velivadas* (Dalit hamlets) on campuses in an Ambedkarite era.

At another level, the past couple of decades especially have seen the rise of Dalit movements and the large entry of Dalit and Adivasi students into universities. We also witness the rising resistance of Muslim students to deeply troubling targeted violence and deep-seated discrimination in the aftermath of the rise of Hindutva politics and government. The gender question has never been stronger and more complex than it is in this moment of churning—with women and LGBTQ persons confronting a misogynist, masculinist, stridently patriarchal gender order steered by majoritarian politics. These students, possessed of the spirit of the Constitution, enter university campuses hoping that these spaces will nurture the power of questioning, and help promote the Article 17 spirit—the annihilation of caste and discrimination. But what they find is that the university is a conflicted space—negotiations around political dissent and free speech intersect with unequal gender and caste orders and hierarchical pedagogic practice. A cogent critique of the ways in which caste is taught in classrooms interlinks with caste as experience and the larger right to political dissent and free speech, with the figure of Ambedkar as the torchbearer of this renewed sensibility. It is this constellation that is very new in the campus movements we witness today. The different resonances of azaadi within university campuses, borrowing from older traditions of resistance for azaadi in Kashmir and in feminist movements, have rocked the foundations of the dominant, authoritarian, majoritarian community that is in control of the governance of the university, the state outside, and the streets—repression, arbitrary rule, the dismantling of institutions (indeed of the Constitution itself), untrammelled powers to the police within and outside campuses, and murder on the streets with the guarantee of impunity are the single method of rule to stem the tide of dissent.

This is also the time for us to recall shards of our engagements with free speech in the Indian sub-continent over the past century—to spin the historical record back into view. The accusation of sedition is not new. The facts of 'incitement to violence', 'clear and present danger', 'persecution' (Gordon 2013) and marketplaces of a different order of ideas are perhaps constitutive of speech in colonial contexts, where there is little evidence that seditious speech was 'chilled' by repressive legislation. Writers demonstrated again and yet again to the colonial government that 'one man's vulgarity is another's lyric'[1]—whether it had to do with obscenity or with the brazen challenge of colonial rule. Speeches by 'itinerant seditious orators' (Sedition Committee 1918: 139), pamphlets, newspapers, poetry, stories, arms, ammunition (sometimes carried back and forth by 'malcontent emigrants' [ibid.: 153]) and address lists of informers strapped the extreme right and the extreme left together in the term 'revolutionary' and pitted them against the state/monarch, challenging the sovereign. There are significant inversions in the conflations as they spread out across the borders of the partitioned sub-continent after 1947 and notable ruptures.

Sedition trials in independent India saw the imprisonment of poets and writers in the 1970s. Then, as now, universities were at the centre of the resistance to authoritarianism. However, in the present conflagration, majoritarian, dominant caste hate speech, the hallmark of the three decades since the 1990s, has gone largely unattended by courts with technologies of cyber communication harnessed in largely unregulated ways, not to speak of murder in the streets of free-thinking intellectuals. The apparent seamlessness in jurisprudence and governmental action—the persistence of impunity—that straddles colonial and post-colonial contexts on the sub-continent is troubling. And yet, free speech on the Indian sub-continent has had a history that is somewhat more complex and layered than is evident from the legend of incidents of state and mob censorship that the PEN International report recounts.

It will take a long time to undo this damage, but authoritarian rule will be defeated by the sheer grit of non-violent resistance—it always has been. And when that happens, there will be a remembrance of another kind—of those who stood unwavering to provide 'freedom's shade' (to echo Kidwai [2011]).

Note

1. Cohen v. California, 403 US 15 (1971) (USA). See also Golash (2010).

References

Ambedkar, B. R. 2014 [1982]. 'On Participation in the War: 3'. In *Dr Babasaheb Ambedkar: Writings and Speeches*, vol. 2, ed. Hari Narke, 261. New Delhi: Dr Ambedkar Foundation. Reprint.

Golash, Deirdre, ed. 2010. *Freedom of Expression in a Diverse World* (AMINTAPHIL: The Philosophical Foundations of Law and Justice, vol. 3). London: Springer.

Gordon, Gregory S. 2013. 'Hate Speech and Persecution: A Contextual Approach'. *Vanderbilt Journal of Transnational Law* 46 (2): 303–73.

Kidwai, Anis. 2011. *In Freedom's Shade*, trans. Ayesha Kidwai. New Delhi: Penguin.

PEN International, PEN Canada and IHRP (International Human Rights Program) at University of Toronto. 2015. *Imposing Silence: The Use of India's Laws to Suppress Free Speech.*

Sedition Committee. 1918. *Report.* Calcutta: Superintendent Government Printing.

38

Mourning the Loss of Gauri Lankesh*

The devastating news of the assassination of senior journalist Gauri Lankesh on 5 September 2017 (Mondal 2017) signals the broken road that lies ahead of us. It is no longer an individual targeting of firm and fearless voices of dissent—it is now the decimation of dissent itself, and the rise of fear as the only emotion that is guaranteed security of life and person in India today. A wave of Hindu fundamentalism marked by murder and mayhem has swept across this country, under the protectorate of governments holding citizens captive—in minds and in actions. We can already see the disastrous effects of self-censorship in our everyday personal and work lives and in institutional deliberations.

But is there a safe space anymore? For after all, violent silencing of disagreement is driven and fuelled by shifting targets.

The deep, deep tragedy of Gauri's death is rendered totally banal with the trading of blame between the BJP and the Congress (Venkataramakrishnan 2017). The new rise of fundamentalist forces in India blurs narrow political boundaries through the violent convergence of ideology with impunity. The fact is that fundamentalist politics operates through the outsourcing of policing to anyone who is willing to kill anyone who disagrees, and all the rest shielding those that kill, overtly or covertly. The guarantee is that there may be no investigation—or there may be an investigation that ensures impunity; there may be no trial, and there may be no conviction. Scrolling through the roll call of those that died for speaking their minds (for example, *Hindustan Times* 2015; Puniyani 2015) in fact shows us that this is the end of the road. There will be an individualising of the 'provocation', the 'trigger' and the murderous act. The question

---

* Originally published in *Indian Cultural Forum*, 14 September 2017.

that will be asked by investigators is, 'What did *she* do to invite the messengers of death?'—not, 'Why are there messengers of death lying in wait in a state of readiness for the next target?' The same story yet again, and we watch—angry, vocal, non-violent, but rendered totally powerless to make a difference.

The flip side of this is that conviction is guaranteed through a 'speedy trial' for putting a name to the evil—through defamation laws, as Gauri's own conviction shows. A defining element in this menacing harassment is to divert and deplete the energies of the critic, even while plans are afoot to wipe her off the face of the earth.

While the acts in each case are outsourced, let us not forget that it is systematic, part of a larger plan, an open conspiracy to annihilate difference on so many different tracks all at once, measured out to make us lose count. What will it take for us to turn this reality around? What do we need to do to set a new balance in public discourse that is framed by democratic values and respect for divergent, even fiercely opposed, worldviews? How do we defeat the narrow bigotry and sycophancy that has come to define politics, religion and everyday life in this country today?

Gauri's assassination is an unprecedented assault on a free press. More direct than ever before. It is a warning of what lies in store for all those committed to free speech. There are mobs on the rampage, killing Muslims, Dalits, women, students, beef-eaters, supporters of beef-eaters, conscientious dissenters, human rights defenders, journalists, professors, political activists, rationalists, union organisers ... We are now citizens of a country being forced into amnesia—the memory of who we are obliterated through the expunging of history, not to speak of its distortion, the fracturing of dissent, and the propagation of banality in the name of religion and faith that sends reason to the gallows, and reduces us all to 'bare life'?

At the precise moment when the Supreme Court of India affirms our right to 'constitutional happiness' (to use Baxi's [2017] words), we plunge into an abyss of hopelessness. The fences are closing in on us, rapidly: demonetisation to assassination is one short road to the end of freedoms for our people, where we see both ends of the conspiracy against citizens in a constitutional democracy work in close concert. In an age of post-truth, accountability is a dead word, as is the rule of law.

The assassination of Gauri must push us to rise and resurrect our power of collective protest—using every method from every strand of resistance we have learnt about. It is time for us to rebuild that road that lies broken ahead of us, if we are to take even a single step into the future.

References

'Rationalist Narendra Dabholkar's Murder Unsolved 2 Years On'. 2015. *Hindustan Times*, 20 August.

Baxi, Upendra. 2017. 'Opening New Doors'. *The Indian Express*, 30 August.

Mondal, Sudipto. 2017. 'Why was Gauri Lankesh Killed?'. *The New York Times*, 13 September.

Puniyani, Ram. 2015. 'Who Killed Govind Pansare?'. *The Indian Express*, 11 March.

Venkataramakrishnan, Rohan. 2017. 'BJP Leaders Condemn Gauri Lankesh Murder and Blame Congress—but Many Right-Wingers are Gleeful'. *Scroll.in*, 6 September. Available at https://scroll.in/article/849757/bjp-leaders-condemn-gauri-lankesh-murder-and-blame-congress-but-many-right-wingers-are-gleeful (accessed 22 June 2021).

39

Taking Aim at the Messenger*

Professor Kancha Ilaiah was again in the eye of a storm—this time so overpowering that he imposed house arrest on himself (Daniyal 2017). There have been menacing threats of violence, police complaints and petitions to the high court at Hyderabad. There are statements out in his support. He has addressed the media, calling for a public debate on the questions he has raised in his writing. The course is open for any of us to challenge his views and ideas, to agree and to disagree.

Challenging the Caste System

In his writing, since the 1990s, Ilaiah has consistently challenged the oppressions in Hindu society that are predicated on graded inequalities and oppressions rooted in the caste system. He is not the first intellectual to do this—he certainly will not be the last. The Indian Constitution is built on the words, ideas and struggles of those who led entire movements for the annihilation of caste—the figure of Ambedkar calling into memory the countless others who marched with him and before him. Ilaiah is a figure in the current moment—following a long and illustrious line of dissenters and critics of the caste order.

Especially at the political moment we are located in—a moment of violent Hindutva assertion—this is an urgent project. Within the Hindu social order that ordains work, occupations, livelihoods and status according to birth and restrains individuals from moving away from their preordained status, it is important to question the

* Originally published as 'Taking Aim at the Messenger: On the Attack on Kancha Ilaiah', in *The Hindu*, 5 October 2017.

fundamental basis of this preordained status if we are to move away from the oppressions of caste.

Not long ago, Bezwada Wilson received the Magsaysay Award for a lifetime of work in pursuance of this same argument (*The Hindu* 2016)—namely, that Dalits have historically been untouchables and condemned to the most degrading occupations, like manual scavenging. Women have a preordained status in the caste order which saw the practice of gruesome violence with impunity—something we have still not been able to annihilate effectively even in the constitutional era, despite a century and a half of the most powerful critiques against the enslavement of women, especially by anti-caste philosophers.

So yes, it is Ilaiah's (2017) argument that Vysyas (the caste, not individual persons) have had a particular place in the caste order that guarantees impunity for the performance of particular caste oppressions that he terms 'social smuggling'. He has previously written about the privileges and immunities granted to Brahmins with impunity by the Hindu caste order. It is useful to look at what he says.

Post-Hindu India

His recent Telugu tract, 'Vysyas: Social Smugglers', is an extract from an older book, *Post-Hindu India: A Discourse on Dalit–Bahujan, Socio-Spiritual and Scientific Revolution* (2009). His preface to the mother publication is important:

> My appeal to Brahmanic readers is that if they want to read this book they must read it without self-righteousness or self-pity. As they begin to read it, it may generate a warlike situation in their minds which are trained in Brahmanic thought. It may indeed result in a "war of nerves" between Brahmanic and Dalit–Bahujan civil societies, the latter having just begun to produce its own organic intellectuals. At the moment there is no large-scale Dalit–Bahujan civil society that could take inspiration from a written text and lead a liberation struggle. The main aim of this book is to create the self-respecting Scheduled Caste (SC), Scheduled Tribe (ST) and Other Backward Castes (OBC) into an intellectual social force that can lead a socio-spiritual and scientific revolution.... This book is meant to play a positive role in empowering the Dalit–Bahujan forces of India in all spheres of life. It is also meant to show how spiritual

> democracy and spiritual fascism are opposite systems, and define what roles they play in our lives. (Ilaiah 2009: *xxvi*)

The intellectual trajectory of this book is clear and cogently stated. The productive and creative contribution of Hindu India's most oppressed castes have been systematically appropriated—expropriated—through a dangerous mix of violence (Chunduru, Karamchedu, Melavalavu, Khairlanji and countless others), discrimination (in access to schools despite the Right to Education Act, for instance), and obscurantist arguments that pass today both as spirituality and as science.

Examining the Inglorious Pasts of Caste

If the classes most subjected to injustice are to rise and claim their rights under the Constitution of India—fraternity, equality, dignity and liberty—there must be a clear debate on what ails our social systems and how we might reckon with our pasts; how might we rise above parochial assertions that make us complicit in histories of oppression perpetrated by dominant castes and classes before our time. This is an argument we cannot fault. Nor can personal outrage and 'caste solidarity' be the basis of 'hurt sentiments' for those who have not been forced to suffer the indignities of the caste system.

It must be noted that Ilaiah is not making a brief *for/on behalf of* a particular caste. He begins his argument on the note that suffering and dispossession must be the fulcrum of our understanding and critique of the order we live in—based on the lived *experience* of those at the bottom. There is undoubtedly rage over the gross injustices of the caste order that come through unequivocally in his argument. But this rage is channelled into forging a political and ideological position. It is open to us to debate that position, to disagree even. But we cannot defeat the argument by taking recourse to the same parochialism and bigotry that drives the oppressions in the first place. And for a free and equal participation in the debate, it is important to generate the text in many languages, for otherwise it will again be confined to the elite English literati, which has no representation whatsoever of voices from among those who have suffered these indignities, and this violence.

Within the Constitutional Framework

Justice Bobde observed memorably in the right to privacy judgement of the Supreme Court that '[p]rivacy must also mean the effective guarantee of a zone of internal freedom in which to think.... The vigour and vitality of the various expressive freedoms guaranteed by the Constitution depends on the existence of a corresponding guarantee of cognitive freedom.'[1]

Ilaiah is writing within a constitutional framework. It must be debated within that framework. Elected representatives who demand his hanging because they happen to belong to the caste he critiques are guilty of gross misdemeanour while holding public office—and must be removed from office for making that appeal alone. The appeal on behalf of a caste association to a constitutional court that Ilaiah must be arrested or an FIR registered for engaging in social critique cannot stand constitutional scrutiny. It is caste discrimination that causes disturbance of peace and social unrest. Speaking out against discrimination and injustice is an affirmation of constitutional morality.

Note

1. *K. S. Puttaswamy*, (2017) 10 SCC 1, para. 22 (per Bobde, J.).

References

'Bezwada Wilson, T. M. Krishna Receive Magsaysay Award'. 2016. *The Hindu*, 31 August.

Daniyal, Shoiab. 2017. 'Kancha Ilaiah: "I Don't Feel Safe Anywhere, So I Have Put Myself under Voluntary House Arrest"'. *Scroll.in*, 1 October. Available at https://scroll.in/article/852368/kancha-ilaiah-i-dont-feel-safe-anywhere-so-i-have-put-myself-under-voluntary-house-arrest (accessed 17 September 2021).

Ilaiah, Kancha. 2009. *Post-Hindu India: A Discourse on Dalit–Bahujan, Socio-Spiritual and Scientific Revolution*. New Delhi: Sage.

———. 2017. 'Explaining the "Social Smuggling" That Has Angered Arya Vysyas in Two States'. *The Wire*, 15 September. Available at https://thewire.in/books/explaining-social-smuggling-angered-arya-vysyas-two-states (accessed 22 June 2021).

40

No Rollback on the Right to Dissent*

The refusal of the Supreme Court of India to quash the FIR against Anand Teltumbde in the Bhima Koregaon case has caused widespread distress (*Scroll.in* 2019). Both the refusal and the distress need to be understood in context, if for no other reason than that the Supreme Court takes note of citizens' expectation that it will play a proactive part in safeguarding fundamental rights under the Constitution at a time when the Constitution itself is in peril.

This expectation has been particularly vocal and visible (even desperate, at times) since 2017, when the Supreme Court took an expansive view of its own brief in the right to privacy case (*Puttaswamy*) by 'resurrecting dissents' in cases of state arbitrariness in matters of personal liberty from 1950 to 1976.[1] The preoccupation of the Supreme Court with judicial dissent continued through the press conference convened by senior sitting judges (the present chief justice among them), intimating citizens that the Supreme Court was under threat of being undermined (PTI 2018). This was followed by the spectacular decision in the case of *Navtej Singh Johar*, where the Supreme Court burst into song, poetry and public apology in its unequivocal affirmation of the right of all queer peoples to personal liberty and dignity without restraint or the threat of criminalisation.[2] In the Sabarimala case, the court challenged Hindu orthodoxy (in yet another stunning judicial interrogation of majoritarian rule) in matters of untouchability and upheld anti-caste resistance, quoting at length from Phule[3]—unparalleled in constitutional jurisprudence till that point.

* Originally published as 'Supreme Court's Refusal to Quash FIR against Anand Teltumbde Damages the Right to Dissent', in *Scroll.in*, 25 January 2019.

In what appeared like the discovery of an immeasurable constitutional renaissance in real time, there was euphoria all around, and hope, despite persistent discordant notes in Kashmir, in the Judge B. H. Loya case (Takle 2017), in the case of G. N. Saibaba, in the cases of Surendra Gadling, Shona Sen, Sudhir Dhawale, Mahesh Raut and Rona Wilson (Johari 2018), not to speak of the murders on the streets. For after all, the judicial dissents and queer rights were part of a larger claim to dignity and liberty by the people of this country, and the Indian Supreme Court was no caged parrot—this was the institution that was (especially now) wresting rights for us, the people, in unprecedented ways.

When Justice Chandrachud declared in open court on 29 August 2018 that '[d]issent is the safety valve of democracy.... If it is not allowed, the pressure cooker will burst' (quoted in Ananthakrishnan 2018), everyone seemed somewhat reassured even though there was unease that the dissenting petitioners were placed under house arrest instead of being set at liberty. Both the June 2018 arrests and the August 2018 arrests, ostensibly about the instigation of violence in Bhima Koregaon, have seen criminal lawyers committed to the defence of civil liberties, Dalit intellectuals, and human rights defenders placed under arrest or threatened with arrest. In their own defence, the petitioners and their lawyers have demonstrated cogently the flimsy grounds of arrest: the fabrications in the FIRs, and the bias in the investigation that targeted human rights defenders and architects of free speech and dissent on the left and set at liberty all those aligned with right-wing political formations locally and nationally.

Right from creating law-and-order problems locally to plotting the assassination of the prime minister, the police claimed that it had clinched incontrovertible evidence of a massive conspiracy. A new label was invented and propagated ably by a caged media—'urban Naxal' (Sharma 2018). Any meeting that upheld the Dalit critique of Hindutva, or criticised governmental lawlessness and arbitrary action—whether demonetisation, or university campus occupations, the impunity of those perpetrating violence on the streets, the spiralling of encounter deaths in Uttar Pradesh, Rafale—was seen as part of a sinister plot to wage war against the state.

For a court that poetically and publicly upheld dissent, the rule of law, the right to personal liberty, and anti-caste philosophies as the basis of constitutional morality, this brazen criminalising of dissent should be the simplest to decode. As also the fact that in an environment trapped by an extremely repressive executive that acted with impunity, it is only the Supreme Court that can keep the executive at all levels in check—and must under its obligation to uphold constitutional morality.

This is why the refusal of the Supreme Court to quash the FIR against Teltumbde strikes a discordant—indeed, jarring—note, just as the arrests of advocates Gadling, Bharadwaj and others did.

Is arrest necessary? Slowly, but surely, the repressive state has shifted the burden of proof. We are all guilty until we prove that we are innocent. Our speech has been stolen from us. As senior advocate Rebecca Mammen John pertinently asked in a personal conversation,

> What has happened to first principles of criminal jurisprudence? Why are courts taking an extreme, almost perverse view while assessing evidence? Why are courts insisting that accused persons face trial in cases where it can clearly be seen that the evidence is shaky, perhaps fabricated and false? Why must they insist that the accused prove his innocence after facing a long, arduous, expensive and debilitating trial, when the evidence can be thrown out so easily at the preliminary stage? (20 January 2019)

Given the magnitude of wrongdoing being brought before courts at this time, we have the paradoxical situation of finding no criminality in a case like Rafale despite evidence being brought on record (Rajagopal 2018), but the ratification of an imagined and fabricated criminality in the case of Teltumbde. The scales tilt disproportionately. Given the vital role of dissent in this democracy, and the fact that the dissents that were resurrected in *Puttaswamy* were in fact dissents that took on board the arguments of human rights defenders—from A. K. Gopalan to the civil libertarians during the Emergency of 1975–76—how does the court explain the adoption of different standards of proof for human rights defenders? There will be no dissent left to celebrate very soon because all dissenters are by this token guilty of conspiring to overthrow the state, so the security of state lies in their incarceration.

More fundamentally still, is mobilisation to overthrow the government a crime? Especially pertinent since we are to face a national election under the protection (we hope) of the Constitution.

Why is there a stubborn refusal on the part of those of us committed to the power of dissent to give up hope on the stellar role the court could play in this sunshine moment when dissents have been judicially resurrected? In its upholding of queer rights, the Supreme Court also delineated the principle of non-retrogression. Dissent, we argue, once upheld, cannot be re-criminalised. This is our firm belief. And if the investigating authorities act on the premise that dissent is criminal, there is no recourse for the spiralling numbers of citizens targeted thus, except to appeal to the Supreme Court to step in and correct a grave wrong by scrutinising and reviewing the materials on the touchstone of the fundamental right to dissent. Justice must be seen to be done.

The FIR against Teltumbde must be quashed. There is really no two ways. This is our Spartacus moment—Teltumbde stands for every one of us.

Notes

1. *Justice K. S. Puttaswamy*, (2017) 10 SCC 1.
2. *Navtej Singh Johar*, AIR 2018 SC 4321.
3. *Indian Young Lawyers Association*, WP (C) No. 373 of 2006 (SC).

References

'Bhima Koregaon Case: Supreme Court Refuses to Quash FIR against Activist Anand Teltumbde'. 2019. *Scroll.in*, 14 January. Available at https://scroll.in/latest/909367/bhima-koregaon-case-supreme-court-refuses-to-quash-fir-against-activist-anand-teltumbde (accessed 22 June 2021).

Ananthakrishnan, G. 2018. 'Elgaar Parishad Probe: Dissent Safety Valve of Democracy, Pressure Cooker Will Burst If Not Allowed, Says SC'. *The Indian Express*, 31 August.

Johari, Aarefa. 2018. 'A Poet, a Lawyer, a Professor: These are the Five Activists Held for Sparking Bhima Koregaon Clashes'. *Scroll.in*, 8 June. Available at https://scroll.in/article/881849/a-poet-a-lawyer-a-professor-these-are-the-five-activists-held-for-sparking-bhima-koregaon-clashes (accessed 25 July 2021).

PTI. 2018. 'Supreme Court Crisis: All Not Okay, Democracy at Stake, Say Four Senior-Most Judges'. *Business Line*, 18 January.

Rajagopal, Krishnadas. 2018. 'Rafale Case: SC Refuses to Intervene in Jets Procurement'. *The Hindu*, 14 December.

Sharma, Arnav Das. 2018. '"Urban Naxal" Is a Word Derived from Stupidity'. *The Quint*, 30 August. Available at https://www.thequint.com/voices/opinion/urban-naxal-vivek-agnihotri-rss-bjp-dissent (accessed 27 August 2021).

Takle, Niranjan. 2017. 'A Family Breaks Its Silence: Shocking Details Emerge in Death of Judge Presiding Over Sohrabuddin Trial'. *The Caravan*, 20 November.

41

For Lives Lived in Labour

*An Interview with Kancha Ilaiah**

I call Kancha Ilaiah Shepherd and we talk about meeting and having a leisurely chat about his work and his troubles in recent times. Our phone conversations these past weeks have been short and hurried, moments snatched in meetings, during a commute, or in the middle of other work. Most of these calls have been to check that he is in good cheer and spirits, since I can never be sure when the strain of belligerent attacks can begin to weigh a person down—even someone like Ilaiah. As I think about the conversation we are about to have, my mind goes back to 1989 or thereabouts, when, as a doctoral student interested in questions of caste, I presented what I thought was a cogent and painstakingly argued critique of caste. A minute after I was done, Ilaiah proceeded to take my paper apart most meticulously, chiding me for hanging on to Brahminical anthropology that will always obstruct an understanding of caste. His insistence that day that I must look at a different corpus if I am to make any sense of the structures of caste has stayed with me till today. This is a methodological point he elaborates on in our two-hour conversation. We first agree to meet at his home but that does not seem possible because the family has other plans on the eve of Diwali, and he offers to come over to mine so we can chat without interruption.

His date of birth according to school records, Ilaiah tells me, is 5 October 1952—he is the fifth of seven siblings. In July 1960, his mother sent him and his brother (older by two years) to the newly established single-teacher school in his village, Papaiahpet—the first two children to be admitted in his village. When they passed Class 5, his mother took them to the landlord in Guduru and begged him to

* Originally published in *The Hindu*, 28 October 2017.

admit them in school. After passing Class 8 there, they moved to the *taluka* (district) headquarters, Narsampet. When his mother died in 1967, his brother discontinued his education, was married to a 12-year-old girl, and took charge of the home, while Ilaiah continued studying. During this period, his brother developed a serious heart condition, so Ilaiah moved his brother's family to his home in Hyderabad—they have been together since.

His first memories of college in Warangal are of G. Haragopal, a young and dynamic teacher of public administration with admirable communication skills, who told him at the end of an English debate where he 'closed his eyes and spoke', that his ideas are good but he needed to work on his English. This was the beginning of a long and trying journey to conquer English. He recalls reading *The Communist Manifesto* (1848), not just for its content, but paying close attention to the English, the flow, and the expression. Not having ever had a convent education, he listened to English news on the radio every night, and practised reading and pronunciation in front of a mirror. He also speaks with admiration about seeing Kaki Madhava Rao, who was then collector of Warangal—a Dalit officer whose doors were always open to those who had suffered any manner of injustice or deprivation. Now, in 2017, four decades later, although an accomplished bilingual author, he is more comfortable formulating conceptual ideas in English than in Telugu. It is from his own struggles with breaking into mainstream academia that he has pursued the idea of promoting English education in the villages with missionary zeal—facilitating the setting up of 107 English-medium schools since 2002, mostly for OBC, Dalit and Adivasi children, and beaming with pride over the fact that these children from rural Warangal are able to speak fluent English by the time they reach Class 6, easily substituting rote-learning of the alphabet with active association with animals, plants and artifacts in their immediate surroundings. 'How do kids change if English doesn't go to rural areas?,' he asks.

What is remarkable about the way the children learn the English alphabet is the fact that experience forms the basis of learning. Ant, not apple. Buffalo, not bat. This resonates with Ilaiah's early thesis that one can only understand caste if experience provides the framework for debate—an argument he proposed in 1990 in an essay published in *Economic and Political Weekly* (Ilaiah 1990). His tryst with writing started with contributions to *Mainstream* and *Frontier* immediately after the Emergency in 1977. He, along with a few friends, started a progressive Telugu journal, *Nalupu*. By this time, he was active in the Organisation for the Protection of Democratic Rights, and had been closely associated with the Communist Party of India (Marxist–Leninist–Nagi Reddy) and had not yet begun to study Ambedkar seriously. He was part of the Andhra Pradesh Civil Liberties Committee, where he raised discomfiting questions about caste in organisational leadership. His involvement with civil liberties and left-wing groups opened out a new world of suffering—journeys to Kashmir, to the Northeast, to Parvathipuram, setting up drought relief centres in Andhra Pradesh and addressing hunger on the ground. However, it was the Karamchedu massacre in 1985 that was a tipping point in his articulation of caste in politics of all hues. This was also the time when Ilaiah began to engage with Ambedkar's writing. On another track, he chose to work on Gautama Buddha's political thought for his PhD, a project that he sees as connected to his engagement with Ambedkar.

Ambedkar's writing took Ilaiah back to his explorations of the experiential basis of understanding structures of thought, feeling and sociality. With no context of rigorous academic research, and a very ordinary education, constant comparisons between textual narratives and a structural approach to the village built on personal knowledge opened out the field to an ethnography of a different kind. Childhood, marriage, markets, goddesses, ritual, worship, food, work, and the clear dichotomy between productive lives and lives outside production—the lived village was the best textbook. His celebrated work, *Why I Am Not a Hindu* (1996) grew out of this ethnographic project. His more recent work, *Post-Hindu India* (2009), takes this further through an exposition of the political economy of caste. Importantly, Ilaiah does not see a dichotomy or separation between productive and reproductive labour—he draws intricate connections between the arguments on sexual division of labour by feminist philosopher, Maria Mies, and his mother's understanding of productive and reproductive labour, or even the worship of goddesses like Pochamma—who had healing and regenerative powers. 'The personal is political' is a slogan of the feminist movement. Ilaiah looks at this alongside 'experience as a framework', in order to grasp the full contours of the Dalit-Bahujan experience of caste. For, in the *dalitwada* (Dalit colony), 'labour is tomorrow's survival', and has been for centuries. Lives are only lived in labour, not in leisure, and there is no notion of property. But there is an immense wealth of knowledge and wisdom. How does this compare with lives lived in leisure and material wealth? What are the moral economies of these different life-worlds? The barber's knife is an illustration—a tool that cleanses, not a weapon that kills.

Having taken the academic world by storm, and having immersed himself in progressive politics, Ilaiah, now retired from Maulana Azad National Urdu University, begins to chart a new course with Telangana Mass and Social Organisations (T-MASS), a broad-based political forum that will bring OBCs, Dalits and Adivasis together to fight for social justice.

References

Ilaiah, Kancha. 1990. 'Reservations: Experience as Framework of Debate'. *Economic and Political Weekly* 25, no. 41 (13 October): 2307–10.

———. 1996. *Why I Am Not a Hindu: A Sudra Critique of Hindutva Philosophy, Culture and Political Economy*. Calcutta: Samya.

———. 2009. *Post-Hindu India: A Discourse on Dalit–Bahujan, Socio-Spiritual and Scientific Revolution*. New Delhi: Sage.

42

'They Cannot Stop Me from Teaching Marx and Ambedkar'

*A Conversation with K. Satyanarayana**

On the morning of 28 August 2018, a large police platoon consisting of personnel from the Maharashtra police and Telangana police descended on the home of K. Satyanarayana and occupied it, claiming to have a search warrant to investigate his complicity in the violence in Bhima Koregaon (for an eyewitness account, see Sasikumar 2018). 'Twenty policemen just barged into my house and showed me some paper in Marathi. They did not follow the procedure of even telling me what the charges against me were and giving me the search order in a language I know,' says Satyanarayana, a professor of Cultural Studies and dean at the English and Foreign Languages University, Hyderabad. He has been a teacher here for two decades, and lives on campus in faculty housing with his wife, Pavana, a college teacher herself, and their seven-year-old daughter, Tara. Known for his longstanding work in building the field of Dalit Studies and for his analyses of caste in social and political movements and literatures, Satyanarayana has, by his own account, been totally focused on his professional academic life and work, which have been the site of his political praxis. The arrival of the police, therefore, was unexpected, as was their inquisitorial conduct towards his life and work.

We agree to meet at his home on the EFLU campus on the morning of 1 September 2018, to talk about the consequences of this police action for him and his family, but also about his academic journey to this point—a journey that was utterly incomprehensible to the police force that descended on him.

---

* Originally published in *The Hindu*, 9 September 2018.

Satyanarayana's family belongs to Amalapuram, in East Godavari district of Andhra Pradesh. Through most of his childhood, the family—his parents and their five children, of whom Satyanarayana is the oldest—lived in Tetagunta village, near Tuni, where his father, a clerk in the *panchayat* office, was posted. He went to the village school and passed Class 10 from there—one of four students who passed in a class of 30, securing a first class. 'That was a big thing in those days.' He then studied in Sree Konaseema Bhanoji Ramars (SKBR) College, Amalapuram, for Intermediate, and Pithapur Rajah's (PR) Government College, Kakinada, for his BA. 'Because my father wanted me to become an IAS [Indian Administrative Service] officer, he asked me to go to a "big college", so I had to study there.' After that he came to Hyderabad.

Why Central University, and why a Masters in English? 'My father was a clerk in a panchayat office. He always wanted me to become a DPO [district panchayat officer] or a collector, because those are the two powerful positions in the district. The reason why I came to Central University was because my English was not very good, I wanted to go to a place where there is English medium.'

Till he joined Central University, he thought of himself as a dedicated, good student, not a topper, but a good student. He had never thought about his caste, although he had a vague idea that they were different from others, because his father would caution them against telling people that they ate pork or beef, or that there was toddy in his grandmother's house. However, his father never stayed in Scheduled Caste colonies, but preferred Backward Class (BC) houses. 'Now I understand that as a clerk in the panchayat, he wanted to be somewhere in the middle ground.' But,

> The moment I came to Central University, the first thing that struck me was that I was a reserved category student. I only knew that I was one of the four students who passed. I got a first class in Intermediate also. In [my] degree also I got good marks. At no point of time was I lesser than other people.

This is not to say there was no discrimination in the village, but it was more normalised. Satyanarayana knew where to go, where not to go—so there was some kind of a consensus, guided by his father and others, he reflects, on hindsight. 'But I felt relatively free. It was not very rigid, and you are not always identified with that. Maybe it was because my father had an important position.' But he also realises that there were subterranean discomforts and that 'my father was always trying to hide several things. Now I understand it after reading so much of Dalit writing, but at that time I didn't.'

In Central University, says Satyanarayana, you were told in different ways that you are Scheduled Caste, you are different, you are a Dalit—the star-mark against SC candidates, teachers' assumptions about students from the reserved category, their advice on whether you could do research, whether you should work for some time, whether this course was fit for you; other kinds of harassment. On the other hand, the gap between him and the metropolitan students was huge. He experienced for the first time what it meant to be a Dalit. He entered Central University with the sole aim of joining the civil services. Then, 'Mandal broke and everything changed'. He speaks about Arun Shourie's articles in *The Indian Express* opposing reservations, the suspension of classes in the university, and his gradual realisation through the pro-Mandal movement on campus that these debates were in fact about him and his entitlements to higher education. Inspired by people like K. G. Kannabiran, K. Balagopal, Varavara Rao, Bojja Tarakam, G. Haragopal, Gaddar, he gave up on the IAS. 'We kept going to their houses to talk to them. They wouldn't remember us. But they shaped our thinking and what we wanted to do.' He then made a conscious decision to take to academics after a life of activism. Tejaswini Niranjana and Susie Tharu pointed him in new directions where he could be political in academics.

His father was most unhappy with his decision to take up a lecturer's job in a university. But when the police occupied his home on 28 August, the whole university—faculty and students—stood outside his house in support, in the rain, without lunch. After 5:30 p.m., when he was permitted to go out and speak to them, people from the neighbouring houses cooked food—like in the villages—and made tea for everyone. There were about 50 people gathered and all ate together. That was very reassuring for him, and all over the world, students were writing about this. 'I wanted to tell my father now: Look at this. As an officer, I would not have got this kind of recognition.'

And yet, it was this standing that the police constantly ridiculed that day.

> They kept addressing me as "professor" all the time, but they were also insulting my position: Have you read all these books? Do you need a university like this? What is its use to society? Girl students wear short dresses—this is a campus following foreign values, and so on. The assaultive gaze was travelling from me to my university, my students, my cultural life, my values, and they wanted me to be somebody else. Initially they came for someone, but as they entered, it was very clear that they wanted to humiliate me, and they wanted to book me. My real worry is that they will frame me in [the] Bhima Koregaon case.

The police also tried hard to reduce him to his relationship to Varavara Rao, and embedded in this was the humiliation because he is a Dalit—how was it possible for him, a Dalit, to marry Pavana? But this was not the first time. Satyanarayana recalls the time in 2000 when he applied for a passport, and was told there was an adverse police report. When he approached the high court, Justice Chelameswar called for the police report. The single reason given was, 'He is Varavara Rao's son-in-law.' The court ordered the passport to be issued without delay.

In this search operation, Satyanarayana sees a larger plan to destroy the Dalit perspectives and Dalit knowledges that people like him are actually trying to create, by delegitimising, isolating, stigmatising and criminalising them. But, he is resolute: 'I will continue to teach as I used to. They cannot stop me from teaching Marx, Ambedkar, Phule. If they think by threatening me, by intimidating me, they can stop me, they are mistaken.'

Reference

Sasikumar, Neeraja. 2018. '"Persecuting the Dalit Intellectual": A Student Recounts Police Raid at Prof. Satyanarayana's House'. *Outlook*, 1 September.

43

Hate Speech and the 'Barbarity of False Equivalence'*

I don't subscribe to the view that Judges perform a divine function. To me, jettisoning the prefix "Lordship" and even "Hon'ble" is not a fetish. It is an acknowledgment *of how mortal, temporal, and, if I may venture to add,* fallible we are.

—Justice S. Muralidhar (farewell speech, Delhi High Court, 5 March 2020; emphasis mine)

To show exaggerated deference to a majoritarian Parliament when the matter is one of fundamental rights is to display judicial pusillanimity, for there is no doubt, that in the constitutional scheme, it is the judiciary that is the ultimate interpreter.

—Justice Leila Seth (quoted in *Navtej Singh Johar*, 2018)[1]

In the immediate aftermath of a horrific display of majoritarian violence in which Muslims were the primary targets (*BBC News* 2020a), oddly enough, it is judicial conduct that has come to occupy centre stage, even while the work of relief and rehabilitation proceeds apace. In one instance, we have the stellar display of courage and empathy by Justice S. Muralidhar and Justice Anup Jairam Bhambani. To quote from Justice Muralidhar's (2020) speech, '26 February 2020 was perhaps the longest working day of my life as a judge of this court. It began at 12:30 a.m. with a sitting at my residence with Justice Bhambani . . . to deal with a PIL [public interest litigation] . . . seeking safe passage for ambulances carrying the injured riot victims.' This empathy continued the following day when the solicitor general's

* Originally published as, 'To Accuse Activist Harsh Mander of Hate Speech is to Fall Prey to the Barbarity of False Equivalence', in *Scroll.in*, 17 March 2020.

I borrow the title from Mannathukkaren (2020).

callousness was confronted in open court by the judges playing videos of the hate speeches delivered by BJP leaders Kapil Mishra and Anurag Thakur (Banka 2020).

While ordinarily, the offence of incitement is made out even if it does not actually result in the violence or harm it is meant to trigger, this case was different. There was a clear and present connection between the incendiary speeches by the leaders (in the presence of uniformed police personnel [Abraham 2020]), the mass murder and destruction that followed, and the morphing of the speech into anti-Muslim war cries by a mob in a metro station in broad daylight, even while the violence was just beginning to abate (*India TV* 2020). Why were FIRs not lodged immediately, the court asked, giving 24 hours to the state to respond. In a twist, the judge's transfer was notified, and the government got four weeks to respond. When the matter of the FIRs was taken to the Supreme Court, the air was thick with the aftershocks of the violence Delhi had just experienced, as also with governmental interference with judicial functioning, which was how Justice Muralidhar's transfer was widely perceived (*BBC News* 2020b; *India Today* 2020). Most importantly, on the one hand, there was an expectation of judicial empathy from the victims' families, especially in terms of providing immediate relief, while on the other, there was a claim to impunity from those accused of incitement to violence.

Chief Justice Bobde was quoted as saying, 'We are not saying that people should die. That kind of pressure we are not equipped to handle. We cannot stop things from happening. We cannot give preventive reliefs. *We feel a kind of pressure on us*' (PTI 2020; emphasis mine). How might judges garner strength through empathy and understanding of grave harms when those who have suffered stand before them in court? Can judges afford to allow themselves to 'feel a kind of pressure'? I return to Justice Muralidhar's (2020) speech: 'I am often asked, "Are judges under pressure?" My answer to that is: Not unless they acknowledge it.' The question then is, what is the source, the root of the pressure the honourable judge feels? Might Justice Leila Seth (quoted in the epigraph) have a point?

At a critical juncture like this, in the aftermath of gruesome, unspeakable violence, and entire neighbourhoods laid waste, can the Supreme Court even afford to feel pressure? The judicial prevarication on the matter of the FIRs against Mishra and Thakur is purportedly sealed by the state producing a recording of a December 2019 speech by social activist Harsh Mander, accusing him of inciting violence in Jamia, and of criticising the court, and therefore being guilty of contempt (Tripathi 2020). On the accusation that Mander incited violence, there has been some confusion in the solicitor general's understanding of incitement. The call to reject provocation of any kind, to meet violence with non-violence, to assert the right to citizenship as a birthright and to draw strength for resistance from the Constitution (to paraphrase Mander) inflamed the passions of a ruling dispensation that has consistently undermined basic constitutional tenets. The strengthening of movements of protest against the Citizenship (Amendment) Act, 2019—a manifestly unjust legislation—by people like Mander strikes at the root of fundamentalist mobilisation on the basis of religion. That Indian Muslims, in the largest numbers, were in the leadership of this protest that was being celebrated the world over tipped the scales against the agenda of the Sangh Parivar. So, what in fact the solicitor general has admitted, is that the leaders who made inflammatory speeches saw that mass violence was the only answer to the kind of peace-work Mander and hundreds of thousands of ordinary Indians like him across the country were doing.

The question before the court (and importantly before every one of us in this country) now is: Do we stand by Mander and everyone he represents? Do we stand with those who have suffered enormously this past week in Delhi, before that in Uttar Pradesh (Citizens against Hate 2020), and before that in Assam (WSS 2019)—all on account of this one law that threatens to dispossess ordinary citizens?

While for us ordinary citizens, the time at our disposal is somewhat more lenient and not exacting, this is not the case with the court. The expectations from the Supreme Court are also of a different order, tasked as it is with the onerous responsibility of keeping the Constitution within easy reach of every citizen. The protest against the CAA is closely intertwined with the inflammatory speeches which triggered large-scale violence and continues to send tremors—the expectation therefore is that the court will act with a sense of urgency. Extraordinary times call for extraordinary remedies. The *Puttaswamy* court demonstrated that to us. Further, as a judge of the Supreme

Court has repeated ever so often, '[d]issent is the safety valve of democracy' (quoted in Ananthakrishnan 2018). An important part of dissent is the right to differ with the opinions of judges, with judicial conduct and with jurisprudence. As Justice Muralidhar states so clearly, judges, like the rest of us are not infallible. Speaking of opinions, no matter how much and how strongly we differ from the view of the court, the court cannot say in the nature of a verbal duel, that '[i]f this is what he [Mander] feels about the court, then we have to decide how to deal' (quoted in *The Free Press Journal* 2020).

Whether or not individual judges agree with my view, I have a right to civil disobedience under the Constitution, which no judge in the country, nor any government can dispossess me of. It is the foremost duty of the judge to protect my fundamental rights, especially in the face of onslaught from the government. Is that not the essence of what this very court upheld in the *Puttaswamy* case?

Note

1. Quoted in *Navtej Singh Johar*, AIR 2018 SC 4321, para. 1 (per Chandrachud, J.).

References

'Delhi Riots: City Tense after Hindu-Muslim Clashes Leave 27 Dead'. 2020a. *BBC News*, 26 February. Available at https://www.bbc.com/news/world-asia-india-51639856 (accessed 22 June 2021).

'Delhi Riots: Anger as Judge Critical of Violence Removed'. 2020b. *BBC News*, 27 February. Available at https://www.bbc.com/news/world-asia-india-51644861 (accessed 22 June 2021).

'"Desh Ke Gaddaron Ko Goli Maaro ..." Slogans Heard at Rajiv Chowk Metro Station, 6 Detained'. 2020. *India TV*, 29 February. Available at https://www.indiatvnews.com/news/india/desh-ke-gaddaron-ko-goli-maaro-slogans-heard-at-rajiv-chowk-metro-station-6-detained-593682 (accessed 24 July 2021).

'President Orders Transfer of Delhi High Court Judge Muralidhar Day after He Pulls Up Police over Violence'. 2020. *India Today*, 27 February. Available at https://www.indiatoday.in/india/story/president-orders-transfer-of-delhi-high-court-justice-muralidhar-1650395-2020-02-27 (accessed 22 June 2021).

'Who is Harsh Mander and Why is the Supreme Court Angry with Him?'. 2020. *The Free Press Journal,* 4 March. Available at https://www.freepressjournal.in/india/who-is-harsh-mander-and-why-is-the-supreme-court-angry-at-him (accessed 24 July 2021).

Abraham, Bobins. 2020. 'Delhi Police Claimed Not Having Seen Kapil Mishra's Hate Speech Video, So HC Played It for Them'. *India Times,* 26 February. Available at https://www.indiatimes.com/news/india/delhi-police-claimed-not-having-seen-kapil-mishras-hate-speech-video-so-hc-played-it-for-them-507195.html (accessed 22 June 2021).

Ananthakrishnan, G. 2018. 'Elgaar Parishad Probe: Dissent Safety Valve of Democracy, Pressure Cooker Will Burst If Not Allowed, Says SC'. *The Indian Express,* 31 August.

Banka, Richa. 2020. 'At High Court Hearing on Delhi Violence, Judges Play Kapil Mishra Video Clip'. *Hindustan Times,* 26 February.

Citizens against Hate. 2020. *'Everyone Has Been Silenced': Police Excess against Anti-CAA Protesters in Uttar Pradesh, and Post-Violence Reprisal.* Available at https://citizensagainsthate.org/wp-content/uploads/2020/03/Citizens-Against-Hate-Everyone-Has-Been-Silenced.pdf (accessed 14 June 2021).

Mannathukkaren, Nissim. 2020. 'The Barbarity of False Equivalence'. *The Wire,* 8 March. Available at https://thewire.in/communalism/delhi-riots-communalism-false-equivalence (accessed 27 August 2021).

Muralidhar, S. 2020. 'Justice Muralidhar on the Distinction between Neutrality and Impartiality'. *The Wire,* 6 March. Available at https://thewire.in/law/justice-muralidhar-farewell-speech-full (accessed 22 June 2021).

PTI. 2020. 'Delhi Riots: CJI Bobde Says SC Wishes for Peace but Aware of Its "Limitations"'. *The Wire,* 3 March. Available at https://thewire.in/law/delhi-riots-cji-bobde-says-sc-wishes-for-peace-but-aware-of-its-limitations (accessed 23 June 2021).

Tripathi, Ashish. 2020. 'Delhi Police Accuse Harsh Mander of Instigating Violence and Making Derogatory Remarks against SC'. *Deccan Herald,* 4 March.

WSS (Women against Sexual Violence and State Repression). 2019. 'Statement of Preliminary Findings of a Fact-Finding Visit to Assam on the Updating of the NRC'. *Countercurrents.org,* 27 November. Available at https://countercurrents.org/2019/11/fact-finding-report-on-the-updating-of-the-nrc-in-assam/ (accessed 23 June 2021).

IX

Professions and Civil Rights

44

Of Lawyers and the Law*

The issue of sexual harassment in the workplace is yet again at the centre of debate. This time the focus is on the legal community and on its resistance to even acknowledge the existence of the problem, leave alone the will to abide by the statutory norms laid down in *Vishaka* by the Supreme Court in 1997.[1]

Sangeeta Sharma, a young lawyer practising in Hyderabad, committed suicide on 15 June 2000. In her suicide note, she named three lawyers as being directly responsible for her death (UNI 2000). The cause: sexual harassment.

One of the lawyers named, the prime accused, is a senior lawyer who is fairly well-known. She had also, prior to her death, maintained a diary in which she had named 17 lawyers, men and women. Many lawyers are upset over these names, although her father says that Sangeeta has indicated which of these people helped her at various points. In addition, Sangeeta left behind a letter addressed to the chairman of the Bar Council of Andhra Pradesh, dated December 1999, complaining of harassment, but did not submit the letter.

In February 2000, Sangeeta brought her complaint to Asmita, a women's collective in Secunderabad (where I was involved in legal outreach and counselling), but was not willing to divulge the names of persons involved in public. Before coming to us, she had spoken about the harassment to fellow lawyers, had been asked to 'forget it' by the relatively senior men and had received support from a few women. This was not the first time we had received a complaint from a woman lawyer. Slander and character assassination have been experiences too common to complain against. And it was the same problem yet again. The women who brought the complaints were unwilling to divulge names or were unprepared to fight the issue publicly.

---

* Originally published in *The Hindu*, 9 July 2000.

We then sent a letter to the chairman of the Bar Council of Andhra Pradesh, which said that in the light of the frequency of complaints, the seriousness of the issue and the Supreme Court decision, the code of conduct of lawyers ought to be amended to specifically include sexual harassment within the definition of gross misconduct, and mechanisms set up for dealing with cases, according to the procedure and modalities laid down by the Supreme Court in the *Vishaka* case. We did not receive any response. When we reminded the chairman of the Bar Council of our earlier complaint after Sangeeta's death, we received a reply which said that sexual harassment would fall under the general definition of professional misconduct or any other misconduct. And that we would need to approach the Bar Council of India for a change in the statute or for any specific changes.

Meanwhile, the investigation into the allegations made by Sangeeta was in progress. According to press reports, two people named in the suicide note were arrested and the third, the main accused, had absconded. On 21 June 2000, a senior lawyer appearing for the accused moved the high court and obtained a stay on investigations, which to date has not been vacated. This is unfortunate, because adjournment, whether on counsel's request or resulting from the court's management of work, has always been an impediment to justice. Further, without going into the merits of the case, however arbitrary a claim or an accusation, no conclusion can be reached before the investigation is completed. And courts, over the past 50 years since Independence, surely have to their credit several decisions that block litigation of this kind, whose purpose is to stall investigation, a possible consequence being the watering down of evidence.

Asmita immediately petitioned the National Human Rights Commission and the National Commission for Women (NCW) to intervene in the matter and ensure the progress of investigation, sending them press clippings and details of the case. The NCW responded immediately, with member Shantha Reddy coming to Hyderabad and conducting an enquiry both on the incident and the general issue of sexual harassment in the premises of the High Court of Andhra Pradesh (*The Hindu* 2000). She also met with various women's groups and human rights groups in the city and visited Sangeeta's family.[2]

Lawyers feel cornered and clearly uncomfortable with being in the glare of adverse publicity. There is, as a consequence, a concerted attempt to police women who are willing to speak about the problem, or those who see that there is a problem. The argument is that this is an internal matter that concerns the profession and must not be discussed in public. It is something that must be 'managed' from within.

On another track is the assertion that Sangeeta was of 'unsound mind', which is why she committed suicide. She lacked courage. There are any number of women who have worked with the person she has named 15 years ago and vociferously vouch for his good conduct. There are other accounts that men in the profession give most readily about how this is really a 'woman's problem' (although 'problem' does not adequately capture the nuances of the Telugu word '*godava*'), because some women, apparently, were going around talking about how beautiful they were and yet this person did not so much as make a pass at them—why would he do it to someone as nondescript as Sangeeta? With a postscript: See how silly these women are. There are yet others, 'progressive' lawyers, who whisper between cases: 'Was she beautiful?'

While there are mixed reactions to this entire episode, and the usual slandering and character assassination of Sangeeta by many of her fellow lawyers, some women lawyers too, there are several crucial questions that must be addressed now.

We have been arguing since the early 1980s that the family is no longer a 'private space' outside the reach of the rule of law, evident in feminist campaigns against family violence. Violence, murder (as in the cases of dowry and sati), abetment to suicide, are all matters that are no longer private or internal matters of families. They are criminal offences, which will be investigated and adjudicated in the courts of law, in accordance with due process, so that there is an opportunity for the victim-survivors to establish and prove guilt. In this context, where does the argument that complaints of a criminal nature between members of the legal community are 'internal to the community' stand?

Our experience as women in India has been that the incidence of violence against women (sexual harassment is a form of violence) has been highest in closed spaces. Sexual harassment is particularly high in university campuses, and in professions like the legal profession, to name a few. Each of these spaces has a clearly hierarchical structure in which those in subordinate positions are directly dependant for survival and largesse on those above them, and resistance results directly in the cutting off of survival options. In the university system, harassment is particularly high in the science departments (although it is a cause for concern in the arts and humanities as well), where there is an almost total dependence of research students on their supervisors. This was an observation that was made forcefully by several participants at the National Consultation on Sexual Harassment on University Campuses organised in the Central University of Hyderabad in January 1999 (Indian Association of Women's Studies and University of Hyderabad 1999).

Why is harassment in the legal profession so high and so difficult to speak about? A survey by some law students, of problems faced by women lawyers, about a year and a half ago, elicited a standard response from women lawyers to several questions: 'No comment.' Several have said in private conversation that not only would they be thrown out of the office they were working in if they were to complain about harassment or make an issue of it, but also word would go around that they have created trouble. Silence and tolerance of abuse is the price women pay for apprenticeship.

Come to think of it, being in a profession for women then is not very different from being in marriage, in a family, in a community. As long as things are smooth, as long as women conform and are acquiescent, there is no problem. Even if you do not submit, if you are silent about the pressure on you or someone you know, you are safe. 'No comment' then, is an important strategy for survival. Interestingly, there is a clear divergence between the views of junior women lawyers and seniors. In the depositions before the NCW member, chaos broke out when juniors asserted the existence of sexual harassment while seniors denied it. An easy and complacent explanation that men often give each other is that women are after all their own worst enemies. The present instance has been no exception.

In the course of defending the person accused of harassing Sangeeta, his supporters have said that Sangeeta was of 'unsound mind'. This is a familiar plea taken in almost all dowry death cases. Two questions immediately come to my mind. What proof is there of the fact that Sangeeta was 'mentally unsound', considering that the presumption in law is of soundness of mind, with the contrary requiring proof? And, if she was, does that automatically disqualify her from bringing a charge of sexual harassment? Further, does this imply that women who are of 'unsound mind' cannot be sexually harassed? What is clear is that whether or not Sangeeta was mentally sound, she was consistent in her complaint of sexual harassment over a period of a year, and she was consistent in fixing responsibility. That, presumably, is sufficient grounds for investigation. The accusation of insanity is an instrument of social control. In the present instance, it is one important way of policing women into silence.

To come to the next question. The legal profession, like every other profession, perhaps far more than any other profession, mirrors the cleavages, fissures and conflicts in society. Caste and community are important markers. These were not absent in the issues surrounding Sangeeta's suicide. One of the first issues that was raised by several lawyers was that this is an attempt by a Brahmin woman to take her revenge on a 'lower caste' man. This track had to be abandoned almost immediately because the person who took up the case on behalf of Sangeeta's family is a well-known and respected Dalit intellectual and activist, while the lawyer for the defendant is an equally well-known dominant caste lawyer. Just this presents to us significant intersections of caste, gender and power. But that apart, the fact that a charge of vindictiveness arising from caste was made alone is enough to tell us that the legal profession is not one homogenous, unitary, internally coherent, consensual 'community'. Add to this the fact that although women qualify in equal proportions to men at the entry point of professional courses (this is particularly true of the premier institutions imparting legal education in the country today), there is a progressive decline in the number of women as one moves up the hierarchy. Parallel to this is the progressive decline of professionals as one moves down in the caste hierarchy. Is it unreasonable then to say that the social profile of the self-appointed guardians of honour in the legal profession is predetermined, far from representative, and their capacity to deliver justice is severely prejudiced to begin with? Differences of interest (particularly political), power, caste, community, gender and a contestation for power along each of these lines will determine whose interests will be 'managed', and by whom, when a complaint of sexual harassment is brought before a community that believes it can govern itself.

Finally, all these arguments are, after a point, irrelevant. The Supreme Court, after careful consideration and protracted deliberations, in *Vishaka*, reached the conclusion way back in 1997 that

> in the absence of enacted law to provide for the effective enforcement of the basic human right of gender equality and guarantee against sexual harassment and abuse, particularly against sexual harassment at work places, we lay down the guidelines and norms specified hereinafter for due observance at all work places and other institutions, until a legislation is enacted for the purpose. This is done in exercise of the power available under Article 32 of the Constitution for the enforcement of the fundamental rights and it is further emphasised that this would be treated as the law declared by this Court under Article 141 of the Constitution.[3]

Can the Bar Council of India and the All India Bar Association please take steps to ensure that the legal profession abides by the law of the land? The first and most urgent step being the amendment of the statute with reference to the code of conduct and devising formal mechanisms to deal with complaints and their formal adoption by all branches and units across the country.

Notes

1. Vishaka & Ors v. State of Rajasthan & Ors, AIR 1997 SC 3011.
2. See Sexual Harassment in the Work Place and Suicide of Sangeeta Sharma, Advocate: Andhra Pradesh, Case No. 203/1/2000–2001, National Human Rights Commission (NHRC).
3. *Vishaka*, AIR 1997 SC 3011.

References

'Women Advocates Depose before NCW'. 2000. *The Hindu,* 27 June.

Indian Association for Women's Studies and Human Rights Programme, University of Hyderabad. 1999. *National Consultation on Sexual Harassment on University Campuses.*

UNI (United News of India). 2000. 'Woman Lawyer's Suicide: NCW for CBI Probe'. *The Tribune,* 9 July.

45

Lawyer, Judge and *Aam Aadmi**

First it was Rupan Bajaj from Punjab,[1] then Nalini Netto in Kerala (*Outlook* 2008)—and we learnt that senior women civil servants are as vulnerable to sexual harassment as ordinary women in ordinary workplaces. Also, that nothing separates top cops and ministers from the common man, save the assumption of impunity by the former. Women blew the lid on male impunity, rupturing it in ways that sent waves of shock down the habitations of the common man—'It somehow makes the law of the land look grotesquely odd and incongruous that a man who has done signal service to the country by ridding a state of the dread and oppression of terrorism should have to spend five months in jail for a minute's exuberance provoked by the charms of an attractive working woman,' was the way K. P. S. Gill's misdemeanours were described (*Deccan Chronicle* 1996). And women, of course, are expected to cultivate 'finely tuned, discreet social mechanisms for coping with importunate intrusions on the individual body' (Dasgupta 1996). This was followed by Bhanwari Devi's memorable but distressing struggle against the assault by upper caste landlords, which resulted in the *Vishaka* judgement of the Supreme Court: Justice Verma's court ruled against sexual harassment in the workplace, setting out guidelines for all workplaces and mandating that protections be put in place.[2] This was the year 1997.

While the progress was uneven, workplaces across the country witnessed some rumbling in the redrawing of the norms of appropriate cross-gender conduct. Women were able, with some measure of success, though far from adequate, to push the common man to conform to behaviour in workplaces that did not constitute an infringement of the bodily integrity and dignity of their women colleagues.

---

* Originally published in *The Hindu*, 18 January 2014.

Impervious to Change

In the decade and a half that this churning has been under way, however, courts themselves have been impervious to change. The situation is indeed peculiar. While ruling that sexual harassment constitutes an infringement of the constitutional right to dignity and comes within the meaning of discrimination based on sex, the justice pyramid across the country stands apart as the exception to this standard. Without going into how pervasive practices of sexual harassment are in judicial spaces—that is, the spaces of the bar and the bench—we could pose an even more basic question: If it is mandatory, according to a Supreme Court ruling, that sexual harassment constitutes a specific kind of misconduct which must be dealt with in a specific manner, why has it not been made mandatory for all courts, the Bar Council and bar associations to constitute complaints committees to create the possibility of redress for women who might need it? These women could be litigants, workers in court premises, clerical staff, advocates and judges. Curiously, the judiciary is befuddled by the problem to which it crafted a solution—it has no language or procedure that will kick in the minute a complaint is made.

The recent complaints are not the first complaints women have ever had. These are only the first that have been spoken about. To their credit, these young women are laying down the non-negotiable in no uncertain terms. It is true that we cannot judge anyone (even less a judge) before a transparent and fair enquiry is conducted. Hearing one complaint in a closed, closely-guarded proceeding, the apex court hastens to decide that no further complaints of this nature will be heard. Why?

The trouble does not stop there. The legal profession itself takes its cue from this construction of the exception by the bench. Lawyers are practitioners who do not need to fall in line with the norms they might seek for their clients. Every day, accounts from women in the legal practice speak of how hostile court environments are for women. It is not uncommon to see bar association halls treated as spaces that men will occupy. Women are relegated to the women's bar association room, which, in some cases, is even veiled with a soiled curtain or may be consigned to the deepest and darkest crevices of court complexes.

We can scarcely forget that these are professional spaces that must nurture deliberations on the Constitution and a sense of justice.

Recent incidents in the Calicut Bar Association, reported on social media, crystallise this issue further (Binduraj 2014). If a woman working in the courts—in whatever capacity—finds men's modes of address and behaviour sexist and objectionable (which often they are, truth be told), surely, she has the right to speak her mind. Not just on her blog, but in the bar association hall. Yet, a remark by a woman lawyer on her blog that male colleagues habitually use unacceptable modes of address in speaking to women leads to her suspension from the association after a general body meeting. What is the writ of the bar association? Is it to nurture an environment where advocates are required to conform to the spirit of the Constitution (constitutional morality) or is it to enforce the morality of the mob on the street (public morality)? Should lawyers vote on a sense of justice or should they vote to reinforce the dominance of the pack?

This brings me to my final point. Unless the legal profession and courts restructure themselves in tune with constitutional principles, they will continue to present 'hostile environments' to women as defined by the decision of the Supreme Court in *Vishaka*,[3] a verdict now enshrined in the legislation.

Gender Composition

The numbers only precipitate matters further. Is there a connection between the prevarication of the Supreme Court in the matter of complaints against members of the bench and its gender composition—the fact that the bench comprises almost entirely of 'brother judges' (with negligible exceptions that do not add up)? Is there a gender-appropriate language to refer to women on the bench that recognises their centrality, their competence and their gender? Can we draw a connection likewise between the decision of the full general body of a bar association to suspend a woman who spoke her mind and the fact that the bar association is ruled and constituted by men—the women being mere spectators with no voice or effective vote?

It is time for a cultural transformation in the gender politics of the justice pyramid. It is time for the Supreme Court to redraw the circle of regulated conduct that conforms to the constitutional norm and situate itself within. That is the only justiciable route, as fundamental rights under the Constitution are.

Notes

1. Rupan Deol Bajaj & Anr v. Kanwar Pal Singh Gill & Anr, (1995) 6 SCC 194.
2. *Vishaka*, AIR 1997 SC 3011.
3. Ibid.

References

'Editorial'. 1996. *Deccan Chronicle*, 8 August.

'Ex-Minister Nadar Acquitted in Sexual Harassment Case'. 2008. *Outlook*, 22 July.

Binduraj, J. 2014. 'Bar Association Suspends Kerala Woman Lawyer for FB Comment on Male Lawyers' "Silly Behaviour"'. *India Today*, 2 January. Available at https://www.indiatoday.in/india/south/story/bar-association-suspends-woman-lawyer-for-fb-comment-on-male-lawyers-silly-behaviour-160830-2014-01-02 (accessed 24 July 2021).

Dasgupta, Swapan. 1996. 'Enter Sexual Harassment: Awaiting the Feminist Inquisition'. *The Indian Express*, 10 August.

46

When Professional Associations Start Promoting Narrow, Sectarian Agendas*

Everyone has the right to freedom of opinion and expression; this right includes freedom to hold opinions without interference and to seek, receive and impart information and ideas through any media and regardless of frontiers.

—Article 19 of the Universal Declaration of Human Rights (1948)[1]

In the time since the attacks on students of the Ambedkar Students' Association in the University of Hyderabad and the death of Rohith Vemula—and earlier in the year, in other institutions like the Indian Institute of Technology, Madras, with the Ambedkar Periyar Study Circle (Rajagopal 2015), and now in Jawaharlal Nehru University (JNU)—we have been forced to think afresh on the question of associational freedoms within educational institutions, especially where it has involved the right of students to free speech and expression, and to organise.

What we need to bring forward in the debate is the democratic exercise of associational freedoms by the membership of professional associations in order to defeat the appropriation of these associations by apologists for the mobs that we encounter round every corner today. This is especially critical in an environment of anti-intellectualism, and majoritarian attacks on individual and collective attempts at informed debate and social critique, both within and outside institutions of higher education. The anticipation of violence and the fear of anticipated attacks have served to police the most aware and articulate into compliance, with institutions withdrawing invitations to speakers who might be controversial (what is not controversial

* Originally published in *The Wire*, 2 March 2016.

today, we might ask) and withdrawing permissions for speaking and performance events. There are a host of others that retreat into silence, hoping and waiting for the moment to pass.

In the weeks since Kanhaiya Kumar was arrested (Shankar 2016), we have heard accounts of two membership-based associations: The first on 19 February 2016, when Kanhaiya was to be produced in court, 'Delhi Police had held a series of meetings with local members of the Bar Association [of the Patiala House Court] to ensure "orderliness" in court that day' (Singh 2016). We have several eyewitness accounts and self-congratulatory admissions by a large section of lawyers, in their professional habits, of physical and verbal violence, of menacing behaviour that day, against what they called 'anti-national' elements (*India Today* 2016). The police deployed there were under instructions to exercise restraint in quelling mob violence. No arrests were made although a person in custody was assaulted in the premises of a court. There was also a widely covered march of lawyers in professional garb from this court against 'anti-national elements' (*Hindustan Times* 2016). The New Delhi Bar Association that functions from the Patiala House Court has not denied that these lawyers were members of the association.

The national president and honorary secretary general of the Indian Medical Association (IMA), on 24 February, sent a letter to the home minister, Rajnath Singh, which began with the following words: 'We the Indian Medical Association, of over 2.6 lac members condemn anti national incident taken place recently at JNU.' It goes on to appeal to the government to take strict and necessary actions against any persons or organisations or groups carrying out 'any anti national protests, speeches, debates or writings in the country'. While appealing to the government to conduct fair and free investigations, it also asserts that 'culprits should be punished as early as possible ... so that in future no one can dare to do anti national activities in the country'. What is of utmost significance in this letter is the assurance that 'the 2.6 lac members of the IMA together wholeheartedly extend our support to the government in this matter' (quoted in Narayanan 2016).

Although we also have the case of the Indian Science Congress Association, which earned fame when the 102nd Congress in January

2015 in Mumbai witnessed in silent acquiescence speeches on ancient Indian aviation technology (Rao 2015), this falls in a different category because it is an association set up under the aegis of the government of India. It is, in that sense, not an independent professional association like the others mentioned here. However, the question of why professional scientists fell in line so easily is one that we have no answers to. Or perhaps we do—we have the history of the Association of Scientific Workers of India (ASWI), a trade union established in 1946 with Jawaharlal Nehru as its president. In the words of Pushpa M. Bhargava (2015), one of the founders of the association,

> One of the objectives of ASWI was to propagate scientific temper. It was very active in the beginning, but fizzled out by the 1960s as the bulk of scientists in the country, including many who were occupying high positions, were themselves not committed to scientific temper which calls for rationality, reason and lack of belief in any dogma, superstition or manifest falsehood.

On 24 February, Rajesh Misra, professor of sociology at University of Lucknow, was attacked on campus, with his effigy being burnt outside the department by students belonging to the ABVP (Daniyal 2016). The reason: Misra's support of an article that spoke with pride about Umar Khalid, one of the JNU students under arrest. As a life member of the International Sociological Society, it is important for the society to issue an unequivocal statement in support of Misra.

We have had intellectuals, scientists, sociologists, social scientists, doctors, writers, creative and performing artists, and others band together in protest in the past months. There have been statements circulating online for signatures and several submitted to the president, vice-chancellors and other figures of authority in the hope that the tide will turn in favour of dissent, diversity and dignity through this coming together. It must.

This still leaves unaddressed the other side of the exercise of associational freedoms.

Let us take a brief look at the mission statements of some of these bodies that we constitute as members, even if we are paying but passive members.

Important among the objectives of the Bar Association of India (n.d.) are the following:

- To uphold the Constitution of India, and the representative, free and democratic form of Government and to uphold and promote the Rule of Law;
- To uphold the honour, the dignity and the independence of the Bar and the profession of law;
- To assist the Bar in upholding its rights and dignity in its relations with the executive and the judiciary;
- To apply the knowledge and the experience in the field of law to the promotion of the public good.

Even more significantly, it is committed to building the strengths of the 'legal fraternity' and 'lawyer community'.

The Indian Medical Association, its website declares, 'is the only representative, national voluntary organisation of Doctors of Modern Scientific System of Medicine'. It has three objectives:

- To promote and advance medical and allied sciences in all their different branches and to promote the improvement of public health and medical education in India;
- To maintain the honour and dignity and to uphold the interest of the medical profession and to promote co-operation amongst the members thereof;
- To work for the abolition of compartmentalism in medical education, medical services and registration in the country and this to achieve equality among all members of the profession.

The delineation of the roles and responsibilities of office-bearers of the IMA does not authorise elected representatives to issue statements in the name of IMA in matters not directly connected with medical practice and public health. Clearly, therefore, the president and honorary secretary general acted in excess of their powers and in the name of the entire membership, when there was no discussion or national vote on whether the IMA should intervene in the events unfolding at JNU.

The Indian Sociological Society is a membership-based national association of professional sociologists—teachers, students and researchers—and its primary activity is to provide a forum for sociological discussion and debate through organising meetings and conferences across the country. Sociology as a discipline is meant to foster critical traditions and defend diverse opinions in the classroom and outside. A life member of the society, Misra is attacked for his views and is asked by the university to explain his 'stand on the controversy' (Seth 2016).

What is the responsibility of the membership of professional associations in calling their elected representatives or offending members to account? Is it enough for us to sit back and say, 'But we were not consulted'? Is it enough for us to come together as independent doctors, lawyers, scientists, sociologists or other professionals and make condemnatory statements? Or is it time to go beyond that and act in the name of the associations of which we are part, insisting that there is a contrary view that must be represented and debated by members who wish to do so. It is possible that this move would also strengthen the possibly paper-thin minority within any of these elected bodies so that they do not feel compelled to swim with the tide.

The question before us is simple, really. This is not a case for being allowed to exercise the right to freedom of association as in the case of students who are barred from forming unions or organising events, especially when such events or groups espouse views contrary to parties and governments in power. This is a question of our inability as professional sociologists, lawyers, doctors, scientists to call the office-bearers of our associations to account and our collective failure to resist the appropriation of associational spaces in the name of patriotism and a narrow, sectarian nationalism that promotes hate and intolerance. It is also our (perhaps unintended) acquiescence to the conspiracy of silence and compliance that is creeping across our professional and institutional worlds leaving us no space except the street (which is also manifestly unsafe) to speak out our politics.

We can scarcely forget that these professional associations and the periodic professional events they organise serve an important pedagogic purpose and are the learning ground for students in higher education: they present forums for debate on questions ranging from the meanings of nationalism and the Constitution to the scientific temper, the purpose of scientific endeavour, questions of human dignity and beyond. We have before us the stunning example of the

JNU Teachers' Association in close solidarity with different students' organisations in JNU enabling an unprecedented cascading of resistance across the country and beyond. Perhaps it is time to wrest control over these associational spaces and redefine their purpose in full and responsible exercise of our associational freedoms to promote peaceful non-cooperation and ethical dissent.

Note

1. Universal Declaration of Human Rights, GA Res. 217 (III) A, at 71 (10 December 1948), art. 19.

References

'JNU Crackdown: Lawyers Beat Up Journalists as Student Leader Kanhaiya is Produced in Court'. 2016. *India Today*, 15 February. Available at https://www.indiatoday.in/india/story/jnu-row-bigafzalfight-jnusu-president-kanhaiya-kumar-latest-updates-308812-2016-02-15 (accessed 26 June 2021).

'Lawyers Take Out Protest March in Delhi against "Anti-nationals"'. 2016. *Hindustan Times*, 19 February.

Bar Association of India. n.d. 'Introduction'. Available at http://baoi.50webs.com/Bar_Association_of_India/Welcome.html (accessed 26 June 2021).

Bhargava, Pushpa M. 2015. 'Scientists without a Scientific Temper'. 2015. *The Hindu*, 17 January.

Daniyal, Shoaib. 2016. '"This is Worse Than the Emergency": Lucknow Professor Targeted for Sharing Article on Umar Khalid'. *Scroll.in*, 27 February. Available at https://scroll.in/article/804253/this-is-worse-than-the-emergency-lucknow-professor-targeted-for-sharing-article-on-umar-khalid (accessed 26 June 2021).

Indian Medical Association. n.d. 'About IMA'. Available at https://www.ima-india.org/ima/free-way-page.php?pid=2 (accessed 26 June 2021).

Narayanan, Nayantara. 2016. 'Doctors Protest as Indian Medical Association Writes Letter Supporting Centre against "Anti-nationals"'. *Scroll.in*, 25 February. Available at https://scroll.in/article/804198/doctors-object-to-indian-medical-association-letter-supporting-centre-against-anti-nationals (accessed 26 June 2021).

Rajagopal, Divya. 2015. 'After IIT Madras Ban, Ambedkar-Periyar Study Circle Spreads to Other Campuses'. *The Economic Times*, 3 June. Available at https://economictimes.indiatimes.com/industry/services/education/after-iit-madras-ban-ambedkar-periyar-study-circle-spreads-to-other-campuses/articleshow/47501675.cms?from=mdr (accessed 17 September 2021).

Rao, Yogita. 2015. 'Heard at Science Meet: Ancient Indian Planes Flew to Planets'. *The Times of India*, 5 January.

Seth, Maulshree. 2016. 'Sharing Article on Umar Khalid: Lucknow University Seeks Explanation, Prof. Says He Liked Idea'. *The Indian Express*, 26 February.

Shankar, Aranya. 2016. 'JNU Student Leader Held on "Sedition" Charges over Afzal Guru Event'. *The Indian Express*, 13 February.

Singh, Alok. 2016. 'Patiala House Assault Case: Bar Assured Order in Court, Lawyers Went Back on Word, Says Police'. *Indian Express*, 19 February.

X

Judges are Equal Citizens

47

Parables of Justice and Women Therein*

The decision of the special court, on 31 August 2012, convicting Maya Kodnani, Babu Bajrangi and 29 others for perpetrating grave mass crimes against Muslims in Naroda Patiya (Gardiner and Kumar 2012) is a source of reassurance and restoration for the families of the victims, their neighbourhoods and communities, and to the larger community committed to a just social order in this country. It has been long in coming. The suffering and humiliation of the survivors has been painful to them and to those who have stood by them and for them. Their courage profound. But despite the long night, the judgement restores our conviction that against all odds, the sun will rise and we can continue to persevere to make the system work for the cause of justice.

Almost all reports of this judgement in the press have highlighted the fact that a 'woman judge' delivered it, not just a judge. We have had several milestones in the jurisprudence on sex discrimination in India, where women have wrested spaces at work, in the family, in the education system, in the labour market, as survivors in the criminal justice system, and in public employment, that were previously unavailable to them. These were cases women brought to court—a few represented by women lawyers, but for the most part, represented by 'men advocates' and decided by 'men judges'—good ones, of course. Despite jurisprudential gains then, the legal profession itself has been, for the most part, unwelcoming of women as lawyers, in judicial services and the judiciary, to put it mildly.

Given this larger context, the judgement of the Gujarat special court, delivered by Judge Jyotsna Yagnik, provides an opportunity to recall the enormous odds against which a miniscule number of

* Unpublished essay, 2012.

women in the judiciary and judicial services have managed to forge a critical space for justice through decisions that have been milestones in human rights advocacy in recent times. Without essentialising the contribution of these women 'as women', and without making sweeping generalisations that all women will be just and incorruptible, the attempt here is to point out that the neglect of due diligence in ensuring an adequate presence of women in the judiciary is based on a general bias against women's capabilities and is unsubstantiated.

For the present, we may look at four cases together: The first is the Premananda case in the Pudukkottai Sessions Court, Tamil Nadu, that looked at aggravated mass sexual assault, wrongful confinement and criminal intimidation.[1] Premananda was the founder of the Premananda Ashram in Pudukkottai district of Tamil Nadu, set up in 1989 with the ostensible purpose of providing shelter and care to women and children, mostly Tamil refugees from Sri Lanka. Most of the ashram inmates, numbering approximately 200 young men and 'grown up girls', were Sri Lankan nationals. In 1997, the court of sessions in Pudukkottai, presided over by Judge R. Banumathi, found Premananda and six of his associates guilty of deceiving believers by claiming magical powers and misusing the belief reposed in him by disciples, cheating them and sexually assaulting several young women residents of the ashram, assaulting and murdering a male inmate and arranging forced abortions of several women who had been so assaulted between the years 1990 and 1994 (Subramanian 2003; for a discussion of the case, see Kannabiran 2012: 400–05). One of the seven accused was a woman, all the rest were men.

The second case was the custodial death of Budhan Sabar, who belonged to a Denotified Tribe in West Bengal. The accusation of petty theft, his arrest, remand, torture and death in prison were typical of the routine treatment meted out to the entire community of Kheria Sabars (Devi 2007). In 1998, the Calcutta High Court, through Justice Ruma Pal, found the police and jail officers guilty of torture in custody leading to death. The court also found several procedural irregularities in investigation and during arrest, after a second post-mortem ordered by the Calcutta High Court revealed injuries that negated the claim of the jail authorities that Budhan had committed suicide by hanging. The state was directed to pay compensation of one lakh rupees to Budhan's family and was directed to initiate action against the guilty officers.[2]

The third case is the massacre of Dalits in Chunduru in Andhra Pradesh (APCLC 1991). Judge S. Anees sentenced 21 persons to life imprisonment, and found 56 persons guilty. The judgement, in 2007, was delivered 16 years after the attack—the first major case in Andhra Pradesh to be brought under the Scheduled Castes and the Scheduled Tribes (Prevention of Atrocities) Act, 1989.[3]

The fourth case, the most recent, is the judgement delivered by Judge Jyotsna Yagnik in the Naroda Patiya massacre case of 2002 (Gardiner and Kumar 2012).

Each of these four cases have involved a persistent, sustained effort by groups committed to the protection of civil liberties—Mahasweta Devi and the Paschim Banga Kheria Sabar Kalyan Samity in the case of Budhan Sabar, the All India Democratic Women's Association and human rights groups in the Premananda case, the Dalit Mahasabha and human rights advocates in the Chunduru case, and a coalition of citizens' groups and civil rights advocates, led by Citizens for Justice and Peace, in the Naroda Patiya case. This effort was possible because of the determination and courage of the survivors.

The combination of these aspects has not however led to victories each time an atrocity has taken place in this country. And there are too many in which gross injustice has been meted out by the judiciary.

In contrast, in these four cases, a dispassionate judiciary committed to the rule of law was what tilted the balance towards justice. These were four women, all judges. The cases involved hate crimes against Muslims, Dalits and Adivasi; sexual assault as part of hate crimes against religious minorities; sexual assault of minor girls in a custodial facility; and mass murder, atrocity and democide against Dalits and Muslims. The task of holding the scales of justice unwaveringly cannot get tougher than this, nor can the application of the judicial mind. While the judge ordered a second post-mortem and directed the state to pay compensation for custodial death in one case; another involved a judge slapping a charge of cheating on the assaulter-godman, after a magician proved in court that tricks have little to do with spirituality; while the other two pronounced guilt and conviction, steering clear of the death penalty.

Clearly then, there is neither a shortfall of capability, nor importantly, a shortfall of victim-survivors who need the scales to tilt in their favour. How much longer can we pretend we just don't see?

Notes

1. Sessions Case No. 7/1996, decided on 20 August 1997 (Pudukkottai Sessions Court). Confirmed in Chandradevi & Ors v. State of Tamil Nadu, MANU/TN/2335/2002 [CA Nos 895, 896 and 897 of 1997 & Cr. MP Nos 780 to 782 of 1998, decided on 12 December 2002 (Mad. HC)]. Also confirmed in Kamalanantha & Ors v. State of Tamil Nadu, AIR 2005 SC 2132, decided on 5 April 2005 (SC).
2. Paschim Banga Kheria Sabar Kalyan Samity v. State of West Bengal & Ors, WP No. 3715 of 1998, decided on 6 July 1998 (Cal. HC).
3. State (Sub-divisional Police Officer, Tenali) v. Modugula Sambi Reddi & 218 Others, Sessions Case No. 36/1993, decided on 31 July 2007 (Court of Special Sessions Judge-cum-IV Additional Sessions Judge, Guntur).

References

APCLC (Andhra Pradesh Civil Liberties Committee). 1991. *The Chundur Carnage.*

Devi, Mahasweta. 2007. 'Hated, Humiliated, Butchered'. *Tehelka,* 12 October.

Gardiner, Harris and Hari Kumar. 2012. 'Stiff Sentence for Former Gujarat Minister'. *The New York Times,* 31 August.

Kannabiran, Kalpana. 2012. *Tools of Justice: Non-discrimination and the Indian Constitution.* New Delhi: Routledge.

Subramanian, T. S. 2003. 'A Sentence Upheld'. *Frontline,* 3 January.

48

Privacy, Sequestered Courts and the Place of Dissent*

Those of us who follow developments in constitutional courts suffered a high intensity shock on 12 January 2018, when four senior judges of the Supreme Court of India walked out of the sequestered environs of the court and exercised their fundamental right to dissent at a press conference (PTI 2018). Their collective statement was simple, free of any ambiguities, and easy to grasp by anyone who cared to listen. As an ordinary citizen who does not professionally inhabit either courtrooms or the media, what are the questions this event raises for me? This is not really about the protocols of right and wrong in the act of judicial disclosure, but what connections the disclosure signals to me between courts, politics and citizenship.

The starting point, and one of immense significance, is that in speaking out and speaking truth to power (certainly placing their own interests—personal and professional—at risk), the four judges were dismantling the fundamental architecture that had contained (and protected) the judiciary and placed it outside constitutional scrutiny till that point. So it is a significant and historic break with the past—a necessary one too. While administering the Constitution, and being its custodian, the constitutional judiciary has enjoyed the privilege of exception from the norms that govern the larger citizenry in relation to the Constitution. While this is invisible at all times, when an 'unprecedented' crisis precipitates, the rupture of this exceptionalism is the biggest shock. But it is necessary—not just as the 'discharge of

* Originally published in *The Wire*, 16 January 2018.

a debt to the nation' (Justice Gogoi) or to save themselves the future accusation that they have 'sold their souls' (Justice Chelameswar) (quoted in *Scroll.in* 2018), but to democratise the institutions of constitutional courts and to open the doors to a possibility of a more egalitarian constitutional culture, in the true spirit of the Preamble: 'We the People of India ... do hereby Adopt, Enact and Give to ourselves this Constitution.' Extending this, we could also read this gesture as an assertion that there is no relationship of superiority or inferiority between judges *inter se* (not just within the Supreme Court but at all levels, hierarchies of jurisdiction notwithstanding) and between judges and lay citizens. Judges are only the first among equals in this country.

The recent judgement of the Supreme Court of India in *Puttaswamy* provided us with a renewed sensibility of dignity, dissent, and speech—also of the constitutional value of silences in the constitutional scheme. One of the judges speaking to the press on 12 January—Justice Chelameswar—was an author of this judgement. In speaking of statute, and the Constitution in particular, he observes forcefully that:

> [i]mplications are logical extensions of stipulations in the express language of the statute and arise only when a statute is silent on certain aspects. Implications are the product of the interpretative process, of silences of a Statute.... The implications arising from the scheme of the Constitution are "Constitution's dark matter" and are as important as the express stipulations in its text.[1]

In the absence of any specification or anticipation of the situations leading up to the event of 12 January within the constitutional scheme, the only course open before the four judges was to plumb the depths of their knowledge on the 'four corners' of the Constitution,[2] and unearth the embedded 'dark matter'[3] that is implicit in and belongs within the boundaries drawn by these four corners. In doing this, they redraw the boundaries of courts, by removing the judiciary from a sequestered existence above scrutiny, bringing citizens into the sphere of judicial accountability in seminal ways. Whether, how long and how well we will be able to remain in deliberative dialogue is of course a big question—especially since the dominant environment seems to be one that is forcing a closing of ranks in the legal fraternity.

A second point of immense relevance in the privacy judgement of the Supreme Court is Justice Nariman's observations on the 'Three Great Dissents'. He begins his discussion on the dissents with a quotation from Charles Evans Hughes, before he became the chief justice of the United States of America: 'A dissent in a court of last resort is an appeal to the brooding spirit of the law, to the intelligence of a future day, when a later decision may possibly correct the error into which the dissenting judge believes the court to have been betrayed.'[4] The dissents he speaks of are spread out 12–14 years apart: Justice Fazl Ali in *A. K. Gopalan*, 1950,[5] Justice Subba Rao in *Kharak Singh*, 1964,[6] and Justice Khanna in *ADM Jabalpur*, 1976.[7]

In discussing these cases at length, Justice Nariman observes that at a time when the Supreme Court of India construed Article 21 rather narrowly, 'there were Judges who had vision and dissented from their colleagues',[8] with foresight 'that simply takes our breath away'.[9] Justice Chandrachud is even more vocal in his celebration of dissent and his castigation of the majority view: 'The view taken by Justice Khanna must be accepted, and accepted with reverence for the strength of its thoughts and the courage of its convictions.'[10] And further, 'When histories of nations are written and critiqued, there are judicial decisions at the forefront of liberty. Yet others have to be consigned to the archives, reflective of what was, but should never have been.... ADM Jabalpur is ... overruled'.[11]

The celebratory reinstatement of judicial dissent on points of law may be productively extended to dissent on points of administration of courts and procedure. How can one be good and the other bad? Substantively, they speak to a space enveloped by the 'four corners of the Constitution'.[12] Nor may it be asserted, as it has been, that 21 judges have not spoken. Dissent has always been in a minority of one. And history—in the voice of the Constitution bench of this same court—has held aloft that single expression as the only correct one, against the long rule of the majority. A simple principle of political life of the citizenry applies to courtrooms too.

Finally, on the question of politics. It is naïve to believe that the national government has chosen 'not to interfere' by remaining silent. Absence of speech acts may not be presumed merely because they are not public or expressly stated. This situation is a direct consequence of two fault lines. The first is the arbitrariness in the administrative functions of courts which have had a relatively long and troubled history in India. The second, that in fact feeds on the first, is the brazen, intimidating interference of government in the business of the court, eroding thereby the fundamental principles of the independence of the judiciary. Judge Loya is at the centre of this debate and its tipping point. Not a by-product. And the case of Judge Loya (Takle 2017), together with this Great Dissent by four sitting judges of the Supreme Court is a telling comment on the imperilled status of the rights to dignity, life and liberty of the entire judiciary, from the magistracy to the apex court—core values asserted by the privacy bench.

Notes

1. *K. S. Puttaswamy*, (2017) 10 SCC 1, para. 12 (per Chelameswar, J.).
2. *Navtej Singh Johar*, AIR 2018 SC 4321, para. 4 (per Misra, J.).
3. *K. S. Puttaswamy*, (2017) 10 SCC 1, para. 12 (per Chelameswar, J.).
4. Ibid., para. 19 (per Nariman, J.).
5. A. K. Gopalan v. State of Madras, (1950) SCR 88.
6. Kharak Singh v. State of Uttar Pradesh & Ors, (1964) 1 SCR 332.
7. ADM Jabalpur, (1976) 2 SCC 521.
8. *K. S. Puttaswamy*, (2017) 10 SCC 1, para. 18 (per Nariman, J.).
9. Ibid., para. 21 (per Nariman, J.).
10. Ibid., para. 120 (per Chandrachud, J.).
11. Ibid., para. 121 (per Chandrachud, J.).
12. *Navtej Singh Johar*, AIR 2018 SC 4321, para. 4 (per Misra, J.).

References

'"Democracy is in Danger": Watch the Historic Press Conference Held by Four Supreme Court Judges'. 2018. *Scroll.in*, 13 January. Available at https://scroll.in/video/864863/democracy-is-in-danger-watch-the-historic-press-conference-held-by-four-supreme-court-judges (accessed 26 June 2021).

PTI. 2018. 'Supreme Court Crisis: All Not Okay, Democracy at Stake, Say Four Senior-Most Judges'. *Business Line*, 12 January.

Takle, Niranjan. 2017. 'A Family Breaks Its Silence: Shocking Details Emerge in Death of Judge Presiding Over Sohrabuddin Trial'. *The Caravan*, 20 November.

49

The Court is not above the Constitution*

In the midst of the political turmoil of a testing election season, a former junior court assistant at the Supreme Court sent copies of a sworn affidavit to 22 judges of the Supreme Court alleging sexual harassment by the chief justice of India (CJI) and intimidation of her family members (Yamunan and Sharma 2019). The nature of the allegations is serious, and for a lesser citizen, it would *prima facie* have set the ball rolling on investigations, enquiries and appropriate actions by duly appointed committees. The fact that this is the correct course of action need not, in this case, detract from the cardinal principle of criminal law on the burden of proof—innocent until proven guilty.

Derailing Fair Procedure

The immediate response of the secretary general of the Supreme Court to the affidavit goes along predictable lines:

> The allegations ... are completely and absolutely false and scurrilous and are totally denied.... The motive ... is obviously mischevious [*sic*].... It would be extremely relevant to mention that the concerned individal [*sic*] and her family have criminal antecedents.... It is not only mischievous but a complete afterthoght [*sic*] of her to make these false allegations at this time. In fact ... there were complaints made against her ... to the Secretary General on account of her inappropriate behavior ... Apart from the misconduct formally recorded,... there were other counts of misconduct on her part.... Its [*sic*] is also very possible that there are mischevious [*sic*] forces behind all this, with an intention to malign the institution. (Quoted in *Scroll.in* 2019a)

---

* Originally published in *The Hindu*, 23 April 2019.

In her affidavit, the complainant spoke of specific incidents, harassment of a specific nature, and against a specific person. Nothing in her sworn affidavit can, on the face of it, be construed as a general derogatory statement on the Supreme Court as an institution, nor on the general behaviour of judges of the Supreme Court. If there is an allegation against a specific person who occupies a high office, it is not an assault on the office. Construing it as such would pave the way to arbitrariness and impunity, and would undermine the Constitution that binds the court in irredeemable ways. On the other hand, it is possible that a thorough, impartial and fair investigation that is mindful of the asymmetries of power between the complainant and the respondent might find the complaint without basis. Instead, we find the first response on behalf of the respondent taking easy resort to 'criminal antecedents' of the complainant and her family, as if that by itself negates the possibility of her being subjected to sexual intimidation. To derail the mere possibility of fair procedure is unacceptable by any standard.

The Supreme Court convened a special sitting of the court to hear the case, listed as '*In Re: Matter of Great Public Importance Touching upon the Independence of Judiciary*', by a special bench consisting of Chief Justice Gogoi and Justices Arun Mishra and Sanjiv Khanna (Krishnan 2019). The order passed shows the case as 'Suo Moto Writ Petition (Civil) No. 1', and lists the attorney general and the solicitor general as parties. The result of the special hearing was a gag-like order on the media, signed by Justices Mishra and Khanna:

> Having considered the matter, we refrain from passing any judicial order at this moment leaving it to the wisdom of the media to show restraint, act responsibly as is expected from them and accordingly decide what should or should not be published as wild and scandalous allegations undermine and irreparably damage reputation and negate independence of judiciary. We would therefore at this juncture leave it to the media to take off such material which is undesirable.[1]

The chief justice was not one of the signatories, although he was present and spoke at the hearing.

It is important to understand that although this issue has sent a shudder all around and gasps of disbelief and shock, the manner in which the complaint has been received and handled by sections of the bench and sections of the bar has been disconcerting to many in the legal profession. The Bar Council of India's statement speaks eloquently of its own standard: 'The cock and bull story has been cooked up to plot some big conspiracy against the institution. The Bar is fully standing with our CJI and the Judges of the Supreme Court' (quoted in ANI 2019). The fact is that the Bar Council of India does not speak for all lawyers in the country, as the response of the Women in Criminal Law Association (WCLA) makes evident. The WCLA published a detailed statement demanding a free and fair investigation by a panel that excluded the three judges who constituted the bench in the first sitting and demanded that the CJI not hold office till the enquiry is completed (*The Wire* 2019). The Supreme Court Advocates-on-Record Association and the executive committee of the Supreme Court Bar Association passed resolutions on 22 April 2019 disapproving the manner in which the complaint was dealt with and asserting the urgency of an independent, impartial enquiry (Sachdev 2019). These resolutions must be viewed in the light of the conspiracy theories alluded to by the Bar Council of India, and finance minister Arun Jaitley's statement that this was the work of 'institution destabilisers' who represent 'Left or ultra-Left views' (quoted in *Scroll.in* 2019b). This attempt to impute a conspiracy jeopardises the security of the complainant, her family and anyone who provides support in securing redress.

The court is unlike other institutional settings—the Supreme Court is sequestered and the constitutional office of the chief justice of India is deemed sacred and inviolable. The argument is that an independent judiciary is indispensable to check arbitrariness on the part of the legislature and government. What is often forgotten is that an independent judiciary also importantly acts as a check on itself, and must apply the principles of natural justice and fair procedure to itself with greater rigour than it would to the parties that appear before the court. The expectation of citizens is that the court will lead by example, not by arbitrary diktat. The expectation also is that constitutional morality will guide the court, especially the justices of the court, at all times; the constitutional presumption is that the court is not above the Constitution.

The Time to Dissent is Now

This very court, in the judgement on the right to privacy, observed unequivocally that judges have in the past erred in judgement, in understanding their powers and in their understanding of the Constitution and the rule of law. Can we forget Justice Nariman's emotionally charged recall of the 'three great dissents'? Can we forget Justice Chandrachud's impassioned statement, 'When histories of nations are written and critiqued, there are judicial decisions at the forefront of liberty. Yet others have to be consigned to the archives, reflective of what was, but should never have been'?[2] And it is the thin line of judicial dissents that have moved centre stage in our understanding of India's constitutional history today. Given the recent resurrection of dissents by the Supreme Court, it is important not to foreclose the possibility of judicial dissent by generalising the actions of the three justices to all the judges of the court. For, after all, to borrow in part from Justice Chandrachud, judicial dissent is the 'safety valve' of constitutionalism (Ananthakrishnan 2018). And dissent must be seen to be done. The time is now.

Notes

1. In Re: Matter of Great Public Importance Touching upon the Independence of Judiciary, Suo Moto WP No. 1 of 2019, passed on 20 April 2019 (SC).
2. *K. S. Puttaswamy*, (2017) 10 SCC 1, para. 121 (per Chandrachud, J.).

References

'Full Text: Official Response to Sexual Harassment Allegations against Chief Justice of India'. 2019a. *Scroll.in*, 20 April. Available at https://scroll.in/article/920702/full-text-chief-justice-of-indias-response-to-sexual-harassment-allegations-made-by-former-staffer (accessed 26 June 2021).

'"Time to Stand with Judiciary," Says Arun Jaitley after Sexual Harassment Allegations against CJI'. 2019b. *Scroll.in*, 21 April. Available at https://scroll.in/latest/920847/time-to-stand-with-judiciary-says-arun-jaitley-after-sexual-harassment-allegations-against-cji (accessed 26 June 2021).

'Women Lawyers Question Chief Justice Gogoi's Handling of Sexual Harassment Charge'. 2019. *The Wire*, https://thewire.in/law/women-lawyers-question-chief-justice-gogois-handling-of-sexual-harassment-charge (accessed 26 June 2021).

Ananthakrishnan, G. 2018. 'Elgaar Parishad Probe: Dissent Safety Valve of Democracy, Pressure Cooker Will Burst If Not Allowed, Says SC'. *The Indian Express*, 31 August.

ANI (Asian News International). 2019. 'Story Cooked Up to Plot Big Conspiracy against Supreme Court: Bar Council of India'. *Business Standard*, 20 April.

Krishnan, Murali. 2019. 'The Bizarre Order in the Sexual Harassment Allegations against CJI Ranjan Gogoi'. *Bar and Bench*, 20 April. Available at https://www.barandbench.com/columns/bizarre-order-sexual-harassment-allegations-cji-ranjan-gogoi (accessed 26 June 2021).

Sachdev, Vakasha. 2019. 'Lawyer Associations Criticise Violation of Procedure by CJI Gogoi'. *The Quint*, 22 April. Available at https://www.thequint.com/news/law/lawyer-associations-condemn-cji-gogoi-supreme-court-hearing-sexual-harassment-allegations#read-more#read-more (accessed 26 June 2021).

Yamunan, Shruthisagar and Supriya Sharma. 2019. 'Chief Justice of India Sexually Harassed Me, Says Former SC Staffer in Affidavit to 22 Judges'. *Scroll.in*, 20 April. Available at https://scroll.in/article/920678/chief-justice-of-india-sexually-harassed-me-says-former-sc-staffer-in-affidavit-to-22-judges (accessed 26 June 2021).

50

Redeeming the Constitution*

We have, since 20 April 2019, been witnessing strange and troubling times. In all the troubles we have been through in the recent past in this country, despite very mixed results, the one bastion that stood undiminished and full of hope and constitutional imaginings was the Supreme Court of India. There have been good judgements and bad, there have been well-reasoned ones and others not so seamless or robust in constitutional articulation, but the balance has tilted without doubt in favour of the court as the institution that keeps the idea of justice embodied in the Constitution in view and within reach of every citizen.

On 19 April 2019, a former employee of the Supreme Court of India brought charges of sexual harassment against the chief justice of India—she mailed copies of her affidavit to all the sitting judges of the court, demanding a fair enquiry and due process (Yamunan and Chakravarty 2019; Yamunan and Sharma 2019). Clearly this was a very simple demand placed on the majestic court. There is a detailed account of how the harassment is alleged to have started, culminating in her dismissal and the dismissal of her brother-in-law from employment in the Supreme Court on grounds that would have prompted this very court to slap hefty compensation on any other employer in its place. There were also other details of harassment by the police and a forced appearance before the wife of the CJI.

After the *Rupan Bajaj*[1] and *Vishaka*[2] cases, the Supreme Court heard innumerable petitions setting out guidelines and procedures for all workplaces—government and non-government, mandating compliance. This was followed by the Sexual Harassment of Women at Workplace (Prevention, Prohibition and Redressal) Act, 2013, but

* Originally published in *The Leaflet*, 10 May 2019.

by this time, the idea that sexual harassment constitutes a violation of the dignity of women in the workplace had got firmly entrenched in the bedrock of constitutional common-sense, with the Supreme Court playing a central role in receiving the learnings of women's groups since the late 1970s and absorbing it into Constitution-speak.

The refusal of the CJI to allow due process in this matter and the refusal of the 27 other judges of the court to publicly insist that justice must be done is therefore not a simple matter. In 1980, we were on the streets in front of the Supreme Court screaming for justice in the case of Mathura. Three law professors of the University of Delhi wrote an open letter to the chief justice of India, which is now one of our rare constitutional treasures.[3] But 2019 is not 1980. A thousand women demonstrating in every city and town asking for justice in the case of Mathura in 1980 is very different from all of us pouring into the streets today. We are at a very different point in our constitutional history.

Even if we set aside the affidavit of the complainant for a second, the official response issued by the secretary general on 20 April is deeply offensive to constitutional sentiment:

> The allegations regarding 11 October 2018, as well as other allegations as can be discerned from [the media's] emails, are completely and absolutely false and scurrilous and are totally denied....
>
> The motive behind these false and scurrilous allegations is obviously mischevious [*sic*]. As referred to in your letter, there is a criminal case pending against her, where very serious allegation [*sic*] have been made, of her having taken a bribe to assure employment in the Supreme Court of India. It has been learnt that there is an application for the cancellation of bail earlier granted to her, which is listed for hearing on 20.04.2019 on acoount [*sic*] of her having made threats to the complainant of the said case.
>
> It would be extremely relevant to mention that the concerned individal [*sic*] and her family have criminal antecedents....
>
> It appears that these false allegations are being made asa [*sic*] pressure tactics to somehow come out of the various proceedings which have been initiated in law, against her and her family, for their on [*sic*] wrong doings. Its [*sic*] is also very possible that there are mischevious [*sic*] forces

> behind all this, with an intention to malign the institution. (Quoted in *Scroll.in* 2019)

This statement came at the end of a day of bizarre proceedings in the court before a bench of three sitting judges (including the CJI-Respondent), of which the attorney general and solicitor general are part: to deal with a '[m]atter of great public importance touching upon the independence of judiciary'.[4] The CJI-Respondent, through this action, pre-empted any deliberations in the court by judges who had received the affidavit by hastily constituting a bench of which he was part, but whose order he did not sign—both of which are bad in law and procedure.

To make unsubstantiated derogatory and defamatory remarks before any investigation or enquiry into the matter reeks of the methods of public morality that this very court has uprooted unequivocally. It can scarcely be forgotten that this is a complainant who has carefully set out her case, supported by documentary proof and specific details of time, place and nature of harm suffered in a sworn affidavit. It can scarcely be argued that the secretary general, located as he is on the administrative side, need not be conversant with the language of constitutional morality—it is reasonably presumed that this response had the full approval of the CJI-Respondent. 2019 is not 1980. It is no longer a question of, 'How can a CJI conduct himself in this manner?' This is also no place to hold forth on the 'impeccable' character of the apex judiciary nor the time to counsel the court to adhere to procedure from which it will surely emerge honourably. On the contrary, the challenge is to safeguard the impeccable character of the judiciary—and every individual judge within it—by calling the institution to account and demanding compliance to constitutional principles. The challenge also is the insistence that no complainant shall be prejudged merely because she is powerless and has decided to speak truth to power—in this case, the complainant is a Dalit woman. It is now our assertion that anyone with such a poor understanding of fair procedure, the question of dignity and constitutional morality is unfit to lead the highest court in the land.

An in-house committee was constituted by the CJI-Respondent after public uproar. There was no external member and the complainant expressed misgivings about the presence of one judge on the committee (*India Today* 2019). This is a subjective judgement that may be easily accommodated—as it was. In his letter announcing his recusal, Justice N. V. Ramana stated unequivocally that there was no basis for the fears expressed by the complainant. He went on to assert:

> My decision to recuse is only based on an intent to avoid any suspicion that this institution will not conduct itself in keeping with the highest standards of judicial propriety and wisdom.... *Let my recusal be a clear message to the nation that there should be no fears about probity in our institution, and that we will not refrain from going to any extent to protect the trust reposed in us.* That is, after all, our final source of moral strength. (Quoted in *The Hindu* 2019; emphasis mine.)

What are the steps the court has taken to 'conduct itself in keeping with the highest standards of judicial propriety and wisdom'? The question is not any more about the facticity of the complainant's affidavit. That still remains to be investigated after the matter of due process is reinstated fully. The derailing of procedure, the summary rejection of her request for a lawyer/support person, the absolute opacity of judicial power and arbitrariness in this case and the total lack of even a minimal sense of accountability is beyond comprehension. Justice A. P. Shah observed that like *ADM Jabalpur*, this case has caused long-term damage to the court as the site of constitutional justice (Sheriff and Chishti 2019). The question before us today is different. *ADM Jabalpur* was possible under conditions of Emergency, with the capture of institutions of justice by a rogue government. Even there we had strong dissenting voices outside and a strong dissenter inside the court, Justice H. R. Khanna, who was reinstated with full honours by this very court in *Puttaswamy*.[5] When governments suspend fundamental rights, there is hope that there will be one judge who may need to wait 40 years to be resurrected—but there will be one judge to stand unflinching on the side of citizens and their fundamental rights. When the CJI suspends fundamental rights, and there is a deafening silence in the court on this matter, what hope is there for a future resurrection? Also, after *Puttaswamy*, why must we wait another half-century? 2019 is not 1975.

In the case of *Romila Thapar*, we saw lawyers with a long and impeccable track record as human rights defenders being arrested for practising their profession with integrity.[6] Neither *Vishaka*, nor *ADM Jabalpur*, nor *Puttaswamy*, to name just a smattering of cases, emerged in the judicial mind from a vacuum. The decisions were the result of months and years of tirelessly pushing for a progressive understanding of the Constitution and the questions of liberty and dignity—by 'activist lawyers' and human rights defenders at enormous personal cost. This is part of the rich history of civil liberties advocacy in this country where movements played a critical role in educating the judiciary on rights and new possibilities of constitutional interpretation.

To allege 'conspiracy' by lawyers providing support to the complainant and accuse them of attempts to destabilise the court and order investigations against them is to be plunged into the dark abyss of arbitrariness. In fact, that is the only road that could open up when the first step was taken by the CJI-Respondent on 20 April. He had, by that single action, foreclosed all constitutional routes, as we have seen.

As an aside, is the court unaware that there is an insurgent understanding of conspiracy that has developed through human rights praxis in this country? That conspiracy no longer needs to be whispered or communicated in the dead of night through signals and coded (even feminist activist) tongues. Conspiracy is the exercise of absolute power by those in positions of unquestioned dominance to silence any semblance of resistance to the rules of power. To be aware of one's own power and to step back from it at times like this is an essential quality of a judge. The anger at the conduct of the CJI-Respondent is not an attack on the judiciary. It is the citizens' assertion to safeguard the court from capitulation to the arbitrary whimsicality of one man. For we can scarcely forget that the Supreme Court is part of our constitutional commons. It belongs to us all—lawyers, judges and citizens—and we hold it in trust.

Where do we go from here? Four judges of the Supreme Court, the CJI-Respondent among them, addressed a press conference in a powerful expression of judicial dissent in January 2018 (PTI 2018). The Supreme Court in 2017 held that three particularly significant judicial dissents are, in fact, good law.[7] The judges of the Supreme Court are protected by Article 19 rights to express dissent and freedom of conscience. Justice Chandrachud was reported to have given a letter to the in-house committee led by Justice Bobde—the views expressed therein also conveyed a sense of disquiet among at least 15 judges of the Supreme Court (Singh 2019).

We have reached a critical moment in our collective travels with the Constitution, where an adverse inference will be drawn from any further silence. There must be an open discussion that is recorded and made publicly available on the question of procedure and fair treatment and adherence to the rule of law in this case. And this open discussion must be followed by the constitution of a committee in accordance with the statute that protects women from sexual harassment at the workplace. The records and proceedings must be made public. The dignity of the court at this point rests in revisiting this entire issue with judicial humility, acknowledging and righting the wrongs. That is the only way the Constitution may be redeemed.

Notes

1. *Rupan Deol Bajaj*, (1995) 6 SCC 194.
2. *Vishaka*, AIR 1997 SC 3011.
3. Upendra Baxi, Lotika Sarkar, Raghunath Kelkar, and Vasudha Dhagamwar, 'An Open Letter to the Chief Justice of India', 16 September 1979, (1979) 2 SCC 143, written in the context of Tukaram & Anr v. State of Maharashtra.
4. Suo Moto WP No. 1 of 2019, decided on 20 April 2019 (SC).
5. *K. S. Puttaswamy*, (2017) 10 SCC 1, paras. 120–21 (per Chandrachud, J.).
6. Romila Thapar & Ors v. Union of India & Ors, (2018) 10 SCC 753.
7. *K. S. Puttaswamy*, (2017) 10 SCC 1.

References

'CJI Sexual Harassment Case: Woman Complainant Demands In-House Committee Report'. 2019. *India Today*, 7 May. Available at https://www.indiatoday.in/elections/lok-sabha-2019/story/woman-complainant-cji-ranjan-gogoi-sexual-harassment-in-house-committee-report-1519330-2019-05-07 (accessed 26 June 2021).

'Full Text: Official Response to Sexual Harassment Allegations against Chief Justice of India'. 2019. *Scroll.in*, 20 April. Available at https://scroll.in/article/920702/full-text-chief-justice-of-indias-response-to-sexual-harassment-allegations-made-by-former-staffer (accessed 9 May 2019).

'Full Text of Justice N. V. Ramana's Letter to Recuse Himself from the Judges' Committee to Probe Complaint against CJI'. 2019. *The Hindu*, 25 April. Available at https://www.thehindu.com/news/resources/full-text-of-justice-nv-ramanas-letter-to-recuse-himself-from-the-judges-committee-to-probe-complaint-against-cji/article26945616.ece (accessed 9 May 2019).

PTI. 2018. 'Supreme Court Crisis: All Not Okay, Democracy at Stake, Say Four Senior-Most Judges'. *Business Line*, 12 January.

Sheriff M., Kaunain and Seema Chishti. 2019. '"This Episode is Going to Haunt SC in Years to Come": Justice A. P. Shah on CJI Sexual Harassment Case'. *The Indian Express*, 7 May.

Singh, Sushant. 2019. 'Sexual Harassment Case: Justice Chandrachud Met Justice Bobde, Calls for Full Court'. *The Indian Express*, 6 May.

Yamunan, Shruthisagar and Ipsita Chakravarty. 2019. 'Interview: "I've Lost Everything. Financially, Mentally, Everything," Says Ex-SC Staffer in CJI Case'. *Scroll.in*, 9 May. Available at https://scroll.in/article/922751/interview-ive-lost-everything-financially-mentally-everything-says-ex-sc-staffer-in-cji-case (accessed 26 June 2021).

Yamunan, Shruthisagar and Supriya Sharma. 2019. 'Chief Justice of India Sexually Harassed Me, Says Former SC Staffer in Affidavit to 22 Judges'. *Scroll.in*, 20 April. Available at https://scroll.in/article/920678/chief-justice-of-india-sexually-harassed-me-says-former-sc-staffer-in-affidavit-to-22-judges (accessed 26 June 2021).

51

Juridical Viralities, Courts and the Question of Justice*

Judiciary is the watchdog of the Constitution and its fundamental values. It is also said to be the lifeblood of constitutionalism in democratic societies.... It is a formidable authority necessarily implying an awesome responsibility. A wise exercise of such power requires an efficient and independent Judge.... [W]isdom is to perceive with precision whether the legislative [judicial] action struck the constitutionally demanded balance between the larger interests of society and liberties of subjects.

—Justice J. Chelameswar (2016)[1]

All conversations in 2020 veer around the novel coronavirus pandemic. Using Covid-19 as my point of departure in a vicarious way, I briefly touch upon the major themes that have emerged in courts of various jurisdictions since late March 2020, and the lessons this juridicalisation of fundamental freedoms holds for our understanding of the claims of citizens to the Constitution-as-commons. Does the pandemic invent these regimes of enclosure? How far is the Constitution compatible with carceral governance and enclosure as the method of containment, reinforcement of prejudice, and the method of pre-trial punishment, along a continuum?

The starting point is the arrest and detention on 10 July 2020 of a gangrape survivor and her counsellors in Araria in Bihar (*The Wire* 2020c). The survivor was released after a week on the orders of the chief judicial magistrate in Araria, but the counsellors, Tanmay Nivedita and Kalyani Badola, both members of Jan Jagran Shakti Sangathan, a registered trade union, were held in Dalsinghsarai Jail

---

* A revised version of this essay was originally published in *The Leaflet*, 14 August 2020.

in Samastipur district (a quarantine jail) for close to a month till the Supreme Court granted interim bail on 4 August, with Justice Mishra observing that '[i]t was a totally impermissible order by which they were sent to custody' (quoted in *The Wire* 2020d). Four weeks in jail during Covid-19 without reason. The same *mahila police thana* (women's police station) where the FIR on rape was registered was the thana that registered the contempt case against the survivor. If the order was impermissible in law, should the judicial officer not be held to account? The perpetrators, of course, still roam free.

Covid-19, the Supreme Court directive on keeping prisons decongested (*Business Today* 2020), the trauma of rape, the critical role of caregiving to survivors of sexual violence, Article 21 rights, indeed the Constitution itself was trumped to uphold the carceral masculinity of a judge disregardful of the basic rights and due process in hearing victim-survivors, and unwilling to acknowledge the constructively vital role of caregivers.

Rewind a few months: Even as we were coming to grips with the violent state action against anti-CAA protesters (Citizens against Hate 2020) and in Kashmir post-5 August 2019 (Kannabiran et al. 2020), the pandemic struck. We suddenly saw the bared fangs of the carceral state and the true meaning of 'hostile environments'[2]—hundreds of thousands of workers flung out on the streets in utter disregard of basic humanitarian concerns (Baxi 2020)—forget about state responsibility under the Constitution. We ask here not what were the laws that were flouted, but which law was *not* flouted in this unforgivable inhumanity of the Indian state towards its people, mostly poor workers.

The starkest case before us was that of 12-year-old Jamalo Madakam, who died walking 100 kilometres to reach her home in Chhattisgarh from the chilli farms she worked on in Telangana (Verma 2020).

Can we actually point to a single law or a cluster of laws that were violated? What of Nobel laureate Kailash Satyarthi's solution of granting a three-month amnesty from prosecution to employers in order to access children locked in their factories? And his cry that 'society has failed our children' (Ganguly and Menon 2020)?

As Enakshi Ganguly and Mahesh Menon (2020) have pointed out—and that is the central point of my approach too—the animal that we call 'society' is many things and it is nothing. Where is the state? Is it difficult for the state to access children in factories? Why? Where is the argument of amnesty from prosecutions coming from? Why is there a reluctance to fix responsibility on the state? Why did so many die? Why were states and villages and neighbourhoods allowed to seal their borders? How was it possible for elected representatives to forget Article 19 rights that guarantee freedom of movement and residence in any part of the country? Indeed, how was it even possible for them to brush aside their obligations under the Constitution altogether?

This then is the first part of the problem of the law. The failure of memory of obligations under the Constitution and the refusal of empathy when suffering on an unprecedented scale broke loose. Damage control only meant denials, counter-accusations, more denials, and contradictions. All with the assumption of impunity.

The Constitution does not guarantee impunity. It guarantees every last citizen protection against state impunity.

While workers were being flung out, the pandemic continued to rage. So did carceral politics and carceral governance. Quarantining under police surveillance has been disastrous in terms of our collective experience of human dignity. If spraying liquid bleach on returning workers was at one end of a theatre of horrors (*The Wire* 2020a), at the other end was the custodial sexual assault, torture, and murder of Jayaraj and his son Bennix in Thoothukudi in Tamil Nadu (Koushik 2020). The rampage of the police is seamless in the present time, strengthened by the fact that courts have locked the Constitution out for the most part. The reliefs we ask, for the most part, are minimal. Provide food and free rations. Provide shelter. Provide free transport—beseeching an abdicating state to throw crumbs our way.

The fundamental question of dignity and constitutional guarantees against state impunity goes unaddressed in the process, as every one of us is kept on our toes pleading for a little succour. Some small benevolence to tide over a difficult time. And yet, we understand too well that this is not about 'society'. It is about state impunity and the abdication of state responsibility. It is about state violence in a different form, and we must name it as such.

The Constitution does not guarantee impunity. It guarantees every last citizen protection against state impunity.

Even while the pandemic rages, the carceral state goes on a rampage, and all protest is disabled by the lockdown. There are pre-trial arrests on flimsy grounds. Safoora Zargar (Pasha 2020), Sharjeel Imam (*The Indian Express* 2020), Akhil Gogoi (PTI 2020), anti-CAA protesters (Citizens against Hate 2020), Devangana Kalita, Natasha Narwal (*The Wire* 2020b), Anand Teltumbde and the Bhima Koregaon twelve (Rajput 2020)—now Hany Babu (Tiwary 2020)—too many to name. There is incarceration in prisons that are seething with infection. At least three people we know from among the political prisoners alone have tested positive, and it is possible for the National Investigation Agency to tell the court that 80-year-old poet Varavara Rao, who is seriously ill in custody, is 'using the pandemic situation' to his advantage (Talwar 2020b).[3] State impunity is demonstrated through the mere possibility that a statement like this is made and not severely reprimanded by the court. These arrests and the manner in which they were effected are indeed in contempt of the Constitution.

Travesties in Kashmir have been entirely forgotten in the process, even as advocate Mian Abdul Qayoom, the president of the Jammu and Kashmir Bar Association, aged 73, and very ill in Tihar, waited for the benevolence of the court and state for almost a year before he was released on 30 July (*The Quint* 2020; see LSEW 2020, seeking his release). He was in jail for a week short of one year—the maximum period for which a person may be held under detention under the law.

In ordering his release, Justice Kaul observed, 'Kashmir has been a troubled area. Nature has been very kind to the place. *It is the human race which has been unkind*. It is time for all wounds to be healed and look to the future within the domain of our country.' It is not the human race, milord. It is the state that incarcerated advocate Qayoom and held him in custody for a year with no good reason. The bench added, 'We are sure that the petitioner will also adopt a more constructive approach to the future and the *Government will consider how to bring complete normalcy at the earliest. Hope is something which creates the future and we are hopeful'* (quoted in Talwar 2020a; emphasis mine).

The Constitution does not guarantee impunity. It guarantees every last citizen protection against state impunity. There is no space and this is no time for judicial equivocation.

There are dangers—real, palpable, measurable dangers—of hazards to ordinary people, of the endangerment of the life of healthcare professionals, of the police, of journalists ... Another manifestation of impunity lies here. In the bleeding of stigmas of contagion that is the bane of the rule by caste in this country to every other locale. We saw a resurgence of 'genocidal journalism' (Vijayan 2016) in the pandemic context. The suppression of information by the state of the magnitude of the situation on the ground, and the refusal to be accountable to the people is yet another manifestation of impunity. Which are the specific laws we may point to? Is there any one law?

At the base of it all is the fact that the pandemic makes rule by impunity possible, in a context where courts are so fragile that they lash a whip at critics of bike rides, and seek jurisprudential solutions for state wrongs from the state. Under conditions of Emergency, fundamental rights and the right of citizens to petition courts is not suspended, said Justice H. R. Khanna, in his stellar dissent in the infamous *ADM Jabalpur* case.[4] In 2017, the *Puttaswamy* bench (of which the sitting CJI was part) reinstated that dissent, and exhibited a rare expression of judicial humility and apology for past wrongs.[5] And yet, today, when for the first time the *Puttaswamy* judgement is tested on an unprecedented scale, we see courts leaning on the state and providing answers to citizen petitioners on behalf of the state for the most part—in matters ranging from bail for pre-trial detainees to the condition of migrant workers.

In this process, as citizens making constitutional demands of the court and state, we are dropping our bar lower than ever before. Not release from prison, but information from the hospital. Not freedom, but freedom enclosed in conditions. Not a right that can serve as a precedent, but a humanitarian order in this one case alone. Not housing justice, but a paltry allowance. Not arrest of the perpetrators, but the release of the victim from custody. Not demanding wages, but justifying why food and shelter do not add up to wages.

We need to start over again. From the very beginning. The 'triadic ethical foundations'[6] of the Constitution and the Constitution-as-commons. And we need, in closing, to recall Justice Stephen Breyer's (2013) sage words:

> [W]hen you are a judge ... it's important to be able to imagine what other people's lives might be like, lives that your decisions will affect. People who are not only different from you, but also very different from each other.... And this empathy, this ability to envision the practical consequences on one's contemporaries of a law or a legal decision, seems to me to be a crucial quality in a judge.

Notes

1. Supreme Court Advocates-on-Record Association v. Union of India, (2016) 4 SCC 1, para. 18 (per Chelameswar, J., dissenting).
2. A phrase first used in *Vishaka*, AIR 1997 SC 3011.
3. The petition filed by Pendyala Hemalatha, Rao's wife, before the Supreme Court on 15 October 2020, seeking bail on grounds of age, health and comorbidities, states that 'his continued custody amounts to cruel and inhuman treatment, violating Article 21 of the Constitution of India and violative of his dignity in custody' (quoted in Talwar 2020).
4. *ADM Jabalpur*, (1976) 2 SCC 521.
5. *K. S. Puttaswamy*, (2017) 10 SCC 1.
6. Reliance Natural Resources Ltd v. Reliance Industries Ltd, (2010) 156 CompCas 455 (SC), para. 97

References

'In Bareilly, Returning Migrant Workers Showered with Disinfectant on the Road'. 2020a. *The Wire*, 30 March. Available at https://thewire.in/government/coronavirus-bareilly-migrants-sodium-hypochlorite (accessed 26 June 2021).

'Anti-CAA Pinjra Tod Activist Arrested for Third Time in 10 Days'. 2020b. *The Wire*, 1 June. Available at https://thewire.in/rights/anti-caa-pinjra-tod-devangana-kalita-arrest (accessed 25 July 2021).

'Days after Ordeal, Araria Gang Rape Survivor Continues to Be in Jail for Contempt'. 2020c. *The Wire*, 15 July. Available at https://thewire.in/rights/araria-gang-rape-survivor-jail (accessed 26 June 2021).

'Araria Case: SC Orders Release of Activists, Terms Custody Order "Totally Impermissible"'. 2020d. *The Wire*, 4 August. Available at https://

thewire.in/law/araria-gangrape-case-sc-orders-release-of-activists (accessed 20 October 2020).

'Coronavirus: Supreme Court Orders Release of Prisoners to Decongest Jails'. 2020. *Business Today*, 23 March. Available at https://www.businesstoday.in/latest/economy-politics/story/coronavirus-supreme-court-orders-release-of-prisoners-to-decongest-jails-252784-2020-03-23 (accessed 26 June 2021).

'J&K Advocate Mian Qayoom to Be Released after 1 Year of Detention'. 2020. *The Quint*, 29 July. Available at https://www.thequint.com/news/politics/jammu-and-kashmir-bar-association-president-mian-abdul-qayoom-detention-wont-be-extended-beyond-6-august-centre-tells-sc#read-more (accessed 25 July 2021).

'JNU Student Sharjeel Imam Arrested by Delhi Police in Sedition Case'. 2020. *The Indian Express*, 28 January.

Baxi, Upendra. 2020. 'Exodus Constitutionalism: Mass Migration in Covid Lockdown Times'. *The India Forum*, 3 July. Available at https://www.theindiaforum.in/article/exodus-constitutionalism (accessed 26 June 2021).

Breyer, Stephen. 2013. 'On Reading Proust'. Interview by Ioanna Kohler. *The New York Review of Books*, 7 November.

Citizens against Hate. 2020. *'Everyone Has Been Silenced': Police Excess against Anti-CAA Protesters in Uttar Pradesh, and Post-Violence Reprisal.* Available at https://citizensagainsthate.org/wp-content/uploads/2020/03/Citizens-Against-Hate-Everyone-Has-Been-Silenced.pdf (accessed 26 June 2021).

Ganguly, Enakshi and Mahesh Menon. 2020. 'Kailash Satyarthi Should Know There's No Place for Dilemmas When it Comes to Child Labour'. *The Wire*, 29 April. Available at https://thewire.in/rights/kailash-satyarthi-should-know-theres-no-place-for-dilemmas-when-it-comes-to-child-labour (accessed 8 November 2020).

Kannabiran, Kalpana, Sarojini Nadimpally, Navsharan Singh, Roshmi Goswami and Pamela Philipose. 2020. 'Interrogating the "Normal" in Kashmir'. *Indian Cultural Forum*, 4 March. Available at https://indianculturalforum.in/2020/03/04/interrogating-the-normal-in-kashmir/ (accessed 26 June 2021).

Koushik, Janardhan. 2020. 'Protests in Tamil Nadu Town over "Custodial Death" of Shopkeeper, Son'. *The Indian Express*, 27 June.

LSEW (Law Society of England and Wales). 2020. Letter to Narendra Modi. 'India – Arrest and Detention of Mian Abdul Qayoom, President of the High Court Bar Association of Jammu and Kashmir'. 5 March. Available at https://mcb.org.uk/wp-content/uploads/2020/05/Honourable-Prime-Minister-of-India-05.03.2020.pdf (accessed 26 June 2021).

Pasha, Seemi. 2020. 'Safoora Zargar Denied Bail as Judge Finds Prima Facie Evidence of "Conspiracy"'. *The Wire*, 5 June. Available at https://thewire.in/law/safoora-zargar-denied-bail (accessed 10 July 2021).

PTI. 2020. 'Akhil Gogoi Charged under Sedition, Anti-terror Law'. *Deccan Herald*, 5 June.

Rajput, Rashmi. 2020. 'Elgar Parishad Case: Activist Anand Teltumbde Arrested'. *The Economics Times*, 15 April.

Talwar, Sanya. 2020a. 'It is Time for All Wounds to Be Healed and Look to the Future: Supreme Court'. *LiveLaw*, 30 July. Available at https://www.livelaw.in/top-stories/kashmir-it-is-time-for-all-wounds-to-be-healed-and-look-to-the-future-supreme-court-160718 (accessed 8 November 2020).

———. 2020b. '"Dr Varavara Rao's Health Condition Feeble": Wife Moves SC for His Release on Medical Grounds'. *LiveLaw*, 15 October. Available at https://www.livelaw.in/top-stories/dr-varavara-raos-health-condition-feeble-wife-moves-sc-for-his-release-on-medical-grounds-164515 (accessed 8 November 2020).

Tiwary, Deeptiman. 2020. 'NIA Arrests DU Professor Hany Babu in Elgar Parishad Case'. *The Indian Express*, 28 July.

Verma, Gargi. 2020. '12-Year-Old Walks 100 km, Dies Just Short of Bijapur Home'. *The Indian Express*, 21 April.

Vijayan, Suchitra, 2016. 'Journalism as Genocide'. *The Wire*, 30 March. Available at https://thewire.in/communalism/journalism-as-genocide (accessed 27 August 2021).

XI

'Freedom to Be' in Universities

52

Education, Campuses and Violence*

This chapter will explore the dilemmas that teaching law from the common ground created by the intersection of law, social sciences, women's studies and feminism throws up. It will also attempt, in the process, to trace the boundaries of pedagogy, rather, the rigid confines within which pedagogic practice is forced to locate itself today, in institutions of formal education in general, and the ways in which this confinement can undermine in very direct ways the teaching of law itself. In other words, it will look at the classroom, campus (and different 'internal' spaces therein) and society as territories that, although contiguous and overlapping, are territories nevertheless, each with their own parameters of 'integrity' and normative order and their own rules and constitutions.

As a first observation, it is important to state that each of these territories is, at every level, gendered and structured by power, hierarchy and hegemony; moving inwards, in a sense, from the dynamic of society to the smaller spaces that constitute it—the family, the campus, the hostel, the classroom; each of these spaces constructed as 'internal' spaces, analogous to the family. An understanding of this shifting definition of the 'private' and the use of the familial analogy is important if we are to understand the troubling reality of violence on campuses and our inability to deal with it.

As a result of persistent campaigning by the women's movement over two decades, the issue of sexual harassment and heterosexual violence has entered the mainstream discourse in different ways. Yet, masculinity and femininity continue to be constructed in strictly regimented ways with very little space for women students particularly to raise questions of discrimination, harassment or derogatory/

---

* Originally published in *The Hindu*, 29 October 2002.

obscene representation. This is and must remain a dialogue between male students, and the resolution must also happen between them, with women on both sides being passive spectators. I will return to this point a little later.

Logically, then, it would follow that there has not been any significant decrease in violence and sexual harassment on campuses. The positive side of this is that there is protest and resistance and persistent campaigning by women's groups and small groups of men and women—teachers and students—on campuses, in Delhi (Gender Study Group 1996), for example, and the campaign on the *Vishaka* petition by women's groups in Rajasthan.[1]

To come now to the troubling question of masculinity. This dialogue between male students, whether about women, or about the right of senior students to services and obeisance from juniors, or about a general policing, is by definition violent and involves extreme physical abuse. And masculinity is constructed around the ability to bear pain, the ability to be an active spectator, the capacity for silence, a firm belief in the patriarchies of age and gender, and an utter contempt for any recourse to legitimate redress.

The heroes are those that bear all these characteristics. In other words, there is a complete normalisation of violence in institutions of education, and while we are able to address some, such as heterosexual violence, there are others, same-sex violence for instance, especially battery, that remain invisible, not spoken about and give cause for serious concern. As a law student I once met said to me, '*Yeh toh boys hostel mein hota hi hai*' (This kind of thing happens in boys' hostels), and asserted that these were not matters that the authorities ought to mess around with because they would get resolved within the hostel. And I am sure students of other disciplines would not speak differently.

How does one process this reality as a teacher of sociology in a law school and as a feminist? Processes of discrimination, hierarchy, power, patterns in the use of violence, the criminalisation of some forms of violence and the exclusion of other forms from the definition of violence itself, as also the continuities in these practices and processes across seemingly dissimilar social spaces, are best understood from the standpoint of sociology.

But that is not enough. The feminist slogan, 'The personal is political', opened up the family to public scrutiny in the face of increasing violence against women within marriage in the late 1970s. Despite stiff resistance to any 'interference in family matters', domestic violence has systematically been forced into public view—the courtroom, legislative bodies and curricula in family law. The fact that there cannot be a derogation of rights—to life, to dignity and bodily integrity, to the freedom of expression, to the freedom of association—even within 'private spaces' is one that must be appreciated through the lens of the 'personal is political' slogan. When even the family is no longer a private space, how can a campus or, worse still, a hostel be one? Legal education cannot be confined to the classroom, but must encompass the entire space that teachers and students inhabit in order for it to make sense.

Women students in elite institutions have resisted quotas for women in student unions, and non-Dalit students (men and women), have generally opposed quotas for Dalits as well. I have not yet heard of an instance where Dalit students, on being offered a quota in unions, have refused it. The argument of the women students in at least one instance that has come to my notice was that they were a sizeable number—a little over half in that institution—and that they would get into the union 'on their own steam'. And yet, when the elections took place, 85 per cent of the seats went to the men. This experience outside the classroom ties in with the teaching of the equality provisions in constitutional law and the questions raised in equality jurisprudence: the distinction between formal equality and substantive equality, the wisdom and indispensability of affirmative action, and the fact that the right to equality binds all historically discriminated-against groups. Reservation was not only for Scheduled Castes and Scheduled Tribes, but was necessary for women too.

Violence is both the subject of law and its context. And violence is always embedded in a social context ridden with unequal power and privilege. Witness the constant threat of sexual violence that women are confronted with and the inoperability of the law when it comes to sexual offences.

What happens in the courtroom is mirrored in the classroom, the campus, public spaces and the family. Clearly, the IPC cannot teach us why. Sociology cannot either, on its own. Only feminist sociology can help make sense of this.

The point of this exploratory exercise has been twofold. First, it is an attempt to underscore the indispensability of a thorough grounding in feminist sociology and a commitment to human rights to pedagogical practice in law. Second, and more importantly, it points to the necessity for teachers in undergraduate institutions particularly to break out of the confines of a rigidly circumscribed job, opening up a conversation with young adults on the connections between violence, dignity and learning; drawing these connections for them, both within and outside the classroom.

Note

1. *Vishaka*, AIR 1997 SC 3011.

Reference

Gender Study Group. 1996. *Sexual Harassment in Delhi University: A Report*. Delhi University, Delhi.

53

Disrupting Caste in Class*

The consciousness of caste is constitutive of the self in caste society—embedded in the fact of being, underwriting it in deep-seated yet often unarticulated ways. It is also entrenched in the realities of class, which structure the experience of bare life itself. The caste-class nexus produces an array of articulations that tell stories of the complex contradictions between consciousness and survival, which are also stories of the caste system. This is not to argue that this consciousness cannot be ruptured or that the self cannot be re-constituted. It is necessary even while examining the ruptures, to delineate what elements of caste-class remain solid and unshaken, and what parts allow for a re-constitution. Even while there may be significant ruptures around you, in the normal course, these will have the status of folklore—of stories that you hear, of heroism that you see and believe but cannot 'know'. In order to know what the rupture of caste consciousness means, it is necessary to engage self-consciously in the politics of becoming, regulating notions of the self, de-schooling and politicising the self in new ways that push you to belonging elsewhere (Connolly 1996; Minow 1996). This process of re-constituting the self can only be intentional and the result of a carefully crafted strategy.

Elements of consciousness and practice may be constantly splintered either by direct resistance or by contrary practice, so that even while receiving/'inheriting' a Brahmin subjectivity, it is also possible to craft its negation. It is not the self-conscious practice of Sanskritic rituals and untouchability that mar(k)s the Brahmin, but

* Excerpted from an essay originally published as 'Making the Forked Tongue Speak ... An Ethnography of the Self', in *Economic and Political Weekly* 43, no. 16 (19–25 April 2008): 63–70.

the micro-practices of being in that social location (seemingly—even self-consciously—distant from practices that derogate human dignity), that constitute the self and entrench it in deeply problematic ways.

Displacing Brahminical Pedagogy in Law School

When I began to teach in a law school, I introduced caste through the work of Ambedkar and Phule, and juxtaposed M. N. Srinivas's (1956) notion of 'Sanskritisation' with Kancha Ilaiah's (1996) notion of 'Dalitisation'.[1] Senior students went further, reading critiques of caste through the writings of Mahasweta Devi, Bama and Namdeo Dhasal. The results were stunning. Conversations began to open up in unimaginable ways. These were students between 18 and 20 years of age.

One set of responses pointed to a deep discomfort with the standpoints I was bringing into the classroom. Why did I persist in introducing readings that painted Hindu society in negative terms, although they also conceded that, of course, Ambedkar is the father of the Constitution—a difficult fact for law students with a stated interest in human rights to dismiss? Why did I seem to approve of Ilaiah's obvious irreverence and unconcern for all that is Brahminical—his extreme and irrational views that 'smacked of the Cultural Revolution'; 'Doesn't the notion of Dalitisation sound a bit far-fetched and irrational when compared to the notion of Sanskritisation?' Why, instead of talking so much about caste and untouchability, could I not focus on the greatness of Hindu philosophy? All of this outside class, of course. In class, the lectures were met with complete silence and an occasional inane comment on Manu or the origin of caste in the different body parts of Brahma, the creator, the hierarchy of the body (the head held aloft while the feet bite the dust) reflecting the hierarchy of caste—the Brahmin emerging from the head, the Shudra from the feet. To which, my response—recounting a song I once heard on origins at a meeting to protest against caste atrocities, that the *panchamas* (Dalits) are the only ones born *as human beings are born*—was always met with a shocked, even disapproving silence.

The obsession with caste in the dominant narrative is, after all, the hallmark of those that cannot lay a claim to merit. The meritorious, in this view, exist outside the parameters of caste. Virtual spaces, personal blogs for instance, interestingly, provided a much-needed release from the self-imposed compulsion to assume 'caste-less' or 'caste-free' postures by dominant caste students. They could, as one such blog did, oppose the views of Ambedkar and Ilaiah and defend the interests and concerns of the '20 Brahmins' in the class of 80—questioning, in the process, the logic of introducing a Dalit standpoint in teaching non-discrimination, equality and more fundamentally, caste.[2] The blog in this case was a space that was free from the 'constraints' imposed by the Constitution on imagining equality and entitlements based on caste. It was a space that was private, yet the private was public (didn't feminism say long ago that the personal was political?) and assumed a culturally homogenous readership—Brahmin students. These virtual spaces created the possibility to resist ideas thrown up in the classroom and align unabashedly in defence of caste inequality, and in defence of the exclusionary rhetoric of the dominant castes, not by recourse to the overworn 'merit' arguments, but by simply asserting a Brahmin identity.

A second set of responses used the literature I was introducing as a springboard to reflect on personal predicaments, dilemmas and difficulties. Students began to speak to me—directly and indirectly—about the micro-practices of caste on the campus, in their homes and in the homes of their friends. A non-Brahmin student narrated a conversation that she found troubling, with a Brahmin classmate who uncritically accepted the use of a different set of utensils by her father, an IAS officer, when his Dalit colleague visited him; other students from dominant groups admitted in class to the difficulty of dealing even notionally with the idea that *anyone* who comes to your home must be served water in the same glass that you would drink from; Dalit and Adivasi students spoke of the caricaturing of 'reserved' students ('She looks like a reserved candidate') and of the covert and overt forms of discrimination they faced—in buses when they went home on vacation, in their neighbourhoods and in the schools they studied in.

Some dropped out, unable to cope with the environment and stating only in private what the reasons for withdrawal were; others were on the brink of nervous breakdowns dealing with the realities of caste discrimination in their peer environment; some had to cope with the impossibility of sustaining the economic resources necessary to avail of quality education; and yet others, struggling with English language teaching for the first time in their lives, had to find emotional reserves to cope with being told that they had got into the institution by 'accident', that they did not really deserve to be there. A second-generation Dalit student said, in the course of a small interactive session, that she learned and experienced the realities of caste for the first time in the university.

Through it all, there continues to be a resistance to taking issue with caste discrimination, and naming it as such publicly and on record on all sides. Conciliation, mediation, negotiation, stand-offs are orally manoeuvred, for the most part by students, so that 'caste politics' does not sully the record of inter-student relationships. The dictates of 'batch solidarity' mask the fractures within, and dominance based on caste/community privilege is overwritten by the struggle for dominance between different batches, as it were.

The process of engaging with caste is far from linear. The opening out of the field of caste to discussion, reflection, dissent, conflict and resolutions at the experiential level immediately opened out the fields of academic work in very positive ways.

On the one hand, non-Dalit students in their coursework began to write on manual scavenging, social exclusion on campus, and on migration, with reference to transgender people, LGBT communities, minorities and so on, in the process also attempting to interrogate the basis of their own subjectivities and the sources of their privilege. The process of working on these issues generated a wider debate among non-Dalit students on the realities of caste discrimination and subjugation.[3]

On the other hand, Dalit students wrote papers that interrogated the notion of 'merit', and dominant caste hegemony in decisions on capabilities in institutions of professional education, rupturing standard notions that undergird 'institutions of excellence' and justify their existence. What was, in fact, happening was the trauma and pain of bearing discrimination was now being translated into pedagogy and being used in class and outside to bring home the meanings of discrimination to the larger university community. By laying claim to the space of these institutions *and* dismantling their core ideological premises, these students, miniscule in number, were actually churning the university system and forcing non-Dalit students out of their complacency through the simple strategy of plain speaking.

'Ragging' practices began to include asking a fresher to read and present Ilaiah's *Why I am Not a Hindu* (1996) in five hours in the men's hostel.

There were doubts as well, on how one could balance individual interests against class entitlements. Personally, students asked me, how would I react if I lost my job to a 'reserved' candidate? To which I said, quite honestly, that I welcome the opening out of university employment to Dalit scholars, regardless of any personal implications. I have tried with little success to explain to students that one cannot pit individual predicaments against class entitlements and have tried to unpack the 'merit' argument and demonstrate the hollowness in its core. The question is not really one of loss of opportunity. What is important and necessary is to merge an individual possibility with the larger goal of equality.

For close to a decade, I have received, separately, different sides of the reaction to the curriculum—one side because perhaps I was identified as someone doing doublespeak, someone who 'belonged to them' but was deliberately speaking an alien tongue; the other side because I belonged with them and opened out the space for a different reality and a different articulation of apparently familiar realities in the classroom; yet another because I was attempting to demonstrate the possibility of speaking differently, and in so doing, pointing in the direction of a politics of becoming as distinct from being.

In terms of writing in a substantively different curriculum, the key elements consisted of looking at caste through the prism of Articles 15(2) and 17 of the Constitution (discrimination based on caste and the ban on untouchability) and the SC/ST (Prevention of Atrocities) Act, 1989; equality jurisprudence—reservations that focused on Scheduled Castes and Tribes; to look at family forms other than the familiar patrilineal, patrilocal one; and sexual orientation and critiques of heteronormativity. The idea was to use Articles 15(2) and 17 to crack open fields of social exclusion and marginality, and to use these

Articles to understand the textures of discrimination and violence in Indian society.

Churning the Self

Order in caste society has specifically been based on foundational violence—within the family, in the larger multi-caste communal space and in the terrain(s) of citizenship(s). In interrogating the bases of this violence, it is imperative to radically re-examine the bases of the constitution of non-Dalit consciousness.

The Brahmin (and Brahminical) stream of consciousness, even when it does not overtly participate in the foundational violence or its perpetuation, at several levels encounters choices that eventually lead in one of two directions: to the condonation of a violent history (of which asserting irrationality of an intergenerational view of violence is part), or to foregrounding a Dalit stream of consciousness as the vantage point for an understanding of the ways in which caste constitutes the self.

It is, of course, only the second path that would take us forward in our endeavour to annihilate caste. Reaching the second path involves an enormous struggle with the self. Taking the second path would mean, for non-Dalits across different communities, to excavate the basis of consciousness, to peel off each layer of memory and see what lies beneath it, and to interrogate the location of the self on multiple axes (which is brutally unsettling)—in short, to embark on a process of becoming through a churning of the self that would lead to a radically different site of belonging.

Notes

1. This account draws on responses to modules on caste only. As part of this project, I invited Ilaiah to deliver a guest lecture to students who had read his work as part of the sociology course. Towards the end of his lecture, he is reported to have said that I was completely 'Dalitised' in my outlook.
2. For reasons of confidentiality, I cannot provide details of the link to this blog, nor a full extract. The assumption of privacy on blogs was brought

home to me by the fact that the post was taken down no sooner than the students realised I had accessed it—a full year-and-a-half after it had been on the internet for peer-viewing.

3. This was especially true of students who opted for my seminar course on 'Social Exclusion and Law'.

References

Bama. 2000. *Karukku*. New Delhi: Macmillan.

Connolly, William E. 1996. 'Suffering, Justice, and the Politics of Becoming'. *Culture, Medicine and Psychiatry* 20, no. 3: 251–77.

Ilaiah, Kancha. 1996. *Why I Am Not a Hindu: A Sudra Critique of Hindutva Philosophy, Culture and Political Economy*. Calcutta: Samya.

Minow, Martha. 1996. 'Comments on "Suffering, Justice and the Politics of Becoming" by William E. Connolly'. *Culture, Medicine and Psychiatry* 20, no. 3: 279–86.

Srinivas, M. N. 1956. 'A Note on Sanskritisation and Westernisation'. *The Far Eastern Quarterly* 15, no. 4 (August): 481–96.

54

A Call to Resurrect the Constitution, or What is a University?*

We live in strange and difficult times. The elected national government, holding office under oath of allegiance to the Constitution of India, proclaims allegiance repeatedly, unfailingly and without exception to '*Bharat Mata*' (Mother India), the Hindu scriptures and divine intervention—governing in the name of Hindutva and criminalising all dissent using the slogan of 'national interest'—by which they mean the interest of the Hindu *rashtra* (nation).

Dissent, free speech, freedom of association, freedom to organise and agitate are guaranteed as fundamental rights under the Constitution. The Constitution sets out a plural framework and refuses any scope to define the country in religious terms. The national interest in this scheme is constitutional rule. To recall Ambedkar (2002 [1948]: 484), it is only constitutional morality that must guide government. Not any whimsical invocation of narrow-minded, parochial figureheads and mythical characters.

It is time to remind the holders of public office that once they have formed government, whatever their personal politics might be, they are constrained to rule in strict accordance with the constitutional framework. Mere assumption of political power does not confer the power to propagate narrow party and supra-party ideologies in derogation of constitutional principles with impunity. It is a matter of deep regret that today we have actually fallen to the level where even this simple fact needs to be stated.

It is our right as citizens of this free country to question the government, to question arbitrary and capricious rule and to organise

* Originally published as 'What is a University?', in *The Hindu*, 16 February 2016.

against injustice, demanding the supremacy of the Constitution over all else. For us to allow the untrammelled use of the charge of sedition to quell dissent and freedom of expression, amounts, to reiterate Amartya Sen's words, to be too tolerant of intolerance (*Hindustan Times* 2016). Indeed, I would go so far as to say that it amounts to us abdicating our collective responsibility to uphold the Constitution of India. It is time to recall Gandhi's (1922) historic defence of seditious speech:

> I have no desire whatsoever to conceal from this court the fact that to preach disaffection towards the existing system of Government has become almost a passion with me.... I hold it to be a virtue to be disaffected towards a Government which in its totality, has done more harm to India than any previous system.

We have come full circle.

The orchestrated trigger for BJP parliamentarians and the ABVP in both the University of Hyderabad and Jawaharlal Nehru University was student protest and debate against the death penalties awarded to Yakub Memon and Afzal Guru (see Chukka 2016; MHRD 2016; *Report of the People's Tribunal* 2016; Shankar 2016). These are both issues that have already been subjected to public debate and consist of two parts. First, on whether the death penalty constitutes judicial murder; second, on whether Memon and Guru were given a fair trial. The debate has involved a close study of jurisprudence, international human rights standards and the fair conduct of the trials. A sizeable section of intellectuals and human rights defenders from across the country expressed the view that the death penalty, without exception, violates the constitutional guarantee of the right to life (see Amnesty International India and PUCL-TN&P 2008; Shankar 2016). An equal number held the firm belief that both Guru and Memon were executed without a fair trial (for example, Joshi 2015). This is a debate that must be carried out, not only in this case but in every case where the death penalty is ordered. There was even a debate in the Nirbhaya case and before the Justice Verma Committee on this very question (for example, *Firstpost* 2013). While on the one side, the victim's parents demanded the death penalty in the Nirbhaya case, in the case of the assassination of Rajiv Gandhi, Sonia Gandhi herself wrote to President Narayanan requesting clemency for those convicted for the assassination of her husband (Janwalkar 2011). These are difficult, heart-wrenching, but necessary debates—and no repressive clampdown can suppress the flow of ideas, questions and fundamental interrogations of the meaning of justice.

An important part of education, particularly higher education, is to learn to ask questions and to develop the capacity for disobedience and reasoned arguments. What is the promise of the university? Lest we forget,

> Where the mind is without fear and the head is held high;
> Where knowledge is free;
> Where the world has not been broken up into fragments by narrow domestic walls;
> Where words come out from the depth of truth;
> Where tireless striving stretches its arms towards perfection;
> Where the clear stream of reason has not lost its way into the dreary desert sand of dead habit;
> Where the mind is led forward by thee into ever-widening thought and action;
> Into that heaven of freedom, my Father, let my country awake. (Tagore n.d.)

Vice-chancellors hold charge of the university in trust—not of political powers but of the university community in which students are the core. To call in the police, act on their advice and abdicate responsibility, or to give the police a free hand (see *Report of the People's Tribunal* 2016), militates against the very spirit of the university as a space for critical engagement and free-flowing debate. The reduction of the position of vice-chancellor to being a watchdog of the government on campuses is a danger of unimaginable magnitude and destructive of the fabric of higher education—the structure will determine form, content, possibilities and importantly, futures.

Finally, back to the question of national interest. The Akhil Bharatiya Hindu Mahasabha observed Republic Day as a 'black day' in Meerut and has been consistently organising protests against the Constitution of India. The leaders of this group have also declared their intention to install a statue of Nathuram Godse (Ali 2016). This was a public show of strength in the service of a Hindu rashtra widely reported in national newspapers—but clearly none of our ministerial compatriots saw this either as an assault on national interest or as an incitement to violence. Yet, alleging that Rohith Vemula organised a protest against the execution of Memon when the ASA's assertion was that it had screened a film on the Muzaffarnagar riots (IANS 2016), and when Kanhaiya Kumar spoke out in defence of the Constitution of India (*India Today* 2016), our parliamentarians and ministers rose to defend 'the nation' (*Scroll.in* 2016; Surendran 2016).

Which nation is this? Whose country?

References

'Death Penalty to Juvenile Age: The Verma Committee Approach'. 2013. *Firstpost*, 24 January. Available at https://www.firstpost.com/india/death-penalty-to-juvenile-age-the-verma-committee-approach-600415.html (accessed 25 July 2021).

'Here's What JNUSU President Kanhaiya Kumar Said in His Speech'. 2016. *India Today*, 16 February. Available at https://www.indiatoday.in/fyi/story/kanhaiya-kumar-jnusu-president-speech-anti-national-308986-2016-02-16 (accessed 24 July 2021).

'India Has Become Too Tolerant of Intolerance: Amartya Sen'. 2016. *Hindustan Times*, 13 February.

'JNU Row: Students Want Smriti Irani to Resign, Says Kanhaiya Kumar'. 2016. *Scroll.in*, 15 March. Available at https://scroll.in/latest/805156/jnu-row-students-want-smriti-irani-to-resign-says-kanhaiya-kumar (accessed 24 July 2021).

Ali, Mohammed. 2016. 'Hindu Group Observes Republic Day as "Black Day"'. *The Hindu*, 26 January.

Ambedkar, B. R. 2002 [1948]. 'Basic Features of the Indian Constitution'. In *The Essential Writings of B. R. Ambedkar*, ed. Valerian Rodrigues, 473–94. New Delhi: Oxford University Press.

Amnesty International India and PUCL-TN&P (People's Union for Civil Liberties [Tamil Nadu & Puducherry]). 2008. *Lethal Lottery: The Death Penalty in India*. Amnesty International.

Chukka, Vikram. 2016. 'The Chain of Events Leading to Rohith Vemula's Suicide'. *The Wire*, 19 January. Available at https://thewire.in/education/the-chain-of-events-leading-to-rohith-vemulas-suicide (accessed 9 July 2021).

Gandhi, M. K. 1922. 'Statement in the Great Trial of 1922'. 18 March. Available at https://gandhiashramsabarmati.org/en/the-mahatma/speeches/great-trial-1922.html (accessed 9 July 2021).

IANS (Indo-Asian News Service). 2016. 'Protest over Documentary, Not Hanging Triggered Fracas at HCU'. *The Free Press Journal*, 26 January. Available at https://www.freepressjournal.in/india/protest-over-documentary-not-hanging-triggered-fracas-at-hcu (accessed 24 July 2021).

Janwalkar, Mayura. 2011. 'Death Row Appeal Cites Sonia Letter Asking for Pardon for All Four'. *The Indian Express*, 3 September.

Joshi, Manoj. 2015. 'Why Yakub Memon Should Not be Hanged'. *The Wire*, 17 July. Available at https://thewire.in/law/why-yakub-memon-should-not-be-hanged (accessed 9 July 2021).

MHRD (Ministry of Human Resource Development). 2016. *Laying of the Report of the Justice Ashok Kumar Roopanwal (Retd) Commission of Inquiry and Memorandum of Action Taken Thereon on the Table of Both the Houses of Parliament*. Available at https://www.education.gov.in/sites/upload_files/mhrd/files/document-reports/JusticeAshokKumarRoopanwalReport.pdf (accessed 9 July 2021).

Report of the People's Tribunal on Caste Discrimination & Police Action in University of Hyderabad. 2016. Available at http://sanhati.com/articles/17555/ (accessed 15 June 2021).

Shankar, Aranya. 2016. 'JNU Student Leader Held on "Sedition" Charges over Afzal Guru Event'. *The Indian Express*, 13 February.

Surendran, Vivek. 2016. 'Rohith Vemula's Mother was Dragged on the Streets by Delhi Police. Is Radhika Vemula Incapable of Being Smriti Irani's Mother India?'. *India Today*, 16 February. Available at https://www.indiatoday.in/india/delhi/story/smriti-irani-rohith-vemula-radhika-vemula-delhi-police-assault-310773-2016-02-26 (accessed 24 July 2021).

Tagore, Rabindranath. n.d. 'Gitanjali 35'. *Poetry Foundation*. Available at https://www.poetryfoundation.org/poems/45668/gitanjali-35 (accessed 9 July 2021).

55

Urgent Notes from a University in Crisis*

The events unfolding at the University of Hyderabad are extremely painful, to put it mildly. The sudden and silent entry of the vice-chancellor, Appa Rao Podile, into the campus triggered a massive protest by a large section of students, and a clash between ABVP students and the university administration on the one hand and the protesting students on the other (*The Times of India* 2016; see also *The News Minute* 2016). This was quite unexpected because the university had settled into an uneasy calm and the academic session was near closing for the year.

The first we saw of this was in television news reports, of brutal handling of students and the few teachers with them by *lathi*-wielding police. After this, there was just a repetition of this footage, and the news that close to 30 students and three faculty members had been taken into custody. Professors Tathagata Sengupta and K. Y. Ratnam were among those arrested. There were eyewitness accounts of police beating up Ratnam even while he was trying to intervene and salvage a bad situation (Bhandaram 2016; *Deccan Chronicle* 2016a).

When the arrests were made, I had assumed (rather naïvely) that all of them would be released after a few hours in custody. After they had been in for a night with no release in sight, I made contact with my friend, a teacher in the university, who was keeping close track of the arrested students and faculty. I sent a lawyer to Miyapur police station on 23 March to find out what was happening. From these accounts, I gathered that there was no information on what the police's next move was going to be and every one who asked got a different

* Originally published in *The Wire*, 24 March 2016.

story of what was to happen. It was close to 5 p.m.; there were many lawyers and students waiting at the police station. When nothing seemed to move, I called my friend again around 5 p.m. and heard that they were planning to meet the chief justice. In the meanwhile, at around 7 p.m., my lawyer friend informed me that the reason the detainees were not being produced was that the remand case diaries were not ready. It had been over 24 hours since the arrests had been made. I messaged my friend immediately, conveying this information and suggested that the team meeting the chief justice should bring this to his notice and demand immediate release. I do not know if they met the chief justice.

I had also requested a friend with access to ministers to intervene with the home minister and the chief minister. He did meet the home minister, who expressed his inability to intervene, but the chief minister was not contactable. Since I live at the other end of the city, I had requested a colleague to drop by at the campus and check on what we could do. We had received several appeals for food and water. Bottles would not serve any purpose if water supply was being cut off (see Kadavanad 2016). So we explored the possibility of arranging water tankers for students, but the heavy police presence and barricades led us to abandon that thought immediately. No vehicles were allowed to stop anywhere near the gate and no outsiders were permitted to enter. But I understand that these arrangements were made and friends had been supplying food packets to the campus till late at night. And, of course, the students had been doing some mass cooking as well.

This morning, 24 March, feeling very restless about having people in custody, I went to Miyapur police station. I had received information in the morning that they had been produced before the magistrate at 11 p.m. on 23 March after everyone had left and were remanded to police custody in Miyapur police station. When I arrived at Miyapur around 9:30 a.m., there were a couple of sentries and constables, and the place was quiet. I called my friend, who informed me that it is always quiet, but if I peep around the back of the police station, they will be there—he had found them there in similar circumstances the previous night. So I got into a conversation, introduced myself, was offered a chair, and told that there was no one in custody in that police station. The Gachibowli police station (under whose jurisdiction the university comes) had not had adequate lock-up facilities and so they had kept the group in custody in Miyapur for 'purposes of lock-up and food' (see *Deccan Chronicle* 2016b). They offered to take me around the police station if I wished. I declined and went to Miyapur court, where the bail applications were to be filed. After a long wait there, when there was no sign of anyone appearing on behalf of the arrested students and faculty, I left.

On my way back, I learnt that the group had been produced before the magistrate late at night on 23 March and were sent to judicial remand in Cherlapally jail (see *Report of the People's Tribunal* 2016), not police custody, as I had been told that morning. I further learnt that around 50 more students were going to be arrested and the FIRs were ready—but I do not know this for a fact. This evening, we learnt that the bail hearing has been postponed to Monday, so the group will stay in judicial custody till Monday. One full week in custody, for what reason?

What is most disconcerting about this entire sequence of events is the total indifference on the part of the university administration and its callous disregard for the fact that its own students and faculty had been placed under arrest. And that those that remained were being put through enormous hardship, with no electricity, no water, no food.

I called a friend who is on the faculty and asked why the entire faculty had not risen *in one voice* against the arrests. We may have disagreements and political differences, but there can be no equivocation regarding persons who have been beaten up by the police and placed under illegal detention, and misinformation about the whereabouts of those detained. This is in clear violation of basic principles of criminal law, but I was shocked at the response I received. In response to my troubled queries on the campus situation, I was told that it was a case of media misrepresentation, and that things were going smoothly on campus. When I attempted to probe further on the arrests that had been made and police violence on campus, I was told that there had been an attempt to murder the vice-chancellor and that senior members of the faculty had 'witnessed it'. Attempt to murder? That was nowhere in the allegations or the charges, as far as I knew. What were the actions that amounted to attempt to murder? Were all

30 protesting students involved? According to accounts provided, the trouble had started with a scuffle between ABVP students and protestors. And yet, ABVP students were sifted out by the police and the only students arrested were the protestors. There was no account of any ABVP student being injured in the lathi-charge, in which 200 people were brutally beaten up. Was it necessary to choke off supplies for students on campus? I received no answers. I ended the futile conversation by making my position clear: Even if ABVP students had been beaten by the police in this manner and arrested, I said, I would oppose it strongly and insist that everyone does too.

Let us set everything else aside for a moment. How did the vice-chancellor, his administration and his colleagues (a substantial number with him) even permit the police to exercise disproportionate force against unarmed students (ibid.)? And how are we to understand their complacency in the face of having their own students and faculty in custody?

From a situation where five students (Rohith one of them) faced boycott, we are now witnessing excommunication—the velivada—as administrative strategy for institutional governance. What we see unfolding before us is the Salwa Judum as a method of governance. Our history of caste violence has certainly taught lessons in the most unexpected ways.

References

'25 Students and 2 Faculty Members Arrested for UoH Violence'. 2016a. *Deccan Chronicle*, 24 March.

'HCU Violence: Cops Abused Us, Say Students of Hyderabad Varsity'. 2016b. *Deccan Chronicle*, 29 March.

'Full Text: UoH Alumni's Open Letter on Appa Rao's Return and Campus Violence'. 2016. *The News Minute*, 25 March. Available at https://www.thenewsminute.com/article/full-text-uoh-alumni-s-open-letter-appa-rao-s-return-and-campus-violence-40761 (accessed 9 July 2021).

'VC Returns, University of Hyderabad Erupts'. 2016. *The Times of India*, 23 March.

Bhandaram, Vishnupriya. 2016. 'University of Hyderabad Row: Students Beaten, Campus on Lockdown; 27 Arrested, including University Professor'. *Firstpost*, 24 March. Available at https://www.firstpost.

com/india/university-of-hyderabad-row-students-beaten-campus-on-lockdown-27-arrested-including-university-professor-2693766.html (accessed 9 July 2021).

Kadavanad, Raoof. 2016. 'Inside Hyderabad Central University: "It's Like Being in a Gulag"'. *NewsLaundry*, 26 March. Available at https://www.newslaundry.com/2016/03/26/inside-hyderabad-central-university-its-like-being-in-a-gulag (accessed 9 July 2021).

Report of the People's Tribunal on Caste Discrimination & Police Action in University of Hyderabad. 2016. Available at http://sanhati.com/articles/17555/ (accessed 15 June 2021).

56

The University is Not a Feudal Village*

On Monday, 13 June 2016, two faculty members of the University of Hyderabad, who had been active in their support for the students' movement after the death of Rohith Vemula, were suspended by the executive council, citing a rule that mandates suspension if the faculty member has been in criminal custody for 48 hours or more (*The Times of India* 2016). K. Y. Ratnam, associate professor of political science, and Tathagata Sengupta, assistant professor of mathematics, were arrested on 22 March along with 25 students for alleged 'vandalism' and violence on campus. They were released on bail on 28 March (*The New Indian Express* 2016a). During this period, an FIR was registered naming the vice-chancellor as an accused in Rohith's suicide in a case under the SC/ST (Prevention of Atrocities) Act, on which no action has been initiated to date (*The New Indian Express* 2016b). The question raised instead was whether Rohith was Dalit. In a new development, the collector of Guntur district has declared that Rohith was a Dalit belonging to the Mala caste, as per records of the district. So then there is a serious criminal complaint pending in court against the vice-chancellor, although no arrests have been made as the law mandates. This is not a matter of fixing guilt. That is for the courts to decide. This is just about procedure mandated by law and facts related to that procedure. Two criminal complaints: one is atrocity, the other is vandalism. Neither is proved nor are there convictions. In a strange twist, it is two faculty members of the university who have been suspended for having been arrested contrary to criminal procedure, while the university administration

---

* Originally published as 'Let the University of Hyderabad Not Become a Feudal Village', in *The Wire*, 16 June 2016.

stood watching. This is after the vice-chancellor stated in a letter released to the press on 28 March:

> *I request you to rise above anger and confrontational attitude....* I and my team wish to lead by example in this area, with our willingness to be always open for a dialogue with all students, which we have always been. Let's work towards resolution, instead of confrontation. Let's together build bridges than walls in this university. It's very painful to see some of our students and couple of faculty members from campus spend time in jail. *While I wanted to intervene, legal system is beyond our control and jurisdiction.* (Quoted in Janyala 2016; emphasis mine.)

June is a month of memories of a difficult and challenging time in the life of the country—Emergency was proclaimed on 25 June 1975, marking the beginning of 21 months of fear, unparalleled (till that point) state violence, and the rise of dissent like never before—in courts and outside. It is now 41 years. An entire generation that demonstrated a fearless resolve to restore and repair the democratic fabric has left us. But we can scarcely forget that the young dissenters—students and very young faculty then—are now in decision-making positions in academia—universities and colleges, in the professions and in the administration. While several lost their lives and livelihoods, several that managed to survive, recuperated and built new lives and stable futures. While many of this generation of the intelligentsia may not be involved in movements anymore, and may even actually oppose movements of students on campuses they teach in today, certainly they have memories of their own predicament and politics—present even if muted or masked.

Suspensions, dismissals, rustications and other punitive measures like this were challenged at several levels during the Emergency—teachers and students were at the forefront with universities then, like now, in the eye of the storm. I still have memories of Cherabandaraju, a teacher-poet in custody with a terminal illness, facing suspension, and challenging that suspension in court. Among those that were arrested were people of all shades—not only people of the left, although they outnumbered the others. But there was no denial of politics—rather the assertion was of a right to politics, the right to dissent and the right to participate in democracy through dissent. The university was a space that offered an opportunity for debate on the meanings and failings of democracy and politics of various hues.

As we approach the anniversary of the dark day when Emergency was proclaimed, we are faced with a peculiarly painful situation in the city of Hyderabad, that was the heart and soul of dissent and free speech. It was here that history was made four decades ago every day, in courts and outside—educating the judiciary and common people who flocked to courts and calling governments and administrative authorities to account like never before. Yet today, we are faced with the suspension of two faculty members for being in custody longer than 48 hours.

This was a manifestly illegal arrest and detention that saw several students and two faculty members in custody for close to a week. Despite this, we have one injustice piled onto another—a spell of illegal detention, during which time the university authorities went on record to say that while they were troubled, they had to let the law take its course (*Deccan Chronicle* 2016; see also *Report of the People's Tribunal* 2016). And close on the heels of the release, a suspension that draws its justification from the arrest (*The Times of India* 2016). Clearly, the law meanders in the corridors of power and discretion is weighted in favour of those in power. We have known that for decades. But we also know that it can take a most unexpected turn towards justice, unsettling dominant complacencies rudely—it is good for us to bear the Emergency and its lessons in mind.

However, what is much more urgent and necessary is for university teachers to come out as a strong moral force committed to the values of the Constitution. There are cases of students, intimidated by overt or tacit 'velivada strategies' within institutions of higher education, who have often needed support or external intervention in order to cope; several others have quietly left, unable to cope. The difficulties and hostile environments that teachers have faced is not discussed as often—hostility to do with gender, social location, or ethnic/caste/religious identity, for instance. Peer support has been crucial for their capacity to cope. This university is not an exception.

It is this peer support and moral authority that teachers must exercise in the largest numbers in order to express unequivocal rejection of administrative arbitrariness and vindictiveness against faculty.

For the administration, also driven by teachers, setting a humane, accommodative principle of governance that completely eschews personal animosities and disagreements, welcoming opposing political standpoints is the only way to restoring a climate that is conducive to learning. Silence and distance at this crucial time can erode the fabric of an already beleaguered institution irreparably.

Can we afford to forget that we are not here sitting in a feudal village with a velivada into which we periodically oust students, faculty, non-teaching staff and others in many ways? It is intensely painful to see photographs of Ratnam and Sengupta sitting on strike in front of the university gate with garlands and a small group of supporters (PTI 2016). Rohith called this a velivada (see Aravind and Kumar 2016)—how many teachers have, at various points in their term in this university, found themselves stigmatised and isolated, seeking help from outside and praying for support within? How many others have bought their peace through silence and distance?

It is time that we recognise and resist cultures that ghettoise people into velivadas rather than hastily distancing ourselves from it. This is a university that every one of us has a stake in safeguarding *as* a university. Insisting on the unilateral and unconditional revocation of the suspension of Ratnam and Sengupta of the University of Hyderabad is the only non-negotiable way forward. This insistence must come from the entire faculty in one voice. The 'law' should not instil fear in us or take away our voices and our moral strength—we can imbue the law with moral fibre through our collective voice. It is also necessary to understand the law and understand the gradations of seriousness and gravity therein. And this is not a call for political agreement among all. It is a call for singular action across differences.

References

'Action against UoH Professors an Act of Vengeance'. 2016. *The Times of India*, 17 June.

'HCU Violence: Cops Abused Us, Say Students of Hyderabad Varsity'. 2016. *Deccan Chronicle*, 29 March.

'UoH Vandalism Row: Court Grants Bail to 25 Students and Two Faculties'. 2016a. *The New Indian Express*, 28 March.

'UoH JAC Members Trash Roopanwal Commission's Report'. 2016b. *The New Indian Express*, 8 October.

Aravind, Indulekha and K. P. Narayana Kumar. 2016. 'Dalit Suicide Case: Why Rohith Vemula's Death is the Tipping Point in Caste Bias on Campus'. *The Economic Times*, 24 January.

Janyala, Sreenivas. 2016. 'Hyderabad University Row: 25 Students, Two Faculty Members Get Bail, Classes Resume'. *The Indian Express*, 29 March.

PTI. 2016. 'UoH Faculty Members' Relay Hunger Strike Enters 2nd Day'. *The Times of India*, 15 June.

Report of the People's Tribunal on Caste Discrimination & Police Action in University of Hyderabad. 2016. Available at http://sanhati.com/articles/17555/ (accessed 15 June 2021).

57

A Year after Rohith Vemula's Death . . .*

It is one year since Rohith Vemula shook the foundations of higher education in this country by his words and tragically irreversible action (Chukka 2016; *Firstpost* 2016). This is also a year that has seen the disembowelling of higher education by a national government doggedly pursuing its objective of forcing the bar of intellectual engagement in institutions of higher learning so low that it will take years to undo the damage and rebuild institutions from the rubble (see Singh 2018). The happenings at the University of Hyderabad portend a larger problem that casts a long and dark shadow on individual and collective dignity and self-respect, intellectual engagement, free speech and institutional autonomy.

The last 12 months began with Vemula's painful decision to travel 'from shadows to the stars' (quoted in *The Times of India* 2016). But this is only the beginning of our descent into an abyss—in that alone, Vemula, through his protest and his writing, has forced national attention to the stranglehold of authoritarianism of which the University of Hyderabad is but a microcosm.

Faculty members have asserted that the University of Hyderabad is primarily a liberal arts institution. How then did it lose its way so badly that students interrogating state and judicial action in the exercise of dissent and free speech were hounded and pursued and hunted down? Skirmishes, violent disagreements and deep-seated prejudice are normal to any institution and certainly not restricted to students. The constant reiteration of unacceptable student conduct,

* Originally published as 'One Year after Rohith Vemula's Suicide, a Deepening Crisis in Hyderabad University', in *The Wire*, 16 January 2017.

especially on the part of protesting students in the university would almost have us believe that all other categories of persons—teachers, non-teaching staff, other groups of students—in the university act in complete harmony and peace. Nothing is further from the truth, as is evident in a complaint by a professor that caused security personnel to forcibly enter the residence of a woman faculty member on the university campus in May 2015 (Karri 2015).

Several questions have been raised in the context of the disturbances in the University of Hyderabad. I have elsewhere (Kannabiran 2017) reflected at length on the question of 'certification' and the untenability of the position of the vice-chancellor Appa Rao on the applicability of the SC/ST (Prevention of Atrocities) Act in his case. I will not touch on that very crucial issue here that has again come to the fore with reports of administrative action in support of the vice-chancellor by the government of Andhra Pradesh (Mitta 2016).

The questions I attempt to look at here centre around the dismantling of institutions and processes guaranteeing autonomy that lie at the core of the idea of a university and the specific implications of these processes for Dalit students facing caste discrimination, public debate and real-time experiments in the playground of impunity. By 31 December 2016, we saw this spiral upwards in an alarming fashion through a consolidation of the scaffolding of a post-truth era with the proliferation of tools for the stripping down of all institutional processes in the country (that goes by the name of 'demonetisation'; see Reddy 2017b) with a callousness towards human social suffering that was first signalled to us in the events leading to the death of Rohith and its aftermath.

As in the country, so too in the university before it, the power of post-truth prevailed over the facts—'extremism', 'radicalism', Dalit anti-caste activism dubbed as 'casteism', 'pro-Muslim sentiment', 'anti-Hindu, anti-national activities'—all these terms are used to describe the activities of students organising discussions and film screenings on contemporary politics, justifying harsh and disproportionate punishment in abrogation of procedures and rules by an administration eager to appease a government. The direct trail of communication on this matter between elected members of the ruling party, the national government and the university administration is on record (see MHRD 2016).

The problem of arbitrariness has dropped deep roots, which need to be cleared completely if any semblance of sustainable peace is to return. I am aware, of course, that classes are in progress, teaching schedules are on course and university life has limped back to 'normalcy'. What I think we need to open out for debate is the definition of 'normalcy'.

For this, I will begin with the Indian Science Congress held in Tirupati in early January 2017. The vice-chancellor of the University of Hyderabad, Appa Rao, received the Millennium Plaque of Honour from Prime Minister Modi in recognition of 'his outstanding contribution in the field of biotechnology and also for his work in higher education'. The university issued a press statement that the award was in recognition of his work as an 'institution builder'. It is important to understand this, especially since the spokesperson for the department of science and technology asserted that this was a decision of the Science Congress and not the ministry, since it was an 'autonomous' body (Mukunth 2017).

Reports in the press in April 2016 revealed charges of plagiarism against Rao in 2007 and 2014, both of which he has admitted to: '[It] wasn't a deliberate attempt.... If we have plagiarised others' data, we will retract the paper with regrets' (Mukunth 2016). There was no categorical denial of the plagiarism charge. On this one count alone, the claim to outstanding contribution falls short. But Rao is not to blame since he did not apply for the award, he was nominated, and therefore accepted it. Is this the 'normal' that we seek to build upon in this university? Is this our benchmark? After all, the head of the institution leads by example, or ought to. So before we slither down the slippery slope of 'merit' among students who come in through reservations, let us re-examine our own equivocation of the 'merit' that resides in dominance—caste, social location and institutional position.

However, the declaration of outstanding contribution to the field is mentioned alongside his work in higher education, which the university, in its statement, asserts is 'institution building'. What is his record of institution building?

The fact-finding report of a group of scientists released to the press earlier this month has observed that 'the University, under Prof. Appa Rao, failed to take several important steps in protecting the freedom of students and faculty to register their dissent' (Raju, Shastri and Banyal 2017: 10). In general, the scientists' group observes:

> It is clear that the University administration failed to discharge its responsibilities in a non-partisan manner, and failed to protect academic freedom on campus. Instead of amicably resolving the dispute between the ASA and the ABVP students, the administration succumbed to pressure from the BJP and the central government and took ill-advised and one-sided decisions that led to prolonged agitations and disquiet among a large section of students. Prof. Appa Rao himself failed to act on Mr Rohith Vemula's letter in December 2015, displaying an alarming lack of empathy. Furthermore, the administration failed to prevent the brutal assault by the police on dissenting students on 22 March 2016. We feel that, as the head of the University administration, Prof. Appa Rao should accept responsibility for these failures.
>
> We wish to emphasise that this issue is not about individuals. Any administrative post in an academic institution is about serving the community. In fact, sincere academics are commonly wary of administrative positions, since they are a distraction from academic work. Therefore it makes sense for an academic to continue in an administrative post only to the extent that he or she is able to contribute constructively to the institution. (Ibid.: 6–7)

While there is a deep disquiet within the university over the continuing implications of all that has happened, dialogue, disagreement and debate are already redundant in this age of post-truth, as D. Narasimha Reddy (2017a) observed in a lecture on demonetisation on 9 January. It matters little if you are a liberal arts university. This is an age of post-truth and mythology—there are little mythologies (of academic excellence in the face of charges of plagiarism, and institution building in the face of the thorough dismantling of established procedures) and big mythologies (that it will no longer be Gandhi spinning on the *charkha* [spinning wheel] [*NDTV* 2017] and that *notebandi* [demonetisation] is a war against the wealthy and their ill-gotten wealth will travel to the bank accounts of the poor [Reddy 2017b]). Post-truth politics works through a system of rewards and punishments. For handing

Rohith and others with him the ultimate punishment—dehumanising, humiliating and violent—and demonstrating total acquiescence to the project of policing universities, a moment of glory with the honourable prime minister himself and an award from his hands.

This brings me back to the point where I began. Experiments in the universities that are playgrounds are upscaled with mind-boggling speed to impact every citizen in the country in unimaginable ways. For the university, however, the bar has truly dropped far, far too low and it will take all our collective energies as citizens of a democratic country with a large stake in the resurrection of higher education, and as people who believe in the power of a robust liberal arts tradition to revive a small fraction of what we have lost.

References

'Before Suicide, Rohith Vemula Wrote to the VC: "I Request Your Highness to Make Euthanasia Facility Available"'. 2016. *Firstpost*, 19 January. Available at https://www.firstpost.com/india/rohith-vemula-suicide-cong-trains-guns-on-bjp-rss-wants-bandaru-dattatreya-sacked-from-cabinet-2589482.html (accessed 9 July 2021).

'Full Text: Dalit Scholar Rohith Vemula's Suicide Note'. 2016. *The Times of India*, 19 January.

'PM Narendra Modi Replaces Mahatma Gandhi on Khadi Calendar, Diary; Employees Protest: Report'. 2017. *NDTV*, 13 January. Available at https://www.ndtv.com/india-news/pm-narendra-modi-replaces-mahatma-gandhi-on-khadi-calendar-diary-employees-protest-report-1648360 (accessed 9 July 2021).

Chukka, Vikram. 2016. 'The Chain of Events Leading to Rohith Vemula's Suicide'. *The Wire*, 19 January. Available at https://thewire.in/education/the-chain-of-events-leading-to-rohith-vemulas-suicide (accessed 9 July 2021).

Kannabiran, Kalpana. 2017. 'Of Law, Resurrection and a Future'. *Seminar* 689 (January). Available at https://www.india-seminar.com/2017/689.htm (accessed 17 September 2021).

Karri, Sriram. 2015. 'At Hyderabad University, Both Teachers and Students are on Strike – with Different Grouses'. *Scroll.in*, 3 September. Available at https://scroll.in/article/752995/at-hyderabad-university-both-teachers-and-students-are-on-strike-with-different-grouses (accessed 9 July 2021).

MHRD (Ministry of Human Resource Development). 2016. *Laying of the Report of the Justice Ashok Kumar Roopanwal (Retd) Commission of Inquiry and Memorandum of Action Taken Thereon on the Table of Both the Houses of Parliament*. Available at https://www.education.gov.in/sites/upload_files/mhrd/files/document-reports/JusticeAshokKumarRoopanwalReport.pdf (accessed 9 July 2021).

Mitta, Manoj. 2016. 'How This Self-Proclaimed Pro-Dalit Government Has All but Buried the Rohith Vemula Case'. *Scroll.in*, 31 December. Available at https://scroll.in/article/825545/how-this-self-proclaimed-pro-dalit-government-has-all-but-buried-the-rohith-vemula-case (accessed 25 July 2021).

Mukunth, Vasudevan. 2016. 'Hyderabad University VC Admits to Plagiarism'. *The Wire*, 5 April. Available at https://thewire.in/education/hyderabad-university-vc-admits-to-plagiarism (accessed 9 July 2021).

———. 2017. 'Science Honour for "Partisan" Hyderabad University VC Charged with Plagiarism Triggers Row'. *The Wire*, 4 January. Available at https://thewire.in/politics/appa-rao-science-congress (accessed 9 July 2021).

Raju, Suvrat, Prajval Shastri and Ravinder Banyal. 2017. *A Fact-Finding Report on the Events at the University of Hyderabad*. Available at http://www.suvratraju.net/openscholar/suvrat/files/report.pdf (accessed 9 July 2021).

Reddy, D. Narasimha. 2017a. 'Demonetisation, Black Money and Corruption: Truth, Post-Truth, Mythology'. Public lecture. Council for Social Development (CSD), Hyderabad, 9 January.

———. 2017b. 'Demonetisation, Corruption and Black Money'. *Frontline*, 24 November.

Singh, Vikram. 2018. '4 Years of Systematic Destruction of Education under Modi Regime'. *NewsClick*, 15 June. Available at https://www.newsclick.in/4-years-systematic-destruction-education-under-modi-regime (accessed 9 July).

58

'I Don't See What is Happening within Universities as Separate from What is Happening in the Political Arena'*

REBECCA BOWERS: Given a growing number of incidents on university campuses, what can be done to ensure that freedom of expression is upheld in India?

KALPANA KANNABIRAN: The troubles of university campuses are linked to the threat that higher education poses to political orders. This is not the first time that students have been targets, it happened during the Emergency of 1975, where students were disappeared, there was arbitrary arrest and torture in custody and a number of people died. All of those cases were brought to court and enquiry committees were set up. Since the post-Emergency mobilisation against state violence, there have been incidents, but this kind of systematic targeting of campuses is quite unprecedented.

There are two aspects to this that I think that are important. One is that in this intervening period, we have seen the rise of Dalit movements and the large entry of Dalit students into universities, both through reservation policies and through the general quota (so it's not true to say that Dalit students have come in only through

---

* This interview was originally published in *South Asia @ LSE*, the official blog of LSE South Asia Centre, on 17 May 2017, and is reproduced here with permission from LSE South Asia Centre.

This interview was conducted by Rebecca Bowers on 30 March 2017 in New Delhi, during 'India @ 70', the London School of Economics (LSE) South Asia Centre's summit to mark the seventieth anniversary of India's independence. At the time of the interview, Bowers was a final-year PhD student in the anthropology department at LSE.

reservations). All of these students have come from families and social backgrounds where they have actually witnessed and experienced discrimination, and they bring the seeds of resistance with them to university campuses hoping that university campuses will nurture the power of questioning.

The university is a transformative space and Dalit students come with aspirations of social justice and with the idea that they can—through the medium of university education—transform societies and in the process transform the university as well. But what they find is that there are problems with interpersonal relations, whether it is between faculty and students or between different students, and with the curriculum and the approach to the curriculum. There are also deep-seated prejudices around reservations, particularly on the part of the administrative and academic community. There are exceptions and exceptions are important, but on a broad level, you have a mismatch between their expectations and aspirations of what a university should be and what a university turns out to be.

The university is then a conflicted space because you are dealing with outside social conflicts within the university space, but you are also contesting the terms on which this education is delivered to you and insisting they change. This brings in a cogent critique of caste and linking it to the larger right to political dissent and free speech. It is that constellation that is very new in the movements that you are witnessing in the universities and the linkage of these movements to rights and political movements outside.

As a result, you hear the different resonances of azaadi within the university campuses and this can be quite unsettling for a dominant, authoritarian community that is in control of the governance of the university. So, of course, when you are threatened and you do not understand what and how pedagogy of practice needs to be reshaped within these spaces, you turn to repression. Either the police will not take your permission when they enter, or you will give the police your permission to enter, as we witnessed in the University of Hyderabad. You will have the lathi-charges and student arrests, as you witnessed both in Hyderabad (Bhandaram 2016) and in JNU (PTI 2016). The conservative student elements can never reach this height of violence if they are not shored up by the administration, the police and politicians. The source of their courage is the guarantee of impunity. So I actually don't see what is happening within universities as separate from what is happening within the political arena. They were never separate.

The second point is that whatever violence you see within universities and whatever reduction and negation of association or free speech you see within universities, is also tied to governmental policy on higher education. For example, you have a directive that all of the centres of social exclusion and inclusivity are to be shut down because you have refused to renew their grants (*The Wire* 2017a). They are on Plan grants every five years, but with no notice they are terminated. Those centres were first established by an extremely proactive chairman of the University Grants Commission, Professor S. K. Thorat, in response to this pattern of education within universities where questions of exclusions and discrimination do not enter the formal curriculum. He tried to bring in a social consciousness, by mandating centres that would then function within schools of social sciences and that would link up with different departments but focus on exclusion and discrimination (see Mishra 2013).

If you shut down these centres at this political moment then you are making sure that all that work goes out of the window. It's not only centres of social exclusion, it's also centres for human rights and women's study centres. These are the centres that have promoted and nurtured dissent in fundamental ways and that have posed a challenge to the status quo. So actually, what you are doing is that you are choking off higher education.

At the same time you have a Rashtriya Swayamsevak Sangh (RSS) leader calling a meeting with vice-chancellors and senior academics, several of whom attended this meeting in order to talk about how they are going to change the course of higher education (*The Wire* 2017b). So it's not a small thing that's happening, you know? It's a very concerted political movement, with people losing their lives, and others losing jobs or the right to higher education.

RB: In the panel you mentioned the educational value of Article 17 of the Constitution. How might this be recognised and incorporated in legal education?

KK: I taught in a law school for a decade and found that constitutional law was a very potent subject. There were some parts of the Constitution that were taught: Article 15(3), which talks about special provisions for women was taught a little bit, and 15(4), that talks about reservations for Scheduled Castes and Scheduled Tribes, were taught. But Article 15(1), which defines discrimination, was not taught. Even with teaching law around reservations, you are never taught the principle of reservation without immediately skewing it by talking about the 'creamy layer'. Similarly, you don't talk about Article 17—the abolition of untouchability—at all. Upendra Baxi (2010: 63) has called it the only constitutional criminal law provision, which it is, because the Constitution does not have any other bans of conduct.

I knew for a fact that my students were not taught Article 17 in their constitutional law class. So from my second year onwards, I started to look at the parts of criminal law that are not taught. Which parts of the Constitution are not on the curriculum? I incorporated these with the readings from social movements in my sociology of law class. Once I started opening the field out, many of the students got quite excited by what they were learning. Sexual offences were very often not taught, and the SC/ST (Prevention of Atrocities) Act was never taught in criminal law. I used to teach those in sociology too. There is a huge issue around how formal law teaching structures itself along lines of the status quo. You will find a handful of teachers, perhaps more now, but between 1999 and 2009, there were very few who touched disability, or caste, all of these issues.

RB: How might the law be able to identify and address discrimination in its intersectional forms?

KK: The standard approach of courts has been to see non-discrimination in silos. Article 15(1) has an interesting structure that talks about nobody being discriminated against on grounds of sex, caste, religion, race, place of birth 'or any of them'. One of the arguments which I elaborated on in my book on constitutional law (Kannabiran 2012) is that Article 15(1) is a provision that coaxes you to take an intersectional view of discrimination. When I looked at a dictionary of legal usage, I found that the term 'or' can be 'more' or 'and' in legal usage.

I argue that you never have discrimination on one ground only. In its manifestation, it is always intersectional and just because it's intersectional, you can't refuse to look at it. So you can't be discriminated against on these grounds or any other. Both intersectionality and analogous interpretations are written into Article 15. I don't know how many takers I had but I did make that argument.

RB: Finally, would you say the Disabilities Act goes far enough?

KK: Following a major process, we have a new one.[1] There are many contestations, one of which is that it is not strong enough on gender and disability—the gender provisions are rather weak (Banerjee 2017). On the other hand, if you look at what we had prior to this, it is a huge jump and I guess it is the best that we have for the moment.

I was a part of the team that made submissions to the parliamentary standing committee for the new act. We conducted a national consultation, got opinions on the draft legislation and then submitted written submissions to the parliamentary standing committee and so on. I was an interested bystander because a lot of my work also focuses on people with disabilities in rural areas and urban poor neighbourhoods. If I look at it from that standpoint, and the responses of people who were organising on the ground, those groups welcomed the advance that it represents. It is a huge leap forward from what we had: it incorporates a lot of the provisions, whether it is due diligence or the definition of disability, which has expanded considerably, and the non-discrimination provisions are strong. We will need to work this through, but at least they didn't just repeal the act and leave nothing in its place.

RB: And this can potentially be further amended?

KK: Of course. It is a statute and can be amended further. I think increasingly we need to bring disability within the purview of constitutional jurisprudence because courts are adamant that Article 15 cannot be read analogously and grounds have to be specific. I took a case to the then Andhra Pradesh State Human Rights Commission on reserving seats for disabled candidates in the local bodies' elections and they said, 'You can't argue this under [Article] 15, it will only go under

16 [equality of opportunity in matters of public employment].' I said, 'I want to argue it under 15 as an analogous ground being immutable.' I pointed them to the fact that Article 15 does not mention tribe. Article 15(1) says race, caste, sex, place of birth or any other, but tribe has been brought under 15(1) right at the founding of the Constitution. It hasn't registered that it has been brought in analogously because people tend to think of Scheduled Caste and Scheduled Tribe as twin categories and so, although caste is mentioned, you read tribe into that but tribe is not explicitly mentioned.

So we have a history of analogous interpretations in Article 15, but you still need a judge who will accept the argument. I constantly make a distinction between the text and what we, as academics, invested in the Constitution: What are the ways in which we can throw light, new light, on the text of constitutional conditions? Which are the interpretative traditions that we celebrate and which are the ones that we would discount in our reading of the Constitution? I think that's really important.

Note

1. The Rights of Persons with Disabilities Act, 2016.

References

'UGC Cuts Funding for Social Discrimination Research Centres across the Country'. 2017a. *The Wire*, 17 March. Available at https://thewire.in/education/ugc-funding-social-discrimination (accessed 9 July 2021).

'RSS Holds Workshop at Delhi University to Make Education System More "Indian"'. 2017b. *The Wire*, 27 March. Available at https://thewire.in/education/rss-du-workshop-indian-values (accessed 9 July 2021).

Banerjee, Poulomi. 2017. 'Does the New Act for the Disabled Represent the Needs of Differently Abled Women?'. *Hindustan Times*, 8 January.

Baxi, Upendra. 2010. 'The Judiciary as a Resource for Indian Democracy'. *Seminar* 615 (November): 61–67.

Bhandaram, Vishnupriya. 2016. 'University of Hyderabad Row: Students Beaten, Campus on Lockdown; 27 Arrested, including University Professor'. *Firstpost*, 24 March. Available at https://www.firstpost.com/india/university-of-hyderabad-row-students-beaten-campus-on-lockdown-27-arrested-including-university-professor-2693766.html (accessed 9 July 2021).

Kannabiran, Kalpana. 2012. *Tools of Justice: Non-discrimination and the Indian Constitution*. New Delhi: Routledge.

Mishra, Alya. 2013. 'Apex Body Slammed for Move to Shut Down 32 Centres'. *University World News*, 13 July. Available at https://www.universityworldnews.com/post.php?story=20130711164322120 (accessed 9 July 2021).

PTI. 2016. 'JNU Row: Umar Khalid, Anirban Bhattacharya Surrender to Delhi Police'. *Mint*, 24 February.

XII

Human Rights Cultures

59

Development, Justice and the Constitution*

Three judgements by the Supreme Court in the month of July 2011 mark a sharp departure from pedantic legalism and point to the possibilities of a transformative constitutionalism that sustains and elaborates the idea of constitutional morality developed in the *Naz Foundation* judgement of the Delhi High Court in 2009.[1] The three cases are also very different pieces that speak to different realities in a similar fashion: *Ram Jethmalani*,[2] *Nandini Sundar*,[3] and *Delhi Jal Board*.[4] It might be argued, and rightly too, that radical jurisprudence by the Supreme Court is not a recent phenomenon—it has an older history rooted in struggles for civil and political rights. While that is the genealogy of this jurisprudence, we need yet to celebrate each signpost in the development of deliberative jurisprudence that responds not merely to the manifestations of a case, narrowly construed, but sees the larger socio-political context as an inextricable part of the bare facts, so to speak.

The guarantee of public goods—security, infrastructure for governance, law-making and enforcement, provision of material and cultural goods especially for classes that lack the power, privilege and status to secure these for themselves—is a state obligation. Neither markets (which cater to self-centred activities of individuals and groups) nor purely private social action can be expected to stand in for the state and provide public goods.[5] Tracing the link between the existence of perennial channels for unaccounted monies abroad and the erosion of developmental goals of the state, the Supreme Court contextualises the need to reign in cash flows and ensure

* Originally published in *The Hindu*, 27 July 2011.

total accountability with reference to the structure of a neoliberal economy. Gunnar Myrdal's caution about the dangers of a 'soft state' that spawns an 'unholy nexus between the law maker, the law keeper, and the law breaker' is immediately relevant.[6] Central to the delineation of the problem in these cases is the opening out of the idea of constitutionalism to include a broader idea of justice that enables the mapping of injustice in all its complexity.

> Carried away by the ideology of neo-liberalism, it is entirely possible that the agents of the State entrusted with the task of supervising the economic and social activities may err more on the side of extreme caution, whereby signals of wrongdoing may be ignored even when they are strong. Instances of the powers that be ignoring publicly visible stock market scams, or turning a blind eye to large-scale illegal mining have become all too familiar, and may be readily cited.[7]

The framework of justice by this token stretches illimitably beyond the narrow confines of constitutional law and decides cases to the letter and spirit of the Constitution.

'Modern constitutionalism posits that no wielder of power should be allowed to claim the right to perpetrate state's violence against any one, much less its own citizens, unchecked by law, and notions of innate human dignity of every individual.'[8]

In Chhattisgarh

The court locates the heart of the conflict and repression in Chhattisgarh in the amoral political economy endorsed by the state and the departure of state policy from Nehruvian socialism in favour of a free-market economy, the natural corollary of which is 'muscular and violent statecraft'.[9] The intimate connections between neoliberal economic policy and a violently authoritarian state have been demonstrated in one country after another. The routine derogation of fundamental rights and human rights, large-scale displacement and dispossession of primarily indigenous tribal communities is an inseparable part of this process.

Courts have more often than not insulated themselves from philosophical and political frameworks of justice, ploughing the over-trodden, unproductive furrow of strictly applied 'constitutional law' instead. Drawing on a wide range of writing—from Joseph Conrad's *Heart of Darkness* (1899) to reports prepared at the instance of the Planning Commission—the Salwa Judum judgement puts back into focus the constitutional scheme with socialism and the Directive Principles of State Policy at the centre. It is against this backdrop that the Supreme Court frames the issue of compliance to Articles 14 and 21, and Article 355 with specific reference to the large-scale occupation of schools and hostels by security forces, ostensibly to combat Maoist forces; the deployment of the 'Koya commandos' or the Salwa Judum, and the arbitrary use of extreme violence by this militia armed by the state; the arbitrary terms of employment of this tribal workforce that violates constitutional safeguards; and the obstruction of citizens' peace missions by the state. The adverse impact of this entire scenario is directly on the Adivasi communities of Chhattisgarh—both as gun-toting Special Police Officers and subjugated villagers.

Sewerage Workers

The *Delhi Jal Board* case points to the predicament of sewerage workers in a globalised economy where essential jobs are outsourced by the state, which then refuses to take responsibility for the health or safety of workers, and challenges claims to reparations. The specific questions placed before the Supreme Court by the state authorities concerned the *locus standi* of the National Campaign for Dignity and Rights of Sewerage and Allied Workers; the appropriation of legislative powers by the high court; and the validity of the high court's order of interim compensation to families of workers who had died after inhaling noxious fumes while cleaning manholes. That the state needs judicial intervention (which ironically, it challenges) in order to provide the barest of safeguards and entitlements to the most underprivileged category of workers is cause for concern, throwing, as it does, the entire range of constitutional guarantees and obligations to the wind.

While upholding the decision of the Delhi High Court, the Supreme Court, importantly for us, asserts that social action litigation is an important part of constitutionalism. In a situation where the implementation of the goals set out in the Preamble to the Constitution has been halting and sporadic over six decades, the court observes, arguments against judicial activism and on judicial overreach have the sole object of tiring out those who espouse the cause of the weak and the poor.[10] Yet, private social action can only force public accountability—remedies are and must be part of state obligation (as the *Ram Jethmalani* bench reminds us).

Each of the three cases considered here demonstrate the significance of social action—the campaign against state repression and the Salwa Judum in Chhattisgarh, the nationwide campaign against corruption that began, in a sense, with the movement for the right to information, and the movement for dignity of workers engaged in hazardous and stigmatised forms of labour. The judgements draw important connections between courts, social sciences and social movements, connections that are often forgotten or negated in courts.

These judgements take a radical view of 'development', thereby addressing not just fundamental rights, but importantly, rendering the Directive Principles justiciable in effect—by resisting a disaggregated reading of the Constitution. At the other end, what the constitutionalism approach to the problem of development accomplishes is the framing of development as a bounded endeavour—and hence of justice as spatially and socially hedged in, to be held together by the state, through clear measures of protection against harm, distribution of good and the realisation of capabilities. These are not responsibilities easily or willingly borne by any government, but are undeniably state responsibility and must be used to discipline governments.

Notes

1. *Naz Foundation*, (2009) 160 DLT 277.
2. Ram Jethmalani & Ors v. Union of India & Ors, (2011) 8 SCC 1.
3. *Nandini Sundar*, (2011) 7 SCC 547.
4. Delhi Jal Board v. National Campaign for Dignity and Rights of Sewerage and Allied Workers, CA No. 5322 of 2011, decided on 12 July 2011 (SC), arising out of SLP (C) No. 12345 of 2009.
5. *Ram Jethmalani*, (2011) 8 SCC 1, para. 7.

6. Quoted in ibid., para. 10.
7. Ibid., para. 15.
8. *Nandini Sundar*, (2011) 7 SCC 547, para. 3.
9. Ibid., para. 8.
10. *Delhi Jal Board*, CA No. 5322 of 2011 (SC), para. 15.

60

Regulating Cultures through Food Policing*

The controversy over the beef festival on 15 April 2012 organised on the campus of Osmania University in Hyderabad and the threat of professors being investigated by the police for 'instigating' the organisers (*The Hindu* 2012) needs to be understood in the context of the larger politics of food and policing of food practices.

Across the country, different communities in different regions have widely varying food habits. It is also well known that food is closely linked to ideas of the sacred and the profane—and must vary along the scale of social diversity. The dense nesting of beliefs related to food extends from what vegetables may be consumed, whether meat may be consumed or not, which kinds of meats are considered food and which not, which kinds of meat are deemed vegetarian, and whether animal products come within the definition of meat or not.

Ideas about Eating

Ideas about food also extend to who can eat together; within a family, who consumes which parts of an animal's body; what is the sequence in which people in a family eat, depending on gender, generation and social status; whether vice-chancellors, judges and peons can partake of the same feast at the same time—or in earlier times or even today, in more self-declaredly caste-ridden locales, whether the '*chuhri*' (woman belonging to the Valmiki caste) can even dare to ask for freshly cooked food from 'Chowdhriji'—to recall Omprakash Valmiki's *Joothan* (2007). And further in the caste context, who must not be sighted by a Brahmin man while he is in the vulnerable state of ingesting

* Originally published in *The Hindu*, 1 May 2012.

food—the Shudra, the menstruating woman, pigs, dogs—all to be equally banished from sight.

Because food is surrounded by thick religiosity, there are days and times of the year and cycles in a month or in a reproductive lifetime when certain foods are proscribed and others mandatory. There are also rigid rules around the slaughter of animals and the preparation of meat for consumption—meat consumers do not eat all meats and do not eat the same meat at any place. The acceptance of meat as food is determined by whether the slaughter of the animal has been appropriate. And there are castes who were condemned to eat only carrion, not animals freshly slaughtered for consumption. There are communities in Andhra Pradesh that share the hunt with the tiger—they believe the tiger leaves enough of its prey for its human kin—with a delicate balance in mutual food security in the deep forests. When religions proscribe the killing of animals, communities of believers who live in hostile and difficult mountainous terrain may drive a herd off a cliff and strip and dry the meat to meet a year's supply of meat. Even with people and communities that eat meat, there are places and times when meat may be eaten—and these vary widely as well. While a religious occasion for some may be marked by the abstinence from meat, for others it is marked by the sacrifice of an animal, its ceremonial preparation and its distribution in a prescribed manner among kin.

Attitudes

Ideas of purity, danger, potency, malevolence, uncleanness, tastes (not individual but social) and aesthetics thickly overlay our attitude to food. Faint-hearted but Brahminical consumers of meat can swoon or get terribly sick at the sight of a butcher at work, or the sight of 'unclean' parts of the animal body—entrails, head, hooves and so on. The same could be the case with lovers of fish when they see a beach overlaid with dry, pungent fish or the baskets of fish vendors on the train on their way to the market. Similarly too, it is not uncommon to find strong negative reactions to snake gourd, bitter gourd and several other vegetables, not to speak of cooking oils, from vegetarians. There are, of course, caste hierarchies in vegetables and oils too.

Its life-giving and life-sustaining quality also makes food the medium through which faith is expressed, through sharing on particular auspicious, festive occasions. Who food is shared with and how is determined by status and social location ranging from 'poor feeding' to mutual exchanges of festive food. There is then the renunciation of certain foods as acts of faith (temporarily or permanently) or as an acknowledgement of loss and mourning. It is not uncommon to hear of people giving up their favourite food on the death of a loved one. And of course, giving up food is a way of renouncing life itself.

Change in Habits

There are also histories of food habits that show that they change over time: the beef-eating Vedic Brahmin (Ambedkar 1990 [1948]; Jha 2009) is a well-known example.

Among the meats that are consumed in India are chicken, goat, fish and other aquatic creatures, frog, dog, pork, monkey, beef, buffalo, a variety of insects, field rats, deer, a range of birds, some reptiles and many, many more. Across this entire range of food, there are some we might love and relish, and others we might recoil at the mention of. What we relish and what we find unthinkable depends on religion, caste, tribe, and social location, after which individual taste plays a role. The diversity in food habits is part of the plurality of cultures, and the right to consume, accept and share food, privately and in festivity, is part of cultural expression.

To the extent that culture is a matter of politics, food becomes the mobilising point for politics. We have sizeable communities in India who eat beef and pork—and these are the two meats on the Indian subcontinent that are used to stoke collective emotions in ways that present polarised stereotypes. Yet we know that the realities of beef and pork consumption defy these stereotypes. Both are traditionally consumed not just by non-Hindus but by subaltern castes and some meat-eating castes as well, a reality that is denied by the Brahminical dominant castes.

In this context, if there is a hegemonic cultural formation across or within a religious group that proscribes or stigmatises the consumption of certain kinds of foods, a central part of resistance and of cultural assertion is to share that food publicly. Acquiescing to one proscription will pave the way for another, and the intolerance to diversity in food habits and through food to plural cultures will spiral upwards.

The choice of whether or not to partake of the feast is one an individual makes. In the recent beef festival organised on the campus of Osmania University, there were no reports of any coercion or force-feeding of beef to unwilling people. The people who were there went because they wanted to be there and were people for whom beef was not taboo. The argument on the need to take action against spreading hatred can scarcely be sustained. Even more irrelevant is the suggestion that professors were instigating students—it was a gathering of consenting, free-thinking adults.

The organising of a food festival is not a matter for courts to interfere with or order an investigation into. There are more pressing matters related to life and liberty that wait endlessly to get a hearing.

References

'Beef Festival Turns Varsity into a Battlefield, Student Stabbed'. 2012. *The Hindu*, 17 April.

Ambedkar, B. R. 1990 [1948]. *The Untouchables: Who Were They and Why They Became Untouchables?* (Dr Babasaheb Ambedkar: Writings and Speeches, vol. 7). Bombay: Government of Maharashtra.

Jha, D. N. 2009. *The Myth of the Holy Cow*. New Delhi: Navayana.

Valmiki, Omprakash. 2007. *Joothan*, trans. Arun Prabha Mukerjee. Kolkata: Samya.

61

Paresh Rawal Must Be Asked to Forfeit His Seat*

Actor and BJP MP Paresh Rawal tweets: 'Instead of tying stone pelter on the army jeep tie up Arundhati Roy!' (quoted in Dasgupta 2017). His reference is to the degrading and inhuman treatment meted out to Farooq Ahmed Dar, who was tied to a jeep by army major, Leetul Gogoi, as a human shield against stone-pelters during the recent elections in Kashmir, for which Gogoi has received a commendation card from the army (see Bagriya 2017). Rawal's statement is particularly serious as it is not restricted to the specific action, but is an incitement to further violence of that nature against civilians at large. With each passing day, we see the escalation of violence at every level against persons belonging to marginalised social groups, particularly against Muslims in the recent spate, in the orchestrated pogroms of cow vigilantism (for example, Raj 2017). This incitement to deploy degrading and inhuman treatment, and brutal violence against a writer—incitement that is tacitly supported by the ruling party—has the immediate danger of escalating the gruesome violence that we are already witnesses to. This is violence being propagated on social media by a Member of Parliament, of the ruling BJP.

The Constitution of India binds us to democratic political traditions based on a respect for universal values, especially concerning life, liberty and dignity and importantly, dissenting political views—these are non-negotiable. The right to dissent is at the core of Article 19, guaranteed to all citizens under the Constitution. Incitement to violence and propagation of such violence against

* Originally published as 'By Inciting Violence, Paresh Rawal, MP, Must Surely Forfeit His Seat', in *The Wire*, 26 May 2017.

persons who dissent—an incitement that has the clear and proven danger of escalating violence indiscriminately on the ground, against dissenters and all those who do not subscribe to narrowly prescribed Hindutva ideologies/diktats—is a grave derogation of both Article 19 guarantees, and the guarantee to life and personal liberty under Article 21. At a time when ordinary citizens who approach courts for ordinary relief are told that the ignorance of the law is not an excuse, what do the honourable courts say about this incitement to violence which, in fact, constitutes perjury of the constitutional oath taken by the legislator?

Under the Third Schedule III(B) of the Constitution of India, the oath Rawal took would have read:

> I, Paresh Rawal, having been elected (or nominated) a member of the Council of States (or the House of the People) do swear in the name of God that I will bear true faith and allegiance to the Constitution of India as by law established, that I will uphold the sovereignty and integrity of India and that I will faithfully discharge the duty upon which I am about to enter.

Every elected representative, importantly, by token of taking this oath, carries the specific responsibility to uphold the integrity of India, which is measured by the degree of their allegiance to the values embodied in the Constitution, the degree to which they represent the spirit of the Constitution, and the degree to which it guides their conduct in public life and their approach to governance. Full allegiance to the Constitution is non-negotiable in order to stay in public office.

What should be done when sitting members of the legislature incite or propagate violence in direct violation of the law and in derogation of their constitutional oath of office? What are the measures we as citizens may take to restrain gross misdemeanour on the part of legislators? At several points in our history post-Independence, courts have stepped in to craft a stunningly innovative jurisprudence of constitutionalism. Perhaps, yet again, the time has come.

The law governing elections and conduct of candidates running for election are set out in the Representation of People Act, 1951. Grounds for disqualification of elected members are prescribed in Article 191 of the Constitution of India, but courts have held that this Article is not exhaustive, allowing for the inclusion of hitherto unanticipated grounds. Public misdemeanour, incitement to violence, wilful disregard of the law and international standards in public conduct, insofar as they signal an assault on the fundamental right to life with dignity and personal liberty, and insofar as they signal the incitement to commit a war crime under international humanitarian law, certainly fall within the most minimal framework of accountability under the Constitution.

Rawal is guilty of perjury of the constitutional oath on which he assumed office. The punishment for perjury of the constitutional oath is immediate loss of office. As the Kerala High Court observed in the case of *K. C. Chandy* (1986):

> The oath of office insisted upon under the Constitution is the prescription of a fundamental code of conduct in the discharge of the duties of these high offices. The oath binds the person throughout his tenure in that office, and he extricates himself from the bonds of the oath only when he frees himself from the office he holds. Breach of this fundamental conduct of good behaviour may result in the deprivation of the very office he holds.[1]

A remedy is implicit in every fundamental right. The remedy implicit in the right to vote is the right of recall, which is not restricted to mere disqualification, but extends importantly to forfeiture of office for failure to satisfy the grounds of continuance.

Following K. G. Kannabiran's insistence a decade ago on opening out this possibility in another context, it is perhaps time to invoke the ancient English writ of *scire facias*, which was replaced by *quo warranto*—a writ which prescribed a proceeding for the forfeiture of office on grounds of misbehaviour, the assumption being that office may only be held 'during good behaviour' (Kannabiran and Kannabiran 2007: 3607). According to Raoul Berger (2002: 131), '[w]hen the framers employed "good behaviour", a common law term of ascertainable meaning, with no indication that they were employing it in a new and different sense, it might be presumed that they implicitly adopted the judicial enforcement machinery that traditionally went with it.'

Constitutional morality may guide us along unanticipated paths, if only we are willing to unfetter ourselves and imaginatively open institutions of justice out to the meaning and essence of the Constitution. This is now indispensable to our collective survival and our collective claim to dignity and full citizenship.

Each utterance or action like this diminishes each of us by the day—it utterly strips the perpetrators and their cohorts of any claim to the right to political office, occupied increasingly only through coercion, lawlessness and radical evil. One day soon enough, the little child in the crowd will cry, 'But the emperor has no clothes on!' Impunity is never a permanent guarantee, and has never been so in history. I am, of course, extremely concerned about the slow death we are dying by being helpless bystanders bearing mute witness to this mayhem, which has the imprint of the state.

The use of human shields (whether prisoners of war, protected civilians or civilians in general) is a war crime under international humanitarian law prohibited in international and non-international contexts (for a detailed discussion, see Varadarajan 2017). Yet, as citizens of the 'world's largest democracy', one that has prided itself on gifting philosophies of non-violence to the modern world—that have, in important ways, as Baxi (2002: 27) has argued, become the *jus cogens* of international law—we are confronted with a situation where the army publicly uses a human shield in Kashmir, and an elected legislator of the ruling BJP tweets his endorsement. Both in gross and brazen violation of accepted standards and protocols on the treatment of persons in situations of combat/occupation/army actions, as the case may be both in international and non-international contexts.

Today, the repeated utterances of elected representatives of the ruling party with impunity makes this exercise of our right to full and informed citizenship with dignity even more urgent. At a more immediate level, there must be an urgent initiation of criminal proceedings against Rawal for these utterances, and forfeiture of his seat. The larger question of collective/command responsibility for this brazen disregard of the Constitution by a person in constitutional office, and the violation of standards set out in international humanitarian law in the case of Farooq Ahmed Dar in Kashmir remains to be addressed.

Note

1. K. C. Chandy v. Balakrishna Pillai, 1986 AIR Ker 116.

References

Bagriya, Ashok. 2017. 'Army Major Gogoi Who Tied Kashmiri Man to Jeep Has Legal Trouble Headed His Way, but Can't be Arrested'. *Hindustan Times*, 26 May.

Baxi, Upendra. 2002. *The Future of Human Rights*. New Delhi: Oxford University Press.

Berger, Raoul. 2002. *Impeachment: The Constitutional Problems*. Cambridge, MA: Harvard University Press.

Dasgupta, Binayak. 2017. '"Tie Arundhati Roy to Army Jeep": Paresh Rawal Kicks Up a Storm on Twitter'. *Hindustan Times*, 26 May.

Kannabiran, K. G., and Kalpana Kannabiran. 2007. 'Taslima Case: Accountability of Elected Representatives'. *Economic and Political Weekly* 42, no. 36 (8–14 September): 3605–08.

Raj, Suhasini. 2017. 'Hindu Cow Vigilantes in Rajasthan, India, Beat Muslim to Death'. *The New York Times*, 5 April.

Varadarajan, Siddharth. 2017. 'Why International Law Matters, from Kulbhushan Jadhav to Kashmiri Human Shield'. *The Wire*, 22 May. Available at https://thewire.in/diplomacy/icj-india-kulbhushan-jadhav-human-shield-kashmir (accessed 26 June 2021).

XIII

Futures of Citizenship

62

Of Law, Resurrection and a Future*

Complex and difficult debates around law have burst to the surface yet again in India with a cluster of very troubling issues—some old debates that persist in sliding back each time in Sisyphean fashion; some new troubles with a new law; some interpretations of law that border on absurdity, foregrounding the fragility of constitutional morality within constitutional courts—but all pointing to the precarity of dignity and survival in a society with graded inequalities and deeply entrenched patriarchies that remain rooted, after decades of struggle against caste and religious fundamentalism, movements for civil liberties, law reforms and feminist engagement.

The context for the current debates, we must never forget, is set by the rule(s) of 'law' in a larger environment of a total constitutional breakdown and counter-factual assertions as the bedrock for the interpretation of 'law' and 'justice' in the everyday—from the 'counterfeit grief' of the 'Supreme Leader' (to borrow from Apoorvanand 2016) to the canonisation of mobs on the rampage (the tricolour adorning the body of the prime accused in the murder of Mohammed Akhlaq in Dadri [*India Today* 2016]) to the celebration of the courage of police officers who kill unarmed prisoners in custody (the chilling murder of undertrials from the Students Islamic Movement of India [SIMI] in Madhya Pradesh [Ghatwai 2016]) and the criminalisation of an entire people (Kashmir [Waheed 2016]). Muslims are at the centre of this entire routinisation of dispossession, loss of life, dignity and security as never before. And finally, the absurd interpretation, in a constitutional era, of the duties of a Hindu son to his parents, where the Supreme Court held that a suicide bid by a wife is cruelty to the husband since he will be entangled with the law for life; and

* Originally published in *Seminar*, January 2017.

that asking the husband to set up a matrimonial home apart from his parents is cruelty, since it obstructs the Hindu son from his pious obligation to his parents.[1]

Precipitation of conflict when it comes to food cultures (for example, Noorani 2016), the rise in practices and technologies of stigmatisation, and the spiralling collective, targeted, aggravated violence deployed through a convergence of state and private actors, fold the Dalit and Muslim questions together even while they remain separate and distinct in all other respects.

It is against this larger context that I will attempt briefly to flag my concerns around gender, law, civil liberties and society, yet again.

Speaking of Women

The periodic reporting under the UN Convention on the Elimination of All Forms of Discrimination against Women has opened out possibilities for debate, discussion and negotiations around law and policy for women's rights among women's groups across the country.[2] While the process might have its limitations, what is very evident from the deliberations is the energies women's groups put into providing the Committee on the Elimination of All Forms of Discrimination against Women with the evidence, data and testimonies to counter government claims of full compliance to all articles of the convention. The concluding observations of the committee in 2014, a fairly accurate statement of the problem, serve as a useful point of departure to revisit current debates on a range of questions.[3]

While placing on record the positive measures taken by the government of India towards eliminating gender-based discrimination, the committee expressed concern 'at the absence of a comprehensive anti-discrimination law addressing all aspects of direct and indirect discrimination against women and all the forms of intersectional discrimination'.[4] That the situation in India presents a bleak picture of security for women, for the committee, is evident in the rise in violent crimes against women; the retention of the exception of marital rape in the new legislation protecting women from sexual assault after the deliberations of the Justice Verma Committee;

the escalation of caste-based crimes, especially sexual assault against women and girls; the poor implementation of the Scheduled Castes and the Scheduled Tribes (Prevention of Atrocities) Act, even in cases that involved gruesome violence against women; the persistence of 'honour crimes' by family members of women and girls; the rise in dowry-related deaths since 2008; the increasing number of acid attacks against women and girls since 2002; and the criminalising of same-sex relationships by the Supreme Court of India when it overturned the *Naz Foundation* decision of the Delhi High Court.[5] We need not multiply examples to assert that every one of these forms of violence against women is rising in alarming proportions across the country.

Radhika Vemula and the Matrilineality of Caste Location

Ten months after she lost her son Rohith Vemula to caste discrimination and dehumanising exclusion in one of the most acclaimed university campuses in the country (Chukka 2016), Radhika Vemula is battling the judicial system, government and university administration, asserting her claim that her son's death be treated as caste atrocity (Mitta 2016; Apparasu 2017). Interestingly, neither the university administration (the serving vice-chancellor, in this case, a direct party) nor the government has denied that Rohith was forcibly evicted from hostels and other public spaces in the university. Nor is there a denial that his occupation of the open space in the university campus, which he called the velivada,[6] was unambiguous in calling out caste discrimination and deep-rooted practices of untouchability on campus (see Aravind and Kumar 2016)—for what other name can we give the conduct of those that reign in a 'republic of the touchables' (Ambedkar 2002: 330)?

However, when a case of atrocity was sought to be registered under the SC/ST (Prevention of Atrocities) Act, 1989, with the vice-chancellor named as accused, the contestation was not that the vice-chancellor was not complicit, but that Rohith was not a Dalit. The insidious circulation of the dominant narrative that this 'Dalit' was not in fact one—*he masqueraded as one*—and that his mother was perpetuating this myth, sought to undermine the credibility of anti-caste collective action, and through that means reinstate the vice-chancellor to a position of dignity, authority and power. But this is a mother who has lost her son, a woman who has refused monetary compensation, and who has demanded that the vice-chancellor meet her in full public view on his own campus, not in secrecy, in a furtive visit to her home—a demand that has not to date been met. Most importantly, this is a woman who has had the courage to stand up and demand that the vice-chancellor be tried for atrocity leading to the death of her son (*Deccan Chronicle* 2016). It cannot be forgotten that her tenacity has been pitted against an unprecedented attack from the highest quarters: Union ministers, Members of Parliament, legislators, police, the entire university administration (Mitta 2016; Surendran 2016) and regrettably, a sizeable proportion of the teaching community in the university, used disproportionate power to delegitimise the single claim Radhika Vemula has been making, that as a Dalit woman of Mala caste, a survivor of domestic violence and desertion, possibly also of bonded domestic labour, who was a single parent, she had raised her children as Dalits in the environment that she belonged to by birth. The woman who 'adopted' her did not deny this fact; and the discovery of her caste by birth was the reason for her desertion by her violent husband, leaving her to fend for herself and her three children with no resources, assets or education. Therefore, while she may have been married to a man of Vaddera caste, which is not an SC, her early separation, and her sole responsibility in the upbringing of her children supported her claim that her children bear her caste and not their father's (Mondal 2016).

What we need to determine is whether Rohith's suicide raises the question of abetment by a non-Dalit. Rather than address this, the entire legal discourse around Rohith's death has circulated around whether he was Dalit at all—the matter left unaddressed and still stands confronting the vice-chancellor is that abetment to suicide is a crime in any case under the Indian Penal Code. It is a targeted crime—an atrocity—if a non-Dalit (especially one in a position of power to take decisions that have a direct bearing on the survival and dignity of a Dalit person) discriminates against a Dalit, and is thereby complicit in his suicide.

Be that as it may, the question of matrilineality is at the core of the justice claims in the case of Rohith. In a caste order, and in sociological/anthropological literature in India, matrilineal kinship is addressed in a manner that seals off related caste groups through the insular parcelling off of claims to inheritance along several axes. Therefore, while restricted and rigidly controlled social (and sexual) intercourse across castes is socially sanctioned, inheritance (of name, property, identity, privileges, dispossessions) is insulated within caste, negating the possibility of cross-caste inheritance claims. This is not only the case with known 'matrilineal' cultures, as in Kerala (Abraham 2011) and Lakshadweep (Dube 1993), for instance. In a patrilineal caste society, where hypergamy is the norm, the access to privileges, and identity for the children of Dalit and Adivasi women who marry/cohabit with men of dominant castes is only at the pleasure of the men and the dominant community. Crying foul and generating hysteria around misrepresentation and false claims is part of this same politics of dominance—as we witness with the incessant undermining of the credibility of Radhika and Rohith Vemula by alleging that his certificates are 'false' *because* the father is not a Dalit. The fact of the vulnerability of Dalit women to violence and exploitation by dominant men *on the basis of caste* forms part of the framing of atrocity itself. What then is the false claim? That a son ended his life unable to bear the humiliation, depredations and dehumanisation of caste (annihilation *by* caste)? That any sense of restoration or healing or justice for the mother is possible only by naming the humiliation and the attendant violence and seeking accountability and responsibility? Can we even begin to understand the politics of the 'false case' accusation?

Justices Alam and Desai in *Rameshbhai Dabhai Naika* (2012), addressed the issue: '[W]hat would be the status of a person, one of whose parents belongs to the scheduled castes/scheduled tribes and the other comes from the upper castes[?]'[7] The question the judges posed to themselves in addressing this was whether the petitioner's father's non-Dalit status gave him an 'advantageous start in life', or did he suffer 'the deprivations, indignities, humilities and handicaps like any other member of the community to which his/her mother belonged[?]'[8] Additionally, was he treated like a member of the community to which his mother belonged not only by that community but by people outside the community as well? Because, conclude the judges,

> in an inter-caste marriage [that is, a marriage between an SC/ST person and a non-SC/ST person] the determination of the caste of the offspring is essentially a question of fact to be decided on the basis of the facts adduced in each case.... [I]t is open to the child of such marriage to lead evidence to show that he/she was brought up by the mother who belonged to the scheduled caste/scheduled tribe.[9]

This is the law as it stands for now. And yet, the case of Rohith Vemula has made no progress. Radhika Vemula stands firm but to no avail. And life goes on, unhampered by the utterly avoidable death and the inexcusable violence against students and faculty, sanctioned by the university administration.

Justice in Times Bereft of Speech

We have news now that charges of murder and criminal conspiracy have been filed against Nandini Sundar, Archana Prasad, Vineet Tiwari, Sanjay Parate, Mangalram Karma and Manju Kawasi in Chhattisgarh for the killing of Shamnath Baghel, an Adivasi man (NHRC 2016). There is no basis whatsoever for this charge, except that these are people who have over the years been tirelessly documenting human rights abuses in this state and petitioning courts for relief on behalf of Adivasis who have been irreparably affected by the conflict.[10] We have already witnessed the burning of effigies of these and other concerned citizens by Inspector General S. R. P. Kalluri (*Firstpost* 2017). In the neighbouring state of Madhya Pradesh, we saw with horror the gunning down of eight unarmed undertrial prisoners (Ghatwai 2016). In Kashmir, over months, we have seen the murder and grievous hurt inflicted on civilians—men, women and children (Waheed 2016). And of course, these are only the most recent in a long list, over the past two years especially, that have opened up the festering sores of hatred and raw violence that know no limit. There is no attempt to answer questions any more, much less fix accountability. State responsibility is a matter of chest thumping and arrogant declarations, with no fear of prosecution. After all, the killing fields spawn 'national heroes'.

Conflict is never episodic, isolated or discrete. There is a cumulative deployment of technologies of violence and the perfection of impunity. I have written in the context of events that unfolded in the University of Hyderabad that Salwa Judum and the creation of velivadas were the new methods of rule (Kannabiran 2016). We see a proliferation to other locales in the formal extension of the guarantee of impunity to private actors: whether these are ABVP foot soldiers on campuses or law-violating lawyers or hate-speaking TV anchors or mobs on the prowl searching for people, bodies, condoms, writing … Just about anything that can loop into the next spiral of hate crimes.

We have laws and procedures established by law. However, when state action takes a sharp turn towards vesting formal power in the mob to kill, maim, humiliate; and when the 'speech of the nation' folds into the violence of the mob, which is indistinguishable from official declamations, we witness a new turn in the history of impunity. This vesting of formal power by representatives of government and agencies of state in private actors (whether the RSS, the ABVP, the VHP, or any other) takes us over the edge of the precipice. The guarantee of impunity to private actors puts the state beyond impunity. State actors—especially the police and armed forces—can then burn effigies, shoot down unarmed prisoners, shoot-to-kill unarmed protesters and mourners, register false FIRs implicating human rights defenders in murder and criminal conspiracy charges, and write directly to university administrations (that are already heavily compromised on questions of autonomy) objecting to discussions on the human rights work by the faculty and students in the university. With a Supreme Court ruling setting out the legitimacy of this very work of these very people,[11] a full-bench decision of a constitutional court on 'encounters' (which, although indefinitely stayed by the Supreme Court, sets out the reasoning for making the police accountable for their actions),[12] a Constitution that guarantees fundamental freedoms, including, importantly, the right to dissent and criticise the government—it is still possible now to offer no explanations at all about threats to arrest, actual arrests and murder of persons in custody. It is possible today, despite the Geneva Convention, to boast about the mutilation of the bodies of dead enemy soldiers with no fear of condemnation, forget prosecution for war crimes (Sukumar 2016). Hard-won gains of protracted battles for civil liberties are consigned to distant memories, caricatured in the strident public discourse driven entirely by the state.

And while the fields of impunity proliferate, conversations around law in and around courts are twisted into tunnels without light or destination: the debates around triple *talaq* (unilateral divorce by a Muslim man through the declaration of 'talaq' thrice) (for example, Sherin 2016) and carceral feminism especially speak to the complex terrains of hostile environments in times of conflict, where narrow prescriptions of identity are forced to determine speech, especially on women's claims to justice. Unsurprisingly, the sexual/conjugal behaviour of women (as the case may be) is the focus of delegitimation yet again—irrespective of the specific and situated claims women make.

Resurrecting Speech and Rights

Yet, this arbitrariness is not anarchic. There is a plan and a pattern that pushes towards constitutional breakdown in our case, similar to the constitutional exception that US filmmaker Ava DuVernay speaks about. The Thirteenth Amendment to the Constitution of the United States of America declared that '[n]either slavery nor involuntary servitude, *except as a punishment for crime whereof the party shall have been duly convicted,* shall exist within the United States, or any place subject to their jurisdiction' (emphasis mine).[13] In *13th* (2016), a brilliant documentary on how modern practices of incarceration and the prison labour system in the US are, in fact, an extension of slavery, DuVernay opens out to stunning view the exception clause in the Thirteenth Amendment. The lesson for us is in the unimaginable interconnections between law and lives, the intersectional histories of oppression/subjugation/prejudice and the fraught and dangerous politics of carcerality in sharply divided social orders. The lesson too is in speaking to and about these intersectional histories and their bearing on the present.

This past year we have also witnessed a churning in the university system, and connected to this, in society: Rohith Vemula and Jignesh Mevani (Vaya 2016) epitomise a stunning new collective articulation of communitarian life, conviviality and sociality—that builds on the core of anti-caste sensibilities of the politics of the possible.

We have a Constitution. In fact, that is our only possession now, which even in times of breakdown gives us slim hope of resurrection. And resurrection itself is always on the horizon, not as far away as we imagine it to be. But the road is rough and unnavigable. Do we have a choice?

The figure of Iqbal Bano in her black *sari* in 1985 singing Faiz's '*Hum Dekhenge*' (see Ahmar 2016) spins into memory, as if showing us the way.

Notes

1. Narendra v. K. Meena, CA No. 3253 of 2008, decided on 6 October 2016 (SC).
2. Convention on the Elimination of All Forms of Discrimination against Women, 18 December 1979, 1249 UNTS 13.
3. Committee on the Elimination of Discrimination against Women, 'Concluding Observations on the Combined Fourth and Fifth Periodic Reports of India', 24 July 2014, CEDAW/C/IND/CO/4–5.
4. Ibid., para. 8.
5. Ibid., para. 10.
6. See also, collection by Dalit poet, Madduri Nagesh Babu, *Velivada* (Narasaropet: Sreeja Publications, 1995).
7. *Rameshbhai Dabhai Naika*, (2012) 3 SCC 400, para. 1.
8. Ibid., para. 43.
9. Ibid.
10. The claim of Inspector General Kalluri was that the wife of Baghel named these six persons in her FIR. However, she has since denied naming these persons and has said she could not identify any of the armed persons who attacked her husband. See *The Wire* (2016).
11. *Nandini Sundar*, AIR 2011 SC 2839.
12. *Andhra Pradesh Civil Liberties Committee*, 2009 (2) ALD 1.
13. US Const. amend. XIII, sec. 1.

References

'Bastar IG S. R. P. Kalluri to Go on Leave, Chhattisgarh Govt Appoints New DIG'. 2017. *Firstpost*, 2 February. Available at https://www.

firstpost.com/india/bastar-ig-srp-kalluri-to-go-on-leave-chhattisgarh-govt-appoints-new-dig-3243538.html (accessed 9 July 2021).

'Dadri Lynching Accused Dies in Jail, Villagers Drape Coffin in Tricolour, Refuse to Cremate Body'. 2016. *India Today*, 6 October. Available at https://www.indiatoday.in/fyi/story/dadri-lynching-accused-dead-jail-mohammad-akhlaq-tricolour-345327-2016-10-06 (accessed 9 July 2021).

'Mother of Rohith Vemula: Do You Want to Give Us Justice?'. 2016. *Deccan Chronicle*, 26 March.

'Wife of Murdered Bastar Villager Denies Naming Nandini Sundar and Others in FIR'. *The Wire*, 11 November 2016. Available at http://thewire.in/79602/wife-bastar-fir-nandini-sundar/ (accessed 11 November 2016).

Abraham, Janaki. 2011. '"Why Did You Send Me like This?": Marriage, Matriliny and the "Providing Husband" in North Kerala, India'. *Asian Journal of Women's Studies* 17, no. 2: 32–65.

Ahmar, Muqbil. 2016. 'Remembering Faiz Ahmed Faiz's Revolutionary Poem'. *Daily O*, 20 November. Available at https://www.dailyo.in/arts/faiz-ahmed-faiz-revolutionary-nazm-hum-dekhenge-zia-ul-haq-iqbal-bano-iskander-mirza/story/1/14129.html (accessed 15 July 2021).

Ambedkar, B. R. 2002. 'Outside the Fold'. In *The Essential Writings of B. R. Ambedkar*, ed. Valerian Rodrigues, 323–31. New Delhi: Oxford University Press.

Apoorvanand. 2016. 'The Chief of Counterfeit Grief'. *The Wire*, 2 November. Available at http://thewire.in/77325/chief-counterfeit-grief/ (accessed 9 November 2016).

Apparasu, Srinivasa Rao. 2017. 'Rohith Vemula Not a Dalit, Says Collector; Andhra Govt to Cancel SC Certificate'. *Hindustan Times*, 14 February.

Aravind, Indulekha and K. P. Narayana Kumar. 2016. 'Dalit Suicide Case: Why Rohith Vemula's Death is the Tipping Point in Caste Bias on Campus'. *The Economic Times*, 24 January.

Chukka, Vikram. 2016. 'The Chain of Events Leading to Rohith Vemula's Suicide'. *The Wire*, 19 January. Available at https://thewire.in/education/the-chain-of-events-leading-to-rohith-vemulas-suicide (accessed 9 July 2021).

Dube, Leela. 1993. 'Who Gains from Matriliny? Men, Women and Change on a Lakshadweep Island'. *Sociological Bulletin* 42, nos 1/2: 15–36.

DuVernay, Ava, dir. 2016. *13th*. Netflix.

Ghatwai, Milind. 2016. 'Madhya Pradesh Police Kill 8 SIMI Undertrials Hours after Jailbreak; Lawyer Wants CBI Probe'. *The Indian Express*, 1 November.

Kannabiran, Kalpana. 2016. 'Urgent Notes from a University in Crisis'. *The Wire*, 24 March. Available at https://thewire.in/education/urgent-notes-from-a-university-in-crisis.

Mitta, Manoj. 2016. 'How This Self-Proclaimed Pro-Dalit Government Has All but Buried the Rohith Vemula Case'. *Scroll.in*, 31 December. Available at https://scroll.in/article/825545/how-this-self-proclaimed-pro-dalit-government-has-all-but-buried-the-rohith-vemula-case (accessed 25 July 2021).

Mondal, Sudipto. 2016. 'Rohith Vemula: An Unfinished Portrait'. *Hindustan Times*, January.

NHRC (National Human Rights Commission). 2016. 'Allegations of Hostility against Human Rights Defenders'. Press Release. Case No. 667/33/20/2016). Available at https://nhrc.nic.in/press-release/allegations-hostility-against-human-rights-defenders (accessed 25 July 2021).

Noorani, A. G. 2016. 'The Ban on Cow Slaughter'. *Frontline*, 24 June.

Sherin, B. S. 2016. 'Shortcomings in the Triple Talaq Debate'. *Outlook*, 6 November.

Sukumar, Arun Mohan. 2016. 'Beheading Dead Soldiers is a War Crime, Bragging about It Does No One Any Credit'. *The Wire*, 10 October. Available at https://thewire.in/diplomacy/beheading-dead-soldiers-war-crime-bragging-no-one-credit (accessed 9 November 2016).

Surendran, Vivek. 2016. 'Rohith Vemula's Mother was Dragged on the Streets by Delhi Police. Is Radhika Vemula Incapable of Being Smriti Irani's Mother India?'. *India Today*, 16 February. Available at https://www.indiatoday.in/india/delhi/story/smriti-irani-rohith-vemula-radhika-vemula-delhi-police-assault-310773-2016-02-26 (accessed 24 July 2021).

Vaya, Surabhi. 2016. 'A Conversation with Jignesh Mevani, a Dalit Activist and Leader of the Uprising in Una'. *The Caravan*, 7 August.

Waheed, Mirza. 2016. 'India's Crackdown in Kashmir: Is This the World's First Mass Blinding?'. *The Guardian*, 8 November.

63

Constitution, Hostile Environments and 'Atrocious' Interpretation

*A Sign of Our Times**

The decision of the two-judge bench of the Supreme Court of India in *S. K. Mahajan*,[1] delivered on 20 March 2018, forces a counter-constitutional judicial amnesia with respect to atrocities suffered by the Scheduled Castes and Scheduled Tribes, and the historical/constitutional background of the SC/ST (Prevention of Atrocities) Act and its continuing and increasing relevance today. In the process of attempting to wipe out judicial memory on the question of atrocities and structural violence based on caste discrimination, the court takes easy recourse to the language of public morality, setting aside the centrality of constitutional morality to constitutional reasoning. In this brief comment, which does not go into all the aspects of the judgement that are deeply problematic, I will look at the major assumptions the judgement makes and its mis-readings.

It is useful, although painful, to begin with the approach of the Supreme Court to this case, which concerns the 'fear' of 'false accusations' and 'allegations' against 'innocent people' who are at the mercy of 'unscrupulous' elements out to trap and 'stigmatise' them through arrest and denial of bail by filing cases of atrocity against these 'unsuspecting' persons.[2] The unsuspecting, innocent persons are persons belonging to non-SC castes in positions of authority/power, either as public servants or employers. The unscrupulous elements are all persons belonging to the Scheduled Castes holding primarily semi-skilled jobs in the cases discussed.

---

* Originally published as 'SC/ST Act: A Hostile Environment and an "Atrocious" Interpretation', in *The Wire*, 26 March 2018.

The specific case before the court concerned a storekeeper who lodged a complaint against his superior officers who had made adverse remarks in his annual confidential record. Sanction to proceed against them was refused by the Director of Technical Education, government of Maharashtra, who, the complainant argued, exceeded his jurisdiction in refusing sanction, and therefore obstructed the course of justice under the act. The intervenor supporting the appeal is a lady assistant professor, who charged the same storekeeper with sexual harassment, against whom the petitioner filed a case under the Prevention of Atrocities Act. This is a case in which specific facts were before the court, and could, in my view, have simply been decided on the merits. Instead, the court embarks on a discussion on the unconstitutionality of provisions under the SC/ST (Prevention of Atrocities) Act, and declares its rampant misuse—with easy recourse to stereotype and selective presentation of facts/evidence. In doing this, it makes a general derogatory comment on an entire class of persons who come under the protective umbrella of this legislation.

The Supreme Court quotes extensively from five earlier judgements of high courts, three from Gujarat, one from Maharashtra and one from Tamil Nadu, that repeatedly use terms (highlighting them in bold) like 'malicious complaint', 'malicious prosecution', 'malicious complainant', speaking of how the act is used 'as an instrument of blackmail' to wreak 'personal vengeance' and settle scores arising from 'personal vendetta', by 'scheming, unscrupulous complainant[s]'—and concludes that the 'above judgements are merely illustrations to show that the abuse of law [is] rampant'.[3] The argument of the intervenor's counsel is that since monetary compensation is available to complainants under the Rule 12(4) framed under the act, it 'is also prone to misuse on account of monetary incentive being available merely for lodging a case'.[4] In not rebutting this serious allegation, nor distancing itself from the plea of the intervenor, the Supreme Court throws itself open to the conclusion that it in fact subscribes to this view.

The next paragraph in the judgement refers to data from the National Crime Records Bureau (NCRB) for the year 2016 pertaining to the Prevention of Atrocities Act. Here again, the court provides a partial account of the data that lends to a distorted reading. Referring to Table 7A.4, 'Police Disposal of Crime/Atrocities against SCs Cases

(State/UT-wise) – 2016', the court points out that 'in the year 2016, 5347 cases were found to be false cases out of the investigated out of SC cases [*sic*]'. This figure is specifically mentioned in the judgement, alongside figures for acquittals and withdrawals. A careful look at the NCRB data show us that the previous column in the same table tells us that 2,150 cases were found to be 'true but [with] insufficient evidence'. The total number of cases for police investigation in 2016 were 56,299. For the same year, according to Table 7A.5 of the report, the total number of cases before courts under (a) the Prevention of Atrocities Act alone, (b) the act read with the IPC, and (c) the Protection of Civil Rights Act, was 144,979; the cases resulting in acquittal or discharge by courts numbered 10,862; the conviction rate was 25.7 per cent; and the pendency rate 89.6 per cent (National Crime Records Bureau 2017: 300–03).

A basic fact of law is that acquittal does not necessarily prove innocence—it may also point to inadequate investigation and evidence on record, or procedural infirmities. The conflation of acquittals with false cases in an account by the apex court is cause for concern. Further, by providing only the figure for false cases, without placing it within the larger context of cases coming up before courts and being decided, the court presents a counter-factual account of cases pertaining to the commission of atrocities against Scheduled Castes and Scheduled Tribes. It engages in a counter-constitutional, reductionist rhetoric that is anecdotal and totally unsupported by evidence and data, and do not reflect the social realities these cases rest on.

It is to the social realities of atrocities against the Scheduled Castes and Scheduled Tribes that we now turn.

As late as 2015, it is still possible in our country for a public university to officially declare a social boycott of Dalit students, soliciting the active intervention of the ruling party and its student body, leading to the suicide in January 2016 of one of the students boycotted—Rohith Vemula (Chukka 2016). In March 2016, V. Shankar, a 21-year-old Dalit man, was hacked to death in broad daylight in Udumalaipet in Tamil Nadu and his non-Dalit wife, Kausalya, murderously attacked by her family for violating caste codes (Kumar and Kumar 2016). In April 2016, a young Dalit student in Kerala, Jisha, was sexually assaulted and brutally murdered in her own home, a 150-square foot house in a canal *poramboke* (commons)—and there were, mysteriously, no eyewitnesses, nor did anyone attempt to rescue her (*The Indian Express* 2017). Since January 2018, Dalits in Vadayampadi, near Kochi in Kerala, have been resisting the building of a 'caste wall' by the dominant castes, which will prevent their entry into common spaces in the village (*The New Indian Express* 2018).

And we can go back year by year to the year of the adoption of the Constitution, travelling from state to state in the country, for accounts of such violence. In its recounting of the logic of the SC/ST (Prevention of Atrocities) Act, how did the judges of the Supreme Court forget that this—*the caste line*—is our present reality and the reason why the act continues to be a critical protection? Can a constitutional court adopt a partisan and derogatory view of a particular class of complainants when *all* complainants in such cases belong to the Scheduled Castes and Scheduled Tribes? Can the apex court ignore the fact that complaints before courts are under a legislation that was enacted to provide protection against structural violence and discrimination to groups rendered vulnerable by the power of dominance and privilege entrenched in the caste order?

The judgement, of course, must base itself on a constitutional reading—it fulfils this requirement mechanically by a restricted reading of basic structures as Articles 14 and 21, declaring that the non-Dalit appellants' rights to equality and liberty stand violated because of these malicious complaints. It is constitutional commonsense that in a case of the protection of civil rights or prevention of atrocities against Dalits and Adivasis, Articles 14 and 21 are only intelligible in their intersection with Articles 15 and 17 (which prohibit vertical and horizontal discrimination and untouchability). These Articles (15 and 17) do not figure at any point in the discussion on the specific reading of basic structure with reference to caste-based discrimination. Instead, a series of untenable comparisons are made between the penal provisions of this act and the (more lenient!) penal provisions in the UAPA, the Terrorist and Disruptive Activities (Prevention) Act, 1985, and offences under the Narcotic Drugs and Psychotropic Substances Act, 1985—particularly in matters of arrest and anticipatory bail.

The biggest travesty is, of course, quoting Ambedkar's last speech in the Constituent Assembly to support its assertion that persons from the Scheduled Castes are perpetuating casteism and eroding the environment of peace and fraternity envisaged by Ambedkar through their false and malicious litigation. In a section titled, 'Further Consideration of Potential Impact of Working of Atrocities Act on Spreading Casteism', the Supreme Court observes that 'it is necessary to express concern that working of the Atrocities Act should not result in perpetuating casteism which can have an adverse impact on integration of the society and the constitutional values'.[5] Two paragraphs from Ambedkar, omitting some text in between, are quoted in support of this view:

> These principles of liberty, equality and fraternity are not to be treated as separate items in a trinity. They form a union of trinity in the sense that to divorce one from the other is to defeat the very purpose of democracy. Liberty cannot be divorced from equality, equality cannot be divorced from liberty. Nor can liberty and equality be divorced from fraternity. Without equality, liberty would produce the supremacy of the few over the many. Equality without liberty would kill individual initiative. Without fraternity, liberty would produce the supremacy of the few over the many. Equality without liberty would kill individual initiative. Without fraternity, liberty and equality could not become a natural course of things. It would require a constable to enforce them.
>
> [...]
>
> In India there are castes. The castes are anti-national. In the first place because they bring about separation in social life. They are anti-national also because they generate jealousy and antipathy between caste and caste. But we must overcome all these difficulties if we wish to become a nation in reality. For fraternity can be a fact only when there is a nation. Without fraternity, equality and liberty will be no deeper than coats of paint.[6]

The ellipsis is crucial because it covers up what the judges do not believe to be true, although they cannot afford to ignore the figure of Ambedkar in a decision on caste atrocity:

> We must begin by acknowledging the fact that there is complete absence of two things in Indian Society. One of these is equality. On the social

> plane, we have in India a society based on the principle of graded inequality which we have a society in which there are some who have immense wealth as against many who live in abject poverty.
>
> On the 26 January 1950, we are going to enter into a life of contradictions. In politics we will have equality and in social and economic life we will have inequality. In politics we will be recognising the principle of one man one vote and one vote one value. In our social and economic life, we shall, by reason of our social and economic structure, continue to deny the principle of one man one value. How long shall we continue to live this life of contradictions? How long shall we continue to deny equality in our social and economic life? If we continue to deny it for long, we will do so only by putting our political democracy in peril. We must remove this contradiction at the earliest possible moment or else those who suffer from inequality will blow up the structure of political democracy which [this] Assembly has [so] laboriously built up.
>
> The second thing we are wanting in is recognition of the principle of fraternity. What does fraternity mean? Fraternity means a sense of common brotherhood of all Indians—of Indians being one people. It is the principle which gives unity and solidarity to social life. It is a difficult thing to achieve. (Ambedkar 2016 [1949])

What does it signal when the highest court in the country asserts, (mis)appropriating Ambedkar in the process, that it is Scheduled Caste complainants who perpetuate casteism and obstruct fraternity, equality and liberty in India today?

Notes

1. Dr Subhash Kashinath Mahajan v. The State of Maharashtra, Cr. A No. 416 of 2018, decided on 20 March 2018 (SC).
2. Ibid.
3. Ibid., para. 22.
4. Ibid., para. 24.
5. Ibid., para. 42.
6. Ibid., para. 43.

References

'Vadayampadi Land Dispute: Wall-owing in a Caste Row'. 2018. *The New Indian Express*, 7 February.

'What is Jisha Rape and Murder Case?'. 2017. *The Indian Express*, 12 December.

Ambedkar, B. R. 2016 [1949]. 'Why B. R. Ambedkar's Three Warnings in His Last Speech to the Constituent Assembly Resonate Even Today'. *Scroll.in*, 26 January. Available at https://scroll.in/article/802495/why-br-ambedkars-three-warnings-in-his-last-speech-to-the-constituent-assembly-resonate-even-today (accessed 10 July 2021).

Chukka, Vikram. 2016. 'The Chain of Events Leading to Rohith Vemula's Suicide'. *The Wire*, 19 January. Available at https://thewire.in/education/the-chain-of-events-leading-to-rohith-vemulas-suicide (accessed 9 July 2021).

Kumar, R. Vimal and S. Vijay Kumar. 2016. 'Dalit Youth Killed for Marrying Caste Hindu Girl'. *The Hindu*, 14 March.

National Crime Records Bureau. 2017. *Crime in India 2016: Statistics*. New Delhi: Ministry of Home Affairs.

64

Through the Clouds of Protest, Sightings of Hope*

Since mid-2014, we have seen an escalation of state violence, from campus troubles being triggered (see *Report of the People's Tribunal* 2016; *The Wire* 2020) to sections of the Constitution being dispensed with (Vij 2019). Is this the face of state terror?

Parliamentary practice has been ignored as major policy decisions that impact dignity, lives, security, livelihoods and survival have been rammed through the lower house with little discussion (*The Wire* 2016; Maanvi 2019; Vij 2019). The state of Jammu and Kashmir was disappeared, and an entire people were blocked from modern communication (PTI 2019a; Vij 2019). During the demonstrations against the Citizenship (Amendment) Act, protesters have been shot and been threatened with having their personal assets being attached in order to compensate for damage to public property (Citizens against Hate 2020). The police have invaded universities and student organisations affiliated with the ruling party have brutally attacked their peers. Justice has been elusive even as the mayhem spreads—impunity reigns supreme.

Though India has comprehensive criminal laws undergirded by the Constitution, we have witnessed a range of horrors: arbitrary detentions, extrajudicial killings by the police (Kurmanath 2019), Dalits on campuses being excommunicated (Rupawat 2019), Muslims being criminally targeted (Citizens against Hate 2020), prolonged internet shutdowns (PTI 2019b).

Battling this ruthless state with unimaginable courage have been India's young people, armed with the Constitution and the courage of conviction it bestows on them. While all those sworn to office under

---

* Originally published in *Scroll.in*, 22 January 2020.

oath of upholding the Constitution rip it to shreds in a hundred different ways, it is these people—the young, the students (of Aligarh Muslim University [Yamunan 2019], Jamia Millia Islamia [Sharma and Bhardwaj 2019], Jawaharlal Nehru University [*The Wire* 2020], Hyderabad Central University [*Deccan Chronicle* 2016], and countless others since mid-2014), the women of Delhi's Shaheen Bagh (Farooqi 2020), the people of Kashmir—who school us all about what the Constitution tells us about who we are and what we ought to be as a people. It is they who teach us its fundamental tenets and demonstrate its power to us.

The policemen who fired on unarmed people in Uttar Pradesh protesting against the discriminatory Citizenship (Amendment) Act, and in Aligarh Muslim University and in Jamia Millia Islamia have not yet been investigated or charged. The Bharatiya Janata Party's student organisation, the Akhil Bharatiya Vidyarthi Parishad, which invaded JNU on 5 January under the watch of a complicit police force (Tiwari and Nair 2020), has not been charged or punished either.

Clearly, although this violence has caused concern around the world, the external affairs minister believes he has no need to address it. As he said at an event on 6 January 2020, 'I can certainly tell you that when I studied in JNU, we did not see any *tukde-tukde* gang'—a term used by some people to define a nebulous group they believe are involved in Balkanising the country (quoted in *Hindustan Times* 2020). What does this even mean? It is lumpen street talk that folds erudition into itself seamlessly. None of the other alumni who sit in ministerial positions in government deemed it necessary to demonstrate their solidarity with students and teachers wounded in the attack on JNU by affiliates of the ruling party.

Clearly, the criminality of mass violence that we saw in Gujarat in 2002 and the derailment of law during the trials of people believed to be responsible for the violence emboldens these current actions (International Initiative for Justice 2003).

As citizens of India, in the context of the struggles against the Citizenship (Amendment) Act, we need to ask, '*Ghuspethiye kaun hai?*'—who are the infiltrators? Those that swear by the Constitution, with the sonorous chorus of 'azaadi' rising to a crescendo their only weapon? Or those who run amok on campuses, bearing deadly weapons?

Those who recite Faiz and the Preamble and draw sceptics into an ever-widening circle of democratic protest and civic engagement? Or those who threaten to hurt and maim in the name of 'Bharat Mata' and 'Hindu rashtra'? Those who assert that their solidarity lies firmly with those who have been targeted, in full knowledge that with this mere expression they risk great personal danger? Or those in positions of leadership who send out dog whistles about who should be targeted in the next round of violence?

Recent events remind us of Telugu poet Sivasagar's poem 'Statement of a Conspirator', written in 1973 ('Devouring Bharat's freedom is conspiracy/the ballot box is conspiracy'; translation quoted in Kannabiran 2019: 32). We may also recall Cherabandaraju's poem '*Vande Mataram*' ('You are the *Bharati* who stands patiently/while rats and bandicoots dig at the roots of crops ripe for harvest./You are the evergreen land that does not reach people's mouths/Vandemataram. Vandemataram.'; translation quoted in ibid.: 33). Like Faiz, countless poets write as they should in opposition to a state that wages wars on its own people without respite. In recounting these poems and stories, this generation is memorialising a radical history of ideas and resistance as the wellspring from which the Constitution draws meaning and its life force.

The university has moved out of its securitised, walled and gated environs. The buildings and vacuous classrooms can no longer resonate a radical constitutionalism as pedagogic praxis. Experience, as never before, now forms the basis of teaching and learning and theorising—we witness a transformation of roles, capabilities and commitment. The student-dissenter is the teacher—an unparalleled one. For decades, some of us have struggled to free the Constitution from the Blackstonian confines of courts, arguing that public constitutionalism is the only route to a robust assertion of equal citizenship. We only succeeded in fits and starts, in miniscule measure and even that made us euphoric. Today, as we watch day after day the public reading of the Constitution, the public schooling in citizenship on an unprecedented scale by people who are most vulnerable to assaults of state terror and criminal labelling, and the steadfast reiteration of constitutional common-sense in the face of serious injury and criminal cases, the sense of healing and recovery returns. Also, a sense of history returns.

For across various insurgent ideas of freedom on the subcontinent, anger and resistance were welded to non-violent disobedience and a deeply ethical politics. Hope rumbles slowly, deep in the belly—the raucous cacophony and utter dishonesty that accompanies these gruesome terror strikes in the name of *deshbhakti* (patriotism) will be vanquished. We have miles to go, but perhaps these are sightings of a hopeful future.

References

'25 Students and 2 Faculty Members Arrested for UoH Violence'. 2016. *Deccan Chronicle*, 24 March.

'Debate on Demonetisation Missing in Parliament as Parties Quibble over Procedural Disagreements'. 2016. *The Wire*, 25 November. Available at https://thewire.in/government/parliament-debate-logjam-demonetisation (accessed 10 July 2021).

'Did Not See "Tukde-Tukde" Gang When I Studied in JNU: S. Jaishankar'. 2020. *Hindustan Times*, 6 January.

'JNU Attack: What the Delhi Police Has Done and What it Hasn't'. 2020. *The Wire*, 9 January. Available at https://thewire.in/government/jnu-attack-what-the-delhi-police-has-done-and-what-it-hasnt (accessed 9 July 2021).

Citizens against Hate. 2020. *'Everyone Has Been Silenced': Police Excess against Anti-CAA Protesters in Uttar Pradesh, and Post-Violence Reprisal*. Available at https://citizensagainsthate.org/wp-content/uploads/2020/03/Citizens-Against-Hate-Everyone-Has-Been-Silenced.pdf (accessed 14 June 2021).

Farooqi, Farah. 2020. 'To Better Understand the Shaheen Bagh Protest, We Must Understand the Locality Itself'. *The Caravan*, 20 January.

International Initiative for Justice. 2003. *Threatened Existence: A Feminist Analysis of the Genocide in Gujarat*. Available at https://www.onlinevolunteers.org/gujarat/reports/iijg/2003/ (accessed 17 June 2021).

Kannabiran, Kalpana. 2019. 'The Struggle is Its Own Reward'. *Seminar* 721 (September): 29–38. Trans. Vasanth Kannabiran.

Kurmanath, K. V. 2019. 'Disha Murder Case: All Four Accused Killed in "Encounter"'. *Business Line*, 7 December.

Maanvi. 2019. 'Parliament Debates Citizenship (Amendment) Bill: Who Said What?'. *The Quint*, 10 December. Available at https://www.thequint.com/news/politics/parliament-debates-citizenship-amendment-bill-who-said-what (accessed 10 July 2021).

PTI. 2019a. 'Abrogation of Article 370 Unconstitutional, People of J&K Bypassed: Petitioners to SC'. *The Economic Times*, 10 December.

———. 2019b. '145 Days of Internet Shutdown in Kashmir, No Word on Service Restoration'. *The Economic Times*, 27 December.

Report of the People's Tribunal on Caste Discrimination & Police Action in University of Hyderabad. 2016. Available at http://sanhati.com/articles/17555/ (accessed 15 June 2021).

Rupawat, Prudhviraj. 2019. 'Rohith Vemula's "Velivada" Demolished, HCU VC Strikes Again'. *Indian Cultural Forum*, 7 January. Available at https://indianculturalforum.in/2019/01/07/rohith-vemulas-velivada-demolished-hcu-vc-strikes-again/ (accessed 9 July 2021).

Sharma, Kritika and Ananya Bhardwaj. 2019. *The Print*, 15 December. Available at https://theprint.in/india/jamia-students-protest-was-peaceful-violence-started-after-local-residents-entered-university/335768/ (accessed 10 July 2021).

Tiwari, Ayush and Veena Nair. 2020. '"They Wanted to Teach a Lesson in Terror": An Account of Sunday Night Violence at JNU'. *NewsLaundry*, 6 January. Available at https://www.newslaundry.com/2020/01/06/they-wanted-to-teach-a-lesson-in-terror-an-account-of-sunday-night-at-jnu (accessed 25 July 2021).

Vij, Shivam. 2016. 'No Debate, No Discussion, No Dissent, and the Constitution is Changed'. *The Print*, 5 August. Available at https://theprint.in/opinion/no-debate-no-discussion-no-dissent-and-the-constitution-is-changed/272436/ (accessed 10 July 2021).

Yamunan, Shruthisagar. 2019. 'Aligarh Muslim University Students Allege They Were Tortured in Police Custody after Sunday Protests'. *Scroll.in*, 18 December. Available at https://scroll.in/article/947178/aligarh-muslim-university-students-allege-they-were-tortured-in-police-custody-after-sunday-protests (accessed 10 July 2021).

65

Retrieving the Idea of Citizenship*

When I suggested in 2012 in *Tools of Justice* that transformative constitutionalism is by definition insurgent, I had not in fact imagined that we would witness an insurgency of these proportions, that carries forth rhythm, sight, sound, musicality, tenacity, constitutional wisdom, collective action and the redefinition of leadership (in terms of caste, religion, gender, class and age especially) in quite this manner in the face of threat, governance by fear and the perpetual anticipation of terror. Just the demonstration of the possibility of this resistance is deeply transformative and moving. Will India and Indianness ever be the same again?

Cruel Ways of the Right

The ways of the Hindu Right are cruel and ruthless beyond measure, disregardful of the rule of law, and utterly anti-national, the 'national' defined in broad, inclusive terms of 'upholding the spirit of the Constitution and respecting its fundamental tenets'. We have seen demonstrations of that as well—especially in Kashmir (Ahmad 2020) and Assam (Singh 2019), also in Uttar Pradesh (Citizens against Hate 2020), not to speak of the violence on university campuses (*Report of the People's Tribunal* 2016; *The Wire* 2020a). Against the brutal reign of terror and threat of more to come, against a future that seems bleak on every score—employment, economy, education (especially higher education) and governance—it is the public and spirited defence of the Constitution-as-commons that has forced accountability on the state and internationalised its depredations.

---

* Originally published in *The Hindu*, 28 January 2020.

This essay was published for India's seventieth Republic Day.

The recitations of resistance range from wresting the national anthem from its empty ritualistic performance by military bands or the ritual flag-hoisting on Republic Day and Independence Day, to reinstalling the tricolour as a symbol of resistance. Recitations of resistance combine Faiz with the Preamble, in the voice of Chandrashekhar Azad on the steps of Jama Masjid before he is arrested for inciting violence (Sinha 2020). The 'incitement to violence' itself acquires a new meaning in the national space of this resistance—the recitation of the Preamble incites the state to violence, forcing a judge to ask the state, 'What offence? Tell me. He'll read the Preamble?' (*The Wire* 2020b).

Radical Reading

Extrapolating from the ideas of Nobel laureate Elinor Ostrom and scholars of the commons (for example, Hess and Olstrom 2007), the conceptualisation of the Constitution as a commons opens it out to radical, insurgent readings that redefine belonging and ownership—it is no longer the property of the state, legislatures and courts to (mis)interpret in the service of political expediency/judicial bias/equivocation. It is the people, who, through collective action and civic engagement, hold institutions to account and provide the tools and experiences that must shape constitutional interpretation. The Preamble sets out the *spirit* of constitutional morality (not its narrow prescription) that guides an understanding of protections set out within. It also makes intelligible to people the legislative, judicial or executive actions that undermine the spirit of the Constitution.

For this public engagement is a 'justice cascade', to borrow from Kathryn Sikkink (2013), that will not (and does not) stop with the recitation—it has forced the government into courts and has forced judicial deliberation on the reach of constitutional protections to discipline the state. Although we see a marked pushback from the spectacular position of the right to privacy judgement in 2017—with no effective relief granted in the Kashmir cases and a deferral on the Citizenship (Amendment) Act, 2019, among others—it is institutions of justice that are now on trial. This is the singular achievement of this historic moment: the rupture of a sequestered 'constitutional jurisprudence' through the articulation of an expansive, inclusive constitutional commons and the performance of lyrical constitutionalism.

Freedoms as Birthright

This insurgency also holds a unique pedagogic moment: it demonstrates a different way of imagining the Constitution and a different understanding of citizenship. In her recent work, *Birthright Citizens* (2018), African-American legal historian Martha Jones argues that citizenship is distinct from and deeper than political rights or voting alone, and embedded in birthright (as African-Americans argued long before they belonged equally in the Constitution). In our context, we must ask, what is birthright? Is it swaraj? Is it freedom or azaadi? Is it the elimination of untouchability (as Ambedkar observed)?

Is birthright embedded in the undisturbed right of forest dwellers to the forest commons—'*maava naate, maava raaj*' (our village, our governance), and Jaipal Singh Munda's (2017) assertions of self-rule in the Constituent Assembly deliberations? Or is birthright embedded deep within the right to dignity and self-respect of *los atravesados*, the migrants, the crossers, that Gloria Anzaldúa (1987) speaks of in her stunning work on borderlands? Is it all of this? For, after all, as Jones (2018: 10) observes pertinently, 'Sometimes citizenship was defined in constitutions and statutes, although most of the time it was not.' Certainly citizenship by any definition is not a dole to be handed out by rulers to compliant subjects nor is its grant an alms deed to be distributed at whim.

Signposts of Change

Since the conversation has now opened up to critical public deliberation, how would we draw constitution-scapes across the rugged terrains of azaadi? The Constitution itself recognises various levels of azaadi, lest we forget. The late B. D. Sharma famously called the Fifth Schedule 'a Constitution within a Constitution' (quoted in Ministry of Tribal Affairs and UNDP n.d.: 2), and prior to 5 August 2019, the Constitution of India recognised the Constitution of the state of Jammu and Kashmir. Areas under the Sixth Schedule in Northeast India similarly have constitutional guarantees of autonomy. The guarantees of azaadi to Dalits under the Constitution are unprecedented. Although each of these is only observed in the breach, mapping constitution-scapes in their specific figurations means keeping these firmly at the centre of debate and collective action. Witness its signposts: Chandrashekhar Azad (Sinha 2020), the *nanis* and *dadis* (grandmothers) of Shaheen Bagh (Farooqi 2020), the Ghanta Ghar resisters in Lucknow (Srivastava 2020), resistance as withdrawal by the people of Kashmir, Kerala's challenge to the constitutionality of the CAA (Rajagopal 2020), the proxy strikes on conscientious resisters, the shutdown of Jammu and Kashmir, incarceration in detention camps and the proliferation of camps (Dutta 2019), the deferral by constitutional courts (*The Wire* 2020c), the languages of rule and resistance, and indeed the languages of jurisprudence trapped in a chokehold that defers the pronouncement of freedom as birthright.

The reinstatement of this experience and ways of knowing, interwoven with a resurgent public constitutionalism, might help us reclaim the idea of citizenship as birthright and inscribe the Constitution-as-commons by 'occupying' them and establishing a shared, collective, inclusive ownership.

References

'JNU Attack: What the Delhi Police Has Done and What it Hasn't'. 2020a. *The Wire*, 9 January. Available at https://thewire.in/government/jnu-attack-what-the-delhi-police-has-done-and-what-it-hasnt (accessed 9 July 2021).

'Court Modifies Chandra Shekhar Aazad's Bail Conditions, Now Allowed to Visit Delhi'. 2020b. *The Wire*, 21 January. Available at https://thewire.in/law/chandra-shehkar-aazad-bail-conditions-modified (accessed 10 July 2021).

'Anti-CAA Pinjra Tod Activist Arrested for Third Time in 10 Days'. 2020c. *The Wire*, 1 June. Available at https://thewire.in/rights/anti-caa-pinjra-tod-devangana-kalita-arrest (accessed 25 July 2021).

Ahmad, Mudasir. 2020. 'How the Public Safety Act Continues to Haunt Kashmir'. *The Wire*, 28 January. Available at https://thewire.in/rights/psa-detentions-kashmir (accessed 9 July 2021).

Anzaldúa, Gloria. 1987. *Borderlands/La Frontera: The New Mestiza*. San Francisco: Aunt Lute Books.

Citizens against Hate. 2020. *'Everyone Has Been Silenced': Police Excess against Anti-CAA Protesters in Uttar Pradesh, and Post-Violence Reprisal*. Available at https://citizensagainsthate.org/wp-content/uploads/2020/03/Citizens-Against-Hate-Everyone-Has-Been-Silenced.pdf (accessed 14 June 2021).

Dutta, Prabhash K. 2019. 'NRC and Story of How Assam Got Detention Centres for Foreigners'. *India Today*, 27 February. Available at https://www.indiatoday.in/india/story/nrc-story-how-assam-got-detention-centres-for-foreigners-1631835-2019-12-27 (accessed 25 July 2021).

Farooqi, Farah. 2020. 'To Better Understand the Shaheen Bagh Protest, We Must Understand the Locality Itself'. *The Caravan*, 20 January.

Hess, Charlotte and Elinor Ostrom, eds. 2007. *Understanding Knowledge as a Commons: From Theory to Practice*. Cambridge, MA, and London: MIT Press.

Jones, Martha S. 2018. *Birthright Citizens: A History of Race and Rights in Antebellum America*. Cambridge: Cambridge University Press.

Kannabiran, Kalpana. 2012. *Tools of Justice: Non-discrimination and the Indian* Constitution. New Delhi: Routledge.

Ministry of Tribal Affairs and UNDP (United Nations Development Programme). n.d. *Land and Governance under the Fifth Schedule*. Available at https://tribal.nic.in/FRA/data/LandandGovernanceunderFifthSchedule.pdf (accessed 10 July 2021).

Munda, Jaipal Singh. 2017. *Adivasidom: Speeches and Writings*, ed. Ashwini Kumar. Ranchi: Pyara Kerketta Foundation.

Rajagopal, Krishnadas. 2020. 'Kerala Files Suit against CAA'. *The Hindu*, 14 January.

Report of the People's Tribunal on Caste Discrimination & Police Action in University of Hyderabad. 2016. Available at http://sanhati.com/articles/17555/ (accessed 15 June 2021).

Sikkink, Kathryn. 2013. *The Justice Cascade: How Human Rights Prosecutions are Changing World Politics*. New York and London: W. W. Norton.

Singh, Bikash. 2019. 'Citizenship Amendment Bill: Why Assam is Protesting?'. *The Economic Times*, 17 December.

Sinha, Jignasa. 2020. 'Again, Jama Masjid, Azad & the Preamble'. *The Indian Express*, 18 January.

Srivastava, Piyush. 2020. 'Ghanta Ghar Undeterred'. *The Telegraph*, 26 January.

66

Safoora Zargar and the Search for India's Soul*

The incarceration of student activist Safoora Zargar and the obduracy of courts in refusing her bail (Pasha 2020) raises some fundamental questions on which the very survival of the Constitution depends. This is about Zargar first, but as she must, she leads us into the deeper, more searching quest for India's soul.

State Brutality

What does the brutality of the state towards a pregnant Muslim peaceful resister during a pandemic lockdown tell us about the deep perils in which our Constitution is mired at this moment? We have reached a nadir. The use of imprisonment and carcerality under conditions of pandemic vulnerabilities to wilfully deny Zargar her right to personal liberty is one part of an exercise of state repression.

Added to this is the move by the state to target her in such a manner as to impose disproportionate punishment that includes imposing the risk of prenatal harm and inflicting injuries that may intergenerationally maim a pregnant resister.

It is far more grave than a violation of Article 21, which protects life and liberty. What does it tell us about the technologies of rule of this state, which presses its armed Hindutva civilian foot soldiers, its supporters in the media, its armed police, and its collusive criminal justice system into service to hold Zargar in custody in the knowledge that she is pregnant, although the case against her is clearly one that is targeted and a display of executive vindictiveness? What does it tell

---

* Originally published as 'The Fight to Free Pregnant Student Activist Safoora Zargar is a Battle for India's Very Soul', in *Scroll.in*, 9 June 2020.

us about the power of Zargar's resistance, and the lack of urgency of intervention on her behalf by constitutional courts in the name of the Constitution? The legitimacy of constitutional courts is imperilled by their tacit deference to indefensible state action.

The Case against Zargar

The Unlawful Activities (Prevention) Act, 1967, under which Zargar has been arrested, like other anti-terror laws in India, is built on the presumption of state impunity, and criminalises any opposition to arbitrary actions by the state. There are two distinct categories of offences: 'unlawful activities' and 'terrorist activities'.

Between 2008 and 2013, amendments were introduced to demonstrate diligence to international standards of combatting terrorism. Section 2(o) of the act defines 'unlawful activity' as:

> any action taken by such individual or association (whether by committing an act or by words, either spoken or written, or by signs or by visible representation or otherwise).... (ii) which disclaims, questions, disrupts or is intended to disrupt the sovereignty and territorial integrity of India; or (iii) which causes or is intended to cause disaffection against India.[1]

Chapters IV–VI (Sections 15–40) of the act focus on terrorist offences and organisations.

The prosecution's case at Zargar's bail hearing in Delhi's Patiala House Court on 4 June 2020 is, and the judge agreed, that:

> [a]ny activity which has the tendency to create a disorder or disturbance of law and order to such an extent that the *entire city is brought to its knees and the entire government machinery is brought to a grinding halt*, such an activity would obviously be treated as an unlawful activity within the meaning of 2(o) UAPA. (Emphasis mine.)[2]

It was alleged that she delivered an inflammatory speech on 23 February 2020 that led up to the riots in northeast Delhi—an allegation denied by her lawyers as inaccurate.

Although in the judge's view it was not necessary to go into the merits of the case, a perusal of the court order shows that the judge 'safely inferred from WhatsApp chats' and statements recorded that there was at least 'a conspiracy to at least blockade the road (*chakka* jam)'.[3] It was an 'unlawful assembly' because a gathering of five or more people with a 'common object to commit any offence' is unlawful.

The court found it could not disagree with the prosecution that 'the accused persons have conspired to cause disruption of such an extent and such a magnitude that it would lead to disorderliness and disturbance of law and order at an unprecedented scale'.[4] There are no details provided in the order.

When the allegation of conspiracy was refuted by the defence on grounds that Zargar was not physically present at the scene, the court went a step further and prejudged the case with the clear observation that since there was *prima facie* evidence of conspiracy, it would be admissible against all, even those not physically present.

When her vulnerable health condition was brought to the notice of the court, it simply instructed the 'concerned jail superintendent' to provide adequate medical attention given her 'precarious medical condition'.[5]

Bail was refused for the third time because, in the words of the learned judge, 'When you choose to play with embers, you cannot blame the wind to have carried the spark a bit too far and spread the fire.'[6]

The court said that it was 'not concerned with the sanctity of the material available on record, however, considering the material available on record, it cannot be said that there is no prima facie case made out against the applicant/accused'.[7] However, although the case made out by the prosecution pertained to Section 2(o) of the UAPA that defines 'unlawful activity', and to unlawful assembly, the court circumscribed its own limits by citing 'the statutory embargo under provisions of Section 43(D)(5) [which] is attracted in the instant case'.[8]

This is a section that sets out conditions for treatment of persons accused of offences under Chapters IV ('Punishment for Terrorist Activities') and VI ("Terrorist Organisations'). As per Section 43(D)(5), the refusal to consider bail must be based (as it should) on the opinion of the court that 'there are reasonable grounds for believing that the accusation against such person is *prima facie* true'.[9]

'Judicial Pusillanimity'

Judicial discretion, which is critical in the matter of personal liberty, is misread by the court to mean 'statutory embargo' in a classic illustration of 'judicial pusillanimity'—a term used by the late Justice Seth, and quoted with appreciation by the Supreme Court in the *Navtej Singh Johar* judgement in 2018.[10]

There are more serious flaws. The discussion of the facts of the case do not allude to 'terrorist activities'. The court admitted that the material on record might have serious flaws, and yet accepted that there was a case serious enough to keep Zargar in custody. The most serious error this order makes is that in colluding with the prosecution's argument and refusing bail under Section 43(D)(5), the court conflated 'unlawful activity' with 'terrorist activity'. The only reference, even by the prosecution, was to 'unlawful activities'.

There is a manifestly arbitrary application of Section 43(D)(5) to an allegedly 'unlawful' activity (not a 'terrorist activity') resulting in disproportionate punishment even before trial. Finally, disaffection against the government is interpreted by the court as disaffection against India, as per the UAPA.

The prosecution, in the bail hearing, submitted a seizure memo from another case of empty crates and bottles, stones and bricks, from an FIR registered in Khajoori Khas police station bearing a different number from Zargar's case. Totally out of context therefore, the court observes that the 'Delhi riots were the result of a larger conspiracy to disrupt the normal functioning of the city and to overawe the government machinery by resorting to force and violence'.[11]

Without any judicial deliberation or attentiveness to the facts, details and inconsistencies on record before it, the court was quick to fix criminal liability on a Muslim woman in this case for mass violence and immeasurable harm to life and property, as also the incitement to violence in northeast Delhi in late February that targeted Muslims. This, despite Justice Muralidhar of the Delhi High Court on 26 February ordering FIRs to be registered against Bharatiya Janata Party leaders, after recordings of their incendiary hate speeches ahead of the riots were played in the courtroom (PTI 2020; *The Wire* 2020).

Minority Rights, Disaffection and State Violence

This needs to be understood and deliberated on publicly. Which are the embers, which is the wind, which the spark, how far is far, and which the fire? This is a case of personal liberty. We live in an era when the principle of non-retrogression of fundamental rights—indeed of constitutional morality—has been affirmed by the Supreme Court, and the right to fair trial and the fullest enjoyment of the right to life and personal liberty was held to lie at the core of the idea of human dignity.

Five foundational figures who shaped the contours of India's soul rise phoenix-like before me. They are figures constitutional courts may only disregard with deep peril to their own legitimacy. B. R. Ambedkar, Abul Kalam Azad, Jaipal Singh, Dakshayani Velayudhan and M. K. Gandhi.

In his monumental *The Framing of India's Constitution: A Study*, B. Shiva Rao (1968: 755–56) records that 'Ambedkar had an interesting suggestion to make; the candidates belonging to a majority community should, before being declared elected, poll a minimum number of votes from among the minority communities in their constituencies. This would have amounted to a minority exercising a sort of veto on the majority communities.' Minorities in the Constituent Assembly included religious minorities, Scheduled Castes and Scheduled Tribes. Ambedkar's suggestion therefore was a cumulative minority referendum on the majority candidate in every constituency (in the immediate aftermath of Partition). His was the lone voice (as was often the case)—and this is prescient, worthy of recall especially in light of questions Zargar places before us and the events that foretold her incarceration.

In her work on Azad, Syeda Hameed points out that he, placing Hindu–Muslim unity before swaraj, anticipated Ambedkar's idea on the right to veto, when in 1940 he declared:

> Any constitution that is framed in future for India, must contain the fullest guarantees for the protection of the rights and interests of minorities. What are the necessary safeguards ...? This judgment rests with the minority not with the majority ... [and] therefore, must be formulated by their consent, not by majority vote. (Quoted in Hameed 2014 [1997]: *xv*)

Shaunna Rodrigues (2020: 126), in her account of Azad's contribution to the framing of the Constitution, draws our attention to the fact that Azad set out the plural foundations of the Constitution by delineating the 'ethical, moral and theological arguments emerging from, among other sources of Indian traditions, Islam, on the nature, justification and critique of a unified rule of law for a diverse people'.

Adivasi leader, Jaipal Singh (2017: 95), spoke to the Adivasi experience under colonialism and under majoritarian rule: 'The new Constitution will be judged not by the provisions for minorities but by the way these are worked to their best advantage.' Finally, Dakshayani Velayudhan, the only Dalit woman in the Constituent Assembly, embodied the collective Dalit experience of resisting untouchability, their resilience and resistance making the Constitution what it is.

Can we forget Gandhi's (1922) statement in court?

> Affection cannot be manufactured or regulated by law.... I hold it to be a virtue to be disaffected towards a Government which in its totality has done more harm to India than any previous system.... Holding such a belief, I consider it to be a sin to have affection for the system.

Ethical Dissent and India's Soul

When Zargar protests against the carceral, Islamophobic, Hindutva regime that passed the Citizenship (Amendment) Act, she is fighting to protect India's soul. She did this, not with guns and inflammable substances and weapons of destruction and torture, but through peaceful demonstration. Not through incendiary speeches that incite mass violence, but through singular focus on the repeal of an immoral, counter-constitutional law. And she protests with hundreds of thousands of others.

This, too, is our inheritance. Ethical dissent and civil disobedience.

Notes

1. The Unlawful Activities (Prevention) Act, 1967, sec. 2(o).
2. State v. Safoora Zargar, Bail Application No. 1119/2020, FIR No. 59/2020, PS Crime Branch (Special Cell), passed on 4 June 2020 (Patiala House Court, New Delhi), 7.

3. Ibid.
4. Ibid., 8.
5. Ibid., 9.
6. Ibid., 8.
7. Ibid.
8. Ibid.
9. The Unlawful Activities (Prevention) Act, 1967, sec. 43(D)(5).
10. Quoted in *Navtej Singh Johar*, AIR 2018 SC 4321, para. 1 (per Chandrachud, J.).
11. State v. Safoora Zargar, Bail Application No. 1119/2020, FIR No. 59/2020, PS Crime Branch (Special Cell), passed on 4 June 2020 (Patiala House Court, New Delhi), 6.

References

'Explained: What the 3 Orders by Justice Muralidhar Meant for the Delhi Riots'. 2020. *The Wire*, 28 February. Available at https://thewire.in/law/explainer-justice-muralidhar-delhi-riots (accessed 10 July 2021).

Gandhi, M. K. 1922. 'Statement in the Great Trial of 1922'. Available at https://gandhiashramsabarmati.org/en/the-mahatma/speeches/great-trial-1922.html (accessed 9 July 2021).

Hameed, Syeda S. 2014 [1997]. *Maulana Azad, Islam and the National Movement*. New Delhi: Oxford University Press.

Munda, Jaipal Singh. 2017. *Adivasidom: Speeches and Writings*, ed. Ashwini Kumar. Ranchi: Pyara Kerketta Foundation.

Pasha, Seemi. 2020. 'Safoora Zargar Denied Bail as Judge Finds Prima Facie Evidence of "Conspiracy"'. *The Wire*, 5 June. Available at https://thewire.in/law/safoora-zargar-denied-bail (accessed 10 July 2021).

PTI. 2020. 'Delhi Riots: File FIR against Kapil Mishra, Anurag Thakur and Parvesh Verma, HC Tells Police'. *Outlook*, 26 February.

Rao, B. Shiva. 1968. *The Framing of India's Constitution: A Study*. New Delhi: Indian Institute of Public Administration.

Rodrigues, Shaunna. 2020. 'Abul Kalam Azad and the Right to an Islamic Justification of the Indian Constitution'. In *Dimensions of Constitutional Democracy: India and Germany*, ed. Anupama Roy and Michael Becker, 125–46. Singapore: Springer.

67

Governance by Annihilation and by Hate*

A 19-year-old Dalit woman was assaulted in Hathras in the most brutal manner and killed by Thakurs from the same village known to her and her family (*The Hindu* 2020). When her mother found her, she was naked, paralysed with indescribable physical injuries, which included deep injuries on her tongue—to silence her from testifying to the attack on her? Yet, in spite of the grave harms, violent humiliation and deep trauma, she made a statement naming the perpetrators. She, a young Dalit woman from a landless Valmiki family, whose only protection against chronic anticipated assault and humiliation by Thakur perpetrators and their henchmen was to stay indoors, never alone, and step out occasionally, never alone. Yet, even this did not give her the guarantee of bare life. Incarceration by caste and annihilation by caste. If we do not annihilate caste, caste will annihilate us.

Can we even begin to understand Article 21 guarantees from the standpoint of this experience? We know the young woman from Hathras is not the first. Khairlanji (Teltumbde 2008), the case of the law student from Ernakulam in Kerala (*The Indian Express* 2017), the young girls in Badaun (*The Indian Express* 2014) ... The roads of this country are strewn with the bodies of Dalit women, young and old, and the bodies of Dalit men. Without multiplying examples of targeted structural violence and assault—for that is a task that is impossible to complete given its sheer magnitude—our collective experience as a people sworn to the Constitution of India in Hathras in 2020, like elsewhere, has been one of *occupation* of Dalit, Adivasi and Muslim homes, neighbourhoods and homelands, of violent death and collective

* Originally published as '#I Can't Breathe: Governance by Annihilation and by Hate', in *LiveLaw*, 3 October 2020.

violence, of desecration of places of worship, of unimaginable suffering, of humiliation as a condition of existence, of the anticipation of violence and murder, and of the trauma of silencing. The first expression of the 'right to maim', as Puar (2017) poignantly calls it, in this instance is the brutal seizure of speech by the Thakur-state.

In a country with people who gave to themselves a Constitution that affirms justice, equality, fraternity, freedom of faith, worship, and conscience, liberty, dignity, unity, and integrity, we have a strident, violent, unabashedly partisan, elected government. We have officers of the government participating in and bolstering genocidal speech by curtailing the invocation of the Constitution (PTI 2020)—by cutting the Dalit's 'tongue in twain and [pouring] hot molten lead in his ears' (Ambedkar 2014 [1989]: 114), ripping apart Article 17 guarantees. Witness the conduct of the district magistrate and the police after the death of the victim. Witness the fortification of the village against 'outsiders' reaching out to her family, while the perpetrators and their families roam free within the village. The murderous assault on the young woman is held in place by the continuing assault on and humiliation of the family—by the dominant Thakurs and the officers of government, now no longer distinguishable from each other in speech or conduct.

This humiliation reaches its most unbearable limit in the manner in which her family was refused the right to her mortal remains—her body broken, wounded and lacerated, but it was what remained of her. Annihilation of the person, the body and the claim to justice. 'No evidence of rape', said the police without any investigation into the crimes that killed her. The right to preserve her body and seek further investigation into the wounds she suffered was denied, and the evidence she carried on her person destroyed in the dead of night by the police (Kumar 2020). We know by now that a forensic report is rarely a truthful record, especially when the case concerns crimes of dominance and crimes against humanity. We saw the Muktadar Commission that enquired into the gangrape of a Muslim woman and the custodial murder of her husband in Hyderabad in 1978 record that the medical and forensic reports had been tampered with to destroy evidence against the accused policemen (see Prasad 1978). In the case of the custodial death of Budhan Sabar in West Bengal in 1998, the Calcutta High Court ordered a videographed second post-mortem that revealed the cause of death as custodial violence and ordered compensation for Budhan's wife.[1] The disposal of the Hathras victim's body therefore is not merely disrespect to the dead person and disregard for the customs of her family in the matter of death rituals. It is destruction of evidence that the Hathras police are guilty of—and there is a record of this destruction. The threats, forced confinement in their homes and fortification are forms of illegal custody that the family have been subjected to—there were armed police and officers of state actively preventing the family from moving out and anyone from meeting them. They were incarcerated in their homes and threatened with greater harm if they did not change their testimonies.

The Allahabad High Court's *suo motu* notice (*The Times of India* 2020) is welcome, and we pin hope on the court as a place that will quell our collective anger at this travesty of justice. The court must name the officers on duty for the 15 days between the assault and their suspension and order them to appear before the court by name. Their suspension should not by default become a release from the burden of appearing before the court. What is required as a first step in reparation is the public acknowledgment by the court of the multiple ways in which the Constitution has been torn to shreds. This is the only route to dignity—for citizens of this country and the courts alike.

Our still raw memories of the brutal violence by the Uttar Pradesh police on unarmed anti-CAA resisters (Citizens against Hate 2020: 21–24), fuelled by the state, is now followed up with the declaration by the Central Bureau of Investigation (CBI) court in Lucknow that there is 'no evidence' against those accused of the large-scale violence, riots, arson, looting and demolition of the Babri Masjid in December 1992, with the elected chief minister releasing a press statement saying, '*Satyameva Jayate*' (truth alone shall triumph) (*The Wire* 2020). That a top BJP elder escaped conviction and heaved the burden off his ageing chest with a 'Jai Shri Ram' is different in its substantive meanings (although his role in the demolition and the violence that preceded and followed it must never be forgotten). And yet, a distinction must be drawn between those accused in the case and the chief minister concurring with the court judgement in which he was neither an accused nor a party.

This is not the first time in our lives as witnesses to state impunity that we have seen complicity in collective/mass violence. And yet, we must insist that this brazen declaration of partisan rule and impunity be signposted. Given the scale of violence, and the volume of documentary and visual evidence available to courts, the Babri Masjid case must go up in appeal to the high court and the Supreme Court and be tried afresh. Through his press release, the chief minister of Uttar Pradesh, a constitutional authority, has seized speech from us all by foreclosing the options to appeal or ask for a retrial. It is an infringement of the Article 19 rights of citizens of this country in their intersections with Article 21 and the Preamble. We just need to look around us to see what havoc this impunity has already triggered.

Clearly, the black letter understanding of the Constitution is woefully inadequate in our situation. It is our responsibility as citizens to alert courts to the incarceration of the Constitution—it is not 'four corners of the law'[2] any more. The Constitution, and by that token, every court in this country and every judicial office, is today in peril. There are no guarantees for the expression of judicial dissent, and indeed no guarantee that this violent seizure of speech will not very soon affect judicial dissent. One experience of this silencing is the decision of the CBI court. There is an even graver harm lurking around the corner—the possibility of the chilling of non-compliant judicial speech that these times signal.

Where do we go as citizens? Who do we appeal to? If our routes to redress are blocked by caste and hate, what are courts going to do to enforce the 'triadic ethical foundations' of the Constitution[3]—the Preamble, fundamental rights and the Directive Principles of State Policy? Or are we going to sit back, fiddling with little reliefs, while the Constitution itself is annihilated—not merely reduced to a farce, as Ambedkar warned?

When *ADM Jabalpur*[4] happened, we waited 40 years for the nine-judge bench of the *Puttaswamy* court to declare: 'When histories of nations are written and critiqued, there are judicial decisions at the forefront of liberty. Yet others have to be consigned to the archives, reflective of what was, but should never have been.'[5] This, our present, is a moment that should never have been. If we let this moment pass, we risk the peril of wiping out the Constitution and the courts that are meant to breathe life into it. The difference between this moment and the one we so proudly consigned to ignominy is that we will not bequeath a *Puttaswamy* moment to our future generations. The choice is ours to make. It is a choice.

Notes

1. *Paschim Banga Kheria Sabar Kalyan Samity*, WP No. 3715 of 1998 (Cal. HC).
2. *Navtej Singh Johar*, AIR 2018 SC 4321, para. 4 (per Misra, J.).
3. *Reliance Natural Resources Ltd*, (2010) 156 CompCas 455 (SC), para. 97.
4. *ADM Jabalpur*, (1976) 2 SCC 521.
5. *K. S. Puttaswamy*, (2017) 10 SCC 1, para. 121.

References

'Badaun Gangrape and Murder: How the Incident Unfolded'. 2014. *The Indian Express*, 2 June.

'Hathras Case: HC Takes Suo Motu Cognisance, Issues Notice to UP Govt'. 2020. *The Times of India*, 1 October.

'Uttar Pradesh Dalit Girl, Victim of Brutal Gang Rape, Dies in Delhi Hospital'. 2020. *The Hindu*, 29 September.

'What is Jisha Rape and Murder Case?'. 2017. *The Indian Express*, 12 December.

'While BJP Celebrates Babri Verdict, Others Criticise CBI for Diluting Evidence'. 2020. *The Wire*, 30 September. Available at https://thewire.in/communalism/babri-masjid-demolition-verdict-cbi-criticism (accessed 10 July 2021).

Ambedkar, B. R. 2014 [1989]. *Dr Babsaheb Ambedkar: Writings and Speeches*, vol. 5, comp. Vasant Moon. New Delhi: Dr Ambedkar Foundation. Reprint.

Citizens against Hate. 2020. *'Everyone Has Been Silenced': Police Excess against Anti-CAA Protesters in Uttar Pradesh, and Post-Violence Reprisal*. Available at https://citizensagainsthate.org/wp-content/uploads/2020/03/Citizens-Against-Hate-Everyone-Has-Been-Silenced.pdf (accessed 14 June 2021).

Kumar, Anuj. 2020. 'Hathras Gang Rape: A Long Caste Feud, a Horrific Crime, and a Sudden Cremation'. *The Hindu*, 3 October.

Prasad, P. S. N. 1978. 'The Police and Rameeza Bee: Muktadar Commission's Findings'. *Economic and Political Weekly* 13, no. 35 (2 September): 1497–99.
PTI. 2020. 'Delhi Riots: File FIR against Kapil Mishra, Anurag Thakur and Parvesh Verma, HC Tells Police'. *Outlook*, 26 February.
Puar, Jasbir K. 2017. *The Right to Maim: Debility, Capacity, Disability*. Durham and London: Duke University Press.
Teltumbde, Anand. 2008. *Khairlanji: A Strange and Bitter Crop*. New Delhi: Navayana.